EGO AND INK

EGO AND INK

THE INSIDE STORY OF CANADA'S NATIONAL NEWSPAPER WAR

CHRIS COBB

National Library of Canada Cataloguing in Publication Data

Cobb, Chris
Ego and ink : the inside story of Canada's national newspaper war / Chris Cobb.

Includes index.
ISBN 0-7710-2173-9

1. Newspaper publishing–Ontario–Toronto. 2. National post.
3. Globe and mail. I. Title.

PN4908.C62 2004   338.4'707113541   C2004-900211-2

We acknowledge the financial support of the Government of Canada through the Book Publishing Industry Development Program and that of the Government of Ontario through the Ontario Media Development Corporation's Ontario Book Initiative. We further acknowledge the support of the Canada Council for the Arts and the Ontario Arts Council for our publishing program.

Typeset in Times by M&S, Toronto
Printed and bound in Canada

This book is printed on acid-free paper that is 100% ancient forest friendly (100% post-consumer recycled).

McClelland & Stewart Ltd.
The Canadian Publishers
481 University Avenue
Toronto, Ontario
M5G 2E9
www.mcclelland.com

1 2 3 4 5   08 07 06 05 04

FOR MARGOT

And for
Rhiannon
Jeremy
Christina
and Julie

CONTENTS

"And of course, there is one thing in all journalists and that's ego. Journalism feeds your ego and this was a big ego trip. . . . In the journalism game you can put issues onto people's breakfast tables and decide what they get to read the next day. That's a rush."

– Martin Newland, founding deputy editor, *National Post*

A new era in Canadian journalism dawned with the launch of Conrad Black's *National Post* on October 27, 1998. By the turn of the century, the *Post* and its conservative viewpoint was influencing government policy in Ottawa and making Prime Minister Jean Chrétien so chronically angry that his wife banned the newspaper from their house.

In ways large and small, the *National Post* had an almost immediate impact on the lives of Canadians, whether they subscribed or not, whether they read a word of it or not. *Post* editor-in-chief Kenneth Whyte and proprietor Conrad Black saw the newspaper as an official opposition during a period in Canadian federal politics when effectively there wasn't one. Their newspaper unabashedly, and sometimes shamelessly, championed a Unite the Right movement on both its news and opinion pages and threw its weight behind a lost cause, the Canadian Alliance.

Within the newspaper business, the *Post* sparked a vicious, economically crippling war, the cost of which has never been fully calculated but by some estimates forced the combatants to spend at least $1 billion between them to shore up their own defences and carpet the streets of Canada's major cities, and especially Toronto, with hundreds of thousands of free newspapers. Black, in his own inimitable way, described it thus: "The *Post* gelignited the fetid little media log-rolling and back-scratching society in Toronto, where the *Globe and Mail*, the *Star*, the CBC, and, like a yapping little dog at the heels of the other three, *Maclean's* magazine, zealously maintained the soft-left orthodoxy."

The *Post* brought upheaval, innovation, and new life to Canadian newspaper journalism. It caused an unprecedented movement of journalists among newspapers, revitalized moribund careers, and created opportunities for dozens of young journalists. The *Post* forced change upon the *Globe and Mail*, wholly owned at the outset by the savvy, mega-wealthy Thomson family. The Thomsons had lost interest in the newspaper business but decided they would spend whatever it took to prevent Conrad Black from prevailing.

It seemed illogical. The Thomson Corporation was never ideological or sentimental and saw its future not in newspapers but in electronic information delivery. Black, at the peak of his prestige in Canada as owner of most of the nation's major daily newspapers, had sound reasons to believe he could get the Thomsons to sell and never stopped trying. In a classic case of business brinkmanship, he was still pushing late in the game, even sending an emissary to the enemy camp with mock-ups of his proposed new daily. The Thomsons didn't blink and, effectively, threw down the gauntlet.

Assorted media observers remained convinced that Black was bluffing and laughed at his efforts to tout this mythical new paper, which by then was commonly known as the "Daily Tubby." Black had never created a newspaper and was well known for his bluff and bluster. But he proved the doubters wrong.

In Greater Toronto, the main battleground, the *Toronto Star* justifiably saw its franchise threatened, and publisher John Honderich, knowing what Black was capable of, sounded the war cry to his managers more than a year before the *Post* eventually appeared. Conrad Black would not be fighting by the Marquess of Queensberry rules, he warned them.

After a remarkable early surge by the *Post* and a confused, faltering reaction from the *Globe and Mail*, the *Globe*'s managers, led by imported publisher Phillip Crawley, adjusted and sharpened their attack on the advertising, circulation, and journalism fronts and transformed their newspaper into a formidable opponent.

Two years later, when Thomson sold controlling interest in the bruised *Globe* to expansion-minded Bell Canada Enterprises of phone-company fame, family patriarch Kenneth Thomson remained chairman of the newspaper – a signal that the family's commitment to the *Globe* was unbending and they intended to finish what Conrad Black had started.

◆ ◆ ◆

Consensus is a rare commodity in this story, which is why, from the outset, I decided to turn these pages over in large part to those who lived, and continue to live, the story.

It is a story of passionate disagreement, differing interpretation, and tantalizing speculation about roads not taken – the myriad of "what ifs." It is also a story of loathing and mutual admiration among many larger-than-life characters, some of who became enmeshed in webs of intrigue that would have taxed Shakespeare's imagination. And among the turmoil, there was warlike propaganda, personal nastiness, intrigue, vindictive gossip, and professional insult.

There was also lots of excitement, fun, and money flying around – more of all three than the Canadian newspaper business had seen in many years.

For an entity so powerful and pervasive, newspaper journalism is a mystery to those who have never practised it. For that matter, it is often a mystery to those of us who do. In the passages dealing with journalism, I have tried my best to be illuminating for those who aren't familiar with the journalism business.

The story told in these pages begins and ends with Conrad Black's ambition — the building of the *National Post*, the subsequent newspaper war, and the impact of Black's *Post* on both Canada's politics and journalism. It was never intended as an obituary. The Conrad Black era is decidedly over, but the *Post* lives on, and it is of no small interest to the country that it continues to do so.

Note: The jobs attributed to the people quoted at the top of each chapter were those they held at the time of this story.

THE END OF THE BEGINNING

"It was the dream job." – Scott Burnside, reporter

I t was September 2001, less than a month since the Asper family of Winnipeg had bought full control of the *National Post* from its founder, the former Canadian citizen Lord Black of Crossharbour, and just six days since the al-Qaeda attacks on New York City and Washington, D.C.

Post employees were uneasy about the new owners, and many had seen Conrad Black's final exit in late August as an act of betrayal, a retreat in the heat of battle. That Black's leaving so shocked and dismayed his troops spoke not only to their passion for the newspaper but also to the remarkable level of trust and respect the larger-than-life press baron had engendered. Black had built the *National Post* on the backs of his thriving Southam dailies with a staff of hand-picked journalists. His newspaper hired established names for big money and nurtured reporters of the ilk he once described as "swarming, grunting jackals of investigative journalism." They thought Black was in for the long haul, which is why some had cried when he said goodbye. Others, angry at being jilted, had fumed. How could they have been stupid enough to imagine Conrad Black would think of anything but his own bottom line?

Columnist Christie Blatchford, who had evolved as the journalistic personification of the *National Post*, wrote touchingly about Black's departure:

As I spoke to Mr. Black yesterday, my own face was wet with tears, he murmured a reassurance that things would be fine.

"It won't be the same," I said.

So in his immediate vicinity, there were three of us in various stages of girlish ruin, and all around him, a variety of other clearly shattered folks.

Mr. Black was composed, as always alarmingly articulate, and dry-eyed (though of course, he may have been inwardly sobbing) and I wondered whether this was what F. Scott Fitzgerald meant about the very rich being different from you and me. As it turns out, it was.

And she quoted Fitzgerald: " 'They possess and enjoy early and it does something to them, makes them soft where we are hard, and cynical where we are trustful.' "

Working at the *Post*, Canada's first new daily newspaper in years, had been a labour of love – less of a job, more of a mission. After a three-year emotional high, and some of the most influential, entertaining journalism Canada had experienced, the wheels on the *National Post* express seemed to be falling off. Black had made reassuring statements a year earlier, in 2000, after he had made his $3.2-billion deal with the Aspers' CanWest Global Communications Corp. He hadn't wanted to part with any piece of the *Post*, but his company was in debt and he needed the money. It wasn't much more complicated than that.

In exchange, the Aspers got the profitable Southam newspaper chain, 50 per cent share of the *Post*, which had racked up $200 million in debt, and the chance to move into a new world of convergence, where TV, newspapers, and the Internet intertwine. CanWest insisted on getting the *Post*, and its national presence, as part of the package.

The sale was traumatic for *Post* employees, but those concerned about the newspaper's journalistic mission had at least been comforted by the initial arrangement that gave Black the deciding vote in the *Post* boardroom.

But now, with the other 50 per cent sold, the old boss had become the object of contempt and the target of colourful epithets from those who felt he had spurned them. The pioneering spirit that had been the engine of the *National Post* all but disappeared. Black said those accusing him of betrayal were not thinking it through. The *Post* was his baby, he said, but for its own good he was handing it over to new parents in a better position to nurture and guarantee its future.

The sale, he said, was in the best interests of the newspaper because it "absolutely guarantees the permanence of the *National Post* as an institution in this country." But Black, never given to public displays of emotion, conceded that the decision to sell had been painful.

The *Post* had been a journalistic phenomenon that strode, well prepared and guns blazing, onto the Canadian daily newspaper battlefield just three years earlier while its main enemy was half asleep. Within weeks, if not days, it was as if the *Post* had been around forever. That alone was a monumental achievement.

Some admired its brash approach, and others dismissed it as nasty, right-wing trash, but denying the *Post*'s growing influence was not an option.

Leonard Asper, the soft-spoken chief executive of his family's CanWest Global Communications company, had said warm, soothing things about the *Post* and about its editor-in-chief, Kenneth Whyte, when he spoke to concerned employees gathered in the *Post* newsroom on the day the sale was announced.

Whyte was "the finest editor of any newspaper I've ever seen," he said in a generous vote of confidence. "This is the finest newspaper in Canada, if not the world," he effused. "We don't intend to mess with that."

And in an effort to allay the inevitable fears among staff, he had added it was not CanWest's intention "to walk into the *National Post* with a machete and start changing the way things are done."

CanWest was going to cut the excesses, however, attempt to turn a profit and give the *National Post* a future. The Aspers had been left with no other choice. Leonard Asper would not specifically rule out layoffs but said there might be other, more productive ways to stop the *Post* from bleeding money – an end to freebies and cut-price subscriptions would be a good start, he suggested. That was three weeks ago, August 24, 2001.

The warning signs were all there, but even the few who had suspected something ill was afoot were not quite prepared for the next piece of news.

❖ ❖ ❖

The *National Post*'s roving culture writer, John Bentley Mays, was at home on September 17 when he received an urgent call summoning him to a mass newsroom meeting ninety minutes later at the newspaper's Don Mills headquarters, a brownish-beige structure in suburban Toronto.

Bentley Mays, among the *Post*'s earliest employees and a high-profile defector from the *Globe and Mail*, might have thought it strange that the call had come from the office bookkeeper. But he didn't give it a thought. He drove toward Don Mills puzzling over what the meeting might be about. Maybe founding editor Kenneth Whyte would be resigning and the Aspers announcing, perhaps even introducing, their new editor. And if Whyte was gone, then his deputy, the dashing Englishman Martin Newland, would likely be gone too. It was normal for new newspaper owners to want their own top people in place.

The sixty-year-old scribe, who had famously chronicled his battle with depression in the best-selling book *In the Jaws of the Black Dogs*, drove into the chronically congested *Post* parking lot confident that he had it all figured out. Sure, Asper had said nice things about Ken, but, as many a hockey, football, or baseball coach knew, a vote of confidence by the owner was often the kiss of death. Or maybe when they got down to how the Aspers wanted the *Post* run, Whyte had decided he couldn't work with them, or vice versa. That happened, more often than not.

And owners often made positive, upbeat statements because they had to comfort investors and shareholders. So it was best to pay more attention to what the owners did, and less to what they said. That much was understood, especially by employees at the venerable Southam, a company that had had more owners and ownership structures in recent years than Elizabeth Taylor had had husbands.

But when the veteran reporter walked into the newsroom, he was stunned at the military-style scene that confronted him. "We were herded into one of three or four rooms because there was no one room big enough to hold 130 people, or whatever it was," he recalls, traces of his Louisiana roots still strong in his accent. "Then Ken walked in and said, 'As of this morning, you don't have jobs here any more.' He looked crestfallen. Then we were all handed envelopes by the human resources people, Ken left, and they took over with their standard routine: 'We have consultants to get you through the transition,' and all this nonsense these companies come up with to try to stop you from thinking about suing them. We were all given declarations to sign, and then we were told we would be escorted out of the building. This was ridiculous to me, so I went upstairs to tell some people goodbye, but I couldn't find anybody. The section editors were in meetings, because even they hadn't been told beforehand what was going to happen."

Bentley Mays left the building for the last time along with 130 other *Post* employees and minus a $90,000 annual salary. He consulted a lawyer, who told him it was worth neither the time nor the aggravation to sue. Mass layoffs weren't personal. "I don't know how they chose the people to fire. In my case, I assume it was a money issue. I was being paid $90,000. But I have no idea how that compares to what others were making."

Situated in the upper middle class but not the aristocracy of the *Post*'s salaried journalists, Bentley Mays rarely ventured into the *Post* newsroom, working either at home or on assignment. Those more attuned to the newsroom *Zeitgeist* had sniffed danger much earlier. There had been discreet construction work happening in the human resources department, which people in the newsroom's special project section could see. They mentioned it quietly to others and there was a little speculation but no full-scale alarm. Two rooms were being spruced up and decorated with tranquil artwork. It was in these two rooms that the human resources specialists held the individual meetings with those who were laid off.

Sports editor Graham Parley had carried a heavy burden all weekend. Martin Newland had given him the bad news on the Friday evening and sworn him to secrecy. "Martin told me my entire department was being closed down. I think it was a sort of heads-up and to make sure that anyone in the department who was out of town was brought back. He was very uncomfortable about it."

Parley, a passionate editor and an early, trusted member of the newsroom inner circle, was both devastated and incredulous. "Don't you remember what happened at the *Globe*?" he asked Newland. "They tried to get rid of sports and had to bring it back. It's one of the classic mistakes in Canadian journalism."

Newland didn't respond.

Parley's first priority was to get hockey reporter Scott Burnside back from Newfoundland, where he had been stuck since September 10. "He'd flown out to Newfoundland to wait for the Maple Leafs to arrive to play their farm team. And then 9/11 happened and the Leafs couldn't get out there, so Scott wrote some 9/11 stories about what was happening in Newfoundland with the stranded aircraft and passengers. Then the Leafs were finally on their way and I told him he had to come back because there was a meeting he had to attend on Monday. The poor guy was totally confused."

"But the Leafs are playing an exhibition game against the Canadiens," said Burnside, thinking that Parley didn't quite understand. "I've got to stay for that."

"No," insisted the sports editor, "you've got to come home."

Shortly before he left St. John's, Burnside sat with a group of his fellow hockey writers. "I might not have a job by tomorrow afternoon," he predicted.

Parley knew what Burnside was beginning to suspect, but the sports chief was also amazed that the list of seventy others from the newsroom who were being let go was still being changed as late as Sunday. "On the Sunday night, after the shift, I was out in the parking lot having a smoke and [writers] Bruce Arthur and Sean Fitz-Gerald were throwing a ball around the parking lot. Ken came out on his way home, looked at the scene, and said to me, 'Sean has been saved.' He didn't say much else. Then he went home. They had to maintain secrecy so everyone could be told at once. Still, it was so secret that even the section heads like me weren't consulted. It all seemed so arbitrary and simplistic."

Ken Whyte had been involved in most of the major decisions since the launch of the *Post*, including non-editorial ones. He says in this case he was not consulted but presented with a *fait accompli*. "I was allowed to cut my own department in a particular way. I had to get to a certain level, but how I got there was up to me. The shape of the product was given to us. We had to cut by a certain dollar amount and a certain number of people. The core product as they saw it was the A section and the *Financial Post*, and anything that wasn't core was seen to be extraneous, and that included *Saturday Night* magazine, the Weekend Post, Arts and Life, and Sports. We had a week to figure out how to do it, but I'm not sure in those situations that more time helps. There was a report in *Frank* magazine that I had left it to human resources to fire people, which wasn't true. We did it ourselves. It was the worst day I've ever had, and it was made worse because people were so good about it. Some were angry initially, but later most people said they had loved working there and were grateful for the experience."

As the morning unfolded, the survivors commiserated with their laid-off colleagues. A parade of *Saturday Night* employees, each holding severance packages, was led along the third-floor atrium to their meetings with the human resources specialists. Newsroom staff watched as they filed past. "It was like watching people being sent to their execution," recalls Parley. "The remarkable thing was that everybody seemed to be taken totally by surprise. You would think that people would have known, but they didn't. When people came back into the newsroom after being cut, none of them seemed angry. They just had these strange half-smiles on their faces. But it was civilized in that way. People weren't forced to leave immediately and could wander back into the newsroom, or wherever, and just hang around and chat."

Shortly before, Parley had been forced to restrain young sports reporter Dave Feschuk, who was agitated at not being invited to the ten o'clock meeting along with everyone else. He assumed his lack of an invitation was a mere oversight, and he felt left out. Parley had met Feschuk by the Starbucks coffee and bagels, a regular Monday-morning fixture in the newsroom. It was a few minutes before ten.

"I should be in there, shouldn't I?" an increasingly troubled Feschuk asked Parley. "Everyone else is in there, it must be some mistake."

"Dave, you can't go in there," hissed Parley. "They're being cut, you're not."

Scott Burnside had arrived from St. John's a few hours before and had stopped at the *Post*'s back door to speculate with his good friend and former *Toronto Sun* colleague Christie Blatchford. He was relieved when he saw Blatchford, the *Post* writer least likely to be laid off. If she had been brought back to town and asked to come to the office, there was no way this mass gathering could be about job cuts. Or so he figured.

The hockey writer sat and waited with about fifty others, including city columnist Joe Fiorito, who had been called at home that morning, where he was busily finishing a post-9/11 piece about a local mosque. Fiorito, visiting the *Post*'s Don Mills headquarters for only the fourth time in three years, had no clue what was about to happen until he walked into the newsroom. "It was a peculiar scene," he remembers, "because half of the people there didn't want to look at the other half, and although nobody would say anything it was apparent that great axes were about to fall."

The silence and tension in the room where Fiorito and others assembled grew with each of the passing twenty minutes they were forced to wait. It became unbearable for the streetwise Fiorito, who was sitting in the front row. He stood, turned to the assembled group, and shouted, "If they come in with box cutters, I say we jump them."

People began to laugh, and were still grinning when Whyte, Newland, and his layoff team entered the room. "You're all fine newspaper people," an obviously mortified Whyte told them. "You are the best of the best."

As Whyte spoke, it became clear that several people in the room had arrived at the meeting completely unaware of what was about to happen. Fiorito, who had no sympathy for Whyte's obvious discomfort, wanted to know how the redundancy list had been decided. He didn't get an answer. "Newland and Whyte looked shaken and were telling us how bad they felt," Fiorito says. "Am I supposed to feel sorry because they were feeling bad? They were still going to be getting paycheques."

The laid-off employees were separated into small groups to be advised by outside human resources specialists. Everyone was given a sign-off sheet and the option of agreeing to a settlement on the spot.

Scott Burnside's group, all obviously stunned, got some unexpected advice. "I didn't tell you this," said their consultant, "but none of you should sign. Take it home and find a lawyer friend and make sure you get what you feel you're owed."

So they did.

Burnside left the building on the verge of tears. Blatchford, loyal to her friend and burning with her own anger, walked with him to his car. "I'll never have a job as good as the one I had here," he told her. "It was the dream job."

They hugged and Burnside drove away.

◆ ◆ ◆

Condemned employees not scheduled to work had been telephoned at home and asked to come to the office for a meeting. Those already in the office received e-mails, and a few others, whom *Post* office staff had not been able to contact, arrived in dribs and drabs for what they expected to be a normal day's work – though the sight of TV satellite trucks and reporters from other media was an immediate giveaway that something out of the ordinary was happening.

The newly redundant were told to remove their belongings from the premises. Personal phone lines and e-mail accounts had been cut before they got back to their desks. Some left the building immediately and gave brief interviews to the reporters outside. Others remained in the newsroom, commiserating and being comforted. Tears flowed, and there were murmurs about the arbitrary nature of the layoffs. "Why's that lazy prick still here?" mumbled one survivor to another as they surveyed the scene, "when she's been let go?" One copy editor hung around the newsroom so long that one of her colleagues congratulated her on escaping the axe. "I didn't," she cried. "I just can't bear to leave."

The layoffs, and the more predictable snuffing out of *Saturday Night* magazine (worth an immediate $7 million savings), had been dictated by secretly commissioned research during which the majority of respondents praised the newspaper's editorial comment and political analysis. Sport, entertainment, and lifestyle coverage was not a driving force for the *Post*, was the conclusion.

Publisher Gordon Fisher, a major behind-the-scenes player in the *Post*'s early development, explained the rationale behind the editorial cuts in an interview with Southam News. He described a new model resembling the *Wall Street Journal*. "The readers of the *National Post* are clearly focused on national and international news – every survey we've ever done proves that. They are also clearly focused on financial news and investment news. Other parts of the paper, while interesting, are not vital to the readership except possibly on the weekend." The *Post* was being stripped down by economic necessity, but as Leonard Asper would later admit, the analysis of the surveys to which Fisher referred was either flawed or incomplete – as major advertisers would swiftly point out.

And so it was that the sports, entertainment, and lifestyle departments of the *National Post* temporarily disappeared. It was also a shock to the *Globe and Mail*, where, in a moment of candid assessment, a bemused editor, Richard Addis, told colleagues he couldn't believe what their competitor had done to itself.

The day ended with the *National Post* lighter by 130 employees, a depression among those who remained, and a chronic parking problem solved in the *Post*'s too-small lot. The newspaper had employed an attendant to shuffle cars around during the day. That expense was no longer necessary.

Leonard Asper arrived to tell survivors that "decisive and swift action was needed to ensure the long-term viability of the newspaper." This wasn't the beginning of the end, he wanted to assure them, it was the end of the beginning. The cuts would make the *Post* a better, more focused newspaper, he said, desperately trying to pump some optimism into the remaining troops.

"Then why didn't they fire another hundred?" a muffled and bitter voice was heard to respond from where the sports department used to be.

But it wasn't the Aspers people were angry at, or felt betrayed by. That much was clear at the drunken wake held later at Allen's Pub on Danforth Avenue, where several hours of unbridled profanity was aimed at the absent Conrad Black.

In an upbeat moment, someone mentioned the tension and excitement of producing that first edition on October 27, 1998, after weeks of dummy runs. The birth and remarkable early life of the *National Post* was pieced together in a jigsaw puzzle of fuzzy bar-room memories. Disasters, near disasters, the fun, the Friday-afternoon office drinking parties, and, most of all, the early victories over the *Globe and Mail*.

"Just think of it," said one drowsy copy editor wistfully. "A year ago, we were talking about the possibility of the *Globe* folding."

"We knew that we were working for Conrad, so we were able to try to see the news as he might see it. He isn't afraid of sex, which Canadian newspapers certainly were, and he isn't afraid of a front-page picture of a nice-looking tennis star bending over."

– Michael Cooke, editor-in-chief, *Chicago Sun-Times*

Conrad Black was angry when he called his *Saturday Night* magazine editor Kenneth Whyte in early October 1996. The daily tabloid *Financial Post*, of which he was a minority shareholder and co-founder, had slipped from his grasp.

In late September 1996, Paul Godfrey, the canny, genial president of Sun Publishing Corporation, which controlled the *Financial Post*, had announced a $411-million management buyout of the company from cable magnate Ted Rogers, who was unloading the *Post* and the *Sun* newspapers he had acquired as part of his company's takeover of cable competitor Maclean-Hunter.

Shortly after Godfrey completed the deal, with the help of several institutional backers, Black called to claim the *Post*, which he said Godfrey had promised to sell him. Godfrey said he had promised no such thing but had merely asked Black, while shopping for buyout money, if he might be interested in doubling his 20 per cent stake should the management buyout plan fall short of the necessary capital. The dispute was never resolved.

The small, dapper Godfrey is an influential former municipal politician who left the newspaper business a rich man to take the helm of the troubled Toronto Blue Jays. He recalled that Black was preoccupied at the time with gaining control of the Southam group of newspapers, a situation Godfrey intended to play to its full advantage. "For a small management group the distraction was good, because Conrad could afford to pay far more for the *Post* than we could," says Godfrey. "We had to view him as a potential opponent. Conrad's version of this is different than mine, but he was under the impression that I had agreed to sell him the *Financial Post*, and after the deal was done he offered to take the *Post* off my hands. He was disturbed that I didn't want to sell, but I had investors who thought the newspaper had upward mobility."

Black had hoped to use the *Financial Post* as a "building block" intended as a solid financial section of some future newspaper. The *Post*, in which Black had been an investor, active board member, and all-around significant supporter, had found a niche in the daily financial journalism market long dominated by the *Globe*'s cash cow, the *Report on Business*. After years of debt, the *Post* – a daily since 1988 – had just turned its first modest profit, and, logically, Black saw it as both a good business prospect and an ideal vehicle for his own political and economic views.

The *Financial Post* was a serious, pro-business newspaper with a good collection of columnists, most of whom had the small-c conservative outlook that Black considered under-represented and essential to the great Canadian debate. Given Black's existing involvement in the paper, it had been an obvious move.

"I'll start my own," was Black's frustrated message to Whyte – and while he was at it, he would ratchet up the competition in Edmonton, Ottawa, and Calgary, where Paul Godfrey's *Sun* newspapers competed head to head with the dominant Southam daily metros.

Kenneth Whyte, soft-spoken and boyish, was relatively new to the *Saturday Night* job and quite unused to speaking to his boss at all, let alone receiving late-night calls from him. He listened but wasn't sure whether Black was serious about starting a new daily or whether he was just venting anger at losing out on the *Post*. "He asked me whether I thought it would be possible to start a new newspaper on the back of Southam, which he called a national newspaper chain without a national newspaper," recalls Whyte. "I asked all the questions everyone else eventually asked. Why does Canada need another newspaper? Who's going to buy it, and who's going to advertise in it? And is there enough talent around to do a really good job? They were all legitimate questions, but they frustrated him even more. He said, 'You're looking through the wrong end of the telescope. I'll call you back in few days and we can talk about what is possible and not what the obstacles are.' "

The call lasted twenty minutes.

❖ ❖ ❖

Winnipeg-born Whyte was thirty-seven years old. He had been western columnist for the *Globe and Mail*, executive editor of the conservative *Alberta Report* magazine under the legendary Ted Byfield, and for less than three years editor of *Saturday Night* magazine. But during that time he had become Black's trusted adviser and observer of the Southam newspaper group. When Black took control of the company, he had asked Whyte for his assessment of the major Southam dailies. Whyte obliged, describing them as mediocre and lacking in opinion and ambition – a view his boss had often expressed in more colourful terms. Black, absent from the country for long periods, asked Whyte for ongoing written assessments of the newspapers and sometimes asked his opinion before appointing editors or making other major hiring decisions.

Within a couple of days of his boss's phone call, Whyte had flipped the telescope and produced a long memo for Black outlining what sort of newspaper might work in the already crowded marketplace. Above all, it would be modest, with an editorial staff of about forty, including only a dozen reporters. It would be conservative in political outlook, and not butt heads directly with the *Globe and Mail*. The working title was "The Canadian," which became the "Times of Canada." Whyte's vision was relatively clear:

> It was going to have to be a second-read paper and an editors' paper that survived on the judgment of what was a good read and what wasn't, what was interesting and what wasn't. It couldn't rely on deep market penetration or classified, career, or grocery ads – or horoscopes and crosswords. It was going to have to be focused on national and international news and not try to be local to anyone, and it was going to have to have three things that we didn't see in other newspapers at the time: a certain level of aggression when it came to presentation, fun, and irreverence. *The Globe*, at that time, considered being a national newspaper meant paying strong attention to national

institutions – the Supreme Court, House of Commons, the National Ballet, National Film Board, and the CBC. We were going to try to escape from that. And we wanted a well-defined small-c conservative point of view. It was always understood there would be a diversity of voices, but overall we wanted to create an alternative.

Among those who had worked with him, especially at *Saturday Night*, Whyte had been something of an enigma, short on people skills but a smart, independent thinker with conservative views and a journalistic sensibility that was not rooted in central Canada. He also had a reputation for changing his mind at the last minute and would delay pages of the magazine as they were about to go to press because he wanted to make changes to a story that had invariably been submitted and edited weeks or even months before. He also showed signs of having a thin skin when it came to criticism, not an uncommon condition among journalists.

For all his apparent complexities, most everyone who met Whyte agreed he could be enormously charming and persuasive, and despite his frustrating management ways he could engender an almost mystical level of loyalty among those who worked for him.

The charm was never to be underestimated, says former columnist Scott Feschuk, who had got to know Whyte when they both worked in Edmonton before Whyte left for Toronto to edit *Saturday Night*.

He's a low-key charmer, sort of an anti–Bill Clinton with a similar effect. It's an intangible thing, but it's impossible not to like him. He has the ability to tell you something and make you feel you're being drawn into his inner circle. There are stories of people leaving his office being convinced that he has just hired them but with Ken actually having no idea that they were thinking that. And people have left his office thinking he had not hired them when in fact he had. It's kind of evil but brilliant. He can make you feel like you have got everything you want from him when in fact you've got nothing. He rarely, if ever, says no. If he could bottle his management style, he would make a fortune. I'm not sure he takes criticism too well. There was a *Toronto Life* article that called him "chunky" and he didn't like that. He sought reassurance from numerous people that he wasn't chunky.

Whyte didn't know that Black had brought other people into the loop, notably Southam's president, Don Babick, and his vice-president of newspapers, Gordon Fisher, former editor-in-chief of the *Ottawa Citizen*. Babick and Fisher enlisted Michael Cooke, the sharp, genial editor of the tabloid *Vancouver Province*.

Cooke would lead a small team to produce the first of the page prototypes that Babick and Fisher would present to Black. Cooke was slightly mystified about the whole project:

> I was sitting in my office at the *Vancouver Province* with the sea and sky glistening when Fisher calls and says Conrad Black wants to launch a new national newspaper. He described it as being a financial paper and would I like to help. I said yes and immediately went out and bought the *Wall Street Journal* and books on the *Wall Street Journal*. I went to Toronto and we put together a small team, including Fisher and Brian Kappler from the *Montreal Gazette*, and we worked for about two to three weeks on various concepts. It was good for me, because I was flying back and forth business class and building up enough frequent-flyer points to fly my family to Jupiter. It was really no-expense-spared from the beginning. You've heard those stories of fire-hosing dollars across the country to put this paper together and it was wonderful.

If Black had told the Babick team about his late-night call to Whyte, it was not obvious to the magazine editor when they all eventually met in the spring of 1997 at 10 Toronto Street, Black's palatial Toronto headquarters. Whyte, who became known as Magazine Boy, had no daily newspaper experience, and on any conventional list of possible editors of a new daily his name would have been low. But the others didn't know about the reports and advice he had been giving Black during the previous two years. For whatever reason, it appears that Black neglected to state clearly at the outset that it was Kenneth Whyte who was to be editor-in-chief of his new newspaper.

Whyte, still happily running *Saturday Night*, was also working on the new newspaper but unaware that Cooke and his team had set up shop at Southam's Don Mills headquarters. Whyte had met separately with Black and his wife, Barbara Amiel, at the King Edward Hotel in Toronto on Good Friday. They spoke several times afterwards and the Blacks encouraged him to begin preparatory planning. "We spent a long time talking about the opportunities for this paper," remembers Whyte. "What kind of editorial position it could take to distinguish itself and what kind of writers would be available. He told me at that meeting to start putting together a wish list of people who would be the right kind of staff. It was at that meeting that they also made it clear – without saying it, they never really did say it – they wanted me to lead the editorial part of it. So I started from that point getting more serious about making lists of names and meeting people at various papers and thinking about what kind of talent we would want."

Whyte, still largely ignorant in the ways of daily newspaper journalism, worked in isolation, attempting to scale a learning curve of Everest proportions. He immersed himself in research data and books about newspapers and newspaper design, and began making detailed notes on the design and possible content of each section of the new daily. The Southam team, still seemingly unaware that Whyte was Black's chosen one, was doing much the same.

When Whyte realized a parallel effort was underway, he became irritated. "Things started to get a little confused between the Hollinger and Southam camps over who was doing what. Conrad often assumes people know things and doesn't always make everything clear. He may have had a good reason, but I don't think he ever explained to them what my role was, except they were supposed to work with me. But they had their own ideas about where it should go and what it should be, and they wanted to run it their way. They knew about newspapers and I didn't. They had their own candidate and Michael Cooke was drafted. They saw my role as more of a consultative one."

Whyte was on holiday in the summer of 1997 when he heard that the Southam team, plus sundry advisers and consultants, was to gather in Hamilton, without him, to produce more prototypes. It isn't clear whether Whyte was deliberately left out or whether he wasn't invited because his role was still not properly defined. Either way, Magazine Boy was having none of it. The would-be editor cut short his vacation and joined the team in Hamilton, driving in every morning from Toronto and returning to work on *Saturday Night* in the evening. He hated the drive and disliked Hamilton but says the group began to work together well.

David Swail, a key Southam business strategist, tried to persuade Whyte not to go to Hamilton. "Swail said at one point, 'Why don't you leave those people out there with Michael for a couple of weeks to see what they can do?' That was the last thing I was going to do. It was difficult for Michael, because I can be a bit domineering and I had my own ideas about what was happening, and I'm not sure I listened to them as much as they would have liked, either. But on a personal level we all got along and were all having fun, even though there was always that tension."

Throughout the summer and fall, the team worked on half a dozen computers in a spartan backroom at the *Hamilton Spectator*, trying to keep their work away from the prying eyes of *Spectator* journalists, which was not an easy task. It wasn't long before someone hacked into the team's computer system and began poking around. The two systems were immediately separated and the door kept locked.

Cooke, appointed editor of Black's *Chicago Sun-Times* in 2000, says it didn't take him too long to figure out that Whyte was more than a consultant. Sitting in his sparsely decorated office overlooking the Chicago River, he laughs heartily at the memory of Whyte's early appearances at the planning sessions. "It was clear to me that I was to be the team leader on a prototype, but when Ken, the big Silverback alpha male, turned up, it took me about a week to figure it out. I was on the 401 at the time, on my way to visit a friend in Kingston. I called Fisher from the car, and he said, Yes, Ken was Conrad's pick. He asked how I felt about it, and I said, Fine, it's too exciting to bail out now. Once it became clear he was Conrad's pick, it was also clear he would be the editor, which was fine. He has challenges with people, but there are others, especially the younger ones, who would crawl over broken glass for him."

The Hamilton team was visited by five newspaper design consultants, all of whom had been asked to come up with proposals for the mix. Clive Crook, creative director on Conrad Black's London *Daily Telegraph*, and his partner, George Darby, an experienced newspaper designer, were followed by Lucy Lacava from Montreal, who was to become a major influence in the eventual *National Post*, Jackie Young from Toronto, and Kelly Frankeny from the *San Francisco Chronicle*, a newspaper Whyte admired because of its imaginative use of colour. Whyte and Cooke both left the dreary confines of Hamilton and travelled to San Francisco to meet with Frankeny. Frankeny then agreed to travel to Toronto and offer her expertise. She caused great merriment among the assembled group when she examined an early mock-up of "The Canadian," which for added patriotic effect had a small beaver placed next to the masthead. "What's with the rat?" asked the puzzled American.

The consultants brought various elements to the prototypes, but Whyte wasn't satisfied. "They were all disappointing. They all had nice elements, but none of them said 'quality broadsheet.' They all said 'middle-market metro broadsheet.'" George Darby's "attics" – the distinctive, brief news items across the top of each news page – were the only element from the early prototype days that survived the design blender.

The core of the Hamilton prototype team – Cooke, Whyte, the *Montreal Gazette*'s Kappler, and designer Carl Neustaedter, seconded from the *Ottawa Citizen* – were joined variously by Kirk LaPointe, who was then editor of the *Spectator*, and Giles Gherson, then editor of Southam News. They all had specific tasks: Kappler, national editor at the *Gazette*, pulled stories from the various wire services; Neustaedter, who had recently led the redesign of the *Citizen*, was a self-described "drone" helping the various design consultants; and Gherson advised on business and political coverage. LaPointe's job was to troll various news services for the best available writers, columnists, cartoons, and crosswords – no easy task because, between them, the *Globe and Mail*, *Toronto Star*, and *Toronto Sun* had most rights worth having already sewn up. (In an early defensive measure against the phantom competitor, the *Globe* had also reserved rights to numerous newspaper titles.)

◆ ◆ ◆

In its various configurations, the group worked long days, drank lots of coffee, ate copious amounts of Indian food, and talked endlessly about the new paper. The prospects of the new national daily's relationship with its sister papers in the Southam chain was a major, and prescient, concern.

If the new paper were to be delivered with the Southam metros, it would have to look different and be different. What if, say, the *Ottawa Citizen* or *Edmonton Journal* had the major news scoop of the day? Wouldn't that make the new national look stupid? But how would you persuade any self-respecting editor to relinquish control of a great story and hand it over to an upstart newspaper most of the metros resented anyway?

"There was great debate over the whole cannibalization thing," says designer Carl Neustaedter. "How would it work, and what kind of reader would it attract? What was the business model? There was lots of discussion about how it would succeed and how it would make money and how long it had taken *USA Today* to make money. And there was worry, too, about driving the local newspapers into decline. It was all very exciting, but at that time I never had confidence that it would come to be."

Neustaedter left Southam and the *Citizen* in December 1997 to travel on a fellowship to Guatemala. He gave his prototype to *Citizen* editor Neil Reynolds on a computer disk and e-mailed members of the Hamilton team telling them he was quitting and wishing them luck. Only Cooke responded with good wishes. But before the designer could leave the country, *Globe* managing editor Colin MacKenzie, soon to be deposed in an ugly newsroom coup, called to offer him a job. The *Globe*, aware of what was happening at Southam, was gearing up for a major redesign and, more important, the introduction of colour, a revolution in the venerable newspaper's grey history. It was then that Neustaedter began to hear from his former bosses at Southam, who were clearly concerned that he would reveal all to the enemy He was warned to keep quiet and told to expect a lawyer's letter to that effect. It never arrived.

MacKenzie and the *Globe*'s executive editor, Sylvia Stead, interviewed Neustaedter, but neither asked him about his work on the opposition's new daily. The day Neustaedter started work at the *Globe*, MacKenzie had been ousted and Margaret Wente had taken his place. "Peggy Wente asked me what I had been doing with Southam," says Neustaedter, "but I told her I couldn't talk about it, so she dropped the subject and nobody mentioned it again."

Losing Neustaedter was a blow, recalled LaPointe, but nothing that subsequently appeared in the *Globe*'s redesign seven months later suggested they had much inkling of what Conrad Black's team had been planning. "If Carl told them anything," says LaPointe, "they obviously didn't give a rat's ass."

❖ ❖ ❖

Black's team got into the daily habit of analyzing the *Globe and Mail*, second-guessing its content, and trying to create a formula to compete – with different political slants and different interpretations on human interest stories. Simultaneously, they worked on a template for a daily front page, which, give or take a few versions, would become the content template for the *National Post*: an exclusive story, a well-written feature-type piece, a sports or entertainment story, and the news of the day. It was, in essence, the same formula that had worked so successfully for Black's *Daily Telegraph* in Britain.

A key ingredient was what Cooke described as the "Holy shit! Hey, Martha, can you believe this?" kind of story. Most of the front-page templates, and subsequently page one of the *Post* itself, invariably carried some example of whacky human behaviour. The overall aim, says Cooke, was to prove a daily template that would be different and appealing to Black.

"Journalists don't like templates, because they like to pretend they just take what happens and put it in the paper," Cooke explains. "But as we get older, we know that news is what we say it is, and if you want to hit five subject areas every day you can find the material. We knew that we were working for Conrad, so we were able to try to see the news as he might see it. He isn't afraid of sex, which Canadian newspapers certainly were, and he isn't afraid of a front-page picture of a nice-looking tennis star bending over."

Canada's new daily was destined to fall head-over-heels in love with well-proportioned Russian tennis star Anna Kournikova, whose fleeting appearances at Grand Slam tournaments would be enough to guarantee her generous space in the *Post*, either on page one or in the sports section. From its embryonic stages, the *Post* would always have room for beautiful women, in the flimsiest of outfits and for the flimsiest of reasons. It was, and is, part of its charm for many readers, and inspired *Toronto Star* executive managing editor James Travers to sum up the *Post*'s content in the memorable phrase "tits and analysis."

But all that was a long way off.

When Whyte, Cooke, and the prototype group had finished the first phase of their work and temporarily parted company, the prospects for Canada's new daily newspaper were modest, at best. There was widespread skepticism regarding Black's intentions, and many of his potential opponents had decided he was simply using the threat of a new daily newspaper as a stalking horse for the *Globe and Mail*, or even the *Toronto Star*. It was just Conrad employing some classic military strategy, probably something Napoleon had done: deploy the armed forces, rattle the sabres, psyche out the enemy, and frighten them into giving you what you want.

It was certainly a suspicion shared by *Globe and Mail* editor-in-chief William Thorsell. "I think that Conrad saw an opportunity for a national paper that would initially serve as a prod to convince the Thomsons to sell, because if you are going to launch a new paper against the *Globe* at the same time as you are trying to buy the *Globe*, you can certainly go up to Thomson and say your paper is worth more now than it's going to be worth in a long time because [the launch of a new paper] is going to hurt your economics. He had the advantage of saying, 'I could probably launch a national paper more cheaply in Canada than anyone, because I've got the whole Southam network to support it in terms of printing, distribution, and news content.' If you had tried to start up something like the *National Post* without owning Southam, it would have been an entirely different proposition."

Kenneth Whyte was operating on a different set of assumptions. He was off to Conrad Black's *Daily Telegraph* in London to learn the ways of daily newspapering and to find skills he had no doubt he would be needing.

3 | MEANWHILE, AT THE GLOBE AND MAIL

"When I arrived from London, I saw the *Globe and Mail* and thought every Canadian had died and gone to hell."

— David Walmsley, political editor, *National Post*

Heading into 1998, the *Globe and Mail* was doing very nicely in its influential, monopolistic grey niche, enjoying handsome profits from the advertising and circulation revenue that rolled in with relative ease.

For years, *Globe* managers had been able to maintain a balance by keeping production costs under control with a steady circulation of around 350,000 – a mix of delivery to subscribers, daily single-copy sales from newsstands, and the relatively new but profitable business of selling cut-price copies to upmarket hotels and airlines. These so-called bulk sales were important for two reasons: they generated between $3 million and $4 million a year and enabled the *Globe* to reach readers while they were captive on aircraft or waking up in the morning at the better hostelries around the country. This mobile readership was a little something extra that the *Globe*'s advertising sales force could offer to advertisers – nice to have when the newspaper wanted to jack up its rates.

William Thorsell, the *Globe*'s editor-in-chief from 1989 to 1999, is an erudite man who liked his office walls turquoise and his newspaper black and white. He had moulded the *Globe and Mail* into his own vision of what a newspaper heading into the twenty-first century should be, and as far as anyone could tell, *Globe* subscribers and advertisers were happy enough with the paper's analytical, often eccentric approach to the daily goings-on in Canada and beyond. Thorsell wasn't universally popular among his staff, many of whom considered him an inadequate, aloof manager capable of a cold nastiness that eventually poisoned the air in the newsroom and embittered dozens of its journalists. Others quite liked him and would enthuse about his stunning intellect and impact on the great issues of the day.

"Thorsell was an interesting choice as editor because he was so radical," says former *Globe* foreign correspondent John Gray. "I distrusted his social judgments and a lot of his politics, but what was wonderful about him was that there was no question he wouldn't ask about how a newspaper should be run. He didn't know a lot about newspapers because he had been an editorial writer. The answer 'because we've always done it that way' was never good enough for him. I didn't agree with a lot of his conclusions, but it was wonderful someone was asking those fundamental questions. But he was a terrible manager."

Thorsell may have been radical within the context of newsroom culture, but his political outlook was decidedly conservative. He came to the job of editor-in-chief from the *Globe*'s editorial board, the place in newspapers where people are paid to reflect and opine on the news rather than immediately react to it. He had limited interest in the traditional ways of covering the news of the day, or "yesterday's routine happenings and recurring tragedies," as he once sniffily described them. His vision of what an upscale daily newspaper should be was commendably well articulated in a magazine celebrating the paper's 150th anniversary:

> Serious readers of serious newspapers need more. . . . They are looking for illuminating patterns in the cacophony of change. They are looking for inspiration in the ability of others to manage common problems. They are looking for early notice about the dangers and opportunities rushing toward them from the future. And with all this uncertainty, they are seeking anchors in principles and values that can withstand and even mould change.

It all sounded a tad pretentious for tomorrow's fish wrap, but the daily newspaper paradigm is prone to lurching shifts in fashion, and Thorsell was writing in a period when there was great concern in the industry over losing readers to television newscasts. Recreating daily newspapers to keep them relevant, and not simply repeating the news that readers had heard before going to bed the night before, was seen as key to the newspaper industry's survival. It was a simple analysis: TV could offer the instant news but only newspapers could delve into the context and examine the trends.

But Thorsell and his publisher, the amiable former American marine Roger Parkinson, were cushioned. The *Globe*, the *Toronto Star*, and the *Toronto Sun* co-existed in relative peace, well entrenched in their own lucrative niches in one of North America's most vibrant newspaper cities. Given the *Globe*'s relative comfort, courtesy of its grip on the high-end newspaper market, Thorsell could afford to challenge the conservative traditions of daily newspapers and play around a little. So he did.

It was all a far cry from the *Globe*'s precarious situation twenty years earlier, when the newspaper had staggered out of Toronto's newspaper war inflicted with potentially fatal wounds to its reputation and slowly bleeding circulation and advertising revenue. Then publisher Roy Megarry, recruited in 1978 as saviour from the *Toronto Star*, knew he had a tough job ahead. "I had been a vice-president at *Star*, and we would sit around the table discussing what the situation in the market would be like when the *Globe* went out of business," recalls Megarry. "It was a very serious discussion that we had a number of times. The *Globe* was in a very tenuous situation."

The *Toronto Star*, which published its first morning edition in August 1981, had emerged supreme and effectively forced the *Globe* out of the local Toronto market. So, in a remarkable show of marketing moxie, *Globe* management leaned heavily on the newspaper's history and what remained of its reputation, referring to it as "Canada's National Newspaper" long before it actually was – and when its sales outside Ontario were barely 10,000 copies and its journalistic representation beyond the province was one bureau. (Science gave this outrageous claim legitimacy when satellite technology emerged in the 1980s and the *Globe* was able to distribute nationally on the day of publication by using regional printing plants and local circulation teams.)

Journalist Robert Fulford, employed at various times in his career by the *Globe*, *Star*, and *Saturday Night* magazine, says the *Globe* had no choice but to reposition itself as a national paper for the country's elite.

"If they had gone up against the *Star*, the *Star* would have beat the hell out of them, so they elected to be the paper for the leadership class and those who imagined themselves to be the leadership class and those who pretended to be. It was a considerable number of people. They were the national newspaper of Southern Ontario and Ottawa – not the city of Ottawa but the Ottawa of myth and deputy ministers. The *Globe* was their paper and the paper for the leadership class."

It was Megarry who appointed William Thorsell editor-in-chief in 1989 in the late period of Brian Mulroney's tenure as prime minister and into the early days of the so-called Common Sense Revolution led by Ontario Premier Mike Harris. Mulroney was given to having friendly chats with newspaper editors whose publications supported his policies and isolating those who didn't. Thorsell got special attention because he was not only friendly to the cause but edited what the Ottawa power elite considered the country's most influential newspaper – though, for the most part, it was only the most influential because they considered it to be. Which may, or may not, amount to the same thing.

The apparent closeness of Thorsell's relationship with Mulroney, and the long phone calls the two shared, made many *Globe* journalists uncomfortable. They felt it compromised the newspaper's independence and their own ability to convince others of their impartiality. Nor was the relationship, which earned Thorsell the *Frank* magazine epithet "Torysell," especially discreet.

In an interview with *Toronto Life* magazine, former *Globe* art director Michael Gregg recalled, "His secretary would announce an 'important call' and William would stop everything to take it. Everyone knew it was the prime minister and we were supposed to know. There was a lot of resentment about the *Globe*'s news agenda being hijacked and our coverage being skewed toward Mulroney, but there was also some envy."

◆ ◆ ◆

So despite its relative prosperity and journalistic successes manifested in copious National Newspaper Awards, not all was well at Canada's venerable, nationally circulated, monopolistic daily newspaper. Complacency was in the air, and during the not-so-secret meetings at sealed rooms across town, members of Conrad Black's prototype team, and their various fleeting consultants, had the enemy pegged as a colourless, ponderous, lifeless, and humourless newspaper ripe for the picking. The *Globe*'s use of news photography was unimaginative, and the lack of sports coverage peculiar, especially for a newspaper designed to appeal to the business community where sports and stocks are common languages.

This version of the *Globe*'s deficiencies, while not universally shared, was the one that would matter, both among the *Globe*'s corporate masters within the Thomson organization and at what would become, a year or so later, the *National Post*.

David Walmsley, a loquacious Irishman and one of several *Post* employees plucked from Conrad Black's *Daily Telegraph* in London, recalled his first look at the *Globe and Mail* shortly after he arrived in Canada in the summer of 1998. His attitude was shared by many of his future colleagues. "When I arrived from London, which is the greatest newspaper city in the world, I saw the *Globe and Mail* and thought every Canadian had died and gone to hell. It was an absolute disgrace. It was a disgrace to journalists. It was a disgrace to the country and to the government it was supposed to be scrutinizing. It was the most boring load of nonsense I had ever read. This was a paper that needed a very serious kick up the arse."

Lack of real competition has many downsides, but chief among them is a chronic and natural unwillingness among those who control the purse strings to spend money they are not forced to spend. Most newspaper empires have been built on parsimony, the Thomson and Black empires included. The *Globe* offices were gloomy, overcrowded, packed with 1970s office furniture, and, compared to the modern technology being introduced at some major Southam newspapers controlled by Conrad Black, its computers were aging relics.

Many loyal *Globe* journalists were unhappy – victims, as they saw it, of managerial lethargy and arbitrary decision-making. The accomplished *Globe* political reporter Susan Delacourt, who transferred to Toronto from Ottawa after covering the June 1997 election, got a gloomy reception. "I arrived there in August, and they had no desk for me, no computer, no phone, nothing. There was a rolling unhappiness around the place. I was sitting at the back of the newsroom with a few others. They called us senior writers, but it was just a bunch of people who sat around doing nothing. So I tested them. I kept suggesting stories, and they didn't want them. So I decided to wait them out and see how long it would take to get an assignment. It was twenty-seven days before anyone spoke to me – twenty-seven days of coming in to work and doing nothing. The morale got worse, and it seemed like nobody wanted anyone to do anything. It was almost like they were discouraging people from working. It was soul destroying."

Delacourt, now Ottawa bureau chief of the *Toronto Star*, wasn't alone in her unhappiness, but for many the situation was only destined to get worse.

Journalists tend to be insecure, and the ones who appear otherwise are frequently the most insecure. But the best reporters also care passionately about their work and keep a frenetic, obsessive pace against fierce daily deadlines and, in some cities, fierce competition. Working with teams of editors who assign and edit stories, photographers who provide art, and design editors who write the headlines and fit stories, pictures, and headlines onto pages, reporters start work every morning with a clean sheet, build a newspaper from scratch, and do it all again the next day. It is manufacturing at its most frenetic and most pressured. Unlike any other business, the new product is out there every day for readers to scrutinize. Each story carries the name of the person who gathered the facts and did the writing. Newspaper writers have no layers of bureaucracy to hide behind, and given the number of facts in any newspaper story or feature article produced under deadline pressure, the level of accuracy is usually commendable. And given the various components that come together with such speed to create a daily newspaper, the description "minor miracle" is not misplaced. Conrad Black was correct thirty years ago when he said that many journalists, especially newspaper people, were alcoholics or close to it, but his accusation that laziness was endemic in the business betrayed the ignorance and arrogance of a young man who had never been put through the ringer of a news cycle at a major daily and had never gone to bed at night terrified that the opposition might have beaten him on a story, or that the story hitting the streets in tomorrow's edition might, in some way, be wrong.

Newspaper people tend to socialize with each other, have affairs with each other, live together, marry each other, have children together, and gossip together, endlessly, about the business. They are at once worldly and insular. It's partly the nature of the business, which throws like-minded people into the same daily maelstrom. It's partly that newspaper work is unique and regularly misunderstood by the public, which puts journalists roughly on the same level as politicians in public esteem – at around about gutter level. Certain segments of society believe that journalists begin each day in conspiratorial meetings deciding whose reputation to tear to shreds today. In truth, journalists rarely have enough time to conspire. It is a unique, addictive business packed with quirky, awkward personalities who, without newspapers, might have nowhere else to go.

It takes special talent to manage, and bring out the best in, such people, and not all newspapers have a brilliant record in preparing or training their newsroom managers, often promoting ambitious people from reporting ranks and hoping for the best. Insecurity and benign neglect can produce bitterness, uncertainty, and misery – conditions a company can live with in most circumstances but are potentially fatal when aggressive, well-equipped, and committed competition is preparing to charge over the horizon and go for your throat. As bad as many thought it was, life at the *Globe and Mail* was destined to become worse.

◆ ◆ ◆

William Thorsell is rather proud of his impersonation of Conrad Black, and during strategy meetings with fellow department heads in late 1997 he got to take centre stage in the role. It was a period when *Globe* management suspected Black was bluffing about a new national newspaper but started planning a defence anyway.

"We knew [Black] had Southam and thought about the advantages he had there and how he would use them," says Thorsell. "We went through scenarios, what he might do, and then we developed a number of scenarios about how we would respond, what we might do in a pre-emptive way to be prepared, should he announce that he was going ahead. We ran various scenarios there and played them out – editorial content, size, costs, advertising. . . . We were strategizing with his musings, and he was musing pretty aggressively. It takes a while to develop strategies, and we thought, 'Let's start planning a war, should the war come.'"

Thorsell was convinced that if Black launched a new newspaper, it would have a Sunday edition, the only day not covered by the *Globe and Mail*. A Canadian version of the Sunday *New York Times* would be an attractive proposition for a newcomer, Thorsell reasoned. Indeed, the *Globe* might have entered the Sunday market itself years before had it not been for the common dilemma facing any newspaper already established in a Saturday market: Sunday papers cannibalize the advertising revenue of the fat Saturday editions, and in most situations generate minimal independent revenue. Years earlier, several Southam newspapers had launched Sunday editions as pre-emptive strikes against competition from *Sun* newspapers ready to fill the seventh-day vacuum.

"When Conrad announced he was going to do a national paper," says Thorsell, "I thought he would definitely do Sunday – seven days a week, or Tuesday through Sunday, or something like that. I'm sure he had good reasons to leave Sunday alone, but in his place I would have been very tempted."

Thorsell's boss, the former Green Beret and Vietnam veteran Roger Parkinson, arrived at the *Globe* from the *Minneapolis Star Tribune* on May 1, 1992, and the new publisher guided the *Globe* as it staggered along with all other newspapers through some lean recession years into decent profit margins – in the *Globe*'s case around 15 per cent.

Parkinson developed a reputation at the paper as a hail-fellow-well-met optimist who enjoyed wearing cardigans. But the impression he had left in Minneapolis was not so benign. He was at odds with most of his reporters and editorial staff – a rift caused by his penchant for a level of community and political involvement that his journalists said compromised the newspaper's journalistic integrity and, in some cases, hampered their work.

Relations at the *Star Tribune* reached a low point when in an election year Parkinson joined forces with state governor Rudy Perpich, who had been dubbed "Governor Goofy" by *Newsweek* magazine and was struggling to get support for his re-nomination from the powerful Democratic Farm Labour party. The publisher agreed to head a task force to bring then Soviet leader Mikhail Gorbachev for a farm tour of the state and helped underwrite the visit with a $300,000 credit note on the newspaper's account. Reporters threatened to withhold their by-lines from stories – a common form of protest – and the union wrote Parkinson, who also headed the newspaper's editorial board, an official note of objection: "Your role as a key player in news-making events makes it difficult for us to explain to our readers that our newspaper is an effective watchdog. It is difficult for us to claim objectivity in covering the governor's race when our publisher is working hand-in-hand with the incumbent."

Given that the eyes of the world would be on the state during Gorbachev's visit, reporters voted against the by-line strike to avoid embarrassing the newspaper. The visit was a huge success and generated much-needed positive publicity for the governor, who romped to re-nomination a week later.

In an article written for the *Newsletter on Journalism Ethics* in September 1990, *Star Tribune* national reporter Paul McEnroe recounted the Gorbachev trip: "The motorcade swept through the Twin Cities, Roger Parkinson in one of the lead limos. At one point when the motorcade stopped, Parkinson got out and, along with KGB agents, pushed the crowd away from the Soviet entourage as Gorbachev worked the crowd. Weeks after what is known cryptically around the newsroom as 'the visit,' copies of doctored pictures still hang. The photograph of Parkinson has been transposed – from a full head of hair, the publisher has become bald in the same fashion as Gorbachev. There is a birthmark imprinted on Parkinson's forehead, in the same spot as Gorbachev's. The birthmark is a perfect outline of the state of Minnesota."

One favourite Parkinson story that travelled rapidly through the *Globe and Mail* jungle telegraph emerged from Parkinson's introduction to recently hired reporter Tu Thanh Ha, who was born in Vietnam, where Parkinson had served with the Marine Corps. The reporter, hired to work in the Ottawa bureau, was in Toronto for orientation when the ever-friendly publisher attempted unsuccessfully to communicate with him in Vietnamese. "Shit," Parkinson was heard to say to the attendant group of managers, "it's been so long. Anyway, all I ever did was interrogate VC."

Recalling the incident years later, Ha says he wasn't offended or embarrassed but clearly remembers that the other *Globe* managers who witnessed the incident were embarrassed enough for him.

"I just thought he was goofy," he says.

◆　◆　◆

When Conrad Black had assumed control of Southam in the fall of 1996, he had felt strongly that the next logical step to strengthen the company's national newspaper franchise was to fill the gaping hole that was Toronto. He wanted to buy the *Globe* but apparently never came close to persuading Kenneth Thomson to sell it to him. Rumour suggested that Black was offering between $400 million to $500 million, which was about half what Thomson considered the newspaper, its good name, and goodwill to be worth. The two men never met, preferring to conduct the game of approach and rebuff through intermediaries. "When are you going to sell me the big enchilada?" Black's partner, David Radler, would occasionally ask Stuart Garner, then president and CEO of Thomson Newspapers. Garner would just laugh.

But Radler never quit trying to buy the *Globe* and was still trying while he was negotiating to buy the *Financial Post* and when plans for the new daily were well advanced.

Radler was working on the assumption that neither company chairman Kenneth Thomson nor his son and eventual successor, David, who was involved in the day-to-day operations of the company, had any interest in keeping the *Globe* for political reasons and were motivated purely by the economics of their business. Given that Thomson had divested itself of all its British newspapers in 1995, Radler was guessing, quite correctly, that the company would eventually do the same in North America. One scenario he explored was keeping the lucrative *Report on Business*, wrapping it into the new Conrad Black newspaper, and killing the rest of the *Globe*.

"One of the advantages of coming with us was the distribution, which they didn't have," he says. "We talked about that. We talked about all sorts of things. We had done preliminary work on the new newspaper, but I didn't care because I was still trying to do a deal."

Radler, representing a company operating with debt, had to take a softly-softly approach with Thomson Corp., a company for whom *debt* is an alien word. Nonetheless, Radler managed to remain optimistic about getting the *Globe* because he knew that Thomson corporate strategy was shifting away from newspapers. He also figured that nostalgia wasn't an issue, either, because Thomson had already sold him the *Timmins Press*, the newspaper upon which company founder Roy Thomson built his empire.

"You don't put pressure on a company that has a net worth of U.S.$35 billion. I didn't try to do that kind of thing, and that's why I had a good relationship with them. But there was no doubt that they were getting out of the business. I knew, and they knew, but I'm close-mouthed, so even when I knew what they were up to, I never talked to anyone about it. I would never do anything to embarrass them. So I knew there was a shot and I kept pushing for the shot."

Black says Thomson offered him – through David Radler – a 20 per cent stake in the *Globe* about a year before the *Post*'s launch, but he rejected the offer. Given what was happening behind the scenes then, and what would happen in the future, an outsider could be forgiven for thinking that Black had seen a chink in the Thomson resolve and had decided to exploit it.

Not so, says Black. "I was never under any illusion that Thomson was going to sell the *Globe and Mail*. They were offering 20 per cent or something, but it wasn't interesting to me. They just didn't want us to start a competing newspaper, which I can understand."

But it seems clear that until the eleventh hour, Black would have ditched plans for his new daily if Thomson had sold him the *Globe*. He told Southam chief executive Don Babick in May 1998 – five months before the *National Post* launch and weeks before he bought the *Financial Post* – to visit Thomson executive Stuart Garner and show him business models for the new daily. It was a militaristic-style play to convince Thomson that the prospect of a competing daily was not just as threat. But Thomson called the bluff and again the answer came back: The *Globe* is not for sale, Mr. Black. Not to you, at least.

But Thomson's reluctance to sell was never about money, even though the corporation was in the throes of ditching all its newspapers and moving into electronic information services that were not dependent on the vagaries of advertising revenue and newsprint prices. Someone close to the Thomson family says that discomfort with Conrad Black's politics was at the root of the reluctance. "The principal reason it didn't happen was because it was perceived that Conrad would try to use the *Globe* as the instrument to achieve political change. I don't believe there was ever a serious discussion of money, but it was never an anti-Conrad Black thing, just pro-*Globe*. There is no personal antagonism. Ken Thomson didn't want the *Globe* used as an instrument in the way Conrad Black was likely to use it. There was no negotiation, never a mention of price, and never any conversation between Conrad Black and Kenneth Thomson. But I think Conrad might have thought he could put the *Globe* out of business."

Publisher Parkinson, who would eventually be pushed out of the newspaper war's front line by Garner, admits that the *Globe* had become a little sloppy in its daily habits because "we had it sort of easy."

Through copious strategy meetings and market research, his management team developed a war plan that, claimed Parkinson, was ready by the time Garner replaced him as publisher with Phillip Crawley, a former workmate from Newcastle, England. "We did a massive amount of research, because we knew that they were doing all sorts of research on us. We wanted to cover every nook and cranny to find out who felt what about us. Conrad is going to know this stuff, so we wanted to know everything that Conrad knew about us. He was going to find where our holes were. So we found our strengths and weaknesses and began plugging the holes."

Garner and Parkinson brought in consultants from the *Guardian*, a newspaper that had survived and thrived in the fallout of a brutal price war between Rupert Murdoch's *Times* and Conrad Black's *Daily Telegraph*. A key adviser imported from Britain to the *Globe and Mail*'s Toronto office was Jim Chisholm, a world expert on newspaper startups and how to thwart them. Chisholm's advice was to prove vital in the *Globe*'s defence.

First Chisholm delivered some good news and some bad: The good news for the *Globe* was that the odds were against Conrad Black, because although there were gaps in the Toronto newspaper market, none was apparently large enough to accommodate a new daily. The bad news was that Black had used clever marketing and circulation strategies to stave off Murdoch in the London war and the *Globe* needed an overhaul.

Chisholm also reminded *Globe* executives of the *Independent*, which faced overwhelming odds when it was launched in 1980 yet still managed to carve itself a niche into the overcrowded world of British daily newspapers by being refreshing and different. In other words, cautioned Chisholm, if Conrad Black launched a new daily newspaper in Canada, passive resistance was not an option. And if Black produced a quality, innovative newspaper, history, tradition, and current position in the market wouldn't be enough to protect any of the incumbents, either across the country or in the critical, reader-rich Greater Toronto Area.

Chisholm analyzed the research and fed his conclusions back to Thorsell. The *Globe* had to be livelier and build on its reputation while appealing to a younger, livelier audience. There was also a lot of debate about whether there should be a sports section.

The launch of any new product into a competitive marketplace has a cost of entry and a price of entry. The cost is the initial capital outlay, and price is what it takes to continue competing when incumbent competitors fight back. Black already owned the Southam newspaper chain, so his cost of entry into the Canadian national newspaper market would be relatively low. He had the printing, circulation, and, to the extent he wanted to use it, journalistic infrastructure in place. The price of staying in the game depended on how vigorously the *Globe and Mail*, the *Toronto Star*, and maybe the *Toronto Sun* fought back. The success of many new products, newspapers or otherwise, is often in the mistakes made by the incumbents.

In the five years before Black's new paper was set to launch, more than 600 dailies and 33 Sunday newspapers were launched worldwide, including 216 in China and 90 in Brazil, 9 in Greece, 8 in Spain, and a couple in France, including *Info Matin*, a smaller-than-tabloid commuter newspaper designed to give people with little time a quick fix of news on the way to work. And there were numerous specialized business dailies and free commuter newspapers springing up. At least two-thirds of all the new newspapers were destined to fail, and most of them sooner rather than later.

In the best strategic traditions of a well-fought war, the two camps each had their spies. If the Canadian newspaper community is a village, the Toronto newspaper community is at the most densely populated centre of that village. Sleeping with the enemy, either illicitly or otherwise, is the natural way of things. Secrets are difficult to keep, because journalists not only love to gossip, but the best of them are among the elite when it comes to digging for information. Traditionally, laid-off, burned-out, or bought-out reporters go into media consulting or government communications jobs, but their talents would be put to far better use on the local police force – in the plainclothes section, of course – or at a detective agency.

The intelligence continued to flow back and forth through the hopelessly porous security and continued unabated on pillows, over family dinners, and at discreet lunches between friends.

So *Globe* executives knew, more or less, what the Southam prototype team was up to, and when they were up to it, but the information was far from definitive, largely because the Southam prototype team was experimenting and prone to changing direction without warning.

"It was a very blurring, seductive idea that [Kenneth Whyte] would fly into town for dinner and fly out again right after dinner. And just to see me. So if that was a Ken manipulation, it was very effective, because it made me feel quite important."
– Edward Greenspon, Ottawa bureau chief, *Globe and Mail*

E d Greenspon left his Ottawa home on a bitterly cold April Fool's Day 1998 and trudged through winter's remaining snow toward La Strada, a trendy Italian restaurant a couple of blocks away on Bank Street in the Glebe. He was burning with curiosity.

Ken Whyte had telephoned the *Globe*'s Ottawa bureau chief earlier in the week. He was going to be in town and wanted to meet for a discreet dinner, away from the downtown to minimize the chances of being seen by prying journalists. The meeting, and what transpired during it, had to be secret. "I don't want to start rumours," said Whyte, showing a charming naiveté toward the newspaper business.

The call came as a total surprise to Greenspon, who only vaguely remembered meeting Whyte once or twice. He booked a table at La Strada and began some serious speculating. He had some idea what it might be about.

The *Globe and Mail* had been getting intelligence reports for months from inside Southam and knew that a small team had been secretly working on newspaper prototypes in Hamilton at the *Spectator* offices and latterly in Don Mills at Southam corporate headquarters. But the prospect of a new Conrad Black national daily had been long treated as a bit of a joke at the *Globe*. Something in Whyte's voice when he phoned told Greenspon that the jokes may have been misplaced. As he approached the restaurant he thought he had it figured out: Whyte had been sent to hire him as either a national columnist for the new paper or some kind of super political writer.

Greenspon was wrong on both counts.

The bespectacled Greenspon, a quintessential *Globe and Mail* man, had impressed colleagues as an intelligent, ambitious person with a clear sight of his professional targets and, through the cultivation of key individuals, an ability to exert quiet influence, and make his views known, in places high above his station. Parallel with his personal ambition ran a vision of the *Globe* and, as he saw it, its integral role in Canadian society and in its political decision-making. For Greenspon, and many similarly minded colleagues, the *Globe* enjoyed a status beyond that of a mere daily newspaper. He took the *Globe*, and his own part in it, very seriously.

Secrecy was vital to Whyte as he began to woo key staff, because he actually wanted to hire some of the people he interviewed, not simply provide them with the opportunity to leverage fat wage increases from their existing employers. But he was in a tough spot. On one hand, he was selling something that didn't exist and asking well-established, comfortable journalists to risk careers and throw their families into upheaval for some speculative venture that could collapse weeks or months after it began. On the other hand, he was about to start a newspaper war and had to be careful about revealing too much to anyone.

Whyte developed a sixth sense when interviewing prospective editors and reporters and pretty well knew when interviewees had already secured their pay raise and were meeting with him on intelligence-gathering missions with the blessing of their bosses. But he could never be totally sure about anybody.

"I could tell early on the people who were doing it to get a raise, but that's what happens in a competitive environment. Anyway, a lot of people had been held back at their own newspapers. Journalistic talent should be worth something. There is a notion we were throwing money at people to get them to come and spending outrageous money. You can't get people to move from one job for another without offering them more money. Most of the people came for $5,000 to $10,000 more, and most of them came from smaller markets. We didn't break the bank for anyone."

When Greenspon and Whyte met at La Strada, Black's choice of editor still hadn't been announced, though the paper itself was by then being referred to in all circles as the "Daily Tubby" or just "Tubby." (Black was first referred to as "Tubby" years before by Geoff Heinricks, one of the original writers at *Frank* magazine. It was an imaginary, private school type of nickname that Heinricks thought might have been bestowed on a younger Black by his well-heeled school chums. In the absence of an official title for the yet-unborn newspaper, *Frank* adopted the Daily Tubby as a temporary handle, and it quickly moved into common lexicon. In a 2001 TV documentary about *Frank*, Black scorned the magazine but asked the filmmakers, almost plaintively, "Do they still call me Tubby?")

Rumours were abounding about who Black would choose for the editor's job, with then *Ottawa Citizen* editor Neil Reynolds an occasional hot favourite, along with then *Vancouver Province* editor-in-chief Michael Cooke. Over time, most senior newsroom managers in the country found their names hanging on the grapevine. Whyte was certainly a contender, but his lack of newspaper experience and comparative youth made him little more than an outsider among the unofficial bookies in the newspaper fraternity. Would Black trust his new multimillion-dollar baby to a rookie? It was a long shot, at best.

But the extent of Whyte's relationship with Conrad Black and Barbara Amiel was not widely understood. He had access and he had influence – and far more of both than any of his potential rivals, or newsroom punters, could possibly have known.

Whyte arrived slightly late for the dinner with Greenspon. Arriving late, and occasionally not at all, was not a rare occurrence for Whyte. The two exchanged a few niceties.

"So what else are you doing in Ottawa?" asked Greenspon.

"I came to have supper with you."

"What do you mean you came to see me?" said Greenspon, surprised and by no means convinced. "You're not doing anything else?"

"Yeah, I flew in to see you," insisted Whyte. "I just came from the airport, and I'm flying back out right after dinner."

Then the enigmatic stranger began to turn on the charm, described by his many and varied professional targets as being magnetic. "He has so much personal charm when he focuses on you and smiles," says former colleague Kirk LaPointe. "It's so hard to resist."

A dinner meeting that Greenspon considered to be kind of strange in the first place had suddenly turned weird. "It was a very blurring, seductive idea that he would fly into town for dinner and fly out again right after dinner. And just to see me. So if that was a Ken manipulation, it was very effective, because it made me feel quite important."

And then things got even weirder. Whyte announced that he had been appointed editor-in-chief of the Daily Tubby and wanted Greenspon to be managing editor, his number two. "Then Ken tells me a couple of stories that make it clear that he is Conrad's guy and how he's had to clean the nose of a few people who treat him like he's Magazine Boy – people who think he doesn't know anything about newspapers and don't understand that he's going to be the guy. After he's sort of established his bona fides with me, he goes on and tells me he wants me to be the managing editor. I'm taken aback. I mean, my management experience at newspapers was pretty thin."

Whyte wanted an answer quickly. Greenspon was flattered both by the offer and the way in which it was presented, but he asked for time to think. He also wanted Whyte to meet his wife – immediately. "Look," he said, "I can't go home and say I'm going to move to Toronto for somebody my wife has never met. So you are going to have to come home with me. Come to the house, I'm about a block and a half away. I'd like Janice to meet you before she and I can have a serious talk about this."

Whyte went to the restaurant washroom and Greenspon called his wife, Carleton University journalism professor Janice Neal, on his cellphone. "In my mind I was going to come home and say, 'So, Ken Whyte just offered me this job to move to Toronto,' and Janice wouldn't even have a mental picture of the guy. I would be married to Ken in many ways and he would be a big part of our lives and I wanted her to have a comfort level and some sense that this was a real person."

While he waited for Whyte, Greenspon began reading a *New York Times* review of La Strada hanging on a wall in the restaurant's vestibule. ". . . [A] well-known hangout for journalists . . . ," it said. Greenspon chuckled to himself. It was news to him. He'd never eaten there before.

At around ten o'clock, after a trudge through the snow, the three had settled into the Greenspons' living room. Ken sat in a wingback chair by the fireplace and they chatted – mostly small talk. Ken spoke lovingly about his little daughter and the Greenspons responded in kind about their three children. But Eddie felt their guest was uncomfortable. "I think he found it weird that I wanted him to meet my wife. I think he finds that sort of thing a little too 1990s or something. And he didn't seem at ease, perhaps because he wasn't as in control of the situation like he had been in the restaurant."

Whyte left about half an hour later for a flight back to Toronto thinking nothing of the sort. "It was the only time during recruiting that I met a spouse, and I found it kind of touching. He obviously had a strong relationship with his wife and trusted her judgment. Anyway, in most of the interviews I knew that at least half of the questions guys were asking were coming from their wives. It's like college basketball recruiting: everyone knows that you've got to get the parents before you can get the kid, and so we took all of the familial considerations very seriously. We even employed an educational consultant on contract to advise people on schools in Toronto."

◆ ◆ ◆

That evening began an intense, month-long relationship between Whyte and Greenspon. During frequent phone calls that sometimes lasted almost two hours, they discussed the type of journalism they wanted in the new newspaper and the journalists they were going to hire. They even discussed in detail the layout of the newsroom at Don Mills – not the ideal location for any newspaper but one that Conrad Black felt would work after the fashion of London's new Fleet Street at the relatively remote Canary Wharf.

At this point, with Black's purchase of the *Financial Post* several months away, the new newspaper Whyte envisioned was a comparatively modest product packed with well-chosen, well-edited wire stories and original pieces from hand-picked staff writers.

Business coverage would be key for any newspaper going up against the *Globe and Mail*'s *Report on Business*. Greenspon, a former *ROB* managing editor, told Whyte he would need a credible business section from day one. "A business section is a very precise kind of journalism. It requires a lot of expertise, because if you screw up and get your A shares and your B shares mixed up, it can send tens of millions of dollars the wrong way."

Like time-insensitive teenagers discussing pop stars or their latest crushes, they talked about their favourite newspapers and magazines and to their joy discovered a mutual admiration for the *New York Observer*, especially the version edited by the Canadian Graydon Carter, by then editor of *Vanity Fair* magazine, who had transformed the plodding community newspaper into a brash, stylish weekly packed with gossip about

Manhattan's professional elite. More than a wisp of the *Observer*'s spirit would drift north and into the pages of Ken Whyte's *National Post*.

Greenspon was impressed.

"Ken had done a lot of work and a lot of thinking. By this time, he knows people he wants to hire and he's been doing intelligence gathering about people in the industry. At that point, he probably had no one to talk to on the basis we were talking, so things picked up momentum."

Greenspon asked to see the mock-up pages for the new newspaper, but the ever-cautious Whyte refused to show them to him.

One of Greenspon's greatest concerns was the Daily Tubby's ideology, and he told Whyte there were some things he would not be comfortable with – anti-homosexual rants, for one. Whyte said the newspaper would have a conservative editorial voice but reassured Greenspon that for any newspaper trying to establish itself in Toronto, exclusion of any group in its news coverage would be plain stupid.

But as the weeks went by, the conversations became negotiations, and Greenspon found himself in contract talks with Tim Peters, vice-president of human resources at Southam, who routinely dealt with details of "the package" after Whyte's part of the recruiting process was done. Whyte was confident that he had found his right-hand man. Greenspon, excited by the adventure of it all, was hooked . . . but he wasn't quite landed.

❖   ❖   ❖

Some Southam executives had advised Whyte not to approach Greenspon, then the *Globe*'s Ottawa bureau chief. In the winter of 1997, shortly before the buzz about Conrad Black's plans for a new national newspaper, Southam had tried to hire Greenspon as editor-in-chief of the Southam News bureau in Ottawa. The bureau was the hub of Ottawa political coverage for Southam newspapers across the country and, for many ambitious newsroom executives, proved to be one step away from being the editorship of major Southam dailies.

Coincidentally, Greenspon had been working on an internal report for the *Globe and Mail* about possible competition from the *Ottawa Citizen* and other major Southam newspapers, which were joining forces under the Southam News umbrella to provide daily federal government and political coverage from Parliament Hill. Black was pumping $50 million into the *Citizen* and seemed determined to transform the newspaper into what reporters were calling a *"Washington Post* North."

Neil Reynolds, recently installed by Black as editor of the *Ottawa Citizen*, was the first to approach Greenspon about the Southam News job. The two met at the Café Toulouse in Ottawa and, according to Greenspon, had a vigorous talk about journalism and got on swimmingly. After a series of negotiations over the phone, Greenspon met Gordon Fisher, the company's then vice-president of newspapers, at a hotel near Dorval airport in Montreal. At the eleventh hour, Greenspon decided not to take the job.

"The Southam guys were very unhappy with how it had ended," says Whyte, "and were discouraging me from talking to him. So too was Conrad, who really had no time at all for him. But I had a need for news, and I had to be able to break national stories, and few people at Southam papers had shown much ability to drive stories that could lead the mainstream of journalistic discourse in Canada. To be successful we had to be able to do that. I also wanted someone young and energetic.

"What was appealing about Eddie was that he could get a particular type of news out of Ottawa. He was well plugged in, solid, and knew what was at the top of the news agenda in advance. He knew how to do news for a quality broadsheet and had a good idea of how Canada works. We had to get our share of the national conversation."

Whyte offered to return to Ottawa to talk more with Greenspon face to face, but Greenspon was travelling to Toronto, so they agreed to wait a few days.

They met in a coffee shop downstairs in a corner of the *Saturday Night* building, near the King Edward Hotel on King Street. It was the day when Southam's Don Babick was to go on national television from Vancouver to announce that Canada would have a new national newspaper by the fall. The choice of Vancouver was a statement: this would be a true national newspaper and not just another organ for the central Canadian view of the world.

Shortly before they left the coffee shop, Whyte got a message on his cellphone, from his assistant at *Saturday Night*, to call Conrad Black in New York. He excused himself and went to a pay phone but didn't tell Greenspon why.

Black was obviously excited. "Well this is the day!" he said.

"We had a really neat little three-minute conversation," says Whyte. "Conrad tends to understate at big moments, but he had a strong sense that this was a great thing to do and would be a romantic adventure. He never gets emotional and never gushes, but he was excited and talked about us embarking on this great adventure. It was touching. Like all of us, he was a little nervous. We didn't know whether we would fall flat on our faces and embarrass ourselves or whether we would create something worthwhile. I remember that conversation with Conrad so vividly because he had such a strong sense of purpose and mission. It was something we felt needed to be done, and it might not work but what a great thing to do anyway."

Whyte returned to the table and excused himself to Greenspon but said only that he had just been told that the official announcement of the launch of a new national newspaper would happen that day. He didn't tell him who had been on the other end of the phone.

Greenspon sent Whyte an e-mail after Babick's televised announcement was broadcast. He had watched it at the *Globe and Mail* offices on Front Street surrounded by colleagues who laughed while Babick spoke. Technical problems that dogged part of the announcement made them laugh even louder. Greenspon told Whyte it had looked Mickey Mouse and made him nervous.

Greenspon listened to colleagues speculate who might be involved in running the new daily. Whyte would not be officially named editor-in-chief for another month, but that appointment had already reached the status of open secret. Who would be Whyte's right-hand man? That was the mystery. Greenspon listened while his *Globe and Mail* colleagues speculated. Names flew back and forth, but Ed Greenspon wasn't on anyone's list. His well-kept secret suddenly felt like a heavy burden.

Adding to Greenspon's confusion was the terrible state of morale at the *Globe*. He was in Toronto to attend a Policy Forum dinner and, later, the farewell party for one of his best friends, Colin MacKenzie, who had been forced out of the *Globe* and was off to join the *Toronto Star* at the invitation of his former *Ottawa Citizen* colleague and friend John Honderich.

The party was a morose affair and as teetotaller Greenspon drifted around the room, he thought to himself how the binds of loyalty to the *Globe* were becoming unravelled. And he was no exception.

Whyte didn't respond to Greenspon's comment about the launch broadcast until they met face to face the next day. The remark seemed to have stung. "Look," he told Greenspon, "there will be bad days in this enterprise. There will be days when things don't go well and people are going to be looking to the two of us to be positive. The great thing is that there is nothing there yet. You get to create it and get to shape it. It's all part of the adventure, not something to worry about."

"I can be a positive leader," Greenspon responded, "but I also want to be honest with you about how I'm feeling, and I wonder whether you know what you're up against." The new relationship had hit its first major bump, and in the hours since his brief chat with the buoyant Black, Whyte was beginning to have his own doubts about Greenspon. "Eddie was getting edgy. He had a lot of trepidation and no enthusiasm or excitement at all. I started to get worried, because at that point it was going to be our job to get everyone onside, optimistic, and raring to go. I didn't want to drag him into it kicking and screaming. I sent him a note back to say it was just a press conference, not the launch of the new newspaper. The problem was, a lot of people still thought the new newspaper wasn't going to happen and was just Conrad's sabre rattling to get control of the *Globe* or the *Financial Post*."

The pair took a cab to 10 Toronto Street, where Don Babick, who would be president and CEO of the new newspaper, and Gordon Fisher, Southam's editorial vice-president, were waiting to meet Greenspon.

As chief executive of Southam newspapers, Babick had been one of the first people brought into the loop by Black when he was throwing ideas around for a new daily. Black was failing to convince the Thomsons to sell him the *Globe* and had lost the *Financial Post* over the "misunderstanding" with Paul Godfrey. Babick had been on vacation in Palm Springs in March 1997 when Black called him to propose the idea of starting a new daily of his own. Babick's reaction was much the same as Ken Whyte's: "You wanna do *what?*" Not that either of them actually put it so boldly.

"I thought it was a little Looney Tunes at first," says Babick, a savvy newspaper veteran, "but he was obviously dead serious and wanted us to come back with some semblance of a business model and do it quickly, within the next three or four weeks."

Babick and his team had produced the business model, and after much back and forth with Black figured the thirty-two-page, modestly staffed paper they were planning would have a circulation of 100,000 and lose money for at least five years. With a cushion of money from the profitable family of Southam dailies, they agreed that a loss of up to $150 million would be okay. Black called meetings of his executives, including a final one at his Toronto home in the winter of 1998, and allowed them to second-guess. But it was Black's dream they were dealing with and Black was the boss.

The boss wasn't unwilling to hear contrary opinion and called Babick before a final executive get-together to further test his resolve. "Are you comfortable moving ahead with this?" he asked Babick. "You're not just coming along for the ride because the rest of us want to do it?" Babick, now genuinely convinced that the new daily could be viable despite the possibility of the economy going sideways, said he was fully committed. Shortly afterwards, Black gave Babick a lift home to Toronto in his private jet after a reception to announce plans for new presses at the *Montreal Gazette*.

"Don, who's going to run this new national newspaper?" asked Black, looking up from his paperwork. They discussed a few names but resolved nothing. The next day, a Saturday, Black phoned Babick and asked him to take the job.

The meeting between Babick, Fisher, Whyte, and Greenspon was congenial. Greenspon asked about the newspaper's financial prospects and an upbeat Babick said the Southam cash flow was strong enough to absorb the expected initial losses.

Greenspon returned to Ottawa still feeling uneasy, and Whyte was now having severe doubts about whether he was the right person for the job. "The Eddie thing had pretty much gone off the rails . . . and everyone at Southam started saying, 'I told you so, I told you so.' I was feeling a bit embarrassed and frustrated."

Greenspon's contract negotiations were not going well, and he worried that the longer they went on the greater the chances his involvement would leak to the *Globe* before he had a chance to tell Thorsell or his national bureau colleagues, with whom he felt especially close.

His fears were well founded. By mid-April, Greenspon-to-Southam rumours were rampant. He got a call from then news editor Margaret Wente on Friday, April 17, and knew immediately that head office had at least an inkling that something was happening.

"Peggy calls me, and I can tell she knows, but she can't bring herself to say it. We talk about a *Globe* scoop on the CIBC-TD bank merger, and then we talk about Black having just hired Isabel Vincent as a roving correspondent. She never mentions the rumours that are rampant about me and

Black but just kind of talks around it for about half an hour and tells me how valuable I am and all this kind of stuff, but she can't bring herself to actually ask me the question, and I don't volunteer it. It was a very weird conversation."

Greenspon and his wife had spent Saturday looking at houses in Toronto, and on the Sunday he called Whyte to tell him he was ready to make the jump but wanted more money. "Look," he said, "the whole thing's going on far too long. If you really want me, let's wrap it up."

Whyte didn't hesitate. "I'll take care of it," he said.

The same night, after two conversations with Peters, Greenspon got a new contract offer. Peters took pains to emphasize what an excellent package it was. Greenspon agreed; it had everything he wanted. While these final negotiations were going on, Greenspon also fielded his first "please don't go" call from Thorsell.

Greenspon returned to the Ottawa bureau the following day to meet his colleagues. They congregated in the bureau's "living room," a communal area with a couch and comfy chairs. As they peppered him with questions, Greenspon began to choke up. But he still didn't tell them he had already made up his mind to leave. "I've got some tough decisions to make," he said. And then, in an outburst of emotion, added, "If I go, I want you all to come with me."

Some indicated an immediate willingness to do just that.

The *Globe*'s veteran political columnist Jeffrey Simpson worked on Greenspon next. Several years earlier, Simpson had been on the verge of becoming editor of the *Ottawa Citizen* before being lured back into the *Globe* fold with more money and some nice perks, including membership in the prestigious Rideau Club.

"I harangued him for an hour," recalls Simpson. "I urged him to imagine what it would be like working for Conrad and Barbara – not that I really knew what it would be like working for Conrad and Barbara. But I raised other issues about the *Post*'s chances of survival and what would obviously be its political bent. I told him that it was certain that whatever happened to the *Post*, whether it succeeded or otherwise, the *Globe* would still be around. He was on the verge of leaving, and in the interests of the newspaper I thought every effort should be made to keep him. He just sat there and mostly listened."

After he left, Simpson phoned Thorsell in Toronto: "Eddie is two feet and one arm out of the door," he told the *Globe* editor, "and we shouldn't lose him for lack of making an effort."

Thorsell immediately phoned Greenspon. Aside from the merits of hanging on to Greenspon, he knew that one high-profile journalistic defection could lead to more, especially in a newspaper where so many journalists were chronically unhappy. And as Greenspon had sensed, among the first to follow him to Black's new enterprise would be members of the Ottawa bureau. That wouldn't look good.

Thorsell asked point-blank, "I hear you're going to leave us. Is it true?"

"I'm about to," Greenspon replied.

Thorsell urged him to stay and told him that the staff in the Ottawa office had sent a memo, signed by them all, urging management to do everything possible to keep him.

Publisher Roger Parkinson called with what Greenspon described as a slap-on-the-back, let's-go-get-'em speech and also asked him to stay.

Thorsell tried hard over several phone calls but couldn't get Greenspon to change his mind. He offered the bureau chief more money, extra perks, and a greater say over the editorial direction of the newspaper, and then asked him to stall his decision for twenty-four hours. Greenspon agreed but promised nothing.

With the contract he wanted in hand, Greenspon had decided to defect.

"On Monday night, April 20, Janice and I are talking, and I say, 'I've got to go, I'm going to do it. This is an exciting adventure.' I went to bed and said, 'We are going to do it.' Then I slept like a baby, woke up on Tuesday, and said, 'I'm going to call Ken now and tell him that I'm not taking it.'"

His wife was shocked. "What are you talking about? You said last night you were going to do it."

"It just doesn't feel right."

❖ ❖ ❖

Greenspon says he still doesn't know why he turned down the offer, but long before he became editor-in-chief of the *Globe and Mail* he felt he had made the right decision.

"I didn't know them well and I was putting my life in their hands. And there would be no going back to the *Globe* once I had done the dirty deed on them. For me, it was ultimately a very visceral thing. It just didn't feel right. And it became a very ideological paper and I am not an ideological person. Things I might have believed in journalistically would have got squeezed."

Greenspon phoned Thorsell first to make sure he still had a job. His delighted boss spoke effusively and emotionally about the *Globe* being a family – a severely dysfunctional family, many newsroom employees would have added.

The call to Ken Whyte was next. It was a short conversation.

Whyte politely accepted Greenspon's decision, hung up the phone, and started work on Plan B. He had lost twenty days and didn't have time for reflection. He thought about the people he'd met at the *Daily Telegraph* and recalled the guy who had taken him to lunch and whose news judgment and enthusiasm had so impressed him.

He picked up the phone and dialed London.

"This is *Ken Whyte* calling from *Saturday Night* magazine in Canada. Do you remember me?"

"Ah, yes," came the reply. "I remember. It's Ken from Canada."

5 KEN FROM CANADA

"We knew he was linked to some Canadian magazine owned by Conrad, and so we thought he might be some kind of spy reporting back. That's why I took him to lunch."

— Martin Newland, editor of news, *Daily Telegraph* (U.K.)

Kenneth Whyte had spent a week at the *Daily Telegraph* in the summer of 1997 to get the feel of a major daily news operation. He had never worked in a newsroom before. The visit to London, arranged by Conrad Black, would prove unexpectedly important in the future development of the *National Post*.

Journalists at the *Telegraph* dubbed him "Ken from Canada" and those high enough in the newspaper's hierarchy to have jobs that might appeal to him became immediately suspicious of his intentions. The reasons for his sudden appearance at the *Telegraph* were shrouded in mystery. "They didn't know if I was an efficiency expert or a stalking horse for Barbara [Amiel]. They were all very polite and let me go to their meetings, which I did for a couple of days, but it quickly became clear that their meetings are just like everyone else's. After a couple of days I got bored and started hanging out with Martin Newland, a former seminary student and devout Catholic, who was running their news operation."

Whyte and Newland, both in their late thirties, quickly hit it off, chatting about newspapers, journalism, and their own careers. But Newland was determined to find out what Whyte was doing at the *Telegraph*, and Whyte was equally determined not to tell him, but he did drop a few hints.

"Nobody quite knew why Ken was there," says Newland, "but he has always had a sense of power around him, a sort of 'don't-fuck-with-me' aura. We knew he was linked to some Canadian magazine owned by Conrad, and so we thought he might be some kind of spy reporting back. That's why I took him to lunch. I wanted to find out what the hell he was doing there."

Newland, a man of bubbling enthusiasm with a serious passion for news, was born in Nigeria to a Spanish-born father. His mother, a countess from Northern Italy, moved to Argentina with her family, and it was there she met Newland's father, an oil company executive and naturalized Briton. Newland was raised in England a devout Roman Catholic, has dashing Mediterranean looks, a manic giggle, and an uncontrollable penchant for profanity, which, among his future Canadian colleagues, would become one of his more endearing features. He, too, was ambitious but considered his lack of English pedigree a detriment to advancement at the *Daily Telegraph*, a staunch pillar of the English establishment, albeit the least stuffy broadsheet newspapers.

Whyte spent some time with the *Telegraph*'s Old Etonian editor Charles Moore, gathered some information on staffing, and generally got the feel of the place. But he spent most of the week sitting with Newland and his colleagues and watching how the newspaper was put together. "There were rows of people all talking and working together," he remembers. "They had a lot of fun."

During one of their lunches, Whyte casually asked Newland if he envisioned spending the rest of his life in England or whether he would consider moving – to Canada, for instance. Newland, married with three young children, was open-minded. But it was just pub talk, a fleeting fraction of conversation he quickly forgot. Whyte, still putting the pieces together in his own mind, was simply asking – perhaps just to file away the name.

Of more immediate importance, Whyte also met the *Telegraph* creative directors Clive Crook and George Darby, experienced designers who had worked on newspapers and magazines around the world. The two had often worked together as a team and Whyte subsequently brought them twice to Toronto to work with the others on his prototype.

❖   ❖   ❖

Newland didn't hear from Whyte again until the phone call in April 1998, about nine months after they had first met. Nor did he expect to.

"Ken said, 'We're launching a national newspaper over here. Would you like to come and help us do it?' My first thought was my wife and family, my second thought was, 'Well, they'll understand,' and my third thought was how quickly could I get out there. I never once thought about not doing it. When you get the chance to launch a new national newspaper in a major G8 nation, you don't pass it up. I didn't know much about it, but I knew Conrad and the *Telegraph* and knew the project was very dear to Conrad's heart. This wasn't Mickey Mouse, it was Conrad Black. I could see it was some serious shit. It wasn't the *Botswana Gazette*."

Whyte explained that the newspaper would be modest, about the size of the *International Herald Tribune*, with a staff of about forty editorial people. And he needed a deputy. Newland said he would think about it overnight and get back to him.

"I thought it was a polite way of telling me to fuck off," says Whyte, who fully expected that to be Newland's reaction. "But he called me in the morning and said yes. It meant moving himself and his three kids to a country he had only visited once. And he hardly knew me. I was astonished and absolutely delighted. I knew he was perfect. I had seen him motivate people and respond to stories. We agreed on what was a good story or not and our politics were similar. And I liked him. . . . He had absolute confidence and I felt much better about the whole thing from that point."

But *Telegraph* editor Charles Moore was annoyed at Whyte's poaching and tried to persuade Newland not to leave. Moore, former editor of Black's *Spectator* magazine, pulled Newland out of an afternoon news meeting, led him out to his chauffeur-driven Jaguar, and ordered him into the back seat. The editor was pressed for time and late for an appointment at the BBC, where he was booked for a radio interview. He sat in the front passenger seat, bent awkwardly around the headrest, and berated Newland for contemplating such a foolhardy move.

Newland laughs heartily at the memory of Moore contorting himself to get a view of his backseat passenger. "It's very strange having a one-to-one conversation around a headrest. Charles told me that I had a good future at the *Telegraph*, that the move would be tough on my wife and family. And, you know, the British have an attitude toward Canadians that is slightly down-your-nose. They still have the image that you have to beat off a polar bear at every downtown corner."

"Thank you, Charles," said Newland. "But I think this is something I really must do."

As they approached The Embankment in downtown London, it began to pour with rain, and Moore, realizing Newland was a lost cause, ordered his chauffeur to stop the car. "You don't mind if you find your own way back, do you?" he asked, leaving Newland on the sidewalk staring at the rear of the Jag as it drove away into the distance.

But Newland meant it when he said it was something he really had to do. "You couldn't say no, and even if you did say no for very good reasons, you would regret it for the rest of your life. If I saw the *Post* now and thought that someone else had actually gone and done it, that would drive me mad."

Still, Newland had his demands. "I had no idea about the Canadian standard of living, but I didn't want to lose money. And I didn't want to answer to anyone but Ken. We agreed then on the title Deputy Editor, which was something I could understand. You have an editor and a deputy editor, a number one and a number two. I couldn't have done what I was asked to do unless there was no bullshit around the lines of command. So I had to be Ken's man and have total power on the newsroom floor. This was a totally different thing we were doing, editorially, culturally, everything. So it makes for clear understanding if everyone knows that when I say something I speak with the voice of the editor. I was very insistent on that."

Given that Newland's influence on the day-to-day content of the *National Post* would be profound, it's tempting to speculate, as many have, on the road not taken: what would have happened had Greenspon, the total opposite of Newland, accepted the job.

❖   ❖   ❖

Rumour buzzed around the *Telegraph* newsroom that Newland was leaving for a job in Canada, something that intrigued a young reporter named David Walmsley, an Irishman with a Canadian mother and Canadian citizenship. He slipped a note to Newland saying if the Canada rumour was true, he would be interested.

Walmsley was working on the *Telegraph* news desk two nights later when the phone rang. "Can you talk?" asked Newland secretively. "I take it from your note you're interested in going to Canada?"

"Bloody hell," thought Walmsley, "he took the bait."

Newland said he had orders not to poach anyone from the *Telegraph*. "I don't want to get into shit with Conrad," he said, knowing that Black had made a commitment to Moore not to hire from the *Telegraph*. "I'd like you to come, but you're going to have to speak with Mr. Kenneth Whyte. I can't give you any guarantees."

"I had this impression that Mr. Kenneth Whyte was some bloke in his sixties with grey hair and tiny spectacles," says Walmsley. "So Martin gives me Mr. Kenneth Whyte's phone number and I go into this ante room where nobody could hear me. Mr. Kenneth Whyte comes on the phone and there is a tremendous silence. He was doing the classic interviewing technique of saying nothing while I babbled on. Then he did this long, drawn-out 'yesssssss,' and said, 'I suppose you require some compensation.' It was a two-minute conversation."

So Walmsley, destined to become political editor of the *Post* and charged with overseeing the newspaper's parliamentary bureau, dusted off his Canadian passport and prepared to head for Toronto.

He would not be the last of Whyte's *Telegraph* imports.

6   THELMA AND LOUISE

"It was like having an affair, because we didn't want other people to know we were meeting."

— Rosie DiManno, columnist, *Toronto Star*

Roy MacGregor, one of Canada's premier newspaper journalists and a successful author of a long list of books for both adults and children, was covering the NHL playoffs for the *Ottawa Citizen* when Kenneth Whyte first approached him. They met for breakfast on April 16, 1998, at the upscale King Edward Hotel in Toronto, across the street from Conrad Black's Canadian headquarters and close to the offices of *Saturday Night* magazine, where Whyte still had his day job.

Along with *Edmonton Journal* sports columnist Cam Cole, Christie Blatchford, and freelance feature writer and broadcaster Allen Abel, MacGregor was on Whyte's instant credibility list – relatively expensive and high-profile writers who would show that the new newspaper, whatever its title, would be a formidable journalistic force.

Whyte, now into frenetic hiring mode, took two cellphone calls during the hour-long breakfast and charmed MacGregor, who was in no particular hurry to leave the *Citizen* and was already being courted by James Travers, by then executive managing editor at the *Toronto Star*. Still, MacGregor was swayed and, along with most everyone else Whyte attempted to woo, quite impressed.

"Ken was very seductive, laid-back, fairly open, and self-deprecating. He has a kind of boyish innocence but is far deeper than that. He's an ideas person, and if you listen to him long enough he could probably persuade you of almost anything." (Michael Cooke, Whyte's temporary colleague during the *Post*'s formation and master of the succinct, describes it this way: "Being stroked by Ken is like being massaged by one of those young Thai girls – not that I've ever been massaged by a young Thai girl.")

MacGregor was not about to jump into the unknown without a serious pay increase and contractual parachute should the new newspaper crash and burn. But he was also puzzled. "You must be making some mistake," he said, "I'm a left-wing loonie."

"Diversity," replied Whyte quickly. "We want diversity of voices."

Whyte said he would get back to him, and MacGregor continued on the Stanley Cup trek, landing in Dallas a few days later. A fax from Southam human resources chief Tim Peters was waiting at his hotel.

"They offered me $4,000 more than I was earning at the *Citizen*, which, given the risk, wasn't worth it. I called and said I wasn't interested, but thanks for the offer."

The phone rang in MacGregor's Denver hotel room three days later. It was Whyte. He came straight to the point. "What will you come for?" he asked.

By the end of the phone call, Whyte had topped MacGregor's *Citizen* salary by $30,000, plus a $10,000 car allowance. Another contract was waiting when MacGregor arrived in New Jersey on April 30. Along with salary, car allowance, and vacation details, there was a parachute clause: "Should your position at the new national newspaper be eliminated within two years of your start date, you may elect either another position offered to you by Southam or severance payment based on your uninterrupted service with Southam companies."

MacGregor scratched out "two" and replaced it with "five," the number of years he had agreed to, and added a whole new clause to reflect what he considered to be more likely: "Or should the national newspaper be folded within eight years, may elect to another position offered to you by Southam, with best effort applied to the Ottawa area or severance pay."

MacGregor initialled what he considered to be his critical changes and faxed it back to Toronto. Whyte, sounding delighted, phoned to say everything had been agreed.

"So that was that. Two months after I started with them, I discovered they had never received my final acceptance. It had been lost on a desk somewhere. The only thing it really tells you is how some of us were not sure. There was excitement, but not a lot of faith. But there was a lot of money. I guess the salaries for those hired early were between $125,000 and $180,000."

MacGregor, author of a phenomenally successful series of children's hockey stories, had signed to write for a new newspaper that would be a sort of daily news magazine in which he would write his trademark essay-style columns on a variety of subjects and then, each spring, join the Stanley Cup tour.

"If you were starting a newspaper," Whyte asked MacGregor, "which sports columnist would you hire?"

"Cam Cole," replied MacGregor without hesitation.

"Oh, I'm so glad to hear you say that," said Whyte. "I've been a fan of his since I was young."

Cole was a fixture at the *Edmonton Journal* in Whyte's hometown. He had been courted by both the *Star* and the *Toronto Sun* in the early 1990s but was happy in the west covering major national and international sporting events for the *Journal* and other Southam dailies.

An edict had come from Southam head office, however, that local editors could not bid against the new newspaper to keep any employee. "The way it was put to me," says Cole, "was that I didn't have a lot of choice. Conrad was putting together an all-star team and I had been anointed as the sports columnist. Ken had said, 'I want him,' which was all very flattering, but the original terms wouldn't have allowed me to keep my head above water in Toronto, so I kept saying no."

Journal editor Murdoch Davis explained to Cole that Whyte's offer was one that he probably couldn't refuse and that the advent of a new *National Post* columnist, and consequent shift of resources, would likely mean a severe curtailment in Cole's travels as an *Edmonton Journal* columnist. It was an important message. "Murdoch was being very honest and explaining what the individual papers were fearing from the coming of the *National Post*."

Cole resigned himself but heard nothing from Whyte for another six months and was feeling somewhat relieved. The call eventually came when he was covering the Masters Golf Tournament in Augusta. They arranged to meet at the King Edward Hotel when Cole was on his way back to Edmonton.

They kicked around ideas, and Cole, unaware that Whyte was a huge Toronto Raptors fan, said pro basketball was a non-issue outside Toronto and a national newspaper should resist stuffing it down readers' throats. Whyte told Cole that Conrad Black really enjoyed his golf coverage and considered it better than any he had read in Europe. Cole didn't know whether Black had ever held a golf club, but the compliment seemed genuine enough. He left the meeting with the promise of an improved offer and a lasting impression of the meeting. "When you sit down with Ken any length of time you are struck how out there he is. You don't get a lot of eye contact and he tends to talk into the distance about ideas and so on. It's not like having a regular conversation with a buddy. So at the end of it I was a little unsettled about what I had actually heard and had to take it on faith that I was actually the guy he wanted. It was never said with much conviction."

Whyte had established a working relationship with the veteran writer and author Allen Abel while editing *Saturday Night*. Abel, one of Canada's better known journalists and authors of the 1970s and 1980s, had submitted a travel article to the magazine "on spec" without phoning in advance as most established writers would do. The article ended up in Whyte's "slush pile" reserved for unsolicited, mostly unusable articles.

"In a month, we had a hundred pieces come in," says Whyte, "and almost all of them were garbage. Junior people would read them, but when I was on my game I would make a point of reviewing all the ones we were saying no to in the hope of finding one gem. And I found this article of his. I couldn't believe that a writer of the calibre of Allen Abel would just send something in by mail."

Abel, who had been a *Globe and Mail* columnist for a dozen years and a TV documentary reporter, had never written for a magazine before and didn't know anyone at *Saturday Night* so had addressed his submission "To the Editor." Whyte's fortuitous find led to a long-term working relationship between the two, during which Abel travelled the world for the magazine. Whyte had also made him a contributing editor, which meant, in the *Saturday Night* definition, an annual lunch with the editor. It was at their lunch in mid-1997 that Whyte mentioned the new daily.

"Conrad Black's going to start a new paper and you're going to write for it," said Whyte.

"No, I'm not," said Abel. "I'm not going to do daily newspaper stuff any more."

"Yes you are," insisted Whyte.

"You haven't heard my demands."

"Okay, let's hear them."

"I want business-class travel for any flight over three hours."

"Done."

"I want a flat in London."

"Nobody is getting apartments."

"I want a car."

"Nobody's getting a car."

Whyte asked Abel how much money he would want and exclaimed when the response came back. "Nobody gets that much money."

"*You* will when you're my age," responded Abel.

New York–born Abel, now a park ranger and documentary scriptwriter living on the edge of the Grand Canyon in Arizona, had no interest in working on staff for the *Post* because he was having fun, and happily employed on contract by the CBC. So he and Whyte compromised and Abel agreed to write thirty-six feature articles a year for a fixed sum that put him in the best-paid league at the *Post*. He would travel Canada and the world, from London to Timbucktu (literally), from Sydney to Beijing.

Gossip appeared in *Frank* magazine a couple of years later that *Post* colleagues, most of whom Abel had never met, were resentful that Whyte had given Abel use of an apartment in London.

"It was transmuted into gospel," says Abel, "but it wasn't true."

He won't say how much he was paid but agrees it was a handsome amount. "If they wanted to spend the money, they might as well give it to me. Stories are commodities, and by writing a cheque to me they must have thought they could promote and sell the newspaper."

❖   ❖   ❖

With his Big Four and a deputy in place, the hiring of section editors and writers continued and the newspaper business began buzzing. A call from

Ken Whyte was much sought after, even among those who had no particular interest in changing jobs. And for Whyte, selling only promise, the
effort to persuade those he wanted to come work for him continued to be
monumental:

> It surprised me how few people actually called me and how many of
> the people I hired *I* approached. I was disappointed in that, because
> I didn't think it was very enterprising. I thought it was a great oppor-
> tunity to do journalism a different way.
>
> It was fucking hard work. Every night I would go to dinner with
> somebody, or drinks with someone else, for two hours going over the
> same spiel, talking about the same doubts and problems. With some
> people I would have twelve meetings and end up getting nowhere.
>
> People were at newspapers that had been around for 120 years.
> They knew who their editor was, knew who their publisher was.
> They knew who sat to the right of them and left of them, knew what
> they would be doing for the next four years and how much they
> would be making. We had Conrad saying he was going to launch a
> newspaper. We had a lot of skepticism about whether it was actually
> going to go ahead and, if it did go ahead, whether it would fall flat
> on its face in six months. We were selling adventure. You could tell
> by the end of one lunch or dinner whether a person was coming over.
> There are some people I should have given up on sooner because
> they weren't suited for it.
>
> It was sales, that's what it felt like – a shoestring and a smile. It
> was like pre-selling condos before they have been built, but it was
> so much fun and it's not such a bad thing to offer people opportu-
> nity. It's far better than cutbacks or laying people off.

After Martin Newland arrived, the two began interviewing in tandem
in the desolate surroundings of the offices of recently laid-off Southam
vice-presidents. "We had some scrap furniture and a dead plant in the corner," says Whyte. "The place looked like a neutron bomb had gone off.
We were dragging people in, doing ten or fifteen interviews a day and listening to one another saying the same thing over and over. We got sick of
being so predictable when really we should have been more upbeat and
treating people how they deserved to be treated and not just as interview

number eight that day. I went everywhere a couple of times. I had never been out east and I saw the Maritimes. And I met a lot of people. I probably know more journalists than anyone else in the country."

◆ ◆ ◆

Among the names on Whyte's most-wanted list in the spring of 1998 were *Toronto Sun* columnist Christie Blatchford and her best friend, and often fiercest competitor, Rosie DiManno of the *Toronto Star*.

The two high-profile women, both tough Toronto newspaper warriors and among the most recognizable names in city journalism, would be major catches. They would bring the yet-to-be published newspaper much-needed credibility among both industry watchers and other prospective employees. Whyte also calculated that Blatchford and DiManno defections would badly wound the opposition. This was, after all, the prelude to war.

Whyte had good reason to be confident he could lure Blatchford and DiManno, if for no other reason than they were both restless and unhappy in their jobs. Although he desperately wanted to hire both women, he gave it a soft sell, pitched primarily at DiManno, who was going to be the most difficult to persuade. "She's got the *Star* tattooed on her ass," comments Blatchford affectionately.

Blatchford was more amenable to change and had already sent a note to the *Post*'s deputy publisher, Gordon Fisher, signalling her willingness to at least think about switching from the *Sun*. The two met briefly in February 1998, and Fisher promised to pass her name onto Whyte, which he did. Whyte promptly forgot. It was Blatchford's former *Toronto Sun* colleague Barbara Amiel who jogged the editor's memory.

"I wasn't familiar with Christie's work," says Whyte. "It was several months after Gordon mentioned her name that Barbara [Amiel] told me that she had heard Christie might be interested in working for us. I asked Barbara, 'Do you really think she is worth a look?' Barbara just said, 'Yes, as far I can remember.' So I dutifully went and pulled a bunch of Christie's work and was astonished at what she was doing at the *Sun*. She had such a powerful voice and such range as a columnist. She had written a column about the differences between bad boys and bad men and how bad men were really bad, but bad boys were kind of fun. She had a nice conversational style, a good, well-argued point of view, and a great sense of humour.

She was obviously a broadsheet voice working in a tabloid format. I didn't find out till later that she had worked for the *Globe* and the *Star*. So I called her up."

The Blatchford column that had so impressed Whyte was published January 28, 1998, at the height of the Bill Clinton–Monica Lewinsky "Zippergate" affair. Blatchford's refreshing lack of moralizing, and her original take on a well-chewed story, captured a spirit that Whyte wanted throughout his new newspaper.

The column appeared under the headline "THE WORLD NEEDS MORE BAD BOYS":

> While Bill Clinton is merely an alleged bad boy, the U.S. president has certainly managed to put the breed on the map again. Thus, what follows, which is to say, Thoughts On Bad Boys:
>
> A key point to remember is that bad boys are not to be confused with bad men, who tend to be bullies who prey on the vulnerable, whether that be a wife, child, secretary, underling, waitress or person in the service industry or merely someone smaller than they are. Bad boys, on the other hand, indulge in rather more benign boyish activities, such as outrageous flirting, overlong lunches, martinis . . . and what another generation used to refer to as "knee tremblers" and other spirited sexual positions.
>
> Before there was phone sex, there were bad boys, who have always appreciated dirty talk and who do it for free. . . .

And so it went.

Whyte recalls the evening he first met Blatchford:

> We met on College Street at the Bar Italia, in that funky part of town where she lives. She was nervous as hell, smoking and drinking. She had about fifteen cups of coffee. We had a great conversation. We talked about what she would do for us, but she wasn't convinced yet that she wanted to leave the *Sun*.
>
> I had been talking to Rosie at the same time, because I was looking for a strong voice with credibility in the Toronto market. I was particularly interested in her as a sports columnist, because that's where she does her best work. I then found out that they are best

friends and share everything. My individual conversations with each of them were going back and forth from one to the other.

When Whyte first met Rosie DiManno, she was emerging from a dispute with the *Star*. She was feeling underappreciated and unloved by the newspaper she calls home. This "journo-depression" is a condition little known outside newsrooms, but it is one that visits itself upon most journalists who stick around the business long enough. Usually, it's a temporary, though not necessarily short-lived, condition and will pass when the aggrieved supervising editor moves on. But in untreated cases it can become chronic and cancerous, mutating what was once a keen, driven journalist into someone horribly bitter and intellectually atrophied.

Penance, for sins real or perceived, can take many forms in newsrooms, but its most degrading manifestation is the humiliation of being deliberately sidelined and deprived of good assignments. A pecuniary punishment does not have the same effect, because journalists do not become journalists for the money.

As horribly debilitating as this journo-depression is, it can be cured with miraculous ease by a few kind words from the right person, by a plum assignment, or by having a byline above a page-one story. Even better than a byline above a page-one story is a byline and small headshot of the journalist. This is the water of Lourdes because it says two things: one, they love the story, and two, they think you're a star. (*Globe and Mail* readers might have noted the newspaper's full-bodied byline photo phase, when disproportionately large columnists posed next to their words like giants warning off potential intruders.)

The columnist's conflicts at the *Star* had come to a head during the Paul Bernardo trial, which she had been covering for three months. Crisis loomed when DiManno and her managing editor, Lou Clancy, clashed loudly over nightly rewriting of her Bernardo trial pieces.

> I had to be at the court early every morning, because I didn't have my own press pass. The *Star* had a couple of passes, but I didn't get one of them. I would be at the court until five and then go to the office to work and then I would be rewriting until ten or ten-thirty, until the first edition went off. They couldn't make up their minds about what could stay in the pieces and what should be left out. I was doing six

or seven rewrites a night and after three months was exhausted. They were making life difficult for me and didn't give a damn. One night, Clancy had a copy of my story sent to him at the ball game and yet again ordered stuff be taken out after it had been vetted by a lawyer. I had a meltdown and went AWOL from the trial for two days. I stayed in my house yelling at the walls and crying and screaming. I didn't answer the door when they sent people over to see if I was still alive. I showed up on Monday ready to go back to work, and they said I had to pay for what I had done. I understood.

DiManno's penance was a suspension, followed by the revoking of her accreditation for the Atlanta Olympic Games. The suspension she could live with:

The *Star* was very unkind to me given what I had done for them over more than fifteen years. It reinforced my belief that the *Star* didn't care about me. It was always, "What did you do for me yesterday?" Well, yesterday I went AWOL, but you didn't cut me any slack. I wore the suspension as a badge of honour, but then they banned me from going back to the trial. And then they took away my credentials for the Atlanta Olympics, which were a year away. I thought that was excessively vindictive and punitive and all meant to show me who was in charge. But what you always have to remember when you work at the *Star* is that if you work for an editor you despise, or have no respect for, you only have to wait. They will be gone before you. This period of discontent with the *Star* was lingering, and I felt unhappy and unloved. Then along came Ken Whyte, who sounded like he really wanted me to work for him and who liked and respected my work. And I was really turned on at the prospect of going to a new newspaper and starting fresh.

In theory Whyte's timing couldn't have been better. He was offering the world, more money, a car, and, overall, likely the best deal offered to a journalist anywhere in the country for years.

DiManno and Whyte had their first secret meeting at Nami, a Japanese restaurant on Adelaide Street, in the spring of 1998. Whyte asked for the table reserved in DiManno's name and after a flicker of recognition from the official greeter was led down a labyrinth of corridors to a small room with paper-thin walls. DiManno was waiting. "Is this discreet enough for you?" she asked.

DiManno had never seen Whyte before nor experienced the attention of a better salesman. But he was going to have his work cut out, and while she would rather enjoy the get-togethers she was more risk averse than her good friend Blatchford.

"It was like having an affair," she recalls fondly of her first meeting with Whyte, "because we didn't want other people to know we were meeting. I certainly didn't want anyone at the *Star* to find out. We were in the back part of the restaurant where they have those little individual dining areas. And I was very surprised when he appeared, because he looked so young and not at all like a person capable of putting together a newspaper."

She was intrigued and flattered at the intensity of Whyte's interest. "I don't get headhunted much. In fact, I don't get headhunted at all. But I liked him very much, right off. I liked his demeanour and enjoyed his enthusiasm for this newspaper they were going to be slapping together. He seemed like a very thoughtful, graceful, and intelligent person. He was very persuasive and had such bold ideas. He described the paper in vivid terms and made it sound like a paper I really wanted to work for."

Despite exhibiting the patience and skill of an expert fly fisherman, and despite DiManno's upset at the *Star*, Whyte found the columnist tough to persuade. He told her about other journalists he was trying to talk into coming to the *Post*. He made it sound like an adventure that no sane, self-respecting journalist could afford to miss. "He said he was primarily interested in putting together a writer's newspaper, which interested me, because I come from a very editor-oriented newspaper. He said he was interested in telling stories that would have a literate quality. He also gave me a choice of what I could do for him – anything, basically."

But DiManno, who in addition to her professional unhappiness had also recently ended a long-term personal relationship, wasn't even sure she wanted to stay in the newspaper business. Even that didn't deter Whyte.

"What I really wanted to do was go and live in Afghanistan," DiManno says. "This was long before 9/11. I've been interested in Afghanistan since I was a kid and always wanted to go there. So Ken said, 'Well, I'll put you on the payroll and you can go to Afghanistan and you don't have to write anything for six months.' I thought it was so peculiar. I'm not used to newspapers throwing money around like that, but it said something about those days of largesse at the *National Post*."

Whyte eventually upped the ante and offered DiManno a new VW Beetle as a signing bonus. The subject of the new bugs had come up during one of their evenings out, and DiManno said the prospect of owning one might even be enough to inspire her to get her driver's licence. "I thought they were so cute. So Ken said, 'Well, I'll give you one.'"

They agreed to meet again after she had thought things over and discussed the offer with Blatchford, who hadn't committed either.

"Christie and I discussed it endlessly, every day for several months. Would we have the guts to do it? We used to joke that we were like Thelma and Louise – you know, that movie where they both hold hands and jump over the cliff. So we began referring to ourselves as Thelma and Louise, but in the end only Thelma jumped."

DiManno's clandestine meeting with Whyte was the first of many. "Sometimes it was he and I, sometimes it was he and I and Christie. I'm not sure how much was wooing, because we liked each other's company and just enjoyed talking about the new newspaper. We would go out frequently and drink a lot, although it was mostly Christie and I who were drinking, because Ken hardly ever drank anything but coffee. That sort of annoyed me, because I would get increasingly pissed, as would Christie, and yak, yak, and yak, revealing all kinds of things. Lord knows what I said. And he just listened, because he is a very good listener. I don't know how much he revealed about himself – not much. We went to smoky bars, because I smoke, and as the supplicant Ken would have to put up with where I would choose to go. It was mostly smoky bars around Front and Sherbourne close to where I lived."

There were days when DiManno was convinced she would join the *Post* and other days when the prospect of the unknown, and the *Star* finding out about her meetings with Whyte, terrified her and she felt like running away from it all. The idea of a bigger paycheque didn't make it any easier.

"I never talk about money and don't even know how much I make now. I never even open my pay stubs. I don't know how much money Ken offered me, but at one point he did offer me a contract, because I had told him I would go work for him."

The eventual offer from Whyte would have made DiManno the *Post*'s Toronto sports columnist. He sent a contract to her house by courier and waited for a response. And waited.

DiManno was thrown into even more angst. "It was in a manila envelope, and I sat with it for a week without even opening it. Other than Christie, and one or two other close friends, there was no one I could talk to about it, because I didn't want the *Star* to find out. Not that I was doing anything duplicitous, but I didn't want the *Star* to come after me and start making me offers that would affect my decision."

It was an offer any newspaper journalist would have killed for. For DiManno, it was a horrible nightmare. She called Bert Bruser, the *Star*'s lead lawyer, and over lunch told him about Whyte's offer. He was aghast. "Why do you want to do this, Rosie?" he asked.

Two days later, John Honderich phoned and asked her to lunch, but by then she had changed her mind again and had decided to stay at the *Star*. She went to lunch anyway, reluctant and embarrassed at the fuss she had been causing. "We went someplace on the waterfront, and he told me he hadn't been aware of some of the things that had been happening to me at the *Star*. He said he was sorry and said he very much didn't want me to leave. I said, 'I'm not leaving.' I wanted to make a clean breast of things and change what I was doing, but going to the *Post* was too dramatic of a change. The *Star* has been very good to me, but it will never love me back as much as I love it. I have been fired and suspended. They like me now, but the day will come when they don't like me a whole lot. I could draw up a list of people they used to like."

So despite Whyte and Blatchford's entreaties, DiManno stayed at the *Star* and became a full-time sports columnist and a full-time page-two columnist, writing on subjects as she pleased, from locations she chose. "The *Star* granted me the privilege of doing two jobs for one salary," she says, "and the privilege to choose to do just about anything I want to. When I want to go somewhere, they rarely say no."

Blatchford signed the contract Whyte offered her. But after months of daily chatter and indecision about whether they should jump to the new daily, Thelma didn't tell Louise she had made the leap.

Whyte recalls the scene between the two women the night Blatchford signed on and DiManno found out. He tells the story with a mix of bemusement and amusement:

They had both seemed to be waiting to see what the other would do, and sometimes they gave me the sense that it had to be a package deal: "Either both of us come or neither of us come." Finally I got a concrete offer to Christie and she sent it to her accountant and we went back and forth a couple of times and then eventually she sent it back. That very night I was having a drink with Rosie at a bar on Richmond Street. Rosie and I were talking, and eventually Christie comes in and joins us.

Rosie says, "What's new with you?"

Christie says, "Well, I'm going."

And Rosie just looks at her and says, "You cunt."

Blatchford says she does not recall the encounter, but that if Ken remembers it she won't deny it.

"We swear all the time, so it probably did happen, but what's shocking to Ken is not necessarily shocking in my world. I don't know why Rosie would have been mad at me."

DiManno's recollection of the confrontation is clearer. "We went out – to Vox, I think it was. Christie had made up her mind and had told Ken. But she hadn't told me. And she hadn't told me that she had told him. So there were the three of us, drinking, and only two of us knew what was going on. They knew and I didn't. Christie was kind of giddy and highly strung, and I thought something odd was going on. About an hour into this drinking session, she told me. I was stunned that she would tell me like that. I might have sworn at her, because I tend to swear a lot. So does Christie. But that doesn't mean I was angry at her."

Whyte had racked up about a dozen meetings with Blatchford and DiManno and emerged from all the smoky bars and clandestine evenings with one win, one loss, and irritated allergies. He'd genuinely enjoyed his encounters with the two women, both of them streetwise and great conversationalists, and spent more time working on them than most. But he was philosophical about the outcome. It takes more than one lunch to sell a skeptic on something that doesn't exist.

"First of all," he says, "you had to meet someone and go through the basics of what do you do, what do you want to do? Then people typically asked about the newspaper and whether Conrad was really serious. How are you going to do it? Who's going to work there? What's the philosophy?

The second meeting, or second series of meetings, was to talk about the job. You don't just give people a take-it-or-leave-it offer. You have to find some creative ways to give them what they want. It isn't always money. Christie came for what she was making at the *Sun*. You often have to find ways of accommodating people, and the more time you spend doing that, the better chance you have of winning them over. A lot of the time it was about building trust, getting to know one another, and answering questions – generally getting them comfortable with the idea. Some were quite easy – and excited about coming. I'd send them an offer and they accepted."

For Blatchford, the pull of working for a new paper was too great to resist:

> It is probably the only newspaper that will start from scratch in my working lifetime. I was in school when the *Sun* started, so I didn't get that chance. That opportunity alone was enough, but I was also intrigued by Conrad Black. I had interviewed Conrad when I was at the *Star*. I can't remember what the interview was about, but I do remember hanging up the phone and turning to my deskmate and saying, "Fuck, does that man ever speak the language beautifully." I was also in awe of his skills as a writer, so I thought it would be fun to see what he could do with a newspaper. So I didn't need much persuading. I wanted to be in a more competitive environment where I had to work every day to be the best. I signed a contract and went back to the *Sun* and told them I was leaving. They offered me more money to stay, but it wasn't a race by then, because I just wanted to go to the *Post*.

DiManno and Blatchford got over their spat, remained firm friends, and accompanied each other to all the *Post*'s parties. At the newspaper's first anniversary do at the Royal Ontario Museum, Blatchford introduced DiManno to Conrad Black.

"Ah, yes," he said, "you're the one that got away."

"It is fair to say that the war got my juices going." – John Honderich, publisher, Toronto Star

Get ready for the Black Attack and prepare for a dirty fight. That was the gist of a presentation by *Toronto Star* publisher John Honderich to his executive team at a three-day retreat five months before the launch of the *National Post*.

"The Black paper will be coming directly after our market," Honderich told his executives. "It will be well executed, well designed, well written, and colourful. It can be expected to go after our retail-advertising customers. The people who own this newspaper are not afraid to stoop to certain levels to achieve what they want. In short, they aren't restricted by the same Marquess of Queensberry rules we have been accustomed to playing by."

They were fighting words. Honderich was probably the first major player to use the phrase "newspaper war" to describe arrival of the *National Post*. His warning that Black and his people would play dirty was a tad on the histrionic side, but as one member of the *Star* team said, "If there's one thing that the Honderichs don't like it is somebody trying to take their newspaper away from them."

The *Star*, the largest circulation newspaper in Canada, had an iron grip on the Toronto market. It could boast tens of thousands of exclusive readers, meaning people for whom the *Star* was their only newspaper purchase.

Loyal readership of this sort is a prized asset for any newspaper, and if it comes in large-enough numbers, it translates into a newspaper advertisers can't afford to ignore.

With his dramatic mix of war and sporting metaphors, Honderich made it clear he considered the *Star*'s dominance to be under attack, and that failing to prepare accordingly would be "sleepwalking to disaster."

"There are no battles you win," he intoned, "only battles you lose. We must adopt the mentality of a long-distance runner, not a sprinter."

Conventional wisdom had it that the new Black daily would focus on the *Globe and Mail* and take sideswipes at the rest. That assessment eased public pressure on the *Star*, but Honderich never believed it. He was convinced the *Post* would come after his newspaper and target his rich band of economically upscale readers. Not everyone agreed with him at the time, but he wasn't far off the mark. From the *Post*'s perspective, the battle against the *Globe* had great potential, but short of the *Globe* folding or selling out to Conrad Black, the spoils of that victory had its limits. The purpose of the *Post*'s second prong of attack was to capture a piece of the *Star*'s readership.

In the spring of 1998, the *Star* was very much in Kenneth Whyte's sights, and he was, more or less, still expecting to produce a newspaper without any significant business news content. "You can overestimate the degree to which we were thinking about the *Globe* at that time. We never designed the paper to steal only from the *Globe*. It was certainly one of our targets, but we wanted just as much to attract readers from the *Star*."

The coming of the *National Post* sparked a golden era for polling companies, research analysts, and marketing specialists. Newspapers wanted to know what their readers liked and didn't like, how loyal they were, and what the new newspaper might do to seduce them. For the *Globe* and *Star* it was about launching pre-emptive strikes. For the soon-to-be *National Post* it was about finding holes in the opposition's coverage and exploiting the dissatisfaction of their readers.

Much of the research simply supported what the players already believed and made everyone feel more confident, but from studies by the Angus Reid Group, one chilling phrase would emerge for the *Star*: "Loyalty is now the absence of something better," which seemed to suggest that the existing readership was a fickle bunch who would transfer their subscriptions at the drop of a free paper on the front doorstep.

But it was more complicated than that.

The *Toronto Star* is not only Canada's largest circulating daily, it is a traditional metro newspaper designed to be all things to as many people as possible. Covering local news, especially sports, politics, and crime, is the *Star*'s strength, but people who wanted some depth in business and national news, for example, might be inclined to drift to a competitor.

The newspaper, launched in 1892 by a group of hard-up printers looking for a way to make money, is unique in that its journalism is guided by a firm set of principles that are, quite literally, a sacred trust. Launched as a "paper for the people" by its blue-collar founders, the *Star* cemented that tradition when Joseph E. Atkinson took over in 1899. Atkinson was publisher of the newspaper for five decades, to 1948, and it was under his watch that a young writer named Ernest Hemingway got his start in 1920. (He wrote for the *Star* for three years before leaving for Paris to pursue other opportunities.)

More important, Atkinson was determined that the newspaper would continue its campaigning ways after he had gone. He left all his shares in the newspaper to a charitable foundation with instructions that the foundation should run the newspaper for the benefit of the public. The foundation was barred by provincial law from owning the newspaper, so Atkinson's son, Joseph, and four other senior managers of the newspaper, including John Honderich's father, Beland, formed Torstar Corporation to buy the *Star* and established a voting trust to hold their controlling interest.

The editorial principles of the *Star* reflect Atkinson's belief that a progressive newspaper should contribute to the advancement of society through pursuit of social, economic, and political reforms. The so-called Atkinson Principles guide the newspaper's coverage to this day. The *Star*'s competitors are fond of saying that the principles are at the root of the most biased journalism in Canada. And maybe so, but in essence they advocate motherhood and the interests of the common people. And thereby would hang a huge point of controversy in the forthcoming newspaper war.

These are the Atkinson Principles:

1. *A strong, united, and independent Canada.* Atkinson argued for a strong central government and the development of distinctive social, economic, and cultural policies appropriate to an independent country.
2. *Social Justice.* Atkinson was relentless in pressing for social and economic programs to help the less advantaged.

3. *Individual and Civil Liberties*. Atkinson always pressed for equal treatment of all citizens under the law, particularly minorities, and was dedicated to the fundamental freedoms of belief, thought, opinion, and expression and the freedom of press.

4. *Community and Civic Engagement*. Atkinson continually advocated the importance of proper city planning, the development of strong communities, and the active involvement of citizens in civic affairs.

5. *The Rights of Working People*. The *Star* was born out of a strike in 1892, and Atkinson was committed to the rights of working people, including freedom of association and safety and dignity in the workplace.

6. *The Necessary Role of Government*. When the public need was not met by the private sector and market forces alone, Atkinson argued strongly for government intervention.

Owners of other newspapers have been known to get all puffed up and defend themselves against accusations of interference in the journalistic content of their own publications by pointing to the Atkinson Principles as the most egregious example of corporate influence on a newspaper's journalism.

The *Star*, with a storied history behind it, headed into the newspaper war well funded, with a huge editorial staff of 420 and an editorial budget of about $40 million a year, slightly less than the *Globe*'s, which at the height of the war peaked at about $48 million. The *Post*, which would spend spontaneously and large on travel for its reporters and columnists but had no permanent bureaus outside North America, reached $35 million.

But, like the *Globe and Mail*, the *Star*'s internal workings were encrusted in tradition and the paper was by no means a place of contentment. It had a reputation as a quirky, sometimes unhappy workplace with Byzantine office politics and a system of punishment for perceived transgressions that could result in employees being sent into a sort of internal exile before being restored to favour months or years later.

"The art of management at the *Star*," one loyal and relatively happy employee says wryly, "was basically this: once the rats learn the maze, change the maze."

This pithy analysis was not delivered as a criticism, merely a statement of fact.

❖ ❖ ❖

According to colleagues past and present, to say that John Honderich has a strong familial attachment to the *Star* is to understate his commitment. Honderich lives and breathes the newspaper. So it was no surprise that from the moment he knew Black was serious about starting a rival, he adopted a dramatic "kill or be killed" stance. It was a matter of personal and family pride that the *Star* should emerge victorious with its readership, reputation, and revenue intact.

Honderich also relished the fight, especially against the formidable Conrad Black, with whom he shared mutual personal indifference. The two had frequently dined together at Black's Toronto mansion – pleasant occasions that ended after Black married Barbara Amiel for reasons Honderich declines to explain. More recent, tentative inquiries from Black about the availability of the *Star* had not been well received.

"It is fair to say that the war got my juices going," says Honderich, who would resign as publisher in early 2004 after an apparent high-level executive battle. "Going up against Conrad Black was a wonderful incentive for motivating staff. I know he wanted to attack the *Star* for what we stand for. Yes, my family has a large stock holding and to some degree that has to be part of the motivating factor, but I didn't need that. I believe in the traditions of this newspaper."

Honderich hired James Travers, who had been summarily ousted from the *Ottawa Citizen* by Black after he took control of Southam Inc. in 1996. A seasoned foreign correspondent and newsroom manager, Travers had spent thirty years with the Southam company and was well connected in the opposition camp. He knew better than most what kind of newspaper to expect Black's people to produce. "We knew it would be somewhat different. It would be more neo-con and libertarian than the *Globe* and obviously much further to the right. It would be in the British tradition – the kind of paper you are happy to be seen reading in a café but one that also gives you the entertainment, the sports – a nice blend of tabloid titillation and serious broadsheet, a very serious newspaper that won't miss a single dirty vicar story. We also knew that the target paper of record was the *Globe*, but to be successful it would have to capture *Star* readers."

Travers's task was to implement the centrepiece of the *Star*'s strategy: making the local franchise impregnable. Despite being around for more than a century, and growing up with Canada's largest city, the *Star* still didn't have a separate Toronto section. Travers changed that. He also made plans for an Ontario section – a so-called big-foot strategy, suggesting more comprehensive coverage in the newspaper than it actually contained – and a reconstruction of the Sunday edition, which, in common with many Sunday sections, was a poor relation, a place to put the stuff that didn't make it into the fat Saturday edition. Plans went ahead to boost special investigative series, once the *Star*'s greatest strength. When the Daily Tubby arrived on the scene, the *Star* would have a year's worth of these special projects either finished or in progress in the expectation that the Tubby would be similarly armed.

The *Star* introduced an intern system aimed at introducing younger faces and a varied ethnic mix into the newspaper. It was, said Travers, all part of the effort to boost the *Star*'s local image. "The Toronto content was always our ace in the hole, and they could never match that," Travers explains. "It is like the *Star*'s problem on business: in order to compete with the *Globe* on the business side, you would essentially need another *Report on Business*, which would be like hiring another city staff. It's enormously expensive and not financially doable unless you want to sacrifice a lot of other things. But we were always going to be the Voice of the Leafs, Voice of the Jays, Voice of the Raptors, and Voice of the Argos. They couldn't ever match us in terms of the size of the staff and size of the coverage. They couldn't compete with us on entertainment or local news, which was key. So no matter what you read in other papers, you couldn't do without the *Star*."

Honderich brought in the marketing and advertising company J. Walter Thompson to create an integrated marketing strategy that focused the *Star*'s local coverage. An advertising campaign built around the slogan "It's where you live" emerged shortly afterwards.

Honderich was deeply concerned about losing his younger and higher-income readers to Conrad Black, and when he saw Ken Whyte talking with his *Star* columnist Rosie DiManno at a National Newspaper Awards banquet in the spring of 1998, he had to start worrying about his journalistic talent too. Whyte, he figured, would attempt to entice key *Star* employees away: for positive motives, to enhance his own staff; or for purely destructive motives, if poaching would damage the *Star* and its reputation. Snagging a marquee name like DiManno would achieve both. Honderich was having none of it. "I got personally involved," he says. "We had to keep our stars and all our main people. We opened the vault, so to speak, and made sure we kept all our significant people. The excitement of going to work for a new newspaper, a new venture with lots of money flying around, is a wonderful lure. And that's what we had to counter. Ken was very persuasive and even came after the *Star* switchboard operators, who are famous for being able to find anyone, anywhere, at anytime. We have six. One went and came back."

It speaks volumes about the degree of sensitivities that the publisher of Canada's largest daily newspaper was keeping such close tabs on the movements of his switchboard operators.

8 A MASSIVE UNDERTAKING

"Ken . . . if this venture fails, your career will be in a hole so deep it will take you years to crawl out of it."

– Conrad Black, CEO, Hollinger International

The early prototype work was finished, but the speculation about whether Conrad Black intended to go ahead continued unabated well into the early part of 1998. The occasional mention appeared in the *Globe and Mail*, and gossip drifted through the nation's newspapers, but most of it was still edged with skepticism if not derision.

Even editor-designate Kenneth Whyte was unsure whether the project would go ahead. Launching a national newspaper is a massive undertaking, even for a company with so much printing and circulation infrastructure already in place. And it was Black, the newspaper magnate who had never created a newspaper, whose reputation was most at risk.

By Christmas 1997, Black appeared to have made up his mind. He invited Whyte to dine with him and Barbara Amiel at their Toronto mansion. Whyte had the flu but dragged himself out of bed and got through the night running on adrenalin.

"Something had changed by then. It was different than our previous conversations. They were drilling me this time. Conrad said I struck him as a laid-back individual and asked me if I knew how much work was going to be involved. We had a really good chat, and they seemed very serious and sure about it. We were all pretty excited. They had obviously been talking about this together. Barbara would chide him for his unbounded optimism and he would chide her for her pessimism. At that point, I don't think she ever thought a small-c conservative paper would work in Canada. She thinks Canadians are hopeless in terms of their politics and figured to the extent it was conservative it would fail. So for her it was more about the tone and spirit of the paper than the politics. But it was something Conrad had been working toward for ten or twelve years and he was convinced there were enough people out there who wanted an alternative."

Black and Amiel spoke intently and in great detail about the *Globe and Mail*, *Toronto Star*, and the major Southam newspapers. Black demonstrated his remarkable memory for the work of individual journalists; he seemed to remember everything they had written. Amiel, who had spent much of her writing career close to Canadian journalism, also had a few opinions on the subject. They gave Whyte a short list of assistant editors, reporters, and columnists they didn't like and did not want to be part of the new paper.

"Conrad was so determined by then and thought so clearly," says Whyte. "Most entrepreneurs work that way: you have to have a vision, something you believe in and then you take a risk. But you can never know. Look at the numbers and you can talk yourself in or out of something. It's all projections, but you can never know."

Black says his motives were both political and commercial, but the desire to exert some influence on the country was his driving motivation. As he saw it, the only media outlets with any influence at all on the federal Liberals were the CBC, the *Globe and Mail*, the *Toronto Star*, and, to a lesser degree, *Maclean's* magazine – all of the same ideological ilk. He also thought the Southam family, which once controlled the company, and later the various executives hired to run the company, had missed too many opportunities to establish the company in Toronto.

"We had the national newspaper company," says Black, "but the ancient lacuna of Southam was that they were not in the leading city in the country. They were in Montreal when, for a time, it was ostensibly the leading city in the country, but they weren't able to make an arrangement with the *Star*, and sat on their hands while the *Sun* was founded, and they didn't buy the *Telegram* when they should have. And I thought there was a need to offer an alternative view. So I had a variety of motives."

It was an opinion poll about Quebec that convinced Black once and for all that he had to give his newspaper group more political heft if he was to have any influence on federal politics. The poll, which ran in Southam newspapers with little impact, suggested that the majority of Canadians inside and outside Quebec wanted the federal government to adopt a tougher attitude toward the province's separatist regime. Says Black,

> I'm the last person who could be accused of being anti-French, but I am also fairly famous as an unambiguous federalist. We had a very interesting, comprehensive poll showing the great majority of Canadians, including a surprising number of French Quebecers, supported the principle that if Canada is divisible, Quebec is divisible. So if Quebec voted to secede, those Quebec counties adjoining other provinces that voted No [in the referendum] would secede from Quebec and remain in Canada. It doesn't sound like such terribly hair-raising stuff now, with the PQ collapse, and the Clarity Act in place, but it was a radical thought in those times, because it was a departure from the conventional wisdom, which was essentially an appeasement view of Quebec. But we couldn't get into the national media with that story. It illustrates my point that if we wanted to present an alternate way, an alternate general course in public policy, we were going to have to do it from a national newspaper and not the regional papers we had.

Key to Canada's problem, in Black's view, was its attitude and policies toward the United States – a problem he would want his new newspaper to address:

> I think this country has made a tragic error in buying into the theory that the *raison d'être* is to be a government to the left of the U.S., to be a kinder, gentler more sharing place than the U.S. When you get right down to it, that is essentially the rationale for Canada, and the problem with that is that you end up with ambitious people leaving, and that's why the leadership cadres of the country are so weak in most fields. It's a good population, and a very rich country, but the leadership groups in almost every field are weak because they are so easily assimilated elsewhere, especially in the U.S.
>
> So we felt all along that we should provide an alternative, which was not to run a radical right-wing state, or annexation, but run a

better enterprise state than the U.S. We thought that because Canada didn't have the defence commitment of the U.S. it would be possible to do that while maintaining benefit levels that were more generous than they are in the U.S., but less generous than they are at the moment in Canada. We had to stop defining the country on the basis of its welfare programs, and things like that. It's a less indulgent, apologetic view of native affairs and so on. But the fact is, you can't get anywhere in this country proposing such things without being labelled a crank or an extremist. So we wanted to present an alternative.

Black says that as he made plans for his new daily he was under no illusion that his "alternate view" would wash with the mass of the Canadian public. "I was never for an instant optimistic that it would actually be successful. . . . The country was essentially convinced in its unshakable majority of the wisdom or desirability of continuing the course it was on, and almost everyone of any consequence is complicit in the system. So my view was, 'We'll give it a go, give it our best try. I don't think it's going to work but we would be remiss not to try. And if it doesn't work we can sell it at a big profit.'"

◆ ◆ ◆

Southam's board of directors met in February 1998 at Black's headquarters at 10 Toronto Street, and after hearing a presentation from Whyte and Gordon Fisher they gave the go-ahead. Montreal financier Stephen Jarislowsky, a long-time Black associate, proposed the motion.

"We felt that if we used the printing presses and distribution channels of our own newspapers, the only market that might be difficult to crack would be Toronto," says Jarislowsky. "Compared to the start-up of *USA Today*, which didn't have all these printing installations in place and was built from scratch, we figured that within a year we would be at a break-even point. The Canadian public was poorly served in many ways and most of the other newspapers were pretty much rags. There was a place in this country for something more sophisticated."

There were other meetings at 10 Toronto Street, including one memorable get-together of all the executives who would be part of the newspaper's team. Black went around the table and each of the executives told

Black that if the product was right, the new daily was a viable proposition. Then he reached Whyte.

"Ken," he said, "given that if this venture fails your career will be in a hole so deep it will take you years to crawl out of it, think for a moment and tell me, Do you think this idea has merit?"

9 THE MD PRESCRIBES A TABLOID

"I didn't want to get caught in this war. It was two Goliaths against one David, and I'm not sure we even had a slingshot."

– Paul Godfrey, CEO, Sun Media Corporation

Toronto family doctor Bernie Gosevitz was medical adviser and sometimes listening post to an array of Canada's rich and powerful, including Conrad Black; Blue Jays CEO and former *Sun* newspaper chain chief Paul Godfrey; cable king Ted Rogers; Canada's wealthiest individual, Kenneth Thomson; former Ontario premiers Mike Harris and David Peterson; former prime ministers Joe Clark and Brian Mulroney; and various movers and shakers in Toronto media. It was an upscale list.

"The practice is worthless," jokes the gregarious Gosevitz, "because it's all based on personal contacts. But it does open up boardrooms to me."

Gosevitz had known Conrad Black for fifteen years or more and enjoyed his company. He felt similar warmth toward Paul Godfrey and was godfather to two of Godfrey's sons. His credentials as a go-between for Black and Godfrey were immaculate.

Gosevitz understood better than most that the two men did not enjoy the best of relations and knew, too, that Black was still fuming with Godfrey for having denied him the *Financial Post*. It was all a misunderstanding, said Godfrey. As Gosevitz saw it, that anger was the barrier to a business deal Godfrey and Black both desperately needed to do. "They had some kind of side deal a year or two earlier and Conrad felt that Paul had back-doored him – that Paul had made a promise and reneged on it. He was very ticked off. Conrad needed the *Financial Post*, because he wanted to launch that national voice, but he was so angry he wouldn't talk to Paul. It was very personal. The standoff was preventing the deal."

Like most people, rich folks talk to their doctors about professional ups and downs, and Gosevitz more than most hears a lot about executive stress and intercorporate conflict. He knew that Black and Godfrey had made baby steps toward a *Financial Post* deal – a deal that would give Black his missing Toronto piece and Godfrey a convenient exit from a forthcoming newspaper war in which the *Financial Post* would likely be the first casualty. Godfrey was also under some pressure from nervous members of his own board of directors to get a deal rolling. Some had been discreetly warned by Black's people about the *Financial Post*'s prospects should another well-funded opponent appear on the scene. And those around Godfrey saw that his relationship with Black had become progressively acrimonious. Both men insist that is an exaggeration.

Black's partner, David Radler, says it was somewhere in between. "I wouldn't call their relationship poor. For a time it was just non-existent, but it wasn't as if, had they met on a street, they wouldn't have been friendly to one another. Either Conrad misunderstood Paul, or Paul misunderstood Conrad, but Paul and I had no misunderstandings."

In June 1998, Black invited Gosevitz to the Hollinger annual meeting in London and, at the last minute, to the prestigious Hollinger dinner, to be attended that year by British Prime Minister Tony Blair and the former prime minister, and Black favourite, Margaret Thatcher, who once famously enthused that "Conrad" was the only person she knew who was more right wing than she.

Gosevitz lodged at the Blacks' Knightsbridge house. He was due to return to Canada before the dinner, but Henry Kissinger, a Hollinger director in town for the occasion, fell ill. Black asked Gosevitz to stick around and help the former U.S. secretary of state to recuperate. He also got to go to the high-class dinner, wearing one of his host's shirts and black bow ties.

"Later that night," remembers Gosevitz, "we were sipping white wine in one of Conrad's libraries. We talked about the newspaper industry and the *Financial Post*. Conrad is truly a journalist. Unlike most proprietors, he has ink under his fingernails and running through his veins. I had known him since the early 1980s, so we could speak pretty frankly. It was a long night, and I think we went on until four or five in the morning."

Gosevitz offered to intercede in the Black-Godfrey standoff.

"Do you want me to make some phone calls when I get back?" he asked.

"If you think it's worthwhile," responded Black, who had sold his long-held share in the *Financial Post* the previous fall after his dispute with Godfrey.

Gosevitz returned to Toronto midweek and immediately went to see Godfrey, whose office was in the same building as his own. He went into Godfrey's office and closed the door. "Look, Paul," he said, "I smell a deal here. Your employees are nervous and worried about their jobs. You and Conrad have got to talk."

"I'm not selling," said Godfrey, who had been at the helm of the *Financial Post* since 1992 and had hauled it out of an ocean of red ink and into modest profitability. "Conrad will not buy this paper. If he wants to, I am prepared to talk trade."

Gosevitz asked Godfrey's permission to call Hollinger general counsel Peter Atkinson to get the ball rolling. Atkinson was also a Gosevitz patient.

"The call you probably should make is to David Radler," suggested Godfrey.

Shortly afterwards, Sun Media lawyer Dale Lastman approached Atkinson, who then called Radler, Hollinger president and Black's business partner of more than thirty years.

Suddenly, there were hints that a deal might be possible. Bernie Gosevitz's work had been done.

Radler called Godfrey. "I understand from mutual friends that we should talk," he said.

For Godfrey, the call was a psychological victory of sorts, and one that could only give him an upper hand. But he was in a precarious position and was anxious to make the deal. It was a game of high-stakes corporate poker, with a lot of ego, tens of millions of dollars, and hundreds of careers on the table.

"I figured that if I picked up the phone and called Conrad, it would have meant an immediate discount for him. But I didn't want to get caught in this war. It was two Goliaths against one David, and I'm not sure we even had a slingshot."

Godfrey told Radler what he wanted and they found enough common ground to meet that weekend in Toronto. Time was tight for both of them. The new newspaper was to be launched in less than six months.

◆ ◆ ◆

The *Financial Post*, a weekly publication for most of its existence, first published in 1907 and was a cornerstone of Maclean-Hunter until that company got into the cable TV business and the *Globe and Mail*'s *Report on Business* section went from weekly to five days a week in the mid-1980s. The *Globe* gradually got a lock on lucrative career ads and began threatening the *Financial Post*'s dominance. Before the *ROB*'s expansion, the *Financial Post*'s one weekly edition had carried more business ads than the *Globe* carried in its six daily editions.

The Toronto Sun Publishing Company, formed in 1971, made the *Financial Post* a daily in the winter of 1988. Conrad Black's Hollinger, and the British company Pearson (owners of the *Financial Times* of London), owned 19.9 per cent each of the newspaper, along with majority shareholder Maclean-Hunter, which owned 61 per cent of Toronto Sun Publishing. For the next five years, through brutal economic times and intense competition from the *ROB*, the *Financial Post* lost about $20 million a year.

Douglas Knight, who became publisher in 1992, likened his appointment to getting the keys to the *Titanic*. But under Knight, the newspaper was redesigned and aimed squarely at the investing public, a fast-growing area that *Financial Post* research suggested the *Globe* was neglecting. Every story in the *Post* was related in some way to investors.

"We thought that losing $20 million a year was really big news," says Knight, "but we came from the Maclean-Hunter culture, where you threw nickels around like manhole covers. But Conrad was always supportive and never a naysayer. He took a particular interest in strengthening the editorial content. We didn't steal *Globe* readers. There were two distinct markets. Between the *Globe* and *Financial Post*, advertisers finally had a way of getting at this elusive audience without going through all kinds of advertising vehicles."

The *Financial Post*'s circulation climbed to 100,000 on weekdays and twice that for the Saturday edition. In an audacious move, Knight resisted the expensive option of increasing circulation and instead increased the single copy price to $1 a day – the first newspaper in North America to do so – and in just a couple of years increased the subscription price from $80 to $200. "We did subscriber breakfasts across the country, and all kinds of other promotional stuff, and ended up with the highest subscriber renewal rate in North America," Knight explains. "So from there we were able to convince advertisers this core 100,000 subscribers were important and loyal. Our ad revenue went from $20 million to $40 million over the next five years after being flat for the previous five. Advertisers were prepared to spend a high premium to reach those 100,000 subscribers."

By the time David Radler approached Godfrey, the newspaper was making $15 million EBITDA (Earnings Before Interest, Taxes, Depreciation, and Amortization), and outselling the *Globe* in Vancouver, Edmonton, and Calgary, and running close behind in Montreal. According to *Financial Post* intelligence, the *Globe* was making $25 million from the business market, and both were on track to add $5 million each to those totals. Between them, the *Globe* and *Financial Post* were coming close to pulling about a $50-million profit out of the Canadian newspaper market.

Godfrey wanted more newspapers to add to his *Sun* tabloids in Toronto, Ottawa, Edmonton, and Calgary, so at the initial meeting with Radler they discussed trading the *Financial Post* for Southam titles in Vancouver and Southwestern Ontario. But they disagreed on the value of the *Post*. Newspapers usually sell at around ten times their EBITDA, which is a measure of a company's cash flow. But Godfrey was angling for more, because, he argued, the *Financial Post* was a speciality daily and on the rise.

Douglas Knight figures that Southam might have made a move for the *Financial Post* earlier had it not been for some bias against the tabloid format, and a basic misunderstanding of how much advertising revenue the business market could provide.

"Non-*Globe* broadsheet guys, who for the most part were not financial newspaper readers, never really took the *Financial Post* too seriously or understood the impact it had in the market," says Knight. "I think this was because the financial elite, and the sophisticated investors targeted by the *Post* and the *ROB*, represented such a tiny fraction of a general newspaper's target readers that we were not on their radar screen. Our advertising market share, apart from Careers, where the *Globe* did dominate, consistently beat the *ROB*. While the *Financial Post* was a new daily, the *Globe* was still relatively new in serious financial and economic coverage, and the

Post had greater bench strength in the newsroom. Even today in the *ROB* newsroom you will find a disproportionate number of former *FP* people running the place."

So the scene was set for that game of corporate poker. Godfrey knew that Black wanted the *Financial Post*, and although Radler was less enthusiastic he figured he had been sent to get the job done. Radler hoped that the gentle lobbying his people had done with Sun board members had prepared his path.

❖ ❖ ❖

Radler, Godfrey, and their entourages of advisers met for two hours on July 7, 1998, at the Toronto law offices of Goodman Phillips and Vineberg to thrash out the details. Godfrey and Radler had already dealt with some of the minor aspects of the deal, and now it was time to focus on the nitty-gritty: who would get what and how much would it cost? The room at the law offices was large, offering lots of space for pacing and for discreet chats in corners.

The Sun management team was excited and confident. They had branched out into the broadsheet market the year before, buying the *London Free Press*, and it was doing well. After some initial discussion over whether to push Radler for the tabloid *Vancouver Province*, the Sun group decided to add to their major broadsheet collection, and given that Conrad Black's Southam owned most of them, this was the perfect opportunity.

In exchange for the *Financial Post*, Godfrey pushed Radler for the *Hamilton Spectator*, the *Kitchener-Waterloo Record*, and its two satellite newspapers, the *Cambridge Reporter* and *Guelph Mercury*. This would give the Sun guys a lucrative corner of southwestern Ontario. In exchange, Hollinger would get the *Financial Post* and some money.

They began arguing about the value of the *Hamilton Spectator* and the real worth of the *Financial Post*. Was the *Post* worth twelve or fourteen times EBITDA or less?

Radler turned his attention to the *Spectator* in an effort to persuade the Godfrey team of its "true" value. "It is a 55 per cent newspaper," insisted Radler, meaning that its profit margin had potential to be a lot greater than it was. The claim was met with a mix of amusement and disbelief on the other side of the table. They knew that even in its most parsimonious days, the Thomson group had never been able to squeeze more than 45 per cent, and they only achieved that by nearly throttling their newspapers to death.

There was dead silence. A relatively convivial meeting, punctuated with bantering and jokes, had suddenly turned very serious.

Radler angrily gathered his papers and, in a flourish, rose from the table. "I'm not paying that," he said. "You're not going to take me for that." He headed for the elevator. Lawyer Dale Lastman chased after him, calmed him down, and brought him back to the table.

Sun executive Wayne Parrish, who was in the room, says Radler's display didn't faze them. "I remember thinking it was great theatre, but that's all. I never had a sense that Radler was going to storm off and the deal would be dead. It was more for effect."

Radler admits it was all in a day's negotiating, but was it a ploy or was it genuine? "I can't remember, but you've always got to walk away at some point. They have to know you're capable of walking away, and I was capable of doing that. I'm sure Godfrey was too."

Things moved quickly after that, says Godfrey. "We agreed to get everyone out of the room except Dale Lastman, myself, Atkinson, and Radler. We talked about a number of issues, about value, who would print the *Post*, because they didn't have a plant in Toronto. It was very complicated. But after about three-quarters of an hour we had agreed on everything."

The details were hammered out during the next couple of weeks, allowing Conrad Black to emerge with the *Financial Post* plus $150 million, and Godfrey with the *Hamilton Spectator*, the *Guelph Mercury*, the *Kitchener-Waterloo Record*, and the *Cambridge Reporter*. The deal was finally done, after approval from the Sun board of directors, on July 18, the weekend of the Toronto Molson Indy. It was officially announced on Monday, July 20. Rumours had bubbled, but news of the deal caught most everyone by surprise, not least members of the Southam team who knew nothing of the negotiations and were merrily working away on a model that was now redundant.

Parrish says the Sun team had a sense of the position Radler was in. "Black wanted the *National Post* and David did not. Conrad believed in it, David did not. So David was there negotiating a deal to create a strong platform to launch a newspaper he didn't believe should be launched. That coloured the meeting. We never met face to face with Conrad, but my sense was that they felt the need to get the *Financial Post* was moderate to great.

What they gave up and the price they paid is the only way you can measure how much they wanted to do the deal."

Looking back on the transaction at the Toronto SkyDome in the midst of his career as president and CEO of the Blue Jays, Godfrey can't resist borrowing a baseball cliché to express his continued pride at a deal he considers well done. "I thought I had hit a home run with the bases loaded and he [Radler] was happy, because he was sent by his partner to get the *Financial Post*. I knew Radler had agreed to things that, God, I wouldn't have agreed to, but he is a man of his word. I knew Conrad needed our circulation base and a stable of good writers, but I don't think Conrad was bluffing. He was a good operator of newspapers, but I think he would have gone ahead without the *Financial Post*."

When the dust had settled, billionaire industrialist Peter Munk called Bernie Gosevitz and ribbed him a little. "If you'd have done for Barak or Trizec what you've done for Godfrey and Black," laughed Munk, referring to his own companies, "you would have got a million dollars' commission."

But Gosevitz didn't get a commission. "I helped broker the idea," he says, "but for the employees, really. I didn't get anything out of it."

◆ ◆ ◆

Barbara Amiel delivered the news of the *Financial Post* deal to Kenneth Whyte in an e-mail less than twenty-four hours before the official announcement. After months of building a magazine-style five-days-a-week daily newspaper to be run by a relatively small, hand-picked staff on a modest budget, Whyte and his managers were suddenly in the big time: faced with the enormous task not only of starting from scratch but also of integrating an existing publication, and its staff, into the new newspaper – all in a little more than three months. Black had stated publicly that October 1998 would be the launch month, and in an atmosphere of universal skepticism about his intentions he was not about to change his mind. The most he would allow was to push the launch date from October 3 to October 27.

But Whyte was not wildly enthusiastic. "I immediately sent back a note to Barbara saying, 'I suppose that's a good thing.' She sent me a short and dismissive note back. She is [normally] a pessimist and she took my note back to her as my having outdone her. Conrad called late that night at home and walked me through it. He was absolutely convinced it was the right thing to do and made me realize that our scale of ambition could immediately increase and we could aim at higher circulation figures and more advertising. We would have more staff and more money and were now a more serious competitor. The whole thing was suddenly at a different level."

Amiel also phoned Whyte, still frustrated at the editor-in-chief's apparent lack of enthusiasm. She wanted to emphasize that both she and her husband considered the addition of the *Financial Post* a great thing. And from the business perspective, it was. They had gained existing advertising revenue, an existing subscriber base of close to 100,000, with names, addresses, and phone numbers – plus a ready-made, tightly edited business section with marquee, conveniently right-of-centre columnists such as David Frum and Diane Francis.

Research commissioned after the grand newspaper swap revealed that not all the *Financial Post*'s loyal readers were likely to remain loyal. Some liked the paper's tabloid format, others were happy with the quick-read, no-frills stories, and many others were unmovable once-a-week buyers. Still, it was a solid base to start from.

The purchase also solved the problem of a name, which Whyte and Gordon Fisher had been struggling with for months, if for no other reason than they needed to develop a marketing campaign. As a spoiling tactic, the *Globe and Mail* had registered some of the more obvious names, though apparently none that were serious contenders. (The name *National Post* was not unveiled until just a month before launch day, and to create a little mystery employees were banned from sending e-mails on the company system. Not that it was a well-kept secret or especially difficult to figure out, but people outside the newspaper business were kept in some suspense, if they thought about it at all.)

Another question the *Financial Post* purchase put to rest was whether Conrad Black was still angling to buy the *Globe*. Until then, the many skeptics were still convinced that the promise of a new daily was a bluff designed to extract the *Globe* from the Thomson Corporation. Indeed, that possibility was still in play at Thomson, where executives knew their bosses wouldn't be selling but were not sure whether Black had come to terms with the fact.

On Sunday, Whyte told his deputy, Martin Newland, about the new addition and swore him to secrecy. In the journalistic community, only Howard Intrator, the *Financial Post*'s industrious, well-connected deputy editor already hired by Whyte, seemed to know for sure. He called Whyte just a few hours after Whyte had opened Amiel's e-mail. The editor-in-chief declined comment and made plans to call his first staff meeting at the suburban Don Mills plant in what was to become the third-floor newsroom.

It wasn't a large gathering. Only fifteen or so of Whyte's people were working there – among the exposed wires, dead plants, and detritus of company vice-presidents past – when Whyte delivered the news.

"Hollinger has just acquired the *Financial Post*," he told them.

The staff had the same initial doubts, and Whyte explained it to them the way Black and Amiel had explained it to him. It was a good thing, offered a clearer journalistic vision, and, most important, all but guaranteed that the new newspaper wouldn't wither and die after six months – something that everyone involved was seriously afraid would happen. It all seemed to make sense.

"We felt far more confident after we bought the *Financial Post*," says Whyte. "The *FP* took some of the originality out of it but also removed some of the risk. It became bigger, but the design was basically the same. When the *FP* came on the scene, a lot of other things fell into place very quickly."

The staff accepted the logic of the decision, but some, including sports editor Graham Parley, had nagging regrets. "When they bought the *Financial Post*, the new newspaper ceased to be an exclusive club of hand-picked employees, and the dream faded a little."

◆ ◆ ◆

With the *Financial Post* deal came a staff of eighty or so mostly nervous newsroom employees – nervous except for the few who had already been hired by Whyte at salaries in excess of their *Financial Post* pay, only to find themselves back at square one, slightly richer.

Whyte offered all the paper's newsroom employees jobs, with guarantees of severance or, in some cases, placement elsewhere if the new newspaper didn't make it. After much wooing, Whyte had dealt a blow to the *Globe and Mail* by hiring away business columnist Terence Corcoran as the marquee business writer, but the *Financial Post* deal also brought the high-profile Diane Francis into the mix and two other senior editors, Maryanne McNellis and Tim Pritchard, who was already favoured by Whyte as a possible business editor. Francis agreed to be editor-at-large and continue under the new regime, but Pritchard rejected Whyte's offer of the senior position and McNellis left shortly afterwards to become editor at the *Hamilton Spectator*.

Whyte's executive editor, Kirk LaPointe, who had recently resigned as *Spectator* editor to join the new daily, was in full hiring mode, lunching with reporters and copy editors from both the *Financial Post* and the *Spectator*, attempting to woo them over. His intent was to create a crack investigative team, but the ownership flip-flop meant that the *Financial Post* people no longer needed persuading and the *Spectator* folk were no longer as accessible – or as cheap.

Whyte put hiring on hold until the *Financial Post* pieces fell into place. The tabloid had to be kept buoyant while the building of a new broadsheet continued. Whyte, who quickly grew to admire the *Financial Post*'s reporters and editors, asked *Vancouver Province* editor-in-chief Michael Cooke to take over at the tabloid until the fall launch.

Whyte knew it could be a tricky job.

"The *Post* people were nervous, because they didn't know what we were doing and who was going to be in charge. They were also tough people who had been through so many changes of ownership they just blew it all off. They were a culture unto themselves, but watching them in the weeks approaching launch, and on launch night, they were as excited as anybody else."

The culture inside the new *Post* would be influenced greatly by the old *Post*, which in turn came from the *Toronto Sun* culture developed by founder Douglas Creighton. His enlightened approach to employee relations was a proven motivator but rarely replicated.

"I talked to people from the *Star*, *Globe*, and Southam," says Whyte, "but without exception the *Sun* people were the happiest bunch of workers. They liked their employers the most and their jobs the most. They were just a happier bunch. It was the little things, like getting a day off on your birthday, and sabbaticals – just being treated well. They were worried about losing that culture, but it influenced us. We wanted to make the *National Post* a fun place to work."

Cooke's time at the *Financial Post* as executive editor wasn't without incident. He had been given permission to occupy the office of editorial director McNellis, but she had been reluctant to vacate. Cooke, unwilling to exert his authority and quietly amused if nonplussed by the impasse, took the path of least resistance. Four years later, it remains one of his strongest memories of the period. "I had appointed myself executive editor, but because she wouldn't leave, I had to sit outside the office at the desk where her secretary had sat. It lasted a week. She would arrive in the morning, shut the door, and start typing. I assumed she was working on her resumé. She was perfectly pleasant and clearly very upset, but short of getting a security guard to escort her from the building, there was nothing I could do. She came out once and said, 'You don't mind, do you,' and I said, 'No, you go right ahead.' Tim Pritchard, who was an absolute gentleman, offered me his office, but I refused." McNellis says it was all a misunderstanding, because nobody at Southam had bothered telling her how the takeover would affect her job. She was simply waiting for someone to call and was, she says, in limbo for that week.

Cooke's main concerns were reassuring the staff, keeping the *Financial Post* circulation buoyant, and generally smoothing the transition from old tabloid to the new broadsheet – "not quite D-Day," recalls Cooke, "but certainly a major operation."

With security, or the illusion of it, a major concern, the initial separation of *Financial Post* staff from the main goings-on at the Don Mills plant was convenient.

There was, says LaPointe, a deliberate policy of telling *Financial Post* people only what they needed to know about plans for the new newspaper. "We didn't want anything spirited out before launch. And we weren't sure about the *FP* people and how many were just staying until they got an offer from the *Globe*. We were paranoid, but we still gave them a taste of what was to come. And I think that taste persuaded a lot of people to stay, because they saw how [the new paper] was designed and how much space they would have. And space was a huge issue for the *Financial Post* writers, because they never got any space for their major stories. The *Financial Post* was in the black, but to get there they had to make some bloody-minded decisions, like no travel for the reporters."

For varying reasons – worry about the new daily's prospects and antipathy toward Don Mills among them – some of the recently acquired *Financial Post* people cut deals and left.

LaPointe organized a meet-and-greet lunch at Don Mills for those who remained and laid on a couple of buses to haul them up the Don Valley Parkway. The visit to a non-existent office to talk about a non-existent newspaper was decisive for some, recalls LaPointe. "Tim Pritchard stayed for ten minutes, said, 'We can't do it out of here,' and left. Maryanne McNellis didn't seem to want to be a part of it if she couldn't run it."

◆ ◆ ◆

And then there was the physical newsroom, the nerve centre of the journalistic operation. That had to be built from scratch. Much of the work fell to executive editor Kirk LaPointe, former chief of the Canadian Press and Southam News Ottawa bureaus, who also had responsibility to keep an eye on newsroom spending. "We wanted the most sophisticated newsroom in the country," says LaPointe, "with high-speed Internet access, an electronic library, terrific photo technology, and a couple of satellite dishes on the roof so we could watch sports on the weekend. And we wanted an open concept, not like the *Globe*, where they have cubicles."

He even got to choose the colour scheme. "My wife would never trust me to do that in a million years, and now I was doing it for a national newspaper. But someone had to decide. People would come and show me colours and say that this colour will make them feel better, or this won't show if someone spills a coffee on it. . . . We went with greenish carpets and slate-coloured desks. I didn't really like it."

LaPointe compares the designing of the newsroom for its 110 expected occupants to organizing a country. "The space and position you accorded certain departments played into their sense of status – how close were they to the editor-in-chief, or where they sat in relation to the news desk. By that point, Martin Newland had come along, and he had a very British view of how a news desk should look. We bought a pile of computer programs that allowed you to watch TV on your computer. There was no sense that we had a limited budget. It was 'get what you need.' In a lot of ways we were in a candy store."

The budget, recalls LaPointe, was a moving target, adjusted from week to week as the expenses piled up. The launch budget was initially around $31 million and gradually increased to $35 million – at which point publisher Don Babick began to express concern, whereupon LaPointe managed to work out a spending formula.

◆ ◆ ◆

Whyte had begun to look at the higher potential circulation of his new, full-service daily and concluded that every newspaper was now in his sights, including, rather awkwardly, the major Southam metro newspapers, also controlled by Conrad Black.

The danger that the new newspaper would cannibalize the likes of the *Ottawa Citizen*, *Vancouver Sun*, *Montreal Gazette*, *Edmonton Journal*, and *Calgary Herald* had long irked the editors and publishers of those newspapers. Black and his executive team had formally introduced Kenneth Whyte and Martin Newland to their fellow Southam editors at a meeting in Chicago in May 1998. The message from the top was brutal: We're a national newspaper company about to launch a national newspaper, and although you are not on the team we expect your full cooperation and we reserve the right to hire who we want from any of our newspapers and to take any of your news stories if we decide they are good enough to make our front page. Oh, yes, and the newspaper will be funded from the profits made by your newspapers, and not only that, there's a good chance readers will stop buying your newspaper and buy the new one.

Newland, who had arrived only four days before from England and knew next to nothing about Canada let alone Canadian newspapers, says the Southam editors debated and argued but were essentially presented with a *fait accompli*. "They thought we were elitist," he says, "but it wasn't a game. It was urgent and merciless. So it was a case of 'Get over it, boys. You have a chance to be part of something that has come from you and would not survive but for you. You have a chance to be proud of it, and if you're not, tough shit.'"

After the meeting, host editor Michael Cooke, now at the *Chicago Sun-Times*, offered to organize a cab to get *Ottawa Citizen* editor Neil Reynolds to O'Hare Airport. "A cab?" sighed Reynolds. "I don't need a cab, I need an ambulance!"

Reynolds, who became a staunch supporter of the *Post*, had asked some of the toughest questions of Black and Babick and was especially concerned about losing hold of his newspaper's political coverage. Understandably, he didn't want his Parliament Hill reporters breaking exclusive stories for the sole use of the new national daily.

Babick, who was president of Southam as well as publisher of the new daily, heard similar worries and complaints from fellow publishers who had to overhaul their production and circulation systems to accommodate the printing and distribution of the new daily. Babick's message was clear and uncompromising: "We are going to do this and everyone has to get on the train and make it happen. If you lose readers because of the new newspaper you should probably be looking at the weaknesses in your own newspapers."

There were pockets of quiet resistance, some of which continued for years afterwards, but the most egregious in the eyes of Babick and Black was from editors and publishers who tried to keep journalists from defecting to the new newspaper by offering them more money. Babick was furious. "I had to step in and say, 'Stop this garbage,'" he recalls. "It was verboten but still done by the odd publisher until you hit them on the side of the head and said, 'You can't do that.' The biggest resistance, and most of the double bidding, came from the *Gazette* in Montreal."

Black, David Radler, and Babick took their editors to dinner at the trendy Gibson's steak house, favoured by many Chicago luminaries, including former Bull's star Michael Jordan. Radler, ever the skeptic, drifted over to Ken Whyte and Martin Newland, neither of whom he knew. "I won't blame you if this doesn't work out," he said, confidentially.

◆　◆　◆

After he had completed the *Financial Post* deal, Radler bowed out while the *National Post* took shape. He says he was happy enough with the deal. "We had a good strategy. The *Financial Post* brought us 80,000 to 90,000 circulation, credibility, and instant recognition. I don't know what that's worth. Was it worth its $200 million? I don't know, and nobody ever will."

10 BLOODLETTING AT THE GLOBE

"The managing editor of the *Globe* is the person everyone hates, because you are down in the ditches getting dirty. It's not like being editor, where you can think big thoughts in a big office. You have to be a bit nasty."
                    – Michael Enright, host of CBC Radio's *The Sunday Edition*

On Canada Day 1998, *Globe and Mail* editor-in-chief William Thorsell visited the grave of George Brown, the newspaper's Scottish Presbyterian founder, to deliver him a spiritual briefing on the *Globe*'s conversion to colour, which was due one week later.

Brown, a father of Confederation, was fatally wounded by a disgruntled former employee in 1880, proving, if nothing else, that blood boiled as fiercely at the nineteenth-century *Globe* as it did in the present.

If Thorsell got a response from Brown, he chose to keep it to himself, but in a longish essay in the *Globe*'s July 4, 1998, edition, he shared with all interested readers news of the Coming of Colour – a second coming, as it happened, but one that this time Thorsell would have been unable to deflect even if he had wished to.

The essay was a nicely crafted infomercial, packed with arcane typographical detail of questionable appeal and presented under the headline "NO LONGER BLACK AND WHITE; STILL READ ALL OVER." With the inevitable enthusiasm executives use to persuade the rest of us that change is good, Thorsell explained that the colour makeover, and spruced-up design, would make the newspaper better and in no way prejudice its journalistic content.

Thorsell had developed the *Globe* during the previous decade into a newspaper for elites and, indeed, it was a newspaper widely applauded for its depth and clarity of vision. Maintaining that focus, even with the advent of colour, was understandably important to Thorsell, which was why he emphasized that the coloured newspaper would still have depth and not simply be a warmed-over rehash of what was on last night's TV news. Oddly, he even mentioned the brand names of new computers upon which *Globe* designers had accomplished their task – as if the multibillion-dollar Thomson organization had made great sacrifice in acquiring them. It was quality equipment, the likes of which had long been in use at other colour-converted Canadian dailies.

That the editor-in-chief should travel to a graveyard to commune with a dead guy, then write copiously to reassure readers that the introduction of colour was not the end of civilization as they knew it, suggests the seriousness with which the *Globe* took both itself and the transformation of its image. This was big stuff, and the anxiety was eased only by the knowledge that the perhaps even more illustrious and conservatively designed *New York Times* was in the throes of doing the same thing.

Barely three years earlier, way before whispers of a new Conrad Black daily were heard, the *Globe* had bought new offset presses capable of colour printing and publisher Roger Parkinson committed to colour conversion. Designers produced prototype pages with colour photographs and graphics while Thorsell sought outside opinions from reader focus groups. Then Thorsell shocked his fellow executives by asking for the colour project to be halted so the $2-million annual colour budget could instead be spent on the written content of the paper. "It's the first time an editor has come to me and said he didn't want colour," Parkinson told him.

Given the choice, Thorsell said, pointing to the evidence from the focus groups, *Globe* readers would forgo colour in favour of more sports, more books pages, more investment coverage, and more analysis. The editor-in-chief's strategy also fed into concern about the lean tabloid *Financial Post*, which was making gains on the *ROB* with its no-frills, easy-reading approach to investment news. The *ROB*, which was generating at least 50 per cent of the *Globe*'s advertising revenue, emphasized analytical business journalism, which deservedly won many industry awards but was too long and weighty to read on the subway ride to work. What Thorsell aimed to do, using the funds diverted from the colour project, was to close off the *Financial Post*'s advance by mixing the *ROB*'s traditional analysis with more easily digestible news items.

So one fall day in 1995, in an operation Thorsell likened to Night of the Long Knives, the *Globe* raided the rival *Financial Post* and hired six of its best people in one grab, after cutely placing an ad in the August 9 edition of its own business section seeking "several outstanding journalists to help expand *ROB*'s business coverage." With Thorsell's extra $2 million, *ROB* editor Margaret Wente was able to increase the space available in her section by 50 per cent, an unprecedented forty pages – muscle, they hoped, to deliver a knockout blow to the rival tabloid.

Forsaking colour for content was the right thing to do, insisted Thorsell. "Colour in newspapers," he reasoned, "is sometimes taken too literally. But colourful content of the paper has everything to do with the writing and approaches to the writing."

Thorsell, at the height of his power and influence at the *Globe and Mail*, got his way.

◆ ◆ ◆

Somewhere in England, on January 18, 1996, a combative executive from the Thomson Corporation by the name of Stuart Garner was boarding an airplane to Canada to take charge of Thomson's regional newspapers, the largest of which was the *Winnipeg Free Press*.

Garner, a trim and tough former reporter and news editor from Newcastle in the northeast of England, had overseen the closure of Thomson's newspaper empire in the United Kingdom and, whether he knew it or not when he arrived in Canada, was destined to do the same thing in North America as Thomson withdrew from the print and ink business in favour of selling electronic information. Garner, who was to shepherd that complex and unprecedented $2.5-billion sale through in June 2000, had left Britain with the reputation of an executive who knew the newspaper business inside out, knew what he wanted and how to get there, and didn't care overly much for people who obstructed his path.

On his resumé, Garner boasts of challenging "accepted ways of doing things," of rapidly diagnosing problems, and of being "quick to apply medicine." As editorial director of a group of regional British newspapers in the early 1990s, his medicine had included the removal of twelve out of sixteen editors, fourteen of eighteen deputy editors, and sixteen of twenty news editors. He replaced them through internal and external recruitment.

Garner had a blunt philosophy for the modern newspaper journalist: "The newspaper is a very simple business. You write things people want to read and they reward you by buying the paper, day after day. If the writing doesn't bring them back, you've got trouble."

He accused reporters everywhere of taking ego trips and writing to impress each other rather than readers. And throughout the Thomson organization he imposed his most radical notion of having circulation directors – the people responsible for getting newspapers to readers – take part in editorial meetings where the content of the daily newspaper is decided. Traditionally, the newsroom operates separately from other departments to allow journalists to pursue the news independently and without undue influence from external and internal commercial interests. Or so the theory goes.

Garner challenged the orthodoxy inside his soon-to-disappear newspaper empire and pushed departmental cross-pollination. Circulation directors could bring important information from the street, he reasoned. "They're the ones who hear people saying they won't buy that rag because it's never got anything in it."

The *Globe and Mail* was not to Garner's liking, but because Canada's national daily enjoyed a unique status within the Thomson organization, there was little he could do other than occasionally suggest what he considered to be improvements. Those suggestions were usually received politely then promptly ignored – rebuffs that did little to endear the editor-in-chief to the abrasive, working-class reporter-turned-executive destined to become his nemesis.

Garner was able to exert himself more effectively over the *Globe* a year later when he was appointed chief executive officer of Thomson Newspapers for the United States and Canada. The *Globe*, which represented 20 per cent of Thomson's North American newspaper business, was a natural target of interest for the CEO but of no immediate pressing concern because it was a good economic performer. Still, his opinion of the newspaper's content and presentation didn't change. "The paper lacked élan," says Garner, now a consultant. "It was worthy, and I thought a bit stuffy. It had great content that was not very well displayed and sometimes it was overwritten. But it was a great paper, no two ways about it."

Garner's retrospective assessment is more generous than the messages he delivered to *Globe* management. When the smell of competition from Conrad Black began to drift through the air, his message was clear and blunt: The *Globe and Mail*, in its current state, is not good enough to win a war against a strong new competitor, so I'm sending help whether you want it or not, whether you feel you need it or not. It was the start of a chain reaction that would make life uncomfortable for some, utterly miserable for others, send some away on stress leave, and push others to pack up and leave.

Garner was about to administer some strong medicine, and he wasn't concerned about sugarcoating it.

◆ ◆ ◆

Colin MacKenzie, liked and respected by his newsroom colleagues, had become acting managing editor of the *Globe and Mail* in the summer of 1995 and suffered nine months of uncertainty, not to mention indignity, while Thorsell and publisher Roger Parkinson launched a fruitless, dinner-and lunch-filled nine-month search for someone else to fill the position. In the typical North American newsroom hierarchy, the managing editor reports to the editor-in-chief and oversees all sections of the newspaper, including the daily news pages. It's a hands-on, busy job.

Parkinson and Thorsell searched throughout North America before shifting continents and hiring a British headhunter to dredge newspapers in the U.K. in the faint hope of finding a Canadian, or something close to it, who could legitimately be presented as someone both ethnically and professionally qualified to fill the bill. They failed.

Three times, they came close to finding the perfect Canadian managing editor and three times their choices fell through.

According to Parkinson, former *Kingston Whig-Standard* and future *Ottawa Citizen* editor Neil Reynolds came close, but he refused to take the requisite psychological testing that at the time was both fashionable and an obligatory final step for prospective newsroom poobahs. Popular speculation within the newspaper business was that the tests were designed to guarantee that successful candidates were actually crazy enough to do the jobs for which they were destined.

CBC radio and former print journalist Michael Enright was also a candidate but was rejected by Parkinson after a couple of lunches because of what appeared to be an anti-management attitude, which may have been an asset at the CBC but was perceived as a detriment for a managing editor at the *Globe and Mail*.

Thorsell had approached Enright – the two men liked and respected each other – and after a couple of lunches Enright agreed to meet with Parkinson. Things were promisingly on track and Enright reluctantly agreed to take the psychological tests at a private testing company in Toronto. The first test was mathematical, which for Enright, a self-confessed innumerate, could only be completed by guesswork. He handed his paper back to an amazed tester after just four minutes and was allowed to complete the rest of the tasks while en route to an assignment in Kansas City. He lost interest after reading a few questions, all of which he considered inane.

"I did it partly because I wanted to see how they tested for a managing editor," he says, "but it was a feckless endeavour, because I didn't want to be measured that way and I didn't want to take a job in an environment where they did a lot of testing like that. So I wrote a note to Bill and declined gracefully.

"The managing editor of the *Globe* is the person everyone hates, because you are down in the ditches getting dirty. It's not like being editor, where you can think big thoughts in a big office. You have to be a bit nasty."

John Burns of the *New York Times*, and a former *Globe* writer, was also approached but eventually ruled out because he had never been a manager. He stayed at the *Times*.

Parkinson was aware of the internal upset the uncertainty was causing but considered the search worth it anyway. "It was a hugely important job, and I wanted a potential backup for William [Thorsell], in case he got run down by a truck or something. So we needed the best we could get. Staff was asking why we were looking if we had the best guy here, and Colin was feeling anxious."

After waiting so long and, according to most colleagues, richly deserving his promotion, MacKenzie settled more securely into the job, but with Black on the horizon, and Garner on the warpath, his tenure was to be short-lived.

Parkinson vaguely recalls that the newsroom under MacKenzie wasn't "clicking well," it was "not firing on all cylinders." From MacKenzie's perspective, he was simply in the wrong place at the wrong time and up against too many powerful enemies. "Stuart came around telling us we weren't ready and that real journalists were coming from England and they were going to rip our lungs out," MacKenzie recalls.

In December 1997, MacKenzie got a powerful message that his ticket at the *Globe* was no longer valid. Garner invited eight *Globe* managers to New York for a black-tie fundraising dinner in aid of the Committee to Protect Journalists. The room was loaded with New York's journalistic luminaries. MacKenzie was watching *New Yorker* editor Tina Brown and NBC anchor Tom Brokaw engaged in separate cellphone conversations when a Thomson newspaper editor from Arizona, a Garner associate, sidled up to him.

"Why are you still there?" asked the editor, not unpleasantly.

"What do you mean?" said MacKenzie.

"Why do you stick around? You're a dead man. You're Thorsell's boy."

"I'm not, I'm not!" exclaimed MacKenzie in mock horror.

"Well, everyone says you are. What they say is that the publisher's an idiot, the editor's a faggot, and they don't know what they're doing."

MacKenzie, flush with plans for the newspaper, shrugged it off. Only months later did he realize that it was a deliberate warning he probably shouldn't have ignored.

◆　◆　◆

The *Globe*'s lack of sports coverage, never Thorsell's favourite part of the newspaper, irritated Garner and he wanted it changed – quickly. "The *Globe* was a hell of a good business and financial newspaper," says Garner, "but from my experience of business people in London and New York, to assume that they aren't interested in sport is to miss the point entirely. It's what they talk about in their coffee breaks. Sport is part of the currency of human existence . . . who played well and who didn't. Clearly the *Globe* was doing very badly in that respect."

On the other side of the gender equation, Garner's copious research also told him that the *Globe* was perceived as being not especially appealing to women. It wasn't a problem that could be fixed with a "women's section," but something only tone and style throughout the newspaper could address. The *Globe* never quite managed to shore up that line of defence before the new Black daily came along, and it would hurt them.

The immediate task was to push the *Globe* quickly toward the colour conversion and redesign that Garner deemed an essential weapon in the upcoming war against Conrad Black. He knew that Black's people would produce a newspaper with full colour, boldly displayed photographs, punchy headlines, and brightly presented stories. The *Globe and Mail*, he decided, looked tired and needed a thorough redesign.

A team of outside helpers, comprising trusted consultants and Thomson executives with whom Garner had worked in both North America and Britain, descended on all departments of the *Globe*. Garner's goal was to have a bright, energetic newspaper, packed with consistently high-quality colour reproduction that was pleasing to *Globe*-friendly advertisers and delivered on time to satisfied subscribers.

"Any newspaper that is going to have a radical change to its competitive situation needs to be reviewed thoroughly to ensure it can be as strong as possible," says Garner. "I don't believe that people on staff at the time are best fitted to do that review unassisted, because they will inevitably be familiar and comfortable with what they do and therefore may not ask themselves the uncomfortable questions which may result in the newspaper becoming stronger. If you can ask one or two people you know and respect to go in and help, it is a reasonable action to take."

Jim Jennings, an American from Kentucky, had worked with Garner in Britain before being promoted to Thomson's vice-president of editorial. His mane of long red hair was to earn him the nickname "Lion King," one of the more polite epithets imposed on the outside help by *Globe* newsroom staffers. Terry Quinn, a tough Scot also from the Thomson executive stable, was brought in to focus on reporting and editing.

Their help was not universally welcome, as Jennings, up to a point, admits.

"Was I embraced with open arms without suspicion from day one? No. Journalists are notoriously skeptical. Did everything go smoothly? No. Was there ever a raised voice? Yes. There were moments when I was the outsider and other moments when I couldn't have been more a part of that newsroom if I had been carrying a Canadian passport and been there for twenty years. But the concept of an American walking into a Canadian national newspaper and saying, "This is wrong, do it this way," would be lunacy. To my knowledge, I didn't do that. To some people there, I am somewhere to the far reaches of Genghis Khan; to others, hopefully a bit better than that."

His nationality was not an issue, but people did take exception to what they perceived as the outsiders' arrogance. "They were thugs," says one prominent *Globe* writer. "It was an invasion force. Call it Six Months of the Thugs."

For Jennings, a colour specialist who now travels the world as a consultant, the message from Garner had been clear. "The *Globe and Mail* was a large part of Thomson's portfolio, so naturally if someone declares war on it, you aren't just going to leave the folks on the ground. You are going to give them all the support they need."

But the newsroom managers didn't exactly see it as support. MacKenzie reflects much of the popular opinion around the *Globe* at the time. "Garner didn't like what he saw, so he sent Jim Jennings to do some kind of audit and babysit us. Everything they found out about us was bad. Stuart could not understand for the life of him why we would have so many people in Ottawa producing the most boring stuff in the world. There was no confidence that the people knew what they were doing. They also had to deal with Thorsell, who was trying to control his ultimate self and desperately trying to establish a relationship with Garner, and that didn't work. But to be fair, if you were an outsider looking for arrogance and complacency at the *Globe and Mail*, there was lots to be found."

Garner says that he was not aware of any discord at the newspaper and that he did not concern himself with micro issues such as the newspaper's parliamentary bureau.

Broadcaster and career Toronto journalist Robert Fulford was a *Globe* columnist at the time and heard echoes of legendary *Toronto Star* publisher Beland Honderich in the way Garner was received. "Stuart Garner had barely heard of the *Toronto Star*, the *Globe*, or the *Toronto Sun* when he was appointed," says Fulford, "but as every journalist knows, it is the filtered impressions that are the most important. When I was at the *Star* in the 1960s, Beland Honderich would have a very mild opinion on something, but by the time it reached the level of the night assistant city editor it was as if Honderich was shouting at him through a megaphone. And that's how Garner's message came to *Globe* people. 'This paper is all wrong! I don't like anything about it! I can't think of anything good to say about it!'

After a few months of that, the *Globe*'s will, and the will of the editor-in-chief, was broken."

Whatever the pressure, Thorsell did not show his discomfort to staff. After ten years as editor-in-chief, he appeared capable of sucking up any indignity and toughing it out.

That, says Fulford, was typical. "William plays his cards close to his chest. Once in a while I have known something very bad has happened to him and I have seen him that evening and you would never know. He has an ability to turn those things off, which is an admirable quality in an executive because so many nasty things can happen to you."

◆ ◆ ◆

Jim Jennings had been an occasional visitor to the *Globe*, but from spring 1998 he rented an apartment in Toronto and grafted himself onto the newsroom staff. He was to oversee and guide the *Globe*'s makeover, conduct seminars for newsroom staff, and, as a high-ranking guy from head office, smooth the office politics and ruffled feathers and hire a new art director. He had agreed with Thorsell and MacKenzie that nobody inside the organization was up to the job.

Jennings suggested Robert Lockwood, an internationally renowned American newspaper designer from Maine, who had designed the *Berliner Zeitung*, a newspaper Thorsell admired. Like most travelling newspaper consultants, Lockwood projected a total confidence that some might have confused with arrogance, but unlike many, he got on well with newsroom staff, who were taken with his eclectic range of interests and his love of Canada's north. When he left the *Globe* after six months, the people who had worked closely with him gave him a book on Inuit design.

"There was an incredible amount of money spent on making sure everyone had the tools they needed," says Jennings, "but I spent a lot of time persuading people I wasn't there to dumb-down the paper. The *Globe* was entrenched in its own culture, much of which was very good. It had a structure that had been in place for a long time and they were very happy with it."

The *Globe*'s make-over was rapid, taking a third of the time it normally takes to switch a major newspaper from black and white. Thomson Corp., the same company that penny-pinched its way to wealth – insisting, in its early community newspaper days, that reporters turn in pencil stubs or dried-up pens before being issued replacements – had stuffed its war chest with millions of dollars and was digging in for the long haul.

Even Thorsell, the colour skeptic, was pleased. "We did a very nice job of bringing in colour," he says. "Thomson was willing to spend whatever it cost because of Conrad." Thorsell had taken a keen interest in the redesign and, like his opposite number, Kenneth Whyte, regularly rejected aspects he considered unworthy of a national daily. Despite the help from head office, the incumbent editor-in-chief had significant influence on the final product.

◆ ◆ ◆

Several months earlier, in an awkward, unpopular manoeuvre, William Thorsell, under intense pressure from Garner and his consultants, demoted managing editor Colin MacKenzie after asking – some say pleaded with – his good friend and *ROB* editor Margaret Wente to step up and run the whole news operation.

MacKenzie had tried to liven up the *Globe* within the "serious mandate" he knew Thorsell favoured, and at one meeting of his managers had used the phrase "snap, crackle, pop" in an effort to illustrate how to make the *Globe* less dense, more accessible, and more imaginative in its approach to stories. MacKenzie left the room of confused editors and headed to another meeting. The phrase quickly spread and caused many chuckles on its way to local infamy. MacKenzie, who says he was actually quoting Thorsell, blanches at the memory. "It's a phrase with which I'm associated, but one I will never repeat," he says.

MacKenzie did not see his demise coming. He had taken reporter Susan Delacourt to lunch on an early December Friday to discuss her future at the paper. When Delacourt arrived at work on the Monday, MacKenzie had been demoted and Thorsell had given Wente the title News Editor and responsibility for the news section.

Thorsell delivered the news to a shocked group of managers called together for a Monday brainstorming session. Noreen Rasbach, deputy national editor at the time and now editor of the *Kingston Whig-Standard*, recalls the reaction. "People practically fell off their chairs and just sat there not knowing what to do and say. Colin had been managing editor for less than a year and the loyalty to him was very strong. He was very popular, and when he became managing editor the place had really settled down. But I don't think William and Colin ever looked at newspapers in the same way."

MacKenzie remained as managing editor in name only and had some responsibility for the arts and sports sections but no power. "William decided he would elevate Peggy [Margaret Wente] to rescue him from all these terrible people from Thomson and I was collateral damage. I was allowed to hang around and suggest things if I wanted, but it was a terrible position to be in. It lasted about a month. I wrote a letter and human resources angels wafted in, gave me lots of money, and I went away."

MacKenzie was compensated for constructive dismissal and in April 1998 left to work at the *Toronto Star* at the invitation of his friend and former colleague John Honderich, the newspaper's publisher. Under his three-year severance agreement, he was banned from recruiting *Star* employees from the *Globe*.

Jim Jennings, the visiting executive watching from the sidelines, said the decision to elevate Wente and demote MacKenzie was totally Thorsell's. "It had nothing to do with me. William needed to buy some time and William shot Colin in the hope that people would say, 'Look at that body on the floor' and William would continue. William did that alone, pure and simple. He was trying to buy time for his own hide. Colin was, and is, the best fiscal manager. He was able to read and motivate his people, but he was caught between a rock and a hard place. If he tried to get too creative, William would hit him in the head and if he didn't then he was seen as William's flunky. William is incredibly bright and talented, but as a manager I wouldn't have wanted to work for him because he was prone to popping in, dropping a proclamation, and disappearing."

◆ ◆ ◆

Chicago-born Margaret Wente was a highly rated, if blunt, editor who had developed an excellent reputation directing the *ROB*'s eighty-five staff with her favourite assistant editor, Michael Babad. Wente had moved to Toronto with her family as a teenager, studied English at the universities of Michigan and Toronto, and worked as a publicist at Doubleday Books.

She arrived at the *Globe* after stints at *Canadian* magazine, *Canadian Business*, and CBC Television's business program *Venture*. At the *Globe*, she edited the *Report on Business* magazine before moving to the *ROB* daily section.

She later told friends she agreed to take the job of news editor against her better judgment and "only because Bill asked me. I thought it might well be a suicide mission."

She got off to a bad start. Thorsell had asked her to produce a confidential report on what she considered wrong with the newsroom. She did and it was scathing.

"The Toronto-based national news team," she wrote, "is in exactly the same situation that *ROB* was in 1994. It is starved for good reporters. Key beats are uncovered. Other key beats are staffed with hopeless people. . . . No amount of clever editing or packaging will fix that. The only fix is to hire some top young reporters. No amount of remedial training, rework, or memo-writing will compensate for a basically weak staff."

To Wente's dismay, the memo was mysteriously leaked to the newsroom, and like Colin MacKenzie's "snap, crackle, pop" remark, Wente's *bête noire* was to become "weak and hopeless." The memo left Wente with few friends among the rank-and-file reporting staff, and in some cases permanently strained relations.

Reporters began arriving at work wearing white buttons saying "Weak and Hopeless" in large black letters. It was in that poisoned environment that Wente assumed her challenging duties, with no guarantee she would meet the approval of Garner or his consultants – or, for that matter, Thorsell.

Reporter Susan Delacourt, waiting for approval for a move to the editorial board, met with Wente, who told her outright that the move was not going to happen: she would be staying put in the newsroom and continuing as a reporter. Delacourt's anger and confusion didn't last long. "She said the editorial board thing isn't going to happen. We're not going to allow it, and you're going to work for me. Then Thorsell called me into his office and said, 'Congratulations, you're joining the editorial board.' I said that's not what Peggy just said and he said, 'Well, you won't be surprised to learn that I overrule Peggy.' So I was gone, and watched while Peggy demoralized everybody on staff. I like Peggy, but she was just no good at dealing with people."

Veteran reporter John Gray, one of the *Globe*'s most respected journalists, lunched for two hours with Wente shortly after her appointment – "a detached lunch," as he recalls it. The day afterwards, Gray asked for a follow-up meeting to tell her what he really felt. He told her, frankly, that her top-down management style was disastrous. "We spent another hour and a half having coffee on the roof of the *Globe*, and she said, 'You're quite right, we have to do something about that.' Later that day, or the following day, it was announced that seventeen people were going to be summarily deprived of their beats. It was just simply announced. She didn't try to ruin the newsroom, but she came goddamn close."

Wente's brusque, autocratic style seemed at odds with the person many of her closer newsroom colleagues had known, but the substance of her complaints about the newsroom, its staff, and its structure, was by no means unanimously denied.

Deputy national editor Noreen Rasbach was at least partly sympathetic:

> The *Globe* is not an easy place. People there have some of the best newspaper jobs in the country, and I would say that 50 per cent appreciate it and 50 per cent don't. No other newsroom had as much complaining going on as the *Globe and Mail* newsroom. Peggy wanted to broaden what we covered; news was our bread and butter, but we had to become more expansive and more popular, and she was totally right. But she didn't have any support, and she dismissed half of the newsroom as idiots and thought the superstar writers were not good writers at all. Newspaper newsrooms are rooms full of egos, especially the *Globe*, and you don't just dismiss people like that. She excluded people instead of including them. So she had very good ideas but didn't know how to manage, and there was no way she was going to survive. She put her trust in William, who had to change the paper and needed someone to do it, but in the end William didn't believe in what was being asked of him. So Peggy didn't have all the staff on her side, but she didn't really have the editor on her side, either.

Wente shuffled the newsroom deck and attempted to introduce change where she thought it was needed, but if the rank and file were anxious to see her gone, the feeling gradually became mutual. With increasingly unfriendly pressure from above, budgets temporarily frozen by head office, and problems of an unhappy staff adding to the phenomenal pressure of being responsible for the content of the main news section of a daily newspaper, Wente was reaching the end. She saw Conrad Black's new paper as an express train trundling toward her, and she was tied to the tracks.

It was a year after she was appointed news editor that Wente returned from a short vacation and was asked to attend a meeting with Garner, newly installed executive Phillip Crawley, Thorsell, Sarah Murdoch (whose responsibilities were the opinion pages, the Focus and Books sections, and the popular Facts and Arguments feature), and Doug Gould of the *Report on Business*.

Someone at the meeting asked Wente what her plans were for the newspaper, but having just returned from vacation, and unaware that the meeting had been planned, she had little of substance to offer.

Murdoch describes the encounter with Crawley and Garner as one of the worst meetings she had ever experienced. "We had rehearsed our little enhancements to combat the *Post*, but they were so incredibly unimpressed with our plans and moved on to other things. They wanted a more interesting newspaper, and it was clear at that point that Peggy had about two weeks left as news editor. We fled to William's office and hung our heads. They hadn't even pretended to be polite. Peggy knew she had to get out immediately and resigned three or four days later."

"This isn't my idea of a good life," Wente told a friend.

Thorsell offered her a cash buyout or a job writing a general column. She took the column, flourished, and went on to win two consecutive National Newspaper Awards for her work.

◆ ◆ ◆

Stuart Garner liked the likable Roger Parkinson and credited him with steering the *Globe* through some profitable years, but he didn't think the American was the right man to tackle Conrad Black. The lack of cutthroat newspaper competition culture in Canada, and, with a couple of exceptions, the United States, meant a new publisher had to come from somewhere else. So Garner contacted his old Newcastle colleague Phillip Crawley, who was battle-worn from newspaper wars in the U.K. and Hong Kong and had recently moved to New Zealand, where he was doing very well in the newspaper business. But Garner needed the finest, most trustworthy general he could find to fight the forces of Blackness.

"Clearly," says Garner, "the battle in Toronto was going to be complex because of the *Star*, and although the *Sun* operates in a different part of the market it complicated the situation more. Given my belief that the *National Post* was going to be a very tough competitor, Roger needed someone who was used to the cut and thrust of newspaper competition."

That "someone" was obviously going to *replace* Roger Parkinson, although it was not presented quite like that. Crawley became president of the *Globe and Mail*, a nebulous title that could have been either meaningful or meaningless. In Crawley's case, it was decidedly meaningful. He was the man.

William Thorsell, meanwhile, was dealing with his own set of competitive realities – the threat of unhappy, talented people leaving the newspaper and defecting to the enemy. There was no shortage of prospective defectors.

Thorsell ordered a talent inventory in all sections of the newsroom – writers, photographers, copy editors, designers, and everyone else considered important to the *Globe*'s survival. He then adjusted their compensation, a term newly introduced to the newspaper business. It basically meant wages and, in the *Globe*'s case, maybe a parking space and a cellphone.

Says Thorsell, "If somebody calls one of my really great people and offers them a job worth $15,000 more than I'm paying them, and they come to me and say, 'Hey, I just got this job offer from the *Post* for another $15,000,' and I say, 'Oh, I really love you, I'll pay you another $20,000,' they might well say, 'Well, why didn't you feel that way about me before.' So I wanted to go to our really critical people, right from production through columnists, to ensure they were being compensated at what was now the prevailing market rate."

So, during the spring and summer of 1998, about twenty-five people in the *Globe and Mail* newsroom felt the benefit of competition before it had even arrived. And there were others, ultimately approached by Kenneth Whyte, whose value also increased. Columnist and feature writer Jan Wong was one who met the *Post* editor at least twice. They shared a liking for the afternoon tea served splendidly at the King Edward Hotel.

"At the *Globe*," Wong says, "there was tremendous curiosity to see who was getting wooed – and management was concerned, they thought they were vulnerable. And, of course, among the masses it was like a beauty contest: who was going to get asked to the prom, did you get a date, and who else has a date. It was like, 'Don't go, don't go, we want you to stay. What will make you happy?' So it was very beneficial for the masses, for the reporters, and very much in their interests to have competition. But for senior managers, it was scary, because if the *Globe* failed they would be blamed."

At *National Post* headquarters, almost two years of planning and preparation were coming to an end, and a new uncertain era in Canadian journalism was about to begin. It was going to be a good time to be in newspapers.

11 THE FIRST POST

"I'd hire a one-legged black lesbian if I thought she could write properly."
                                    – Martin Newland, deputy editor, *National Post*

On any given day, what qualifies as news is relative to whatever else is happening in the world, and, relatively speaking, Monday, October 26, 1998, was not a particularly good news day. There were no devastating terrorist attacks, no tragic natural disasters, and no major political scandals. News material for the launch was a bit thin.

But the new *National Post* did have a minor scoop that had been leaked to the newspaper's parliamentary bureau from a source in the office of Alberta Premier Ralph Klein, who was set to make a landmark speech to a United Alternative conference in Ottawa.

Under the headline "KLEIN BACKS UNITE-THE-RIGHT MOVEMENT," the story, by Ottawa bureau staff writer Sheldon Alberts, included an interview with Klein, who said that only the joint forces of the Reform Party and the Progressive Conservatives could topple the Liberals in Ottawa.

The phrase *Unite the Right* had two main qualifications for the front-page, big, bold type treatment: the phrase had a nice rhythm, and it fit into the allotted space. But like most readers, Reform Party Leader Preston Manning wasn't considering the niceties, or technical strictures of headline writing, when he saw the *Post*'s front page. He winced and years later he insists that the irresistible poetry of the phrase *Unite the Right* and its subsequent absorption into Canada's political lexicon, damaged the cause of uniting a common front against the Liberals – a cause at the root of the ambitions of Conrad Black and his closest business colleagues.

Manning considered the right-centre-left political paradigm to be an anachronism – and anyway, many of the people who supported his populist Reform movement did not consider themselves to be right wing. It was Deborah Grey, the first Reform MP, who lamented that if the *Post* wanted a rhyming headline, why hadn't they used "Unite the Bright"?

The Klein story, which was a nod to the *Post*'s small-c political leanings and its future preoccupation with the mythical political coalition that might have defeated the Chrétien Liberals, sat next to a large photograph of U.S. Senator John Glenn, who was embarking on his second space mission. Columnist Allen Abel began his story of the aging astronaut's vanity flight with the memorable sentence: "At T-minus three days and counting, with a thumbnail moon lying low, the engine of human conceit and ambition waits to puncture the sky." The Abel piece, shouting boldly from the front page with the inspired headline "AT 77, GLENN SHOWS THE WHITE STUFF," was another signal of sorts: that the *National Post* would deviate, often radically, from the daily newspaper traditions cast by that other national newspaper, the *Globe and Mail*.

The *National Post*'s statement of intent, written by editor-in-chief Kenneth Whyte, was published on page two of the first edition and held some fighting words for the *Globe* and, significantly, acknowledgment of the role played by other Southam metro newspapers:

Good morning, Canada, and welcome to the first edition of the *National Post*.

We are the creation of Southam Inc., Canada's premier newspaper group, with 33 daily papers from St. John's to Victoria and three million readers daily. We will be printed Monday to Saturday at nine sites across the country, and available in street boxes and for home or office delivery in major centres. The question arose, when Southam announced its intentions to launch this project, why another newspaper in Canada? Here are three answers. Canada has never had a national newspaper. We've had national business papers, and Toronto papers presuming to speak for the whole country, but we've never seen a paper founded to serve the nation as a whole. Southam, with its strong presence from coast to coast, is the only print-media company in the land with the resources necessary to make a success of such a mandate.

Canada has changed. We are, at the end of this century, an increasingly confident and cosmopolitan place. We're adapting to the economic and political realities of the '90s with more fortitude and dispatch than almost any other industrialized country. We're at the forefront of global commerce, free traders of unsurpassed resourcefulness. We've abandoned the cultural timidity of previous generations to become international leaders in many intellectual and artistic pursuits. We need a newspaper that will reflect the new vitality and sophistication of the Canadian people, an articulate, vigorous voice for an exciting future.

People want a quality paper that's not a chore to read. Canadians told us they think an informative and intelligent daily should also be entertaining. We agree. This will be a spirited publication, reporting and commenting on events, issues, and personalities of the day in an engaging and stylish manner.

To that end, we've assembled an astonishing array of journalistic talent – Roy MacGregor, Christie Blatchford, Allen Abel, Andrew Coyne, Mordecai Richler, to name a few. Our corps of roving correspondents will be lead by the highly regarded authors Isabel Vincent and John Bentley Mays. Our Arts & Life section will feature, among many others, the celebrated writers Charlotte Gray, Linda Frum, and Anne Kingston.

We are also delighted to bring to your notice a number of Canadian journalists who have yet to attract the national audience they deserve. For instance, Mark Steyn, the Montrealer whose spectacularly funny and insightful columns have brought him great acclaim in London and New York, will write Thursdays on our editorial page. Cam Cole, easily the best sports columnist in Canada today, leads off our daily sports package.

Southam was fortunate, while preparing to launch the *National Post*, to have acquired one of the country's great newspaper franchises, the *Financial Post*. We have returned the *FP* to its original broadsheet format and smoothly integrated it with the new paper. We have preserved the best of the *FP*'s features, including its Investing section, while introducing new elements such as our U.S. news page and our daily Briefing page.

We now boast the most impressive array of business columnists and writers ever assembled at a single Canadian paper. Terence Corcoran, the new editor of the *Financial Post*, is Canada's most authoritative business columnist. He is joined by the feisty and ever-popular Diane Francis, our editor-at-large, as well as economist William Watson, authors Linda McQuaig and Peter Foster, *FP* favourites Barry Critchley, Patrick Bloomfield, Neville Nankivell, David Frum, feature writer Rod McQueen (author of a best-selling new book on the Eaton dynasty), and a stellar crew of reporters led by Sandra Rubin, Theresa Tedesco and Phil Mathias.

We also have a number of specialty pages we hope will become a daily habit with you. Discovery, full of new knowledge from the worlds of science and the humanities, is on page A17. Our Parliament page seeks to re-establish the relevance of Commons debate to national politics. Avenue, a double-page spread in the Arts & Life section, is the visual highlight of the paper. It will feature the finest in Canadian and international photography and illustration.

Though this is just our first issue, the *National Post* is already off to a great start. In the months leading up to our launch we have dramatically increased daily paid subscriptions of the *Financial Post*. Readers and advertisers, both, have responded to our efforts with great enthusiasm. I hope you enjoy the paper and pick us up again tomorrow.

In closing, I'd like to extend a personal note of gratitude to all the Southam employees across the country who have helped us get off the ground. Thanks, also, to our proprietor, Conrad Black. The creation of a new newspaper on this scale requires vision, courage, and a considerable commitment of resources. He supplied all of that, and by doing so has enhanced the prospects for a genuine national community in Canada.

◆ ◆ ◆

After eighteen months of preparation, and several weeks of reporters writing real stories for dummy newspapers, the wheels and cogs of the new newspaper were well greased and, with the exception of the circulation department that had been naturally deprived of a dress rehearsal, the transition from pretend to real world was expected to run smoothly.

There had been the inevitable nerves to soothe just days before, suffered by someone Whyte describes as "pretty close to Conrad" who was concerned that the design of the newspaper was too radical, that perhaps it should be more conservative-looking, like the *Daily Telegraph*. "It's very vertical, isn't it," said the person (pessimistically). "Are readers going to like that? Perhaps we should consider something else . . ."

Given the army of high-priced design consultants who had contributed to the final effort, Whyte wasn't overwhelmed with enthusiasm at the prospect of a radical eleventh-hour overhaul, so he calmed the fears while simultaneously digging his heels into the industrial-strength pile of the office rug.

Conrad Black had arrived in Toronto a week before to handle any last-minute emergency. Two press runs of 20,000 copies each had been run off the press as part of the pre-launch dress rehearsals. Most were immediately shredded, but Whyte held on to a few, drove them over to Black's house, and left them with him.

At the morning news meeting on October 26, Whyte urged his editors to be encouraged by the success of the dummy runs and not to become overawed by the occasion, historic though it was.

It was executive editor Kirk LaPointe's job to find the page-one picture for the first edition, and, given the paucity of choice, he plumped for the photograph of the geriatric American spaceman-turned-senator, which he correctly guessed would give critics of Canada's new national daily newspaper an easy target. It was the best available, and at least it married with a piece of original *Post* reporting from Abel, but it didn't help that *USA Today* would choose to run the same photograph on its front page on the same day. Critics of the Glenn image were not deflected by the deliberate addition of Canadian content at the top of the page: photographs of Alanis Morissette and Wayne Gretzky in "sky boxes," newspaper shorthand for the illustrated index items (and a design technique the *Globe and Mail* would copy before the end of the *Post*'s first week).

On the inside pages, there was lots of space for the *Post* to strut its stuff. A new national newspaper was obviously going to be a target for advertisers, so to give the editorial department plenty of room to work, limits on the number of ads were imposed on the first few editions.

Because of the demands of the Southam metro newspapers, whose presses the *Post* was using, deadlines for completed sections for the nationally distributed edition were staggered through the early evening, beginning at 7:30 p.m. for the *Financial Post* section and finishing at 9:30 p.m. with page one. By most morning newspaper standards, the deadlines were early, demanded a frantic work pace, and, inevitably, a scramble in the last minutes. Work then started immediately on the Toronto edition of the newspaper, which meant adding new sections and updating ongoing stories until the final deadline at 11:30 p.m.

But the first night's production went relatively smoothly save for a bout of anger by exhausted deputy editor Martin Newland, who had been brought from Britain on the understanding from Whyte there would be a clearly defined hierarchy but whose rivalry with Kirk LaPointe continued to surface. Newland figured that Southam, perhaps reasonably, had insisted on bringing LaPointe into the managerial mix because Whyte had no national newspaper experience and Newland knew nothing about Canada. LaPointe, hardly a veteran himself, had one year's daily newspaper experience, but as former chief of the Ottawa bureaus of Canadian Press and Southam News, he had established working relationships with the editors of Southam newspapers on whose cooperation the *National Post* would depend and who, with one or two exceptions, had been resistant and uniformly skeptical.

In LaPointe, the Southam editorial brass had someone who knew the company, knew the country, and knew something – at least more than Whyte – about their newspapers. In other words, Newland figured that LaPointe was there to help with the newspaper's infrastructure and to keep the editors happy.

"I think," says Newland, "when the Southam side of this operation heard that Ken was going to be bringing some highly expensive person from London to run the paper, they didn't like it. I think Kirk was a concession to that Southam editorial anchor. Two weeks before I came here, I got a call from this guy called Kirk LaPointe, who said, 'How are you? I'm executive editor.' I said, 'Oh, yeah? My last conversation with Ken was that I would report only to him.' Obviously it was a problem. Kirk wanted [control over] content, but that was me. Kirk did a lot of amazing things, but he was never going to get content. I was prepared to shut up about it, because I am what I am. I bludgeon people with personality and carry on."

Shortly before the launch, the senior newsroom management met weekly to assess who had been hired and whom they still wanted to hire. LaPointe was concerned about the ethnic and gender balance of the newsroom, but Newland was bred on an entirely different Fleet Street ethic. "When Kirk came in and talked about the ethnic and gender balance in the newsroom, I couldn't believe it. I thought, 'Do you think this is a fucking game? Do you think Conrad is spending $150 million of his money so we can get our ethnic profiling right?' But Kirk kept coming back to it, so I said, 'I'd hire a one-legged black lesbian if I thought she could write properly.' And Ken was sharklike, sitting at the head of the table like Christ at the Last Supper. I went to him afterwards and said, 'Ken, you agreed with me, I know you agreed with me.' He said, 'Yes, I agree with you, but I'm not going to be seen agreeing with you.'"

The most dramatic showdown between LaPointe and Newland was on launch night, and it was a classic piece of internal newspaper drama. Newland spotted the masthead, where the various newsroom executives had their names listed, and saw that Kenneth Whyte's name was in its rightful place at the top, and that underneath, both on the same level, were the names Martin Newland and Kirk LaPointe. It took the *Post*'s chief executive, Don Babick, to solve the dispute, in Newland's favour. "That was the only time I said, 'Enough, we've got to get this sorted out,'" says Newland. "I said, 'Fine, just put Kirk LaPointe there and take me off. I'm not playing this bloody game.' So that brought it all to a head on launch night."

LaPointe and Newland say they became best of friends and regularly exchanged what Newland describes as "farty" e-mails. LaPointe denies there was friction between him and the deputy editor because they both had plenty to do – Newland firing up the troops and getting the newspaper out on time, and LaPointe running newsroom logistics, alternating Sunday shifts with Newland, and acting as newsroom liaison with the marketing and advertising departments. "People probably suspected there was friction," says LaPointe, "but we could argue in public and buy each other a beer the next day. We are terrific friends. We confided in each other and never betrayed each other's confidences."

❖ ❖ ❖

The new broadsheet *Financial Post* was now the new daily's business section, printed before the rest of the paper. When the first edition was ready to be printed at the downtown *Toronto Sun* plant, Conrad Black pushed a button to start the press and then paced the floor like an expectant father. He waited, then waited some more, but Murphy's Law had struck. Between the Don Mills newsroom and the downtown printing plant on King Street, several pages had vaporized, and although everything was running to perfection at the other eight plants across the country, Conrad Black and Barbara Amiel were not elsewhere, they were in Toronto.

Barbara Amiel relayed her husband's irritation to production manager Patrick Brennan, who was in the throes of the worst night of his life.

"Tell him that things are running smoothly in all other areas," said Brennan.

"I'm not sure that will do," she responded without sympathy.

The newspaper was two hours late out of the Toronto plant, but before that, the front page of the *Financial Post* did make it off the press intact and it was enough for the photo opportunity. The widely used photograph of Conrad Black holding a hot-off-the-press first edition of the *Financial Post* was, in printing plant parlance, a spoil. It had nothing written on the back. But still, it did the job, and Black, with his wife and entourage, headed to Don Mills to greet the troops and celebrate the new birth.

❖ ❖ ❖

There was a band, drinks, and much celebration in the *Post*'s first-floor cafeteria. People hugged and kissed and when someone finally turned up with bundles of newspapers, a clearly delighted Black patiently signed copies and posed for photographs.

Kenneth Whyte was thrilled that his parents came from Edmonton for the occasion, and for his parents it was just as thrilling that they got to meet the local hero Cam Cole, a sports columnist they had read in the *Edmonton Journal* for years.

Sports editor Graham Parley, raised in the London borough of Chelsea and a fan of the local soccer team of the same name – his yappy Jack Russell answers to the name Chelsea – was absorbed in a page of sports results.

Without raising his head, he shouted to a colleague, "Hey, we have a problem here!" Conrad Black was at that moment leading his entourage in single file past Parley's desk.

Black stopped, swivelled his upper body, and stared back at Parley.

"We *have*?" he inquired in mock surprise.

"Er, no, no, we've just solved it," spluttered the quick-thinking Parley, much to everyone's amusement. Black moved on, smiling broadly, leaving Parley to the merciless ribbing of his colleagues.

Shortly before one o'clock in the morning, deputy editor Newland answered the news desk phone. It was a reader calling from Vancouver.

"I've just got your first edition," said the anonymous male voice.

"Oh, yeah?" replied Newland.

"It makes sense," said the caller and then hung up.

The exchange, brief as it was, sticks with Newland. "I didn't know what to make of it. Did he mean that page two follows page one, or what?"

Newland drove home at around one o'clock, leaving the party early, as was his habit. He felt exhausted and close to tears. "It was unbelievable how polished we were coming out of the gate. I went home after the first edition was done. My wife was in a strange land she didn't particularly want to be in, and for weeks I had been working sixteen-hour days. I just wanted to go home and have a good cry. When you're emotional, you go to the one you love, don't you? And then it was a feeling of heart-bursting joy. I felt like 'I'm the man.'"

Whyte was happy with the first edition, but in a deliberate, symbolic statement the two-page Avenue section, published the next day, was devoted to things you can do with an otherwise useless newspaper – wrap fish, make hats, and so on. Whyte wanted to make the point that the *National Post* should not be judged on one edition alone. Launch night was the end of one long road and the beginning of another.

"It was only going to happen once," says Whyte. "It was a special thing, and in a way it didn't matter what happened afterwards. Whether it succeeded or failed, you had at least got it that far and launched a new paper. And much of what was going to happen after was beyond our control. To be able to say you had done it was a nice feeling, but part of me also thought that it was downhill from there. You had got it that far, executed an idea, and now it was time for others to start firing at it and look for its shortcomings. It was no longer an ideal to dream about but a concrete reality with concrete failings and problems. That was one of the great things about the pre-launch period, the sense of possibility – what you could do and how good it could be. But when it became real, you had to focus more concretely on the problems. It became tangible and attackable and you weren't just in the realm of expectations and possibilities any more. It was what it was."

When the party had ebbed, and long after Conrad Black and his group had left, Whyte sat alone with his feet on the newsroom desk, exhausted but pleased with himself. He had a promotional breakfast to attend at the King Edward Hotel five or six hours later.

Aside from memories of the night, he would keep as souvenirs the only existing, wrapped bundle of *National Post* first editions and the printing plates off the press.

◆ ◆ ◆

Publication day brought mixed blessings. Delivery ran smoothly in most parts of the country, but there were major problems getting the *Post* distributed in Toronto. Fortunately, many people attributed the lack of copies to heavy demand and became even more keen to find a copy.

The promotional breakfast was a blur, and Whyte couldn't wait to get back to his office to hear what everyone was saying about the *Post*.

Conrad Black had left a warm message of congratulations on his voice-mail. (It was still on his machine four years later, along with a subsequent, less complimentary phone message from the proprietor who had read something in the *Post* he did not like.)

But the worst was to come that evening on the CBC's *The National*. A segment hosted by Leslie MacKinnon featured an interview with Black and a panel discussion between journalism professor Stephen Kimber of the University of King's College, Halifax, Shari Graydon of Media Watch, a feminist group dedicated to eliminating sexism in the media and elsewhere, and Ian Austen, a former Southam News journalist, who had been laid off in a round of staff cuts.

Presented as "Post Time," the item began with an interview with a buoyant Black and proceeded with the panel, whose job it was to assess the *National Post* on the basis of its first issue. After the broadcast, *Post* executives were furious that the panel had been loaded against them.

MACKINNON: The *National Post* is taking dead aim at one of the oldest newspapers in the country, the venerable *Globe and Mail*. So on day one, how did they compare? On the front page of the *Post*: a photo and feature article on John Glenn, the American astronaut; a story on a Canadian company's links to the Russian mob; an interview with Ralph Klein; and an article about Boris Yeltsin, mad that Jean Chrétien has scrapped a trade mission to Russia. The front page of the *Globe*: a photo of the Canadian autumn; three articles on Canadian health issues; the Canadian army's preparedness for computer problems in the year 2000; and a feature on Yeltsin's rival, Russian politician Alexander Lebed. Inside the *Post*: a section called Parliament, featuring two articles on the parties of the right; one on the APEC inquiry; and one criticizing Jean Chrétien's comments about the constitution on the eve of a Quebec election. *Post* editorials: two items on Chilean leader Augusto Pinochet's arrest; an essay critical of the Trudeau legacy; and an editorial openly dismissive of Joe Clark's bid for the Conservative leadership. Inside the *Globe* editorials: faint praise for Joe Clark; why Chrétien should shut up on Quebec; and why Canadians should worry about health/safety.

Now the view from the readers – and admittedly, these are not your average readers.

Shari Graydon is president of Media Watch, a non-profit organization dedicated to eliminating sexism in the media. She joins us from Vancouver. Stephen Kimber is a newspaper columnist and director of the School of Journalism at the University of King's College in Halifax. And journalist Ian Austen joins us from Ottawa.

Stephen Kimber, we'll start with you. What is the view from the East Coast about the *National Post*?

STEPHEN KIMBER: Well, my fourteen-year-old son I think summed it up this morning when he looked at the paper and he said, "It's nice, but – ," and that was the feeling that I got. We've got another Ottawa-centric right-wing business paper. We already have one of those. I don't know that we actually need this one.

MACKINNON: And Shari, what about you? What does it look like from Vancouver?

SHARI GRAYDON: We've got all these other papers. And, uh, it was nice that they acknowledged that. But it really does beg the question, and certainly from a West Coast perspective, there did seem a couple of self-conscious attempts to acknowledge that we're alienated out here and we want to be included, so they had the double-page two-inch stories running across the top saying from west to east, instead of the east to west. But it didn't really do anything, as has just been said, that we don't have already. And certainly it didn't appear to be a national paper. When you looked at all the folks who were profiled in the glossy brochure included in the paper as key columnists and writers, they were all white folks from Ottawa, Toronto, central Canada.

MACKINNON: Ian, since you're in Ottawa, let me ask you, What do you think of the political coverage of the *National Post*?

IAN AUSTEN: Well, you know I was a bit puzzled by their obsession today with the unite-the-right movement to bring the Tories and Reform together. I mean, the people who say they're Tories on the weekend more or less elected Joe Clark as leader – which doesn't strike me as, you know, that they're about to join Reform yet. We were treated to three stories about this issue today. It was, to me, just sort of baffling.

MACKINNON: Shari, go ahead.

GRAYDON: Well, I was just going to say I thought it seemed unusually predictable. In a paper put out by Conrad Black, I was surprised at how predictable some of the content was. I thought, at very least in their first week, they would make some semblance of attempting not to wear the ideology or their agenda on their sleeves, so to speak. So I found that a little bit surprising.

MACKINNON: Okay, Stephen, let me ask you about the front page, the cover story with the big photo, which is important. It was the story about an American astronaut, John Glenn, who's going to space at seventy-seven. That's a good story, but it's not Canadian.

KIMBER: It's a good story. It was well written by a guy who I'm delighted to see back in newspapers. But this is a front-page story that . . . the people in that newspaper have been labouring at for a number of months. I don't think so. I don't think that was a good opening story. And the picture was awful. I mean, it's a good technical photo, but you know, of him just sort of looking into the camera. This is not a good use of that front page.

AUSTEN: And even stranger was the way they pushed that business story on the front about Magnex . . . I mean, I went and looked on a database today. The *Globe and Mail* had almost all of that story on the 23rd of May, and they [the *National Post*] had "exclusive" across the top. Well, they had a couple of small details that were exclusive, but there wasn't much new there.

KIMBER: I think there's a lot of labouring that goes on. And we should be fair. This is their first day and even if you have a lot of time to do it, it's still very difficult to get any flavour of what the paper's going to be like. We need to be fair and say that in a little while this paper may be quite different. But at the moment, I agree with you. There wasn't much there today that was worth your fifty cents, you know.

AUSTEN: You would think, Stephen, on their first day – I mean they've had months to get ready for this. This is the day that you pull the blanket off and pull the rabbit out of the hat. You know, the hat was kind of empty.

GRAYDON: I think they're waiting. I think the weekend edition might be a better measure of what they're attempting to do, flash-wise. I agree that it did seem odd that with six months to put this issue together, that there wasn't more oomph to it – some great big investigative breaking story, but maybe they're doing the Volkswagen Beetle strategy. Let's hype it, build up the suspense, make it hard to get. In Vancouver, one of the issues was you couldn't find it if you weren't at the gas station or at the box at 6:30 this morning. Apparently many people had difficulty getting their hands on it.

KIMBER: I'm not sure there'll be a lineup tomorrow, though.

GRAYDON: Judging by this one, I'm not sure either. The other thing that I thought was interesting was remembering Conrad Black's statement, when he bought majority shareholdership of Southam a few years ago, he listed . . . a number of things he was going to rid Southam papers of. And looking at this vehicle, it looks like he's been very explicit about making sure that his paper gets rid of all of the socialist "sludge" and the "feminist path" and all of the stuff that he really was setting out to eradicate.

MACKINNON: You all see evidence of that, do you?

KIMBER: Oh, there's no question. The interesting thing to me is that Linda McQuaig apparently is going to be a columnist in the paper.

AUSTEN: Only every two weeks, though.

GRAYDON: It's sort of a token Rick Salutin in the *Globe*, isn't it?

MACKINNON: Let me ask you, How do you think this will change Canadian journalism, if it does?

AUSTEN: It won't. I think it probably has a pretty good chance of surviving. We're going to have to, as consumers, . . . make a choice at some point between the *Globe* and the new *National Post*. And I think they'll both survive, but . . . why do we need this? It'll survive. But why?

MACKINNON: Shari, I don't know whether people in Vancouver think the *Globe and Mail* is a national newspaper, but will they think this, the *National Post*, is a national newspaper?

GRAYDON: No, absolutely not. In fact, the *Globe* in the last couple of years has really, really beefed up its Vancouver bureau. The stories and the columns and the representation from Western Canada has improved significantly, perhaps in anticipation, especially in the last six to eight months, of the new competition. But no, the *Globe* still isn't perceived as a national paper particularly, and this vehicle is certainly no threat to its presence in Western Canada for sure.

Now, I would just like to add that having the opportunity of a new national newspaper would be to maybe address some of the problems that exist elsewhere in Canadian journalism. And that would be to make the paper more reflective not just of regional diversity, but of diversity generally. And based on a cursory content analysis, this paper is still very white; there are still very few women's voices and perspectives, and that's an opportunity waiting to be taken advantage of, from my perspective.

MACKINNON: Did you like anything in the paper you saw this morning?

AUSTEN: Yeah.

MACKINNON: What?

AUSTEN: Well, I thought, in fairness, I thought the *Financial Post* has been improved by returning to being a broadsheet. It really hung together well. The stories still look like a skinny man in a fat man's trousers now that they've got big pages. I think that's going to come. I think it's a big improvement to have the *Post* brought back to a broadsheet.

KIMBER: And I think there are very good writers in this paper who really haven't yet had a chance to show their stuff. Allen Abel gave a little demonstration of it with the piece on what's his name, the old guy . . .

AUSTEN: John Glenn.

KIMBER: Thank you. John Bentley Mays going back to Hot Springs, Arkansas, was a good story as well. I . . . I expect to see those kind of things, that kind of good writing in this newspaper.

MACKINNON: And Shari, did you like anything?

GRAYDON: Well, I agree, there are a couple of good writers. . . . Um, but there certainly wasn't anything that made me jump out of bed in the morning and run to my front door and subscribe to this paper, on the basis of today's very superficial . . . coverage.

MACKINNON: Okay, that's our time. Thank you all very much.

Memory of "the fucking CBC panel" still makes Whyte angry. Newland remains equally incensed. "That day [for us] was all neurosis. What did people think? How is it being received? And then came that CBC thing. You didn't want to just remonstrate with them, you wanted to rip their heads off and shit down their necks. How dare they! We have put so much work into this. It has taken our hearts and minds for months and months, and by God it's worked, and all you can do is criticize."

"It was what you would expect of two gentlemen in a duel to the death."

– John Honderich, publisher, *Toronto Star*

T he *Toronto Sun* greeted the dawn of the newspaper war with a sex-and-relationship survey announced with coloured balloons flapping from their squat red street boxes and a cheeky marketing campaign that proved irresistible to local commercial radio stations, which joined in the fun.

The stories, part of a "sizzling series," were packed with irresistible headlines such as "PREOCCUPATION WITH SEX RAMPANT," "SEX? WHATEVER YOU SAY, DEAR," and "BUSINESS AND PLEASURE: HOT AND BOTHERED IN THE OFFICE." It could easily have been a series the *Post* might have run.

In keeping with the atmosphere of the times, *Sun* management had jealously guarded their plans and, in an effort to keep the survey secret before the *Post*'s launch, had sequestered two university sexperts in a downtown hotel where they were interviewed by *Sun* writers.

The polling firm COMPAS, which would eventually move on to higher matters of state as the *National Post*'s own regular pollster, provided grist for the stories by interviewing a sample of 1,479 Canadians. The series, modelled after an earlier *Financial Post* survey on investing, was a huge success. Circulation jumped an average 30,000 daily during the first week, and, most important, made a statement to the competition that the *Sun* would not be a neutral in the battles to come.

Publisher Douglas Knight wasn't necessarily concerned about direct competition from the *Post* but was worried about the *Sun* drowning in the free newspapers he guessed were about to start flooding the Toronto market. The *Sun*'s weekday circulation depended exclusively on single-copy sales, and Conrad Black's new daily would undoubtedly be distributed free on the streets, for a limited time anyway. And if commuters were getting the new daily free on the *Sun*'s patch, the *Globe* and *Star* would be forced to make the same offer. Knight got it exactly right.

"You actually had to make a conscious choice every day to buy a *Sun*," says Knight. "If you're a regular *Sun* reader riding on the subway and someone gives you a free paper, you might decide not to buy the *Sun* that day. If you lose just a tiny percentage every day, it can mean a significant reduction in your average circulation. A lot of people were taking free *Post*s because it was new and saying, 'Why not? It might not be for me, but it's free, and it has a sports section, and it's big and colourful.' "

The *Sun* managed to hold its own during the early days of the newspaper war and was doing very well when its own corporate earthquake erupted during that remarkable final week of October 1998.

◆   ◆   ◆

Sun Media chief executive Paul Godfrey had been sitting in his office on June 30, 1998, when David Galloway, his counterpart from Torstar, dropped by to see him. Torstar, parent company of the *Toronto Star*, was apparently hearing about a potential deal between the Sun group and Conrad Black's Hollinger/Southam company. It was barely a week before Godfrey and Black's partner, David Radler, finalized the agreement that would deliver the Sun group's *Financial Post* to Black in exchange for the Southam titles in Hamilton, Kitchener, Guelph, and Cambridge.

The call from Galloway emerged from an ongoing relationship between *Star* publisher John Honderich and Sun Media executive Wayne Parrish. The two had known each other for more than twenty years, a relationship that dated back to Parrish's days as a columnist at the *Star*, and they sat together on the boards of numerous industry organizations. Honderich was keen on broadening the *Star*'s horizons and strengthening its defences. He and Parrish discussed various partnerships between the *Star* and *Sun*, including joint purchases of other media and possibilities of the *Star* taking a stake in Canoe, the *Sun*'s online information service.

Galloway had phoned ahead to arrange the meeting, but, according to Godfrey, the proposal Galloway brought with him was a shocker.

"Maybe we could do some business together," suggested Galloway, "and combine some efforts on the Internet and in circulation – and, perhaps later, some other things."

"David, what are you talking about?" asked Godfrey.

"Well, perhaps a complete merger between the *Sun* and *Star*."

"How would that work?"

"I don't know about you, Paul, but I know what I'd be doing. If we do this deal, I will have to get up on Monday morning and go to work, but you'll be a wealthy man and can do what you want."

"Well, I'm already doing everything in life I want to do," replied Godfrey, "and I'm not poor. I'm not wealthy, but I'm not poor. I'm not enamoured by the idea."

Galloway left, saying he would think things over. "The *Star* will never do anything unfriendly toward the *Sun*, but let me work on some numbers and I'll get back to you," he said.

Torstar, whose share price had seen better days, was determined to prevent erosion of its dominance in Toronto and the surrounding reader-rich regions close to the city. The Radler-Godfrey deal was alarming because, at a stroke, it transformed the Sun group into a powerful threat with the potential to topple the *Star* from its pinnacle as the region's circulation- and revenue-generating giant. The potentially destructive arrangement couldn't be allowed to continue. From almost any perspective – income, retail sales, or population – the *Star* and the *Sun* were, in essence, fighting for a quarter of Canada.

By bringing the *Toronto Sun* into its fold, the *Star* would have a lock on the region's lucrative lower-end advertising and leave the *Post* and *Globe* to fight for the remainder.

But pride and ego were also a factor. The *Sun*, born from the defunct *Toronto Telegram*, had lived and thrived against all the odds for nearly thirty years with the *Star* its arch-rival. Any executive who delivered the Sun newspaper group into the hands of the *Toronto Star* would be a traitor

Top: *Toronto Star* publisher John Honderich warned his managers early that they were heading into a war and that the new Conrad Black daily would not be fighting by the Marquess of Queensberry rules. (*Toronto Star*)

Middle: Thomson newspaper executive Stuart Garner thought the *Globe and Mail* was in danger of defeating itself and decided external help was needed. He didn't sugarcoat his tough medicine and neither did he win too many friends. (Courtesy Stuart Garner)

Bottom: Douglas Knight in 1994, four years before the *National Post*. Knight was publisher of the tabloid *Financial Post* as it chiselled a niche into the business advertising market and publisher of the *Toronto Sun* the day Black's newspaper launched. On the *Post*'s launch day, his *Sun* carried a sex survey and adorned its newspaper boxes with balloons. He needn't have worried. (Jeff Wasserman, *Financial Post*)

Christie Blatchford (left) and Rosie DiManno, competing columnists and best of friends, were prime candidates for the *National Post*. After much angst and negotiation during several secret, boozy meetings with Ken Whyte, the women dubbed themselves "Thelma and Louise." But would they both jump to the new paper? (Courtesy Rosie DiManno)

National Post deputy editor and daily driving force Martin Newland catches up on the gossip during the hot pre-*Post* summer of 1998. Columnist Christie Blatchford said she had to stop working in the same office as Newland because his beefy good looks distracted her. (Graham Parley)

Top: As *Post* staff waited for
the newspaper's first edition
on launch night, Black chatted
to editor-in-chief Ken Whyte
while pointing to the main
"Unite the Right" headline
on a dummy sheet. Black
loved the paper but thought
promoting the Canadian
Alliance misguided. Barbara
Amiel is in the background.

Middle: Conrad Black gets
into the party mood on launch
night with Ken Whyte joining
in the fun.

Bottom: Both Black and Whyte
signed dozens of copies of the
first edition for staff members.
(All courtesy Ken Whyte)

Globe and Mail publisher Phillip Crawley, veteran of newspaper wars in London and Hong Kong, was happy as a media executive in New Zealand when his old buddy Stuart Garner tempted him to Toronto. Crawley eventually brought stability to the *Globe* and earned respect – grudging or otherwise – both inside and outside his newspaper. (Phill Snell, CP/*Maclean's*)

Globe editor-in-chief Richard Addis, imported from Fleet Street to battle the *National Post*, was a colourful, much maligned character who provided endless nasty fodder for the gossip pages of *Frank* magazine but found a way into the hearts of Toronto's literary community. (*Globe and Mail*)

Chrystia Freeland, Addis's Canadian-born number two, raised many hackles at the *Globe* among those who thought her youth and lack of managerial experience added insult to Addis-inflicted injury. She lasted two years before returning to London but got to lead the troops through 9/11. (Courtesy Chrystia Freeland)

Edward Greenspon, pictured shortly after becoming the new editor-in-chief of the *Globe and Mail*, spent more than three years frozen out of the newsroom hierarchy by Richard Addis, the Englishman he eventually replaced. The two men disliked each other. Addis, a product of the ruthless ways of Fleet Street, sensed that Greenspon was out to undermine him so did it to him first. (Jayson Gallop)

Mitchel Raphael, in the spikes, with deejay Daniel Paquette at the *Post*'s second anniversary party. Raphael, who covered the Toronto alternative scene for the *Post*, bonded with Barbara Amiel during party chat about hair products. (Courtesy Mitchel Raphael)

Conrad Black, Barbara Amiel, and their new best friends at the newspaper's second anniversary. The *Post* boys were male models gathered for the occasion by writer Mitchel Raphael. (John Lehmann, *National Post*)

Wayne Gretzky asked that writer Roy MacGregor ghost his weekly column for the *Post*. In return, MacGregor got Gretzky's many phone numbers but invariably reached the former hockey great on a golf course in California. The column, often based on a short conversation between the two, lasted a year. (Gordon MacGregor)

Rebecca Eckler, a canny columnist who quickly learned that self-humiliation sells and used that awareness to become a skilled vendor of her own cheeky, irritating/irresistible brand of chick lit. (*National Post*)

Top: The former Canadian citizen Conrad Black found this Patrick Corrigan cartoon touching and has a framed copy on his wall in London. (*Toronto Star*)

Middle: CanWest Global CEO Leonard Asper – enjoying the moment with his father, Israel (Izzy) – saw the purchase of Conrad Black's Southam newspapers as the gateway to the future. The newspapers, including an initial 50 per cent of the *National Post*, cost CanWest more than $3 billion. Izzy Asper, a TV pioneer who built one of the most successful independent broadcast companies in the world, died in October 2003. (Kevin Frayer, CP)

Bottom: *Post* deputy editor Martin Newland, managing editor Alison Uncles, and editor-in-chief Ken Whyte, together for the last time at a party in early summer 2003 shortly after Whyte and Newland were fired and Uncles quit to join the *Toronto Star*. (Courtesy Ken Whyte)

of the highest order, and Godfrey was not going to allow himself to be cast in that role.

Godfrey told Galloway he could visit any time but to forget about the merger. The meeting had, however, set the two camps on a collision course – a pivotal battle in the newspaper war officially declared the day before by Conrad Black.

Torstar became increasingly enthusiastic about doing the Sun deal, but a series of exploratory meetings between the two sides made little progress. Galloway and his colleagues figured there was only one option left. "I did tell Paul that it is not Torstar style to do anything unfriendly, but the more we looked, the more we liked it, but the more difficult the conversations became as to what people's different roles would be. It was awkward, because Torstar was buying the *Sun* and in the end they made demands that were untenable. We decided to go ahead anyway. It embarrassed Paul because it looked like a sellout."

Paul Godfrey was meeting with Ontario Minister of Culture Isabel Bassett when his assistant phoned. It was three days after the launch of the *National Post*.

"You'd better come back to the office," she said. "I've got a letter here from David Galloway to you."

Godfrey asked her to read it to him. The *Star*, she said, was making an offer of $16 for all outstanding Sun Media shares. It was a hostile takeover bid, and as far as Godfrey was concerned a distinctly unfriendly act. But what puzzled him, and what made it such a shock, was that the *Star* had made no earlier attempt to buy Sun shares when the price had been lower.

"My head was spinning," he recalls. "I was very angry and came out all guns blazing."

As the Sun's stock price – which closed at $9.90 on October 18, the day of the offer – began to edge up, Godfrey called members of the Sun Media board and his trusted lawyer Dale Lastman to an emergency meeting. The board issued a statement accusing the *Star* of being "opportunistic." The $776-million offer was "inadequate" and they advised shareholders to reject it. Which, of course, was easy for them to say. The pressure was quickly mounting, and by mid-November the Sun's share price had almost doubled.

Star publisher Honderich felt the *Financial Post* deal with Conrad Black, and Sun Media's existing ownership of the *London Free Press*, had left the

Star no choice but to move on Godfrey. "When they did the swap with Conrad," says Honderich, "what that effectively did was make them the dominant player in southern Ontario, and on some of the larger advertising and promotional deals they had more reach than we did. We realized that in this region we were no longer the dominant player, and it has always been our position that it is better to compete as number one, firmly in charge, than number two and trying harder. That accelerated our view that we needed to do something."

It also accelerated Godfrey's view that he had to find another buyer, but as the share price continued to rise and more investors came along for the ride, the pressure mounted. Godfrey and his board would be forced to sell to the *Star* unless some alternate could be found. Given that tax laws effectively ban foreign control of Canadian newspapers, the options were limited. And to put the squeeze on Godfrey further, Torstar upped its bid to $18.50, which was as far as it was prepared to go. "We raised our bid to scare everyone else off," said Galloway. "I knew if there was another bidder we would get a letter within twenty-four hours. And guess what?"

An indication of how much tension existed between the two sides came, according to Godfrey, in a phone call he got from Galloway at the height of the takeover battle. The two men, then as now movers in the same social circle, were going to be at the same event that night and Galloway said he wanted to avoid any public display of unpleasantness.

Godfrey recalls getting increasingly suspicious as Galloway spoke. "He said 'Look, Paul, I don't want to discuss the hostile bid with you, but we are going to be at the same dinner tonight and I'm going to come over and shake your hand. I don't want to give you any surprises.' I thought about it for two minutes and concluded, 'Oh, oh, I'm being set up.'"

Godfrey suspected that Galloway would arrange for a *Star* photographer to be at the event to record the handshake and publish it next day to create confusion among *Sun* staff. He knew that many *Sun* employees loathed the *Star*, and any public sign of fraternizing with the enemy would immediately alienate him from his own people.

Columnist Peter Worthington, one of the *Sun*'s founders, put it best in an interview published a couple of days after the *Star*'s initial offer: "Some of us have spent our careers fighting the *Star*," he said. "I'm appalled. It would be a betrayal if the *Sun* were sold that way."

Newly minted *National Post* columnist Christie Blatchford, who forged her reputation at the *Sun*, was even more succinct, calling it "a horse's ass of an idea."

Godfrey assured everyone that the *Sun* would "not go quietly into the starry night," and for good measure a gorgeous Page Three girl appeared on the *Sun*'s front page holding a copy of the *Star* and wearing little but a disdainful look.

In the theatre of the national newspaper war, it was a great sideshow.

◆ ◆ ◆

Godfrey's unlikely white knight came in the form of Quebecor, the Quebec printing giant, which emerged on December 9 with an offer of $983 million, or $21 a share. It made instant millionaires of the dozen members of the Sun Media management team that had bought out the previous owner, cable czar Ted Rogers, a couple of years before. According to the *Toronto Sun*, Godfrey made $28 million on the deal. Torstar accepted defeat and Quebecor took control of the *Sun* a week later. In the end, the *Star-Sun* skirmish was a frenetic, emotionally draining, massively expensive academic exercise.

While desperately trying to fend off the *Star*, Godfrey's team had challenged the hostile takeover at the federal Competition Bureau on the basis that the takeover would have given the *Star* 88 per cent of the retail advertising market in Toronto and more than 83 per cent of classified ads. That proved too rich for even the Competition Bureau, which judges media takeovers on whether the dominant player will emerge with unfair access to advertising revenue. Reduction of editorial choice is of no concern to them.

Star executives had done their best to reassure all concerned that the *Sun* would be neither closed nor occupied by the forces of darkness from the *Star* headquarters at One Yonge Street, a high-rise near the edge of Lake Ontario. According to *Star* executive managing editor James Travers, "We always intended to keep the *Sun* going and genuinely intended to run it as an independent entity, reporting to the Torstar group. We didn't want to run a big tabloid, because we didn't know how to do it, and we wanted to keep as much natural competition as possible. So the *Sun* basically beat us on that by saying we weren't telling the truth, but we were."

Sun business columnist Linda Leatherdale added perspective after the sale to Quebecor in an admirably tough column headlined "WHITE KNIGHTS OF THE SUN," in which she harked back to a bout of fear and loathing in 1996 when Quebecor, under founder Pierre Peladeau, had once before been a potential buyer.

Leatherdale quoted *Financial Post* editor Diane Francis, who had said at the time, "Peladeau may be able to legally buy this chain but he won't own a single soul who works here." And combative columnist Allan Fotheringham accused Peladeau of being an ex-alcoholic closet separatist. (Peladeau, never one to back out of a fight, responded in kind, calling Fotheringham a falling-down drunk and wishing, for Francis's sake, that someone other than Quebecor buy the *Sun*.)

Leatherdale also reprised a quote from Worthington, who had described Quebecor as "every *Sun* journalist's worst nightmare." If nothing else, the welcoming of Quebecor two years later illustrated how passionately *Sun* folk felt about the *Star*.

Shortly after the December takeover, Quebecor cut 180 Sun group jobs across the country, including twelve in Toronto, and completed a side deal with Torstar. For $335 million it handed over the *Hamilton Spectator*, the *Kitchener-Waterloo Record*, the *Guelph Mercury*, and the *Cambridge Reporter*. Torstar didn't get the *Toronto Sun*, but it did get peace on one of its two fronts and could now focus on any threat the *National Post* would pose. And there was some satisfaction at *Star* headquarters that arch-rival Conrad Black had inadvertently strengthened Torstar when it swapped Hamilton, Kitchener, Guelph, and Cambridge in its deal to get the *Financial Post* from Sun Media.

It was, summed up James Travers, a remarkable few months. "There were so many unforseen consequences playing out. Between the start and finish of the year, it became a totally different business. We felt far more secure, and rather than just defending ourselves against the *Post*, we had control of a huge chunk of the Canadian market."

It was an especially pleasing turn of events for Honderich, who met Conrad Black periodically at social functions and occasionally engaged in jocular conversation with the *Post* proprietor.

"War is war," Honderich said dramatically. "It was what you would expect of two gentlemen in a duel to the death."

13 RELIGIOUSLY IRREVERENT

"You'd walk past a *National Post* box and you'd feel fangs in your legs, like a mad dog had just bitten you."

— John Bentley Mays, columnist, *National Post*

The *National Post* knocked the 154-year-old *Globe and Mail* off kilter with staggering speed and apparent ease. Perhaps the *Globe* lost its nerve, and its faith in itself, too soon, or maybe it was institutionally ill equipped to face the bright, brash, and sexy package every morning. The venerable daily was obviously trying hard, but it seemed spooked, and in often clever but revealing ways began mimicking some of the *Post*'s design techniques and taking uncharacteristic *Post*-like approaches to news stories and feature articles. Its mix of page-one stories became noticeably lighter and design and story selection on page three of its first section – a particular *Post* strong point – changed significantly. Christie Blatchford, who wrote primarily about criminal trials, had made an instant impact in the *Post* with her coverage of the Gerald Regan trial in Halifax. The former Nova Scotia premier, facing charges of rape dating back forty years, was perfect grist for Blatchford's passionate, opinionated style. The *Post* played her columns well, and for a while at least the *Globe* assigned its own reporter, Erin Anderssen, to cover court cases in a similar style.

But the *Post* was full of daily surprises and would regularly devote copious pages and much of its journalistic resources to one topic. This "Outbreak of Third World War" approach to subjects of sometimes dubious qualification defied Canadian newspaper convention but was an echo, in fact, of what had been happening for more than a year before the *Post* at the *Ottawa Citizen* under the editorship of Neil Reynolds. In fact, Reynolds's *Citizen* also sparked the *Post*'s predilection for photographs of young attractive women.

The *Post* was awash in hubris, its hand-picked, non-unionized staff willingly working twelve-hour days or more for little extra reward other than the pride and satisfaction of being part of the team. There was no happier, more dedicated group of newsroom employees on the planet, and it was giving the upstart daily a significant advantage. There was a buzz around the words *National Post*, and among those who had rejected offers to join the new daily regrets were not uncommon. Like a brash young stranger rolling into a small frontier town, the *Post* was the centre of attention and admired even by those who could only allow themselves to admire grudgingly.

That gave people like Christie Blatchford – people who had gambled by jumping to the *Post* – an extra jolt of satisfaction. "When I left the *Sun*, everyone I knew told me I was crazy. It was never going to get started, they said. And then it wasn't going to last. And then it wasn't going to last a year. And then it wouldn't last two years. But every single son of a bitch who said it wasn't going to get started was knocking on the door and asking, 'Can I get a job?'"

A renaissance seemed to be happening in Canadian daily newspapers, and whether you were in the newspaper business or simply some unsuspecting reader having a free newspaper thrust into your hand at the local gas station or coffee shop on the way to work, it was inescapable.

Globe columnist Robert Fulford, who would eventually create a major upset by defecting to the *Post*, described the *Globe and Mail*'s reaction to the *Post* as "panic and hysteria." "My impression is that they completely mistrusted their tradition as a defence. Instead of playing to their strengths, and building up their best qualities, they panicked. 'We are not good enough' was the feeling. To become more *Globe*ish was not a solution. They had to become something else."

The *Globe* had a useful and consistently helpful spy in the *Post*'s organization – most likely outside the newspaper's Don Mills headquarters – who had slipped the *Globe*'s senior managers a copy of the final *Post* prototype the night before its official launch. William Thorsell passed it around that evening during a *Globe* social gathering at the King Edward Hotel.

"My first reaction," says Thorsell, "was that it was much more conventionally arranged and put together than I expected it to be. I thought it would be more different from a traditional paper than it was. It had a couple of features that were very unusual and magazinelike. Avenue was very expensive but very well done – a luxury really."

Thorsell concedes that the *Post* introduced an impressive mix of news and human interest along with a good sense of when to commit extra resources to an event. "When there was a big story they would devote six pages or so with a tremendous combination of news, photography, and [opinion] columns that might have been a two-page thing in most papers. So when we thought they were going to six pages, we went to four. In their first budget coverage they did about twenty pages and we did our usual four. I was really taken with it, but then again is anyone going to read twenty pages on the budget? So we had those kinds of discussions that were provoked by what they were doing, and sometimes we picked up the cue and other times we said, No, it's their world, and didn't think it was necessary to respond to it. Some of it was about staking out territory – saying [they] are serious, even more serious than the traditional *Globe*."

Thorsell met the early weeks of the *Post* with series on health care and aboriginal issues, deliberate statements of journalistic purpose attempted to instill a steady-as-you-go ethos into his managers. Despite the subsequent, often clever adaptations of certain *Post*isms, he tried hard to shore up the Thorsellian view of what a daily newspaper should be. Senior features editor Sarah Murdoch was struck by the editor-in-chief's determination. "At our morning meeting, we would all compare the *Star*, *Globe*, and *Post* [a ritual at all three newspapers]. William was less complacent than most people and erred on the side of saying that things the *Post* did were pretty darn good. But at the same time he didn't want to make any changes by copying what made the *Post* what it was. He was very clear that we shouldn't deviate from what he considered wonderful journalism. The *Globe* set the agenda for the country with political coverage and he was prepared to leave pop culture to the *Post* because he preferred the higher arts. He had a vision of what the *Globe* should be and never wavered on it. It was admirable."

Not everyone judged Thorsell's *Globe* so positively. Former *Globe* foreign correspondent and *Saturday Night* magazine editor John Fraser agreed with his chum Robert Fulford that the *Globe* was running scared from the *Post*'s opening volley. "The *Globe* had this great franchise that William Thorsell fucked around with for ten years and didn't seem to do any damage because there was no competition. He's not a dumb person, but he introduced some of the stupidest ideas I've ever seen in journalism. It was a boring paper and they miscalculated getting ready for the *Post*. It was a big shock when the *Post* came out with such a comprehensive, comfortable voice that was both more intelligent, more fun, and racier than the *Globe* could ever hope to be. Parkinson and Thorsell were in over their heads. Thorsell had no experience of competition and didn't have a clue how to create an exciting front page."

Fraser, now master of Massey College at the University of Toronto, wrote a weekly media column for the *Post* in which he regularly used goings-on at the *Globe* as grist for his pieces.

Former *Globe and Mail* publisher Roy Megarry, the man responsible for saving the *Globe* from possible extinction in the mid-1970s by reinventing the newspaper as a national daily, considered it inevitable that the *Globe* would stagger at the start. "When you have enjoyed a monopoly for all those years and had the market all to yourselves, it's human nature to start taking things for granted. You are at the top and you are successful. It reflects in your readership research, in your circulation, in advertising revenue, and editorial. Throughout the organization, even though you think you are being innovative, it's still not the same as having a competitor breathing down your neck. It was one thing to strategize and anticipate, but when it actually happened and you read the *Post* for six days in a row, it was obvious that whatever we were doing, we had to do better. They put out a good newspaper."

Megarry, long retired, was brought back to the *Globe* as a special adviser to Phillip Crawley, the Englishman brought in from New Zealand three weeks before the *Post* launched. Megarry took Crawley across Canada as part of a rapid education and arranged lunches, dinners, and meetings for him with business and community leaders. Crawley had visited Canada only once before, on a two-week vacation.

◆ ◆ ◆

The *Post*'s approach to news, features, and photographs had been developed over many hours of conversation between editor-in-chief Kenneth Whyte and his deputy, Martin Newland. Whyte, a small-c conservative but not, he insists, an ideologue, had a clear idea of the issues he wanted the newspaper to emphasize, and Newland, who has an a-pox-on-all-their-houses approach to party politics, had no doubt how it should be done: irreverent but with a seriousness of purpose.

Whyte had seven or eight issues he wanted the *Post* to focus on:

- Parliament and the lack of democratic accountability in Ottawa.
- Taxes, which were too high.
- The brain drain, which was sucking away Canada's future.
- The United Nations (in Whyte's opinion, "one of the most bloated, inefficient bureaucracies ever devised").
- The Supreme Court, whose decisions were not getting the critical analysis they warranted.
- The Chrétien government's use of public funds for political purposes, which siphoned cash from much-needed improvements to infrastructure in cities and towns across the country.

And there were other ongoing issues, the type that former Hollinger president David Radler describes as radio talk-show topics that no other newspaper in Canada was writing about in a critical way – issues such as the rights of divorced fathers, human rights tribunal decisions, Supreme Court decisions, immigration and Crown corporation spending, all of which would find plenty of space in the *Post*.

In essence, they were on a mission to rescue Canadian journalism from what they perceived as drab, humourless, institutionalized reporting that wallowed in the woes of victims of all kinds. Theirs was a newspaper intended to shock, amuse, intrigue, and, when necessary, horrify. They wouldn't be afraid of sex and *totty*, a word Newland imported from England that became part of *Post* lexicon. Totty, which in earlier generations would have been called cheesecake, is photography of beautiful women, personified in the *Post* by tennis star Anna Kournikova. As columnist Scott Feschuk was to record in an article commemorating the *Post*'s one thousandth edition, large photographs of Kournikova appeared 109 times during that period, and with most of those photographs there was a story that referred to the Russian beauty, who had never won a Grand Slam, getting more press than any other tennis player.

Tabloid editor Michael Cooke, who exhibits a remarkable ability to sum up complex subjects in four words or less, said it was the "Holy shit, Martha" stories that would remain unique to the *National Post*. These are stories that provoke outrage or highlight the bizarreness of human behaviour – stories that people are moved to share and talk about at home and work. In more polite company, they are referred to as "water-cooler" stories. Two of Ken Whyte's favourite examples are stories his team used in many of their prototypes. One involved a Saskatchewan boy who was caught shoplifting in a mall. As punishment, the boy's father sent him back to the mall for the afternoon wearing a sandwich board that read, "I Am a Thief."

"Everybody who has a kid or has been a kid knows the shoplifting story," says Whyte. "It was a perfect water-cooler conversation piece. Everyone would think either, 'Hey, good on the father,' or, 'How can you humiliate a kid like that?' The other was a story about a knife fight in a monastery involving two monks in a monastic order where they don't talk but somehow got on each other's nerves in the kitchen. We wanted that sort of story on the front page all the time."

Above all, Whyte wanted to tap into ideas that he sensed had a ready, under-served audience from coast to coast. "There are big problems with the country that people like me have been thinking about for a long time. None of those ideas was original, because there are large pockets of dissent in books, think tanks, universities, and political parties. There has always been an orthodoxy in Canada, on one hand, and people who dissent on the other. It was part of our job to gather all those people who didn't take the official line on things."

The news of the day, how it would be approached, and where it should be placed in the daily newspaper was decided at news meetings, the first of which was scheduled daily at 11 a.m. but rarely started on time because the editor-in-chief was invariably late. News meetings are usually formal, structured affairs with department heads taking turn to list their best story prospects for the following day's edition. The *Post* meetings, held around a ping-pong table in an office adjoining Whyte's, developed early in the newspaper's life into emotional, irreverent, often hilarious, politically incorrect gatherings and a melting pot of ideas. The results were consolidated at another meeting in the afternoon, from which an early form of the daily newspaper emerged. During one period, the meetings were announced by the banging of a Chinese gong, but was ditched because it irritated people.

Whyte would use his favourite phrase – "What if we do this . . . ?" – to push basic stories into different, offbeat directions. Deputy editor Newland educated his Canadian colleagues in profane Fleet Street newspaper language – wanker (loser), bollocks (bad idea), dog's bollocks (good idea) – but whatever was said in the *Post* news meetings, nothing leaked to the satirical press – otherwise known as *Frank* magazine, which was feeding copiously off misery at the *Globe and Mail* and would for several years to come. It was indicative of the happy, collegial nature of the *Post*.

Despite the atmosphere of apparent anarchy, the *Post* meetings were strangely hierarchal, recalls sports editor Graham Parley. "Ken was always very much in charge, and even if he wasn't there people would cram into the room but nobody would ever sit in Ken's chair. It was an ordinary chair at the head of the table, but it was sacrosanct. And Martin would always sit to his left. The mood of the meetings was dictated by Ken's mood. If Ken was looking like thunder when he came in, it would be more subdued, but mostly they were Seinfeldian discussions like a bunch of people would have over a beer."

There was competition at the story meetings to be the funniest person that day, says former Toronto section editor Peter Scowen, who left in August 2002 to join the *Toronto Star*. "It was a freewheeling, fun place and you looked forward to those story meetings. You could say anything. They wanted to hear about the top report of the day but also the stuff that could provide the outrage or fun story. You knew you could get Ken's attention if you had those fun, controversial stories. But we all learned that Ken's attention was too unreliable to vie for, because sometimes he wasn't in the same room as you even though his body was there."

Scowen's quintessential meeting moment came after one of the editors suggested a story about Prince Edward and his wife, Sophie. "The editor who made the pitch finished and then John Racovali, the foreign editor, started delivering this impressive and earnest pitch of great stories. Ken was sitting there with his feet up on the table. John reached the end and there was a long pause. Ken looked across at the person who had made the Edward and Sophie pitch and said, 'Which member of the royal family was it you were talking about?' You just never knew where his mind was.

But he and Martin Newland knew exactly what they wanted. You didn't have to agree with the politics of the paper, and a lot of people who work there don't, but they still enjoyed working at the *Post* because it had such a clear vision of what it wanted to be."

It was Scowen, with a half-serious aside at a news meeting during the Stanley Cup playoffs in the spring of 1999, who inspired one of the *Post*'s most successful stunts during its early years – a stunt, for sure, but a brilliantly simple idea that produced irresistible reading. It was, essentially, a copy of a series of beer commercials, broadcast during playoffs, in which a group of hockey fans purloined the Stanley Cup and showed it off around town to incredulous ordinary folk.

Parley emerged from the meeting smitten with the idea and determined to make it happen. He called the National Hockey League's Toronto vice-president Gary Meagher.

"Gary, we want to borrow the Stanley Cup," said Parley.

Meagher listened to the story proposal intently. "That's the strangest request I've ever received," he replied, "but I like it. Give me an hour or so."

The Stanley Cup assignment fell to sports reporter Dave Feschuk, who travelled from Toronto to Buffalo with the trophy strapped in the passenger seat of a rented gold-coloured Chrysler convertible while photographer John Lehmann brought up the rear with the Keepers of the Cup – two guards, one from the Stanley Cup's home at the Hockey Hall of Fame and another from the NHL. The Holy Grail is never left alone.

Crossing the border, Feschuk was stopped by a U.S. customs officer, who didn't believe his claim that his passenger was, indeed, *the* Stanley Cup. After a brief interrogation, Feschuk took the Cup to a chicken-wing emporium in Niagara, New York, before heading back across the border, where a Canadian customs officer phoned down the line urging all his colleagues to come look, then proceeded to pose joyously with Lord Stanley's treasure while Lehmann photographed him. The story ended with the cup back on the Ontario side and a young boy refusing to touch it. He knew the superstition that he who touches the Stanley Cup will never win it. And he had ambitions.

The idea was subsequently copied by *Sports Illustrated* columnist Rick Reilly and then by *Time* magazine, which credited Reilly for the original idea. Parley assigned reporter Scott Burnside to do the same thing with the Grey Cup, but despite hauling the Canadian Football League silverware on journeys through the Toronto subway system, it didn't quite create the same excitement.

"The Stanley Cup story was one of the few stunts we did at the *Post* that didn't produce a single negative comment," recalls Parley, "and it cost only the few hundred dollars in car rental fees and a few bucks for the chicken wings. Any newspaper would have done the same if they had thought of it, but it was a good example of the pizzazz of the *Post*. That kind of thing came out of the informality of the meetings when people often just sat around talking about their favourite movies, TV shows, or, in that case, commercials."

The creative approach extended to political coverage. Former Canadian Alliance leader Stockwell Day caused a fuss, and was ridiculed by government MPs, when he suggested that the House of Commons should run on a four-day week, closing on Fridays. The *Post*, looking for an offbeat angle on the story, sent Ottawa reporter Jane Taber and photographer Dave Chan to Ottawa Airport on a Thursday afternoon to interview MPs leaving for a long weekend. It may have been news to Day, but it was well known among Parliament Hill journalists that MPs often left the capital on Thursdays if there was no critical House of Commons vote on the agenda. Taber's story, while hardly news, was an entertaining piece of work – "gotcha" journalism with a humorous twist. Underneath a photograph of each MP was "The Excuse," the reason given to Taber for the early departure. If MPs wanted to save money, she suggested in the story, maybe they should share cabs to the airport on Thursdays.

The *Post* also made much of Julia Roberts's armpits. By happy coincidence, Roberts had flashed an armpit full of hair to photographers in London around the same time Australian researchers emerged with a study suggesting that women who didn't shave their legs and armpits had higher self-esteem than women who did. It brought Roberts the handle "Pretty Hairy Woman" in one British tabloid headline and the story and picture gave the *Post* perfect front-page fodder.

Deputy editor Newland is particularly proud of the page-one story about a cat in Orillia, Ontario, that got stuck in a tree for a week and refused all appeals from neighbourhood cat lovers to come down. Tales of cat-stuck-up-tree are among the most basic of local stories and are routinely ignored by the smallest of city weeklies. But the cat's determined attitude and the bizarre human distress on the ground below made the story, in Newland's view, a natural page-one item for the *Post*. The story included quotations from locals who reported minute details of the cat's rare movements.

"News, to an extent, is what people are talking about and what they are curious about," says Newland. "And for all the tut-tutting that went on, Julia Roberts's armpit hair was something people were curious about and talked about. A lot of people read us because they like to get pissed off. All of us live with popular culture and, if we're honest with ourselves, are fascinated by it. Good coverage of pop culture is good coverage of news. We can't be so proud, or so far up our own arses, that we ignore a vast tract of the lifestyles of half the population. And just once, before my career was over, I wanted to put 'Cat Stuck Up Tree' on the front page. It got a huge reaction from readers. Half were slightly baffled and half were genuinely wanting to know what happened to the frigging cat."

As a newcomer, Martin Newland saw Canada as a country of infinite possibilities and, as he put, "one of the highest standards of living in the world, where you have two-car garages and garage doors that go up and down by themselves." He didn't see that country reflected in the newspapers he read when he arrived in Toronto during the early summer of 1998.

"Reading the papers and listening to the CBC, there was such an unbelievable victim-based brand of journalism. News was something that had to leave you rubbing your chin and saying, 'Hmmm, that was a good lesson.' So much of Canadian journalism was based on misery. I remember being struck, during my first month here, about the number of items about cancer on the CBC. It was like you needed that sprinkle of cancer every day to make the cake rise. I find it so hard to define news, but it can be a strange event that evinces a reaction in people – outrage, fear, laughter, even sexual reaction. There is a degree of exploitation in it, because I know the readers we want and I know the readers we need reading the paper. All newspapers target stories to achieve that."

Newland brought a racy, pugnacious tabloid style of writing to the *Post* that had been perfected by Conrad Black's *Daily Telegraph*. It's a no-frills, often adjective-free style of news writing that can make the most salacious of news stories sound respectable without losing any of the spice. The more understated and subtle the story, the more powerful the impact and the greater chance of getting readers outraged or amused, depending on the topic.

John Bentley Mays, one of the earliest defectors from the *Globe and Mail*, says page one of the *Post* was pure Newland. "You'd walk past a

National Post box and you'd feel fangs in your legs, like a mad dog had just bitten you. That was Martin Newland, and it was what the *Globe* got so sniffy about. The front page was vulgar, but it was great, and Newland managed to do it without cheapening the product. He flew in the face of every prejudice that is held by the ruling elite in this country."

The *Post*'s obsession with the United States, exemplified on a daily basis with stories about the brain drain and tax cuts, seemed to get totally out of hand with the eighteen pages devoted to the death of John Kennedy Jr. and his wife and sister-in-law when their aircraft plunged into the ocean off Cape Cod. Newland says it was a subtle way of riling Canadians by prodding them to face the fact that the United States plays a huge role in Canadian lives. "For someone like me, who just floats in never having been to Canada, you all look like Americans; you all dress like them and there on TV is *Friends*. So what is it that you are? For me, one of the biggest questions about Canada was do they love the Queen, or do they love the Queen because the Americans don't have her? Do they love medicare as it is, or do they love it because the Americans haven't got it?"

The persistent pro-American pursuit was a strategy that tarred the *Post*'s reputation, and even Conrad Black, loath though he is to criticize the *Post* under his ownership, was somewhat uncomfortable with that aspect of his newspaper's journalism. Given the chance to start over, it would be one of the few things he would change. "Too many people got the idea that the paper was always critical of Canada," he says, "and it certainly wasn't what Ken and I wanted the perception to be. I think I would assert myself more than I did to try to avoid that perception."

The *Globe and Mail* came in for bouts of ridicule at *National Post* news meetings for its apparent efforts to copy their racier style, but in the months after the *Post* launch, *Globe* editor-in-chief Thorsell decided the competition was surprisingly conventional in its look and biased in its political news coverage – similar, as he saw it, to the *Toronto Star* but conducting its mission at the other end of the political spectrum. The *Post* was allowing its right-wing bias to enter into its news coverage, breaching the traditional wall between impartial news reporting on one side and editorial page comment and opinion columns on the other. Reader surveys, which the *Globe* commissioned continuously on orders from Thomson chief executive Stuart Garner, suggested to Thorsell that people were suspicious of the *Post*'s political mission.

"It was good for the *Globe*," says Thorsell, "because it came back to us in surveys that people saw that as transparent and manipulative and didn't trust it."

Thorsell and his fellow *Globe* executives knew that the *Post* was spending heavily to make a big splash but were still surprised at the daily Avenue section, a double-page photographic or graphic spread and one of Whyte's favourite features. Despite the extravagance, Thorsell figured that the *Post* was doing what it had to do to get noticed.

There is no such charity from Phillip Crawley, brought in by Stuart Garner three weeks before the *Post* launch as president and COO and, in June 1999, formally replacing Parkinson as publisher and CEO.

Crawley and Garner had worked together as reporters and editors at the *Newcastle Journal* in England during the 1960s and 1970s, and at one point in their careers, before heading off to become executives, Garner had been Crawley's deputy. The two men share a passion for soccer and are ardent supporters of the storied English premier league club Newcastle United. They know each other well and speak in the precise, clipped manner of those who have had to work at being understood. The regional "Geordie" accent they share is one of the more attractive in the English language but a decidedly foreign tongue to most ears outside England's northeast. It's also an accent that can be especially chilling when raised in anger, as *Globe* employees would discover when Crawley decided they had to have the fear of God put into them.

Either out of genuine conviction or competitive posturing, Crawley became relentless and brutal in his criticism of the *National Post* and of Conrad Black – a sentiment that quickly became fully mutual. From his arrival in Canada Crawley considered the new daily as little more than an irresponsible indulgence. He still refuses to be impressed by anything the *Post* did or does and considers the *Post*'s design rather old-fashioned rather than radical or revolutionary.

"I detested the Avenue centrespread, which I thought was the biggest waste of space I have seen in a daily newspaper since my time in newspapers, which goes back to 1965. It was a classic example of a magazine editor trying to run a newspaper and seemed to be wholly self-indulgent. You have to question Conrad Black: Why allow that kind of thing to happen when there wasn't the advertising to support it? The amount of space thrown away by the *Post* was incredible. I regard myself as a professional newspaperman, and to me it was unprofessional. There was no business logic being applied. They were being allowed to play with their train set and had a proprietorial indulgence to do so."

Six months after the *Post* published its first edition, the *Globe* began looking for reinforcements from the United Kingdom. The *Post* was wounding the *Globe* journalistically and financially, and after watching Thorsell try to compete on his own terms, Crawley decided he needed a new editor-in-chief to give the opposition a taste of its own ammunition.

"The ghastly, appalling public-school boy that I am, I have to make things appear
effortless. You can paddle hard underneath, but on the surface you must be a swan."
— Richard Addis, editor-in-chief, *Globe and Mail*

ord soon spread around the *Globe and Mail* that Phillip Crawley
hadn't come all the way from New Zealand to be Roger
Parkinson's helper. There had been a meeting of managers to
which Crawley had arrived early, ahead of Parkinson, and settled into the
chair at the head of the table. Parkinson arrived next, looking a little irritated. This was interpreted, rightly or wrongly, as Crawley making a point,
and the speculation travelled rapidly.

Confirmation of Crawley's role as de facto publisher came barely three
months after his arrival, when he called a staff meeting at the usual mass
meeting place, a disused garage next to the *Globe*'s main offices.

It had been a collegial habit at the *Globe* for management to share the
newspaper's business data with the newsroom, urging recipients to keep
the information to themselves, which, predictably, not everyone did.
Crawley made it clear that the days of sharing financial information with
staff were over and threatened dire punishment for anyone caught leaking
information to, or gossiping with, the competition. The benign, gentlemanly days were over. For Crawley, this was war.

Columnist Jan Wong, a former China correspondent who had long before
decided there were reasonable comparisons to be made between the ruling elite in Communist China and *Globe* management, was shocked by

Crawley's blunt presentation. She decided to exercise her democratic rights and push back. "He used military terms and said, 'In this war if you betray us we will execute you.' He talked about executing people who weren't loyal foot soldiers, and I was, like, 'You're telling a bunch of journalists this? It was, like, Hello!' I think he wanted to rev us up, but he certainly revved me the wrong way."

Wong, author of the much reviled, irresistible Lunch With column, was one of the *Globe* journalists Kenneth Whyte had courted and Thorsell had proactively compensated with a pay raise and cellphone. She raised her hand and asked Crawley, "So, how exactly are you going to execute us."

"Hanging," snapped back Crawley without missing a beat.

Reporter Susan Delacourt recalls there had been a mix of bravado and curiosity among her colleagues as they made their way to the meeting. "We were all saying that this Brit would know he was in a room with a hundred bullshit detectors so he wouldn't try to put anything over on us. So then he made this speech about treason and about fraternizing with the enemy being a hanging offence. He said the *Globe* was now at war with the *National Post* and then used lots of military analogies. He was very serious and he scared the bejesus out of all of us big brave reporters. After he finished, we just quietly filed out and went back upstairs. It was something we had been waiting to hear, and wished someone had said it months before."

Crawley laughs when he's reminded of his bellicose lecture but said he decided soon after he arrived at the *Globe* that it was something he had to do:

> I just wanted to stiffen the backbone a little bit. At times like that there are usually two groups: one group who are frightened to death and think the end of the world is nigh, and the other group who will think, "We don't have to worry about the opposition; they can't touch us because we're so good." And in between there is some sensible middle ground. I was talking mainly to the two ends of the spectrum, which needed to understand that change had to happen and I was there to deliver it and if they didn't like it, then tough luck. We wouldn't be operating on a democratic principle. We had been in the habit of being very open – divulging lots of business information to the staff, and I made it very clear from the word *go* that I would not be doing that. It was confidential information that could be useful to

the enemy and I would not be disclosing it in the future because it was ammunition. We were on a war footing, and I said that if anyone wanted to bale out because they couldn't stand the pace, then okay. And if people behaved treacherously and betrayed secrets I would know what to do with them. Journalists and sales people are great gossips, but by and large we protected ourselves quite well.

Shortly afterwards, on January 20, 1999, Crawley visited Ottawa to meet the *Globe*'s parliamentary reporters and take them to lunch at the National Press Club. Word had travelled quickly from Toronto that the new guy, publisher in everything but name, was tough and scary and should be treated with caution, but Crawley's sardonic wit and impressive knowledge of the newspaper business, especially the news side, came more as a relief.

He told the parliamentary reporters that the *Globe*'s use of photography was poor and he intended to do something about it.

Deputy bureau chief Anne McIlroy protested mildly and suggested Crawley was being a little unfair. She cited the photograph on the *Globe*'s front page the day after Pierre Trudeau's funeral the previous October as an example of a good image beautifully displayed.

Crawley fired back. "Do you know who chose that photo?"

"Er, you, I hope," replied McIlroy.

"Yes," he said, much to the reporter's relief.

Before he left, Crawley spoke privately with bureau chief Edward Greenspon, who complained about the newsroom management in Toronto and said that too many good stories from the Ottawa bureau were getting short shrift or falling through the cracks altogether. And the *Globe*, he said, wasn't competitive enough.

After he turned down Kenneth Whyte's offer to join the new Black newspaper, Greenspon had received a mixed reaction from his friends at the *Globe*, some of whom said they were glad he stayed but sorry, too, that he hadn't given management a kick in the pants by leaving. In the nine months or so since, he had developed a better relationship with Thorsell and Wente, but the frustrations never fully disappeared, and the apparently waning interest in political stories from Ottawa was a constant irritant.

Shortly before the *Post* launched, Greenspon and his Ottawa colleagues had been hearing whispers about the new daily's plans for covering the vitally important federal political battleground. In particular, they had heard that the *Post* was in the throes of investigating Prime Minister Jean Chrétien's personal financial links with taxpayer-funded projects in his home riding, what was to become known as Shawinigate. Greenspon wanted to put together an investigative team to prevent the *Post* from scooping the *Globe* on the Chrétien story. The suggestion was rejected by his bosses in Toronto.

At their meeting, Crawley asked Greenspon about his future plans and whether he might be interested in being editor-in-chief. Greenspon said, yes, he certainly would be interested in replacing Thorsell, but he was in no hurry. They left the subject, but Crawley seemed to be struggling with how the newspaper should look and be organized. (Greenspon didn't know that the weekly national surveys ordered by Stuart Garner to keep close tabs on the national and Toronto-area newspaper markets were showing a troubling downward trend in *Globe* fortunes.) Crawley hinted to Greenspon that a crunch could be coming and he might have to make a decision to move from Ottawa to Toronto, sooner rather than later.

◆　◆　◆

Greenspon was enjoying a short family vacation to celebrate his daughter's birthday when Crawley phoned him at the upscale west Quebec resort Chateau Montebello barely two months later. Changes were afoot and he wanted Greenspon to move to Toronto to replace Peggy Wente as executive editor, Thorsell's second-in-command, and run the newsroom. It was Tuesday, and Greenspon asked for time to think. Crawley was holding a management retreat the following weekend and wanted to introduce him then as the new executive editor. Now was the time either to put up or shut up.

Greenspon's wife, Janice Neal, was reluctant to uproot herself and the couple's three children, especially given the turmoil that had become a hallmark of life at the *Globe and Mail*.

"I wasn't happy with the way things were going," says Greenspon, "but nor was I scheming behind anyone's back. On one hand, I had been a critic in the bullpen, bitching about people; now I had the chance to go in and pitch the next few innings. And it is the World Series, because the *National Post* is out there and we are floundering. We are all a bunch of whiners, but there's whining and there's really soul-sapping kind of stuff that makes people not work as well as they should. We were well into that."

Greenspon agreed to take the job if he could keep his home base where it was, returning to Ottawa on Thursday evenings and working there on Fridays. Crawley agreed and they signed a contract.

The changes were announced by Thorsell without much enthusiasm on April 9, 1999, in an internal memo to staff. He thanked Peggy Wente "for the role she has played in leading the changes to the A-section to date" and that she was "currently considering her options." He added, "These changes are being made to ensure we have the most effective organization and processes in place to deliver the best news package to our readers."

Crawley had not promised Greenspon the editor-in-chief's job and was now hinting that he had plans to bring in a senior British journalist with production experience who could produce the consistent daily design of the newspaper Crawley considered necessary to combat the bright displays in the spacious *National Post*. Greenspon understood that the new person would be Thorsell's deputy.

Like most monopoly businesses, the *Globe and Mail* had institutionalized bad habits, and Greenspon found a structure that was often unable to react quickly enough to accommodate new or changing stories. He arrived in the *Globe* newsroom one Sunday evening in May 1999 when staff was trying to decide how to accommodate an exclusive interview with escaped convict Ty Conn, a career criminal and chronic escapee who, two weeks earlier, had slipped out of Kingston Penitentiary in Ontario – the first convict in forty years to do so – and now had apparently killed himself while on the lam. It was the hot story that weekend, and broadcaster Lyndon MacIntyre, who had conducted the interview (and would go on to co-author a book about Conn), was offering the *Globe* a preview. But the space in the Monday edition was spoken for; in some cases, it was filled the previous Friday. Plans were in place to hold the MacIntyre interview and run it in the Tuesday edition, whereas the *Post*, given a similar opportunity, would likely have devoted two or three pages to it on the Monday. Greenspon cleared one page and ran it the next day.

He remembers the Ty Conn story as a breakthrough of sorts. "They needed someone in the centre to say, 'Yeah, I really care about that story. Let's go for it.' So that's what we did. The *Globe* mentality was that if the newspaper is already planned for the next day, you don't tear things apart."

It was a good summer for news, especially in the West, where B.C. Premier Glenn Clark was being accused of ethical indiscretion, Chinese boat people were landing off the coast, and there was scandal at the world-famous Montreux eating disorder clinic, where staff was alleged to have been force-feeding anorexics.

Six weeks after becoming executive editor, Greenspon got an encouraging letter from Stuart Garner, whom he had never met, expressing satisfaction in the change in the *Globe*'s first section and congratulating him on a job well done. Garner's letter may have also been prompted by new research which showed that *Globe* circulation was doing better and readers were more positive about the newspaper.

In the meantime, Phillip Crawley was busy making changes. "I arrived with a fairly clear idea of what needed to be done and knew I would have to move quickly in some areas. It took a little while to effect all of the changes, but within two weeks of getting here I made sure there was a sports section in the newspaper every day. We didn't have a sports section, just a small space at the back of the paper allocated to sports. I knew that sports was going to become a battleground in terms of reader appreciation, and we had some very good sports journalists, but they didn't have a very good platform. Other things took a little longer. We needed some new leadership across the company and some of it was back office and some of it was in the public eye. So, during the first six or nine months, I made some of the changes, and I suppose the most important one was appointing Richard Addis editor in the summer of 1999."

❖ ❖ ❖

Richard Addis was not the first choice to succeed William Thorsell as editor-in-chief.

They had tried, within weeks of Crawley taking over at the *Globe*, to entice Scottish newspaper editor Andrew Jaspan to take the job. Jaspan had been editor of the *Scotsman*, a newspaper in many ways similar to the *Globe*, and Lord Roy Thomson's first newspaper in the United Kingdom.

Stuart Garner, head of Thomson operations in Britain, had persuaded Jaspan to take the *Scotsman* job, but eight months later Jaspan got an enticing offer to edit the *Observer*, a "quality" British Sunday newspaper, and much to Garner's chagrin he accepted. That job, one of the more desirable in British newspapers, lasted barely one year, and after an acrimonious departure Jaspan found himself on the street, so to speak, as publisher of the *Big Issue*, a magazine for street people. In a story typical of the ups and downs of a British newspaper editor, Jaspan was then asked to develop and launch a new Scottish Sunday newspaper, a $30-million project he was in the midst of when Phillip Crawley called him in December 1998 to ask him to become editor of the *Globe and Mail*. Apparently at the suggestion of Garner, Crawley offered the fluent French-speaking Jaspan a lucrative three-year contract, with handsome bonuses, along with the clear message that the war with new *National Post* was not one the Thomson family intended to lose.

They sent copies of the *Post* to Scotland for their chosen editor to peruse. Jaspan, who had visited the *Globe and Mail* three times and had come to know and like William Thorsell, insisted that any new arrangement would have to accommodate the current editor-in-chief. Crawley and Jaspan worked out those details, and despite some mild reservations about the optics of being a British editor running Canada's national newspaper, Jaspan was sorely tempted. He had a written contract, but with the launch of his own *Sunday Herald* only weeks away, he turned Crawley down.

Undaunted, Crawley and Garner invited Jaspan to stay with his Scottish project for a couple of months and then come to Canada. He again refused, offered Crawley a few alternative names, and left the Thomson executives to search elsewhere – a search that would eventually lead them to Richard Addis.

Conventional wisdom, not always the most accurate barometer of things to come in the newspaper business, was that Garner and Crawley were searching for a deputy for Thorsell, not a replacement. The theory had some credence, because Thorsell was to be part of the final interviewing team along with Garner and Crawley.

But former Thomson executive Jim Jennings, who had helped guide the newspaper through its colour conversion and redesign, was not surprised that the demise of editor-in-chief William Thorsell was at hand. "William wanted the paper to go one way, and he and the publisher apparently disagreed, because he was there and then he was gone. William was an imperial editor who would grace the newsroom with his presence but really didn't run the newsroom."

Jennings recalls a discussion about rearranging the design of the *Globe* newsroom to have a central news desk that would allow people easier access to one another, including improved contact with the *Report on Business* department, a floor above the main newsroom. Jennings got the distinct impression that Thorsell was more interested in the look of the staircase than any practical improvements the new set-up might provide, and began to imagine an elaborate Broadway musical set.

"William, I have this vision of you descending the staircase in a long white robe surrounded with smoke from smoke machines," said Jennings.

"Mmmmm," mused Thorsell, "that's a thought."

Crawley had, indeed, decided that the *Globe* needed a different kind of editor-in-chief. Whatever else Crawley felt about Thorsell, he considered ten years editing the same daily newspaper too long. "It is an extremely demanding job, both physically and mentally, and you have a very high burnout rate. We needed a hands-on editor who would take charge of the day-to-day running of the paper, and William was more detached. It was very important to have someone from outside the *Globe*, because anyone from inside would carry too much baggage. The newspaper needed an outsider's eye to see what needed to be done, to drive change – to change the internal culture."

Associate editor Sarah Murdoch saw the relationship between Thorsell and Crawley start well and slowly deteriorate as the imported executive grew less and less enamoured with his editor-in-chief's serious-minded, somewhat eccentric view of what the *Globe and Mail* should be. "Crawley found the *Globe* boring and wanted to make it more sexy and entertaining. I was a big supporter of William's, but he would come into my office saying he wanted a five-part series on productivity or something, and I would talk him down to three parts, but Crawley wanted no parts at all. William loves events like the Giller dinner, and enjoys flitting around Toronto. Crawley is a smart, working-class Brit and hates the poncey, elitist thing that makes life worth living for William. So it was quite obvious that William and Crawley were on different planets and the relationship wasn't going to work. It was plain to all of us that our time on the masthead was limited."

Thorsell said he wanted to hand over the news side of his job by New Year's Day 2000, and, while there might have been confusion over titles, he took part in the recruiting process knowing that the person being hired would take control of the news pages of the *Globe*. It was, he said, all in the cards when he flew to London, met with the headhunters, and then eventually with Addis.

Thorsell hints that he didn't really have the stomach or experience for the different style of journalism he knew Crawley wanted to bring to the *Globe* – a match for the British sensibility that was driving the *National Post*. Thorsell and his managers had a running joke about the amount of female cleavage and space devoted to furry animals on the *Post*'s front page, but the reality was that the *Globe* would be heading at least partially in the same direction and he didn't like it. "It's not really my nature and my sensibility and I'm not going to be very good at producing that. I'm just not that kind of person, and if I went out there and tried to pretend, I'm sure I would have embarrassed myself."

◆ ◆ ◆

The decision to hunt for a new editor in the United Kingdom was a clear admission by Garner and Crawley that they were deeply worried about the journalistic and financial damage the *National Post* was inflicting.

Richard Addis had been editor of the high-profile *Express* tabloid, but like most Fleet Street editors he hadn't lasted long in the position and was soon labouring as a section head at the *Daily Mail*, a job that bored him and was made extra discomforting because his boss, in better times, used to work for him. The knowledge that Fleet Street editors often met in similar circumstances on the great elevator ride of ambition did little to soften the indignity.

The headhunters' call came out of the blue for the ambitious Addis, an upper-class Cambridge graduate and a divorced, devoted father of three young children. He was cool at first, and rejected the first approach, but chronic boredom, and exotic imaginings of the Great White North, gradually warmed him to the idea. Two months later, he got another call from the headhunters, who wanted to tell him more about the *Globe and Mail* and explain how important it was.

Aside from his initial comical ignorance of Canada, Addis was from such an alien personal and professional culture that, in pre-*Post* times, he would have escaped the headhunters' radar altogether. He was the antithesis of a "*Globe* person," and while "*Globe* people" were never above knifing each other in the back when the opportunity arose, they would at least be polite enough to tend each other's wounds. Addis was content to step over the bodies until the human resources personnel dragged them away.

The *Globe*'s new man had been a prominent Fleet Street editor – a mis-nomer really, because Fleet Street, once the centre of British daily news-paper journalism, has long since ceased to be so. After the once-powerful unions were crushed and new technology took a grip, newspapers moved their London operations to other parts of the city. But the words *Fleet Street* still serve as recognizable shorthand for the merciless world of British tabloid and broadsheet daily newspapers – a brutal world where the average tenure of a tabloid editor is around three years.

Addis had held a variety of journalism jobs, the first of which was edi-tor of a magazine called *Homes and Jobs*, which was run, Addis later dis-covered, as a front for a petty criminal organization by two men who had served time in prison for assault.

He went on to write a regular column for *Marketing Week*, a respectable publication that provided him a luxurious life of irresponsibility and long lunches. "I got invited to everything in the advertising business – lunches in Nice, parties in Rome. Quite often I would get up in the morning and meet some tycoon for lunch and have a very good lunch from 12:30 to 4:30 and go back home. My job was to keep in touch with these people, to mock, tease, and interview them, so I lived on caviar and champagne for two years."

He moved to Rome to learn Italian and worked for two years as sports editor for a small expatriate's newspaper called the *Rome Daily American*, even though he knew absolutely nothing about American sport. But his real Fleet Street baptism came as a freelance reporter for Britain's *Daily Mail* when he was sent with a battle-hardened photographer to stake out Sarah Keays, the pregnant mistress of one of Margaret Thatcher's favourite cab-inet ministers, Cecil Parkinson, whose contemptuous attitude toward his parental responsibility had earned him the wrath of Fleet Street and the loathing of almost everyone except, apparently, his boss. Addis shudders at the memory of the Keays stakeout:

> The photographer was a vile barbarian I had never met before, but he taught me how to do a stakeout. Under cover of darkness we invaded the garden of this house, found a little chicken house, got inside, and prised open the wall so there was a little crack we could see through. We stayed in there all night long. I had a new suit that I had bought for my first day at work and it was freezing cold. We sat

there for three days, going to the pub occasionally to eat and get warm, and then, shortly after the photographer had left for another job, Sarah came out of the door, and I called the office as instructed and they said, "You have to follow her now." She got into a Lagonda or Maserati or something and I had a Citroën and couldn't keep up with her. I got back to work and was fired. The penalty for failure on Fleet Street is death.

Addis was eventually forgiven and gradually climbed the Fleet Street ladder. He had been executive editor at the *Daily Mail* for a couple of years when, as he tells it, he was at a dinner party in London seated next to a beautiful and charming Iranian woman who claimed to know Lord David Stevens, chairman of the *Daily* and *Sunday Express*.

"He's looking for a new editor," she said. "Do you know anyone who might be a candidate?"

"I would be a good candidate," replied Addis, without hesitation or expectation.

Lord Stevens, who doubtless hadn't yet told the incumbent editor he was being ousted, phoned Addis the next day and invited him to the first of a series of secret interviews at luxury hotels and houses in London's Mayfair district during which the ambitious thirty-nine-year-old met members of the *Express* board of directors.

Three weeks later, Stevens offered Addis the job and a crack at instant celebrity with a salary of £200,000, £50,000 in bonuses, and limitless expenses, countless parties, and fine dining at only the very best restaurants. Addis also got a chauffeur-driven bullet-proof green Jaguar.

He loved the life and lived it to the full, partly because he knew it wouldn't last too long. It was the existence, he says, of a firefly – glorious for a while but destined for an early end:

> You are expected to act in a very autocratic way. You have armies of secretaries and can order the chauffeur to get you a toothpick if you want one – not that I did that sort of thing. I had a drinks cabinet and champagne in the fridge and my feet on the desk. There is a degree of theatricality about being an editor in England. You have to wear really nice suits and have the occasional dramatic scene in the office,

like ripping up the front page or standing on a desk in the newsroom and exhorting your troops to fight harder, or hurling a typewriter though the window. It all goes with the job. You get to meet anyone you want – prime ministers will see you about once a month, the Queen will see you from time to time, and I lunched occasionally with Princess Diana. Celebrities and pop stars will see you, if you want to see them, and you get at least ten lunch invitations a day. It's very glamorous, very thrilling, and if you're thirty-nine and ambitious it's like heaven.

The longevity of a Fleet Street editor depends on two things: circulation, and the ability to stay on the good side of the right people. The job is long on both hours and intrigue, as Addis discovered:

Twelve hours is a short work day, and it's very cutthroat, because everyone is out to get you one way or another. You have to be tough, resilient, charming, and cunning just to survive. Everyone around you wants your job, because it's such a good job, and they will find any way they can to manoeuvre into position to get it. The rival newspapers are always trying to hire your best people or ruin your best projects and leak personal stuff about you to *Private Eye* or one of the rival gossip columns to damage your character. If you're at a party doing or saying something foolish, it will definitely be in the gossip columns, because the point is to get it on the daily clippings file produced for your proprietor. He won't read the column itself, but he'll have the item provided on this daily file of clippings, and he'll see something like "Richard Addis was seen at the National Gallery last night. He went up to the Cabinet Secretary for Culture and called him by the wrong name." In our weekly meeting with the proprietor, he would say, "I hear you couldn't remember the culture secretary's name." You could say, "That's absolute rubbish, I got it right." And he would say, "Well, that's not what I read in the *Mirror*." You have to accept the job for what it is and enjoy it, and I enjoyed it a lot.

Addis increased his power at the *Daily Express* in the fall of 1996 when new owner Lord Clive Hollick decided to merge the daily title with the

Sunday edition, which, in the British tradition, had operated as a separate entity. Hollick told his two editors to prepare presentations detailing their plans for the merged *Express*. In gladiatorial tradition, the winner would get the big job and the loser would get nothing. Addis won, and as editor of two newspapers with a combined circulation of more than two million copies, he became one of the most powerful editors in the country.

He became notorious for what came next: the laying off, in one day, of eighty newsroom staff, all of whom were angry. Several of them grew loud and threatening before being led away by human resources people to get their severance packages.

A month later, Addis was in the London restaurant Caprice. "A really vile blonde journalist from the *Daily Mail*, who I'd never got on with, came over and said, 'Oh, Richard, it must have been so awful having to fire all those people!' Because I disliked her so much, I said, with heavy sarcasm, 'It was just like cleaning out an old sock drawer.' The quote, of course, went straight to *Private Eye*, as it would have gone into *Frank* magazine. It lived on as a horrible thing to say, but I was just trying to undermine her unctuous sentimentality, which annoyed me. If I had been a really clever person I wouldn't have said it, but there we are."

Addis learned of his own execution at the *Express* in April 1998 when he read a story in the *Times* reporting that Rosie Boycott would be his successor. (She was fired in January 2001.) He called Lord Hollick, his boss.

"I just read that I've been fired," said Addis.

"I can't talk now," said Hollick, essentially confirming the news. "Come and see me at eleven."

Addis got the two year's severance he had negotiated into his contract, packed the contents of his office and left the same day, to the noise of the traditional "Banging Out" by reporters and editors knocking heavy objects on their desks. Banging out is an ancient ceremony, a throwback to the days when compositors in newspaper print shops used lead, which they would bang in unison when a fellow union member retired.

"There was this loud crashing noise as I walked out of the newsroom, because everyone knew what was happening. It was quite moving. So I got banged out, had a party in a nasty big pub across from the *Express*. It was a very Fleet Street party, with lots of tears and hugging and stupid emotional speeches. That evening, I went to a book launch and met Margaret Thatcher, and she said, 'Bad luck.' I went home and didn't have a job."

Addis lived off his severance for nine months before taking a job back at the *Daily Mail*, where he launched a new arts section and ran it unhappily while he wondered when, and if, another editor's job would come his way.

The *Globe and Mail*'s headhunters put an end to his wondering.

◆ ◆ ◆

Garner, in transit, met Addis at a hotel near Heathrow Airport, and Crawley interviewed him three times, with and without Thorsell. Addis flew twice to Toronto and met Thomson family scion David Thomson and, in an unofficial side meeting, chatted by his hotel pool with Kenneth Whyte, whose phone call shortly before had been "a total surprise."

During negotiations for the *Globe* job, Addis had visited Conrad Black at his mansion in Kensington to ask his opinion. Black had phoned Addis, a former employee at the *Telegraph*, to offer his condolences after the editor was fired from the *Express*. Addis recalls,

> We met at his house in a very Conradian room about 300 metres long, lined with Napoleonic history and heavy Sun King–like furniture. There was me, feeling about three inches tall, sitting in a vast chair at one end of the room and Conrad, about nine foot tall, entering through the far door and walking slowly toward me. I told him that I was getting really interested in the *Globe*, and was it a good job. Obviously, I knew he owned the chief rival, but I wanted to know how honest he would be. If he had recommended against it and said it would be a downward step in your career I wouldn't necessarily have believed him, but I would have been interested in hearing it. But he said the opposite: he said it was a very good job and a great thing for me to do. He likes journalists and, like a good warrior, will come and help when you're wounded on the battlefield.

They chatted for half an hour, and Black briefed him a little on Canadian history, focusing on one of his favourite subjects, the late Quebec premier Maurice Duplessis.

In a jocular aside, Addis suggested that the newspaper war in Canada was about to get hotter and more expensive.

"Are you warning me?" asked Black.

"Yes," smiled Addis, "I think I am, because if I do get this job, it will cost you a lot of money."

Black wished him luck and Addis left to consider his options.

When Whyte visited Addis at his hotel in Toronto, the Englishman decided it was an effort on Black's part to scupper the *Globe*'s efforts to hire him. "I think I was in Toronto for just one night, and there was a window of an hour or so. Ken basically offered me the job of their comment editor and had been instructed by Conrad to try to head off the appointment. It was nice to meet him and I was very polite, but it was a pointless offer."

Addis says he was never clear how Whyte knew he was in Toronto, let alone where to find him. "But I think everyone in Toronto knew I was there."

Kenneth Whyte's recollections are different. The impetus for the meeting, he says, came from Addis, not the other way around. Crawley and Garner were genuinely searching for a deputy for Thorsell, and Addis was dissatisfied with that scenario and had contacted Black to sound him out on job opportunities at the *Post*.

According to Whyte, "Conrad said, 'Go talk to Ken Whyte.'"

> Addis and I met for about an hour by the pool at his hotel. He had come with his girlfriend and they were taking it easy. He was very interested in what we were doing and had already sized up the *Globe*. The way he viewed London was like this: there were nine or ten senior editing jobs and about fourteen or fifteen people capable of holding them, and it was a game of musical chairs. You had to keep yourself in play until your turn came up again, and if you had to spend some time in the colonies while you were waiting, so be it. He was very frank about what he was trying to do with Thomson. They were offering him a number-two job, but he wanted it to be the number-one job or have it lead to a number-one job. He told me he was going to tell them he was interested, but only in the number-one job. And it worked. I think Thomson wanted to treat William well, but the only way they could get Addis was to make him the number one. He was looking probably to play one side off against the other and wanted to explore his options.

Whyte sensed that if he had offered the job as deputy editor – the job already filled by the other Englishman, Martin Newland – Addis might have taken it. "If I am Richard Addis doing calculations and my goal is to get back to London as a number one, you're far better able to do that from Hollinger than you are from Thomson, because Conrad owns two number-one titles in the *Daily* and *Sunday Telegraph* plus the *Spectator*."

Addis concedes that the original plan might have been the plan to hire a deputy to Thorsell:

> I successfully turned it around during the interviews with [British headhunter] Spencer Stuart and made it clear that I was not interested in any job in which I was not going to be the editor in the British sense. Which means editor of everything. I wasn't that interested in the job in the first place and certainly would not have become interested had it been anything less than editor. I think that Spencer Stuart told Thomson that they would not find anyone good unless they made them editor. So throughout all the interviews it was understood that if I got the job I would be the editor. There was this thing called the Editorial Board, which we don't have in England. We have leader writers who report to the editor and do whatever they are told. They told me there would be a chairman of the editorial board who would report to me, and that would be William Thorsell. That was fine. As long as he reported to me, I could live with that.

After a week's negotiation, conducted through his Toronto lawyer, Addis eventually got a contract that spelled out clearly that he would be in charge of everything on the editorial side of the *Globe* and Crawley would take care of business. "I had to have it spelled out in British terms so I knew exactly what being the editor meant. Because I knew I had that power, I was more relaxed about it than I would have been had I had to fight William. I was very gentlemanly toward William in the sense that I didn't interfere with him at all. In the six months he ran the editorial board I never interfered, so we got on quite well."

Garner and Crawley showed Addis a circulation chart and told him it was his job to rid the Canadian newspaper market of the *National Post*. In turn, they promised to supply him with the money and troops to do the job.

Addis had already given them a detailed plan of how he intended to do the job. "I gave them a dozen areas that needed to be improved: We had to strengthen the *Globe*, undermine the *Post*, and lock them into a corner and wait for them to shrivel up and die. The strategy I proposed was to keep the high ground in Canadian journalism, which we already had, though it was dwindling, and then push downward. The way I saw it, we were on the top of the mountain and the *Post* had a big army coming up the mountain, so what we needed to do was keep the top and drive them back down by occupying some of their territory and broadening the *Globe*'s appeal. They were a U.K.-style newspaper based on tabloid principles, whereas the *Globe* was a hopelessly slow-witted, cumbersome, boring operation that would be dead in months if it didn't react quickly."

During the course of the hunt, Spencer Stuart had been considering another candidate who had told them that if he got the job, he would bring a young Canadian woman, Chrystia Freeland, to Toronto as his deputy. "The headhunters were very clever," says Addis, "and decided not to hire the person who put himself forward, but they did like Chrystia and said, 'Why don't you take her?' I didn't know her, but I liked her, and she had a tremendous drive and that Fleet Street ruthlessness that I liked. I decided very quickly that we could change things more quickly together than I could on my own."

Ed Greenspon was holidaying with his family in Nova Scotia when Crawley phoned to give him the news about Richard Addis, the imported British editor Greenspon had expected. But there was a sting in Crawley's message: Addis would not be Thorsell's number two; he would replace Thorsell, who was being bumped down to become chairman of the editorial board, where he would be in charge of the editorial and opinion pages, the job he had before becoming editor-in-chief. Greenspon, uneasy at the prospect of working directly for an imported editor, told Crawley he disagreed in principle with a foreigner being editor-in-chief of Canada's national newspaper. They agreed to disagree, but Crawley, offering small consolation, did assure him that Addis had signed a three-year contract and would be gone at the end of it.

But for Greenspon, there was worse news to come. He was walking with his family through a fort when his cellphone rang again. It was a colleague from the *Globe*. "They've hired a deputy editor," he was told.

A call confirming the appointment of thirty-year-old Alberta-born Chrystia Freeland as Addis's deputy came about a half-hour later from Crawley. Greenspon was stunned. Richard Addis, or someone with his professional pedigree, he had sort of expected, but a new deputy, especially one so young and inexperienced, came as total shock. "I wasn't sure that I was totally ready to be editor," says Greenspon. "Richard had a lot of knowledge, and I thought I could work with him and learn things. My unhappiness was with Chrystia rather than Richard – until I started dealing with him."

◆ ◆ ◆

Greenspon, disappointed and angry, felt he had a decision to make.

Ottawa bureau chief Anne McIlroy called to say she would step aside if he wanted to exercise an option in his contract and return to Ottawa. But Greenspon had only been on the job in Toronto for four or five months and feared that leaving so soon would be interpreted as failure, and he did not feel like he had failed.

Greenspon and Addis met for ninety minutes in the *Globe* boardroom, and Greenspon, figuring that Crawley had told Addis to go gently, agreed to try the new arrangement. But until the new editor and his deputy settled in, Greenspon would continue running the news section alone. "I had a lot of power when Richard arrived, and probably I was reluctant to surrender it, but I didn't see anything wrong with that, because I was working for him not against him. But he was very jealous about having all the power."

Addis came to Canada with prototypes for a new-look *Globe and Mail* in his suitcase, created for him by London designer David Hillman, who had, fifteen years before, radically overhauled the *Guardian*. Addis's own redesign plans became a long-running saga, colliding with lots of resistance before appearing in a milder form a year later. In the meantime, he rejigged some sections, shuffled some editors, and, in September 1999, spoke to his highly skeptical troops about his intentions.

While none of them expected Addis to say, "Look, you lot, Garner and Crawley think you need whipping into shape and they've hired me to do it, so let's just get on with it," his was a presentation directly out of the Speeches for New Executives textbook, beginning with some requisite self-effacement: "I hate speaking in public and am very bad at it." And then:

Empathy for the long-suffering staff: "You have all had too much change and uncertainty in the last few years. Plans and people have chased each other's tails. I want to stop all that . . ."

The (sort of) open-door policy: "People with something important to say are welcome to come in and talk. E-mail is an excellent way of getting a decision . . ." (He did not define "important.")

Tepid praise for the Globe *as it was before Addis:* "We have integrity and quality . . . a wonderful reputation and great strengths. . . . Our stories are accurate. These are precious jewels. I firmly support our long-held commitment to clarity, elegance and accuracy. . . . We are different from the other papers in Canada and the world. But we need to feel more different and enjoy our differences."

A light whack at the National Post: "Our boast should be the same as the Costa Rica Tourist Board – No Artificial Ingredients. How different from another newspaper, whose main aim is to be 'provocative' – what could be more artificial than that?"

But let's not kid ourselves: "While I think we should never set our sails by the wind that comes from the *Post*, we should admit that it does some things right. I know it is often very hollow and delivers an awful lot less than it promises, but it is winning credit for being bright, fresh, and new. For reasons that we all know, the national edition has some advantages over us. The Saturday offering is acknowledged to be pretty strong . . ."

This-is-why-they-hired-me criticism of the Globe: "Against this, the *Globe* often looks so forbidding. Despite the improvement that came with the introduction of colour, we somehow still have the problem of 'the great grey Globe' – as grey as a prison wall, some I know described it."

Emphasis on new lines of authority: "Chrystia Freeland is coming this month as deputy editor, and she and I will work together on most things. She will edit the paper when I am away. She has great qualities that make up for my defects and vice versa."

But confidence in the old guard: "Our number three will be Ed Greenspon, who is promoted to executive editor from tomorrow. He will also edit the paper and be totally involved in our inner councils. . . . He has done a wonderful amount for the paper this summer. I am giving him a huge job, which reflects the confidence I have in him."

Tangential self-association with greatness: "Arthur Christiansen, who was Lord Beaverbrook's greatest editor, summed up his memoirs by writing something like this: 'And, with strong language, laughter, and a passion for news, the *Express* came out day after day.'"

Upbeat ending: "I want people to be free to air their passions. I want there to be much laughter as we toil away. At its best, a thriving newspaper is like a good party . . ."

After Freeland's arrival it became clear to Edward Greenspon that he was not going to be part of any triumvirate. "Richard and Chrystia met every morning by themselves. She would go into his office in the morning and close the door and do whatever they would do, and I wasn't part of those conversations. I wasn't taken with Richard's management style, and there were lots of promises unkept to people we would offer jobs. I didn't know whether I wanted to be around this guy."

It was during the first week of the Addis tenure that he made one of many faux pas that would reveal his almost total ignorance of Canada and its geography. "Who's Wayne Gretzky," he asked Greenspon, "and why would we put him on the front page?"

Another hockey faux pas came when Montreal Canadiens great Maurice (The Rocket) Richard died and Addis famously asked, "Who is this Maurice *Richard* fellow?" (as in King Richard). And he was confused about whether Alaska was in Canada.

Greenspon also grew to loathe the way Addis was prone to treat people beneath him. Not long after Addis's arrival a department editor came into a meeting and sat in the chair next to the new editor-in-chief, who immediately told him, "You're not important enough to sit there."

Addis thought he and Greenspon were getting on reasonably well in the first months of their working relationship, and the endorsement he gave Greenspon during his speech was not totally disingenuous. At first, he considered Greenspon enthusiastic, bright, and energetic, but his opinion gradually changed. "I got impatient with him after a month or two. He was stupid in that he was too ambitious and thought he could somehow win a power struggle with me. And, of course, just having that thought is fatal. I could see it was slipping through his mind. He didn't have the skills that were necessary at that time to repair the newspaper. He didn't have a clue how to do it. So it wasn't the right time for Eddie. He was very upset that Chrystia was coming in over his head, and we had long negotiations about what he should do next, and he agreed to be number three, but obviously he wasn't going to be allowed to run things as he had before."

Addis and Greenspon were two cultures, and two specific upbringings, colliding. The Englishman conceded that Greenspon could sometimes be a warm, understanding person, but the rest of the time, he just didn't like him. "That's when I'm more aware of this very ambitious hustler, and that gets right up my nose," says Addis. "Part of it is a cultural thing, because it is not the way anyone I know, with any style, operates. He might say, 'I really like that watch. Can I buy it off you? It looks great.' Whereas I would not mention your watch, but would buy a slighter better one and never mention it. The ghastly, appalling public-school boy that I am, I have to make things appear effortless. Victories must seem effortless. You can paddle hard underneath, but on the surface you must be a swan. It's a chemical difference between us, so when I was editor, if he annoyed me I would give him a kick."

◆ ◆ ◆

One *Globe* veteran in whom the former editor-in-chief occasionally confided says Thorsell was shocked to be fired, because he had assumed he was doing what Garner and his other bosses wanted. "He had never been a hands-on editor but more of a big-picture guy and accepted that the *Globe* needed a hands-on person to drive the newsroom. He went to London as part of the search-and-interview process with Crawley but always under the assumption he was looking for a number two. When it became clear that Addis was being brought in as the editor, William was shocked and saddened but seemed to get over it quickly and was never less than graceful about his demise. But I imagine the blow was cushioned by a pretty good settlement. So he had his column and was back on the editorial board, but nobody ever imagined he was doing anything other than waiting for something else to come along."

The departure of Thorsell, who found a second successful career as head of the Royal Ontario Museum, was expected, but those already uncomfortable with an Englishman running Canada's venerable national newspaper were outraged when Addis, contrary to Canadian journalistic tradition, assumed direct control over the comment and opinion pages. "It's one thing to have someone come from Britain running our national newspaper," one *Globe* editor complained, "but quite another to have someone come from Britain to tell us how to run our country."

National Post editor Ken Whyte admired Thorsell and figures he was lucky to get out when he did:

> He had the last great run of being the last great newspaper in the country. It had better writers, better talent, everyone wanted to be there, and it had a dominant voice in the national conversation. It's like comparing the original six to the expanded NHL. The *Globe* did some things better then than it does now. It had integrity then. I don't think it has integrity now. It had a real sense of what was important in the country and what the important stories were. It had a political point of view under William, and I think it all hung together pretty well. It's certainly more readable now, but that is only part of the game. I think it had more authoritative voices then than it does now – Andrew Coyne, Terence Corcoran, Michael Coren as a counterpoint to Michael Valpy. Rick Salutin was always an effective in-house critic who argued with all those guys. There was a lot going on in Thorsell's *Globe*.

◆ ◆ ◆

In March 2000, while Greenspon was taking a week off with his children, Addis announced that newly hired news editor Fred Kuntz from the *Toronto Star* would take charge of the front section on the afternoon and evening shift. Addis had not discussed the changes beforehand with Greenspon, but it was clear that he was being squeezed out, and not too diplomatically. "I had been stripped of all my power," says Greenspon, "and for the second time while I had been on holidays. It was an unnecessary insult to me."

The resilient Greenspon, down but not quite out, had asked Crawley months before about beefing up the *Globe*'s Web site and now asked to be put in charge of the job. After all, with Thomson dumping its newspapers and refocusing on electronic information, it seemed to fit with corporate strategy. Crawley agreed that it made sense and Greenspon had engineered his out.

But aside from getting nervous about taking holidays, Greenspon also decided that too many of his eggs were in one unsteady basket and he couldn't trust his future to the vagaries and whims of other people. He developed what he called a Brand Eddie strategy to give himself a diversified multimedia presence in books, on TV, and online.

Six months later, with an impressive globeandmail.com launched and in good shape, Greenspon exercised his option and returned to Ottawa as a senior political editor and columnist. Despite his irreparable differences with Addis and Freeland, Greenspon would continue to keep regular contact with Crawley – something that Addis, well practised in the art of self-preservation, knew all about.

"He had never been to Canada before, and had never read anything about Canada, and all of a sudden he was editor of Canada's national newspaper. I didn't work with him, so I can't speak about those horrors, but I can say that morale sank to the lowest level I could remember."

— Jeffrey Simpson, national columnist, *Globe and Mail*

Early in the winter of 2000, Richard Addis accepted an invitation from his soon-to-be good friends Governor General Adrienne Clarkson and her husband, John Ralston Saul, to a Rideau Hall dinner honouring Costa Rican president Miguel Angel Rodriguez, who was in Ottawa on a state visit. It isn't unusual for prominent journalists to be invited into the opulence of Rideau Hall, and unlike previous governors general, former journalist Clarkson knows many of them well.

Veteran *Globe and Mail* columnist Hugh Winsor, a former colleague of Clarkson's at CBC Television, was also at the dinner but didn't realize his new boss was there until people began mingling after the meal. Winsor noticed Addis chatting animatedly to Prime Minister Jean Chrétien, so, his curiosity aroused, he sidled over to listen to what they were talking about.

"Richard was giving Chrétien the gears about why we hadn't invited Tony Blair to Canada, and the prime minister said he sees Blair all the time and he can come to Canada whenever he wants. I didn't think this was a good topic of conversation and not a good way for the new editor of the *Globe* to make an impression. I edged into the conversation to get the topic off Blair and we started to talk about other things, including the *National Post*, which had been publishing the Shawinigate stories. Chrétien started to get into this when Aline came by to tell him the president of Costa Rica was leaving and that he'd better attend to his diplomatic duty."

Chrétien was furious at the *Post*, which had begun publishing stories about his business dealings with Yvon Duhaime, a businessman with a criminal record who received a $655,000 federal loan to develop a hotel adjacent to a golf course in the prime minister's riding of Maurice in Quebec. The stories, which implied that Chrétien may have gained financially from the development of the hotel, were only the prelude to a series of articles that would give the prime minister the worst political grief of his career and subject him to unrelenting bombardment by opposition parties in the daily parliamentary question period.

At the time of the Rideau Hall reception, the *Post* had been in business a little over a year and had been in a running battle with Chrétien for most of that time. The prime minister, angry at the aspersions the newspaper had begun casting in his direction, had, in April 1999, taken the unprecedented step of writing a long letter of complaint to the *Post* defending himself against the newspaper's "false and baseless accusations." Chrétien stopped short in midconversation with Addis and turned to Winsor.

"Bring your friend over for cognac afterwards," he said.

"Sure, but it's a bit late, and we all know you go to bed early, Prime Minister," replied Winsor.

"Ah, that's okay," said Chrétien, "come over."

Winsor, well aware that Chrétien was not a night owl, checked with Bruce Hartley, the prime minister's ever-present executive assistant, who quickly and discreetly checked with his boss.

"He's serious," Hartley reported back.

By then, Addis had moved on and was chatting with Supreme Court Chief Justice Beverley McLachlin and other Ottawa notables, apparently enjoying himself immensely. After introducing his new boss to several movers and shakers, Winsor began to worry about the time.

"Richard, if we're going over to see Chrétien we've got to get out of here," said Winsor to his gadfly editor, who was exhibiting an insatiable appetite for small talk.

Winsor, his wife Christina Cameron, and Addis drove to 24 Sussex Drive, across the road from Rideau Hall. Chrétien and his wife were sitting in their living room, and a maid, armed with a cognac bottle, was waiting for the late-night guests. Addis and Winsor spoke to the prime minister in English while the two wives chatted in French.

Chrétien was not forgoing his early night to engage in social chit-chat. Ever the politician, he wanted to deliver to Winsor and Addis his spin on the *Post*'s so-called Shawinigate affair. Chrétien defended Duhaime and seemed especially upset that the *Post* referred to the businessman's criminal record. The prime minister painted Duhaime as a hero of sorts who had come about his criminal record honourably during a strike by his hotel workers. Addis and Winsor, sensing that Chrétien was feeling the need to get a few things off his chest, sat on the opposite side of a coffee table and just listened.

"He told us the hotel staff had gone on strike and there was nobody to feed the guests," Winsor says. "Duhaime was also continuing to provide meals to an old-age home during the strike and someone threw a rock through the window at his home and the glass hit his kid. Chrétien said that Duhaime came out shaking his fist and the union went to the police, who charged him with issuing threats. Duhaime had gone to court without a lawyer and was given a minimum sentence. Chrétien said he had been hornswoggled by the union and the conviction was not really serious."

Most of the conversation was about the *Post*, and at one point Chrétien, referring to the accusations of conflict of interest, laughed as he said to his visitors, "Not everyone has a son-in-law like I have," meaning André Desmarais, the multimillionaire president of Power Corporation, who is married to Chrétien's daughter France.

"He was basically saying he didn't need the money," says Winsor.

Winsor recalls the prime minister nursing a beer throughout the evening, but Addis recalls sharing a good portion of the cognac bottle with Chrétien.

"We spoke to him about the *Globe* and Conrad Black," says Addis. "He defended his position on the peerage, said he didn't like the politics of the *Post* or some of the things the *Post* had been writing about him. But mostly he talked about himself and his family. He told me he was a tough guy from a big family and, 'I've made it.' He looks full of energy. I met Paul Martin and Allan Rock formally in their offices, Stockwell Day, Brian Tobin, Preston Manning, and other minor figures. Apart from Chrétien I found them all rather boring. They are much less articulate and confident than British politicians. They seem to have less need to be interesting and

would bore you to death with details. British politicians meeting journalists always try to be witty, sharp, and pugnacious and get across some kind
of character. Canadian politicians, other than Jean Chrétien, reminded me
of bureaucrats. I think Paul Martin may be the world's most boring man.
Chrétien may be wrong and infuriating, but he is a great character."

The group chatted about golf, and at around one-thirty Addis, Winsor,
and his wife left.

The *Globe*'s new editor-in-chief was clearly taken with the occasion,
recalls Winsor, though not obviously interested by anything the prime
minister had said about the *Post* and its stories. The columnist was rather
pleased with how the evening had gone. "Chrétien made it seem like I
drop in there for coffee and brandy on a regular basis, and Richard was
mightily impressed by that. As we were driving away from Sussex Drive,
he asked me, 'How can we exploit this?' I said, 'Richard, if we start to
exploit it, we'll never get invited again.' Then he went back to Toronto
and told people that Hugh's got these fantastic contacts. It probably saved
my job."

◆ ◆ ◆

Richard Addis would enrage and alienate dozens of people during his three
years at the *Globe and Mail*, but no internal battle was greater and more
sustained than the one he had with national political columnist Jeffrey
Simpson, who is a *Globe and Mail* institution and reputed to be better connected to Ottawa's circle of powerful higher-echelon bureaucrats than any
journalist working in the capital. Despite his longevity and reputation, the
columnist felt branded, along with other high-profile *Globe* writers, by
members of a new regime from another country and a different journalistic tradition who disliked the old *Globe and Mail*. Despite that, he had sent
Addis a welcoming letter when he arrived and offered to help in any way
he could. The letter went unanswered.

"People who were prominent, or who were headliners, at the previous
paper," says Simpson, "were by definition tainted, because they had been
part of the building of a paper that the new regime didn't like. So people
who were high profile under the previous regime were by definition suspect – the style of journalism they practised, the way they comported themselves, the assumptions they had about the readership and the kind of

newspaper they wanted, were called into question. So here was I, with all my awards and all that bullshit, I was a sitting duck for guys who were in a rejectionist mode about what had gone on at the *Globe and Mail* before."

Simpson first met Addis and his deputy, Chrystia Freeland, in the fall of 1999, when the pair visited the newspaper's Ottawa bureau for the first time. Simpson took them to dinner at the famed Café Henry Burger, an upscale eatery opposite the Museum of Civilization across the Inter Provincial bridge in Hull, Quebec. Simpson wanted his visitors to get a taste, literally and otherwise, of the French side of Canada and thought that the evening had been an agreeable one. Freeland, on the other hand, returned to Toronto apparently feeling she had been treated badly by Simpson.

Addis had begun the dinner by reaching for his ubiquitous red notebook and listening while Simpson spoke about the history of the *Globe* and its role in Canada. Simpson then asked Addis about his impressions of the *Globe*, which the editor-in-chief described as organizationally dysfunctional. He asked Simpson what he thought of asking writers like Margaret Atwood to write for the paper.

A few days later, Simpson got a surprise call from his Toronto editor, who told him that his column was being moved to another page, cut by a quarter, and that he would be required to write only three days a week instead of four, albeit at the same salary. Simpson, unhappy at the affront and anxious to maintain the continuity he had established since he began writing the column more than fifteen years before, fought back.

After a battle lasting several months, Simpson made his case to Addis during a lunch in Toronto. "He didn't like confrontation, so spent most of the time talking about skiing and other chit-chat. At the end of the lunch he said, 'Well, I know you're unhappy so we'll take the column back to four days a week.' That's the way he was." The column would also return to its previous spot.

Simpson was in Vancouver the following summer to give a speech and prepare to promote his new book, *Star-Spangled Canadians*, when a call came from Chrystia Freeland. Simpson's publisher had sent excerpts of his book to the *Globe* hoping the newspaper would publish them, and Simpson assumed that was why she was calling. It wasn't. Freeland was delivering bad news. His column was being cut once more to three days a week to accommodate Eddie Greenspon's move back to Ottawa. Greenspon would be writing a new column on the *Globe*'s other three publishing days.

Simpson was upset that the new arrangement had been devised in Toronto without his input. Freeland apologized on behalf of Addis and explained that the editor-in-chief was on a canoe trip so couldn't make the call himself. She was doing the courtesy of calling, off her own bat, so he would not hear it from other sources. Says Simpson,

> I took her at her word and only later learned that it was all bullshit and that she had been delegated to do it and report my reaction back to the powers that be. Addis didn't have the courage to deliver the news himself. You can only take that as a slap in the face and a complete lack of confidence, and I did not take it very well. I had been kicked in the nuts and responded, as you would expect, very badly. But I didn't want to do anything precipitous in anger, so I went into a shell and considered whether I wanted to stay at the paper. I had a book to promote and a federal election to cover and just couldn't deal with anything else. Eventually, we reached an agreement, but the problem with Richard was that even if you made an agreement you could never guarantee that it would stick. He was very charming, but I don't think he was used to people pushing back hard. I saw him as someone who was fundamentally weak.

In fact, given the circumstances, Simpson had some *mild* sympathy for Addis:

> Let's be fair. If someone from Canada suddenly went over to Britain to be the editor of the *Times*, huge eyebrows would have been raised across Fleet Street. And that was the situation he was in when he walked into the *Globe*. He had never been to Canada before, and had never read anything about Canada, and all of a sudden he was editor of Canada's national newspaper. I didn't work with him on a daily basis, so I can't talk about those horrors, but I can say, as someone who has been around a long time, that morale had sunk to the lowest level I could remember, and there have been some low points in the *Globe* newsroom history. But Richard made an effort to get to know the country. I remember once he said he had been to Montreal to "an ice hockey game and bought a ticket from some touts." Several of us

said to him, "No, Richard, you went to a hockey game and bought the ticket from scalpers."

Two years later, toward the end of the Addis tenure, Simpson was giving a lunchtime speech at the Empire Club in Toronto and was sitting with his editor-in-chief and former external affairs minister Barbara MacDougall. Addis, his relations with Simpson less hostile, mentioned he was going to Halifax and was seeking names of people he might visit in an official capacity. MacDougall, who has a summer home in Chester, Nova Scotia, obliged, and Addis inquired if there was anyone he might meet at the University of Halifax, which doesn't exist. "He was still struggling," recalls Simpson. "Canada is a big, complicated country."

Shortly before he left Canada, Richard Addis reflected on his relationship with Simpson like an old general musing sentimentally about past encounters with a worthy enemy:

> Jeff Simpson was my big battle at the *Globe*, but grudgingly I came to like and admire him. He'll be shocked to hear it, but it's true. I redesigned the Comment page and his spot moved from the left-hand side to the right-hand side, under the readers' letters on the opening page of Comment. He didn't like that and called it a "shrivelled sausage." He is a formidable opponent. He's very bright, well connected, and knows the country way better than I am ever going to know it and knows a certain stratum of *Globe* readers better than I'm ever going to know them. And he is amazingly stubborn and formidable. He didn't talk to me for at least a year. Not once. I compromised eventually and put him back – not where he wanted to be but near where he wanted to be and gave him the days of the week he was happy with because I admired his defiance. If you go a few rounds with someone and they're still standing, you shake their hand and say, "Okay, you haven't won, but you do have my respect." But he probably hates me.

❖ ❖ ❖

Other *Globe*ites adopted less direct methods of contending with Addis, usually via anonymous communication with *Frank* magazine, which became the forum for *Globe and Mail* discontent with a brutal mix of innuendo, fiction, and devastating, well-documented attacks on the new editor. Addis became known in the magazine as "Bluebeard," and after his former wife gave an interview describing him as having "reptilian charm," *Frank* editors took to printing his name as "Addissss." Freeland suffered similarly ugly treatment, her relatively youthful looks and youthful-sounding voice earning her the epithet "Britney," her voice being described as sounding like a "chipmunk on helium."

The old sock-drawer remark Addis made in London after his mass firing of journalists at the *Express* newspapers preceded him across the Atlantic. It was among the first of the many scathing anti-Addis items fed to *Frank* magazine, and despite his explanation of how the remark came about, Addis never made any secret of his dismay that a union prevented him from doing the same thing at the *Globe and Mail*:

> Some of the journalists were entrenched in their jobs, and some were very lazy, and others were talented but bored. But some were talented and not bored and were a great gift to the newspaper and better than any journalist in Britain. So I found a few gems around the *Globe and Mail*, including some who could get jobs in any English-speaking country in the world, but it took more than two years to figure it all out. Some were disheartened and very difficult to deal with. They would always find a million reasons why they couldn't do something, or if they did it, they would do it reluctantly, not very well, and charge overtime. So that's the worst of all possible worlds. It was just a handful of people, but a powerful handful. I tried to put them under a lot of pressure, but in the end it isn't worth it, because you don't get the work that you want anyway, so as an editor it's tempting to avoid them. I still say that the *Globe* would be a better paper if you fired fifteen people tomorrow. It desperately needs that, but before cleaning out the sock drawer you need to get to know the socks.

It would be overstating it to suggest that the *Globe* was a completely hostile zone for Addis, but few of his allies were among the reporting rank and file. The incessant barrage of negative gossipy tidbits sent anonymously to *Frank*, mostly recounting his alleged lavish personal spending and imperious attitude toward his staff, were a manifestation of the resentment.

He claims the leaks never bothered him, even though they invariably painted him as a nasty, conniving, hypocritical, non-caring cad who treated people like dirt, was panic-stricken about the *National Post*, and liked to ingratiate himself with the powerful.

Among the most damning Addis entries in *Frank* concerned his relationship with his secretary, Jan Robson, an Oxford University graduate he treated – if you believe *Frank* – like a skivvy, demanding she fetch his laundry, lend him her car, take his family on outings, arrange for free trips, and make sure he didn't miss lunch dates with high-profile celebrities passing through Toronto. Robson, who signed a confidentiality clause as part of her settlement at the *Globe*, refuses to speak about the relationship.

Robson quit after Addis allegedly ordered her to contact former national ski team member Kerrin Lee-Gartner to ask if the *Globe* editor-in-chief could use Lee-Gartner's condominium at Whistler. Neither Robson nor Addis knew Lee-Gartner. When Robson refused, Addis allegedly accused her of being stupid.

Addis is retrospectively philosophical about the shellacking he got in *Frank*. "It's a shocking thing to say, but life would be worse without *Frank*. I had nothing to lose from *Frank* and maybe a little to gain. It's not a bad thing to be a colourful character in Canada. The worst thing is that it undermines morale in a newsroom if people feel that things that happen in meetings and internal matters will get into print. I used to feel sorry for the other people, who were devastated by what was said about them, but I didn't care about myself. I felt whoever was leaking to *Frank* was betraying the spirit I was trying to create and betraying a loyalty that was building. The leaks eventually became less vicious, but I could never quite figure out where they were coming from."

Former *Frank* magazine publisher Michael Bate is a tall, bald, soft-spoken man who lives in the Glebe, a comfortable middle-class section of Ottawa and an area of the city favoured by many journalists, mid-to-upper echelon public servants, and other members of the national capital's chattering class. His magazine, since sold, operated out of a disused shambles of an office on Sparks Street in the city's downtown. It often contains exaggerations, misinterpretations, unfair and unchecked subjective assessments, and is often dead wrong. But not always.

Frank relies for its media gossip on anonymous contributions, which in turn seem to be in direct proportion to the prevailing atmosphere inside the contributing newsroom. Happy people do not send gossip to *Frank*, and nobody reports positive stuff about their colleagues or bosses, although on occasion some accidental, grudging admiration can filter through the fury. Compared with some of the possible alternatives for venting anger and frustration, *Frank* is a relatively harmless forum, although being on the receiving end of negative gossip is never pleasant. Bate, raised in a military family, enjoyed pricking inflated egos, especially if they belonged to the ruling, or boss, class.

From Bate's perspective, Addis was the victim of his own flawed personality and made for great gossip because he was different, colourful, and loathed by so many people. He was good for business. Bate also liked to focus on the *Globe* because of its prominent position in the country and because the flow of gossip from the *National Post* (or National Putz, as he dubbed it) was almost non-existent:

> Hacks are inveterate whingers and they love to gossip, and this ultimately makes for interesting copy. The *Globe* has had 150 years of tradition to develop the backbiting, backstabbing, dissension-ridden culture that makes it such an entertaining subject, whereas the *Post* is only a few years old and employees there are behind in their pissing-and-moaning development. The *Globe*, as described in the pages of *Frank*, may appear to be a snake pit, but I'm not sure that any newsroom is more discontented than any other. The *Post*ies were much more ideologically driven and at the outset there was tremendous loyalty to Black and to the *Post* cause. In other words, the *Post* was a much more closed shop, more difficult to infiltrate, and more like the *Star* in that it is a less interesting place than the *Globe*. And Addis was a far more entertaining character than anyone at the *Post*.

❖ ❖ ❖

Addis was, in the words of publisher Phillip Crawley, the *Globe*'s "agent of change," charged with the delicate task of responding to the *Post*'s racier journalism while maintaining the *Globe*'s traditional conservative edge and its core readership.

While he was loath to say anything complimentary about the *Post* or its founder, Crawley, in hiring Addis to shake up the newsroom and brighten the *Globe*'s presentation, was saying, in effect, that the *Post* was having an impact that needed to be countered:

> Richard is particularly good at packaging content, and while there was lots of good stuff in the *Globe* before Richard arrived, and the quality of the journalists was often very high, we weren't making the best of their work. So a big part of Richard's job was showcasing the best of the *Globe*'s material. At this time, in the early days, the *Post* was being touted as this wonderful new creation that was going to revolutionize Canadian journalism and how the world had been such a dull and terrible place before the *Post* came along. The arrogance of it all was astonishing. They had the belief that they would produce this magical new product and were claiming before the launch that they would have new types of advertising not previously seen in newspapers. It was pure fantasy. So they jollied themselves along for the first year or more on this self-induced fantasy that this was the greatest thing since sliced bread that would conquer Canada in an instant. It took quite a long time for the penny to drop that it wasn't happening.

Crawley didn't like the *Globe*'s front page, which, at that time, featured a vertical column of brief stories down its left side and, on Saturdays, the largest circulating day of the week, was further restricted by a rigid space at the top of the page devoted to a narrow horizontal photograph. "It was quite a challenge, week by week, finding a picture that actually worked in that shape. The design people were performing contortions every week trying to find one that would fit. They would run pictures of rivers because they happened to be flowing the right way."

Crawley wanted his agent of change to be gradual and subtle so as not to shock loyal readers into cancelling their subscriptions. He wanted to showcase the *Globe*'s foreign bureaus, because the *Post* didn't have any of its own, and expand the newspaper's range of columnists in an effort to emphasize "the *Post*'s blatant right-wing drum beat."

Opinion on how Addis went about that task varies from contempt to admiration with a few stops in between. *Globe* veteran reporter John Gray saw an idiosyncratic micro-manager, the polar opposite in that way and most others of William Thorsell. "People who had done a good job with immense pride found themselves second- and third-guessed, and all of a sudden told that their judgments were no longer adequate. The *Globe*'s response to the *Post* has, in many ways, been to the detriment of the *Globe* and its traditional quality. They made some lamentable news judgments, taking stories out of context and rewriting stories so they could get a headline they wanted. It really pissed me off."

Jan Wong was one of a circle of "star" writers at the *Globe* whose input was initially sought by Addis at Monday meetings. Wong refers to them as the "Prima Donna" meetings, which she would avoid when possible, because she felt Addis wasn't genuinely consulting the writers so much as flattering them to keep them on his side.

"I hate meetings because they waste so much time," says Wong, "but these meetings had the effect of alienating everybody who wasn't invited. Many people who had worked at the *Globe* for twenty or twenty-five years – their whole careers – felt they were suddenly nameless because Richard didn't know or care who they were. It was just another knife in the old culture of the *Globe*, because Richard came with no background in Canada, no background in the *Globe and Mail*, and he didn't care who you were or what you did. The *Globe* was a writer's paper that became this meat grinder, and people's stories were routinely killed. Richard didn't seek consensus, disliked people who disagreed with him, and would retaliate and punish people."

Addis pushed, trying to lighten up the *Globe* with a choice of stories and feature articles, but in his early days especially, they often looked out of place and forced. It was, recalls Wong, a culture alien to almost everyone who worked at the newspaper.

"The *Post* did a wonderful job of being fun and light and finding the quirky features. We came at it with a big sledgehammer called sex and didn't have a clue how to have a light touch. We were people who had always been sober and serious and suddenly we were putting on miniskirts and starting to dance, but we didn't have any rhythm. The *Post* stunned the *Globe* with its light touch and innovation but our stories didn't sparkle or have any taste. They were like sequins on a stripper's panties. The low point was a story we ran about who people would most like to have a shower with. I think most male Canadians wanted to have a shower with Pamela Anderson. That was Fleet Street vulgarity."

Addis knew the turmoil and resentment he was causing, but Fleet Street vulgarity was second nature to him. He had no history and no allegiances at the newspaper and, as he saw it, had been given a fixer's job to do. After his bloody campaign at the *Express* newspapers in London, the *Globe* presented a relatively polite challenge.

"The lesson I learned from some great editors was simply that you had to do what they wanted and you had to do it quickly. We were up against a newspaper that was totally motivated, and I became angry when people at the *Globe* didn't react quickly enough. I had some great battles and I don't regret any of them. When blood gets spilled it's generally a bad thing, but if it's the only way to achieve something then it has to be done. I am not a good shouter, but I can become very insistent. The worst I can be is very cold and harsh. I have a cold nature when needed, and I can be horrifyingly tough, but people often don't realize that I would prefer, I think, to be a nice warm person. But there is some steel deep inside me, which is why I got all these jobs."

◆ ◆ ◆

What continued to irk many *Globe* employees who came into contact with their new editor-in-chief was his brusque management style and his apparent continued lack of understanding of Canada and the role of the *Globe and Mail* in it.

Jan Wong got a phone call from her section editor on a snowy February day during Addis's first winter. Addis wanted a story about the weather, which Wong resisted doing. Snow in Toronto in February was not unusual, she reasoned, and there were no disruptions, no deaths, and public transit was still running. "I don't understand the assignment," she said. "I'm missing the point. [Mayor] Mel Lastman isn't calling out the troops." As she recalls,

> I am badgering and saying every step of the way I don't think it's a story and then, finally, I said, "Tell Richard that the day British newspapers write about the fog in London is the day I'll write about snow in Toronto in February. In August, I would write about snow, but in February it's not news." There was a big sigh on the other end of the phone like I am the problem. . . . They asked other reporters until

someone eventually said yes, but nobody in management would say that the emperor has no clothes. Every time I did it, I was digging a bigger hole for myself, but I feel you've got to kill a stupid story in the bud. All down the line it was, Richard wants it, Richard wants it, instead of saying this is a good idea, because. . . . It would be a nutty, undoable, or unethical idea, but nobody would say so unless a reporter did. People were scared of Richard.

Addis pushed Wong to choose higher-profile people to feature in her Lunch With column, which was a must-read for *Globe* readers but had become notorious among publicists and communications advisers who were warning high-profile clients to decline Wong's invitations. Go for lunch with Wong at your peril, was the message, because chances are she will skewer you. Consequently, the chances of her getting a prominent politician or some other well-known public figure were becoming extraordinarily slim. Addis asked her to get Ontario Premier Mike Harris, who refused. Undaunted, the editor-in-chief continued to suggest public figures Wong considered unattainable.

"Addis was clueless about who would have lunch with me," says Wong, "but I would always try to go through the motions of getting who he wanted, even though it was a waste of time. I couldn't get some people because I have a reputation, so I had to face the fact that people with a public relations adviser would usually say no."

The *Post* and *Globe* went through periods of mutual obsession and wrote about each other's woes with a regularity that may have surpassed any two rivals in the history of newspapers. It has been common for competing newspapers to sabotage or steal each other's stories and engage in dirty tricks behind the scenes, but the *Post* and *Globe* sniped at each other from their own pages with an unprecedented and total disregard for their readers, who couldn't possibly have cared. At one point, all mention of the *Post* was banned in the *Globe*, but that restriction was lifted, unannounced, when Addis asked Wong to arrange a lunch interview with Conrad Black. After much soul-searching, Wong convinced herself that it might not be such a bad idea.

"At first I felt it was such a conflict of interest. How can I possibly interview somebody who is running the rival newspaper? If I'm nice to him, he'll think I'm just looking for a job; if I'm tough on him, then I'm just beating the drum for my employer. I thought it was really a no-win situation. I messaged Crawley, and I said, 'Are you sure you want me to do this?' I'm not going to ask him and then find out we don't want to, because then we'll look really stupid. He said, 'Yeah, go ahead.' So I called Conrad Black, because by then I decided he's a significant person in Canadian society. I had rationalized it."

The angst was hardly worth it. Black's Toronto secretary returned her call, after consulting with her boss, and chuckled a very polite no.

◆ ◆ ◆

In October 1999, Addis appeared with Freeland at the National Press Club in Ottawa to speak about his vision for the *Globe and Mail* and, though he didn't anticipate it, take some serious heat from some of the hundred or so people in the audience.

"No one in my whole life has ever paid a cent to hear anything I had to say before," he began, "and I hope that anyone here who has paid the five dollars won't mind if I pay you back directly after this talk."

Whether deliberately or otherwise, Addis waved a red rag at the *Post* employees present. "As a reader," he intoned, "I have a huge range of choice every morning in Toronto. The wonderful *Globe and Mail*, a highly credible newspaper full of good writing. The *National Post*, unreliable, obsessive, vulgar."

"Tell us what you really think of the *Post*," someone shouted.

"It's wrong about nearly everything," said Addis, not totally seriously. "It gets stories wrong. You can't believe it any more. Nobody believes it."

Post reporter Andrew McIntosh, author of the Shawinigate stories, was incensed.

"You guys ignored, dissed, humiliated, and dumped on a story of mine about Chrétien," McIntosh said, "then you jumped on it. And now you're actually investigating. If we're so inaccurate, why are you matching story for story on that subject?"

Addis, apparently flustered, attempted to flatter McIntosh. "This must be because you are an extremely good reporter, so you've managed to pull –"

"Flattery will get you nowhere," he interrupted.

Addis took another question.

"So you don't regard the *Post* as a worthy opponent?"

"I haven't even thought about it like that, really. It's a nice . . . it looks nice. It's quite pretty."

"You want the *Globe* to be known for its accuracy," said another questioner. "You just made a statement that everything in the *Post* is wrong and you can't even give us one example. Could you or your deputy come up with one example?"

"Well, we don't . . . We're just trying to be polite. We don't want to, uh, rub salt into the wounds here. But there probably is an example."

◆ ◆ ◆

The day after deputy editor Chrystia Freeland's appointment had been announced at the *Globe*, a newsroom wag, reflecting the general feeling of the newsroom, circulated a memo purporting to be from publisher Crawley:

> I am pleased to announce the appointment of Allistair Buffet to the position of inter-departmental editor, effective this fall. Allistair will be an outstanding addition to our editorial team. He is 17, and a native of Manchester, England, where he regularly reads several daily papers. He is also the captain of his Catholic high-school's rugby team, and attends church regularly. He once freelanced a photograph of Princess Diana to the *Daily Express*. Though he has never been to Canada, Allistair received a grade of 88 percent on his high school history final exam. The course included several chapters on the colonies.

Freeland's only contact at the *Globe and Mail* was John Gray, whom she had known in Russia when he was Moscow correspondent and she was a recent Harvard graduate, barely in her twenties, who had gone to the Russian capital to learn how to be a journalist. Freeland, born in Peace River, Alberta, in 1968, was a Rhodes scholar at Oxford and a correspondent for London's *Financial Times* in Kiev and Moscow. She was national news editor of the *Financial Times* when she was recruited by the *Globe* in the fall of 1999. As a reporter of relative youth she would have been accepted into any newsroom of any major newspaper, but as the deputy editor with almost no managerial experience, her reception at the *Globe and Mail* was guaranteed to be hostile. In the words of the *National Post*'s Martin Newland, upper-crust English people have a "down-your-nose attitude" to Canada. That an ultimately failed candidate for the position of *Globe* editor-in-chief should have chosen the Canadian-raised Freeland as a running mate suggests she was intended by that person as some kind of cynical compensation for colonial *Globe*ites.

Freeland's first call, naturally enough, was to John Gray, who would be one of several *Globe* veterans who left the newspaper in a round of voluntary redundancies and cost-cutting at the beginning of 2001.

"Nobody else at the *Globe* had ever heard of her," recalls Gray. "She phoned me and asked, 'What have I got myself into?' People didn't like her because her manner was abrupt. I got along with her fine, but it was said she didn't get along well with women. She looked young, sounded young, and is very small."

Freeland had been interviewed in London by Phillip Crawley and had lunched with William Thorsell and Stuart Garner before she was introduced to Addis. Crawley seemed to be the man in charge, but at the outset no one made it clear to Freeland what position she was being considered for. Because of her age and inexperience, she assumed it was not the editor-in-chief's job.

"It was great. I was happy to be back in Canada, and it was nice to be in a newsroom where everyone was talking with my accent and nice to be working with the people who were journalistic stars from my childhood. I was impressed by the high quality of the newsroom, but it was apparent to me that the *Globe* was a place unaccustomed to competition and not used to the cut and thrust of a newspaper war. It was clear people were uneasy going into that."

Freeland says she felt more discomfort running the national news pages of the *Financial Times* than she did at the *Globe and Mail*, where, despite her relative youth, she was a Canadian in a Canadian newspaper. While Addis worked on his redesign – actually redesigning the redesign he brought from England – Freeland focused increasingly on reshaping the *Report on Business*, a piece of the *Globe* about which she remains effusive.

Freeland says she admired the *Post* on a superficial level, for its design and competitive spirit, but that's about all. Long before she left Canada, she figured the paper was slumping. "I'm from Alberta, from redneck country, but even the people there were saying, 'I don't have to buy the *Post* any more because I know what the splash [main story] is going to be. It's either going to be that medicare sucks or that Jean Chrétien is a terrible prime minister.' That relentless pushing of an agenda is not the job of a newspaper. I didn't like the gratuitous use of titillation – the constant parading of bimbos and the harping on about celebrities. They pushed that too hard. It was like kids aping adult behaviour and not getting it quite right. They saw this slightly racier news mix in the *Daily Telegraph* in Britain and thought they could do the same. The *Telegraph* would occasionally have a picture of Liz Hurley on the front page, but it never pushed so hard in that direction."

Freeland had taken just six weeks off work after giving birth to her daughter and wanted to continue feeding her child breast milk, which meant she had to express it at the office. That meant going through numerous contortions to preserve office decorum and her own privacy. The breast pump, and the attendant palaver, caused a minor stir in the newsroom, as reported in the pages of *Frank*, where Freeland first discovered it had become an issue. Unwaveringly diplomatic in her recollections of life at the *Globe*, she was, nevertheless, hurt at the reaction. "I had a big job, and although nobody was holding a gun to my head, it was not the kind of situation where someone could fill in for me for six months. So I was happy to come back. I set up a system of blinds that I needed to pump my breast milk, but they wouldn't close properly so I had to have brown paper put on my windows. That elicited some comment, but people got over it. I felt the criticism was quite misogynist. There was one week when I was attacked for coming back too soon after my daughter was born and another where I was attacked for expressing milk in my office. What can you do? Damned if you do, damned if you don't. It was hurtful that people you work with would do that."

Addis was glad to have Freeland back and thought it healthy to have "elements of human craziness" introduced into the newsroom. "The more I could make people laugh, and recognize the absurdities in life, the better. So Chrystia had a baby, and she wanted to feed the baby with her own milk, so she brought her pumping machine to work. It wasn't that she brought the baby, but the milk had to be bottled and sent home to her husband, who would feed the baby. We set up a screen in her office so she could go behind it and express her milk. You could talk to her over the screen. So the conversations would be like, 'What are we going to do about that special *ROB* project?' and she would say, 'I'm proofing it now,' and things would fly over the top of the screen. There was some complaint that the screen wasn't positioned properly and you could see her pumping away from the newsroom.

I don't know whether it was true, but I think the whole thing was very charming and lovely."

Jan Wong said the episode did cause a stir, but the objections, such as they were, had nothing to do with the principle of Freeland expressing her milk but more in the way she did it. "It was so in your face and unsubtle and I think that was held against her. It was good that she did it, and I am totally in favour, but she did it more from a position of a Louis the Fourteenth than of a liberated woman in the workplace. Louis the Fourteenth would hold his morning meetings while he sat on the toilet. There was an air of nobility in her attitude and we were the peasants." Freeland had few allies at the *Globe*, and when she left there was much relief and little afterthought from the rank and file.

She returned to England and the *Financial Times* exactly two years after she had arrived. Looking back on the short but memorable experience, she hesitates when asked to recall the low points. She shares the impression of many *Globe* managers that the pundits who appeared on CBC Radio and TV and wrote articles in magazines were generally anti–*Globe and Mail* and willing its defeat at the hands of the *Post*. "I was surprised at the hostility and snarkiness toward the *Globe and Mail* in the great newspaper war. Given the liberal tilt of the Canadian chattering classes I would have thought they would be pro-*Globe*, but they wanted the icon to be shattered, which was based on meanness of spirit. I didn't like that. The *Frank* coverage bothered me at first, but I found it easier to tune out because I was used to a lot worse from the Soviet press. In Ukraine, just before the collapse of the Soviet Union, truly awful pieces would be written about journalists like me – she is a CIA agent type of stuff – so it wasn't totally unfamiliar."

On the wall of her London office, Freeland has a framed copy of the *Globe and Mail*'s front page and special section from September 12, 2001, an edition she supervised because Addis was on vacation in Britain at the time. This, Freeland says unhesitatingly, was her finest hour at the *Globe*.

"People come into my office here, and everyone who does says it is the best front page they have seen from that day. It showed the strength and greatness of the *Globe and Mail*. The newspaper's reaction was fantastic and the richness of commentary superb. September 11 was a Tuesday, and by Thursday we were all exhausted, and at some point that morning huge platters of sandwiches arrived at reception along with a letter from the Sheraton

Hotel saying we all must be tired so they wanted us to have sandwiches and coffee from their kitchen. You don't get that feeling too often, the feeling that you're not just a hack churning out the morning entertainment."

For Addis, it was a terrible experience to be stranded out of the country. "I was visiting the children on September 11 and walking down Blythe Road in Olympia and bumped into a famous New York journalist, Anthony Haden Guest. He was with Alexander Chancellor, a famous British journalist. One of them said, 'Look at those pictures on the TV.' We actually stood and watched through a shop window while the second plane flew into the World Trade Center. Then I phoned the office and Chrystia said it was the biggest story we had ever tried to cover and would I try to get back to Toronto. For four days, I couldn't get anywhere. I called once a day to see if she was okay, and I took on this job of monitoring the British papers and passing ideas on to the *Globe*. It was agony, but I couldn't do anything about it."

◆ ◆ ◆

Addis had rejigged some sections of the *Globe* in October 1999 shortly after arriving from England, combining arts and lifestyle coverage in the weekend edition under a new section called Saturday, and doing the same on weekdays in the Globe Review. As part of the Saturday newspaper, he also introduced a separate weekend Books section, which remains both successful and profitable. And he continued to work on his redesign. The initial plan he had brought from the U.K. had proven too radical and would not emerge until a year later, in September 2000, and then in much-diluted form.

Thomson executive and design guru Jim Jennings was long gone from the *Globe*, but contacts inside the newspaper were secretly sending him copies of various redesign plans and asking for his opinion. Says Jennings,

> The new editor comes in and wants to put his stamp on it. The first thing he wants to do is fiddle with the typography. The fundamental shell of the *Globe* pre- and post-Addis stayed unchanged. What he brought with him from London looked more like the *Observer* than anything in North America and brought a very British voice to the *Globe*. He had decided he wanted to redesign the paper, and although I had nothing to do with it, I did some handholding of certain staff

members and they did some back-channelling. I heard from members of every department who were trying to understand him, and I had copies of prototypes that were sent to me but probably shouldn't have been. I gave comments and waited to see what happened. Nothing was sacred for Richard. He wanted to shuffle the cards, and no matter what you thought about Richard personally he did a lot of good by getting people to think differently. He was never afraid to get his hands dirty.

"I learned very early that you don't discuss content with Mordecai. Sometimes it would work really well and other times it was less inspired, but he is not a rewriter."
— Kenneth Whyte, editor-in-chief, *National Post*

Wayne Gretzky joined the *National Post* stable less than a year after the newspaper's launch. The recently retired superstar was hired to write a Saturday column, which, though he didn't write it himself, was trumpeted as another big gun in the newspaper's arsenal. The Gretzky column was part of a cross-promotional deal between the *Post*, the Hollinger-owned hockey Web site faceoff.com, and MVP.com, an online merchandising enterprise owned by Gretzky, Michael Jordan, and former NHL quarterback John Elway.

Sports editor Graham Parley never saw Gretzky's contract and claims he would have stuck his fingers in his ears had anyone attempted to tell him any of the contents. "I just didn't want to know how much more than me he was getting paid," says Parley. "And I didn't want to have to lie when people asked me how much he was getting paid."

Despite rumours at the time that Gretzky's services were costing the *Post* $100,000 a year, Parley thinks that The Great One was availing himself, at minimal effort, more to boost the fortunes of his own business.

One thing Gretzky did insist upon was that Roy MacGregor be his ghost writer. The two had developed a good relationship during the NHL lockout in 1994, when Gretzky and other NHL stars played in Europe and MacGregor was sent by the *Ottawa Citizen* to report on their travels. On that trip, MacGregor also toured European museums and cultural meccas with Wayne's father, Walter, and the two had got along especially well. (MacGregor had also written *The Home Team: Fathers, Sons & Hockey*, a book that included a chapter on Walter and Wayne Gretzky, and, as the writer would subsequently learn, Gretzky's children were big fans of the Screech Owls, MacGregor's series of hockey mysteries for kids.)

The working relationship between Gretzky and MacGregor involved a weekly phone call, usually on a Thursday or Friday, during which the two would chat informally for anywhere between five minutes and half an hour. MacGregor would then write the column for presentation each Saturday under Gretzky's name and image, in the monochromatic woodcut style the *Post* used for most of its permanent columnists. After two or three weeks, Gretzky told MacGregor he trusted his judgment and not to bother sending him the columns any more for pre-approval. In return for writing the column, MacGregor had insisted on having all of Gretzky's numerous phone numbers to avoid the frustration of not being able to contact the busy, ever-mobile superstar.

"It was often difficult to connect with him. I would phone his home, talk to [Gretzky's wife] Janet, who was always very nice, or a man who works for them. But usually I called his cellphone. I had inside-the-house numbers, cell numbers, and all the personal numbers. I must have had five or six of them. We had some emotional conversations about the passing on of people, such as Marty McSorley's dad, whom we both knew, but we had a lot of laughs too. Wayne would be on golf courses sometimes, and almost always in California, but we did meet a couple of times at his restaurant in Toronto, where we could find a quiet corner and record an interview."

Gretzky's ghosted contributions to the *National Post* were a natural target for enemy sniping and they were often criticized for being too wishy-washy and not carrying the usual columnist's bite. Expectations that Gretzky would suddenly change character to provide some weekly controversy were unrealistic, says MacGregor.

"Wayne's tendency is to be level-headed and non-controversial, and that's how he developed his reputation. That tendency translated into print and a lot of people didn't like the column because he wasn't being the Johnny Miller of hockey or a John McEnroe type. But that isn't the hockey personality. The hockey personality that has been handed down through Jean Béliveau, Gordie Howe, and Bobby Orr – and with Gretzky pre-eminent – is to be more 'aw shucks' and very humble. He got the most passionate when he was talking about kids – his own kids, or the treatment of kids in minor hockey. They were his best columns because they carried authority."

The Gretzky-*Post* relationship hit an embarrassing bump in May 2000 when Gretzky gave Al Strachan, his friend at the *Toronto Sun*, the scoop that he was buying into the Phoenix Coyotes hockey club. It was a big story in the professional hockey world and Strachan's piece appeared in the *Sun*'s Saturday edition, while in the *Post* the same day Gretzky said he was only considering the proposal. It didn't look good.

"The deal happened late on a Friday night," explains MacGregor, "and people noted that he had given the story to a friend at the *Toronto Sun* instead of announcing it in his own column. But what those people didn't know was that the *National Post*'s early deadline was prohibitive and we couldn't have got the story in anyway. There was a call from Wayne on my cellphone at around 11:30 p.m. on the Friday. He had been trying to give me the heads-up, but the phone wasn't switched on."

Being in possession of all of Wayne Gretzky's telephone numbers wasn't without its pressure, much of which came from MacGregor's own *Post* colleagues. But Gretzky had only given them out on condition that MacGregor agree to keep them secret. "When the *Post* did one of those features about what celebrities carry in their purse or wallet, or what famous people are reading this summer – when everyone claims to be reading some obscure South American novel – I would get calls asking me to contact Gretzky and ask him this or that. But I never did it, because I was honour bound to stick by the deal."

The Gretzky column ended suddenly after a year in a decision MacGregor suspects was mutual. "I don't think the *Post* was happy with it because they weren't getting the reader feedback they expected, but then again I can't imagine them phoning him up like any other freelancer and saying, 'Look, sorry, Wayne, it's not working out.' So maybe the initiative came from him and he just got tired of doing it."

◆ ◆ ◆

Also prominent among the *Post*'s marquee guest columnists were novelist Mordecai Richler and former *Saturday Night* editor Robert Fulford, who had been part of the Toronto journalistic establishment for decades. When Ken Whyte first approached him, Fulford was writing for the *Globe* but was unhappy at the way he was being treated during the insecurity immediately after the launch of the *Post* and later by a new editor-in-chief from Britain he didn't like. And he admired the *National Post* and said so in an article he wrote for *Toronto Life* magazine. "I thought it was four times as good as it had a right to be and was amazed they could do such a good job out of the box. I thought it was the best newspaper published in Canada in my lifetime and decided I would really prefer to be there than at the *Globe*. Then things at the *Globe* got scattered and one of the things that was scattered was my column. They had it on Tuesday, then decided they wanted it on Saturday, and then in a different part of the paper. The copy editing fell to pieces and I had an editor who didn't seem to care what I wrote about."

The last straw for Fulford was a run-in with a copy editor – "a maniac," he maintains – who for reasons unexplained added the honorific "Mr." to about half-a-dozen historic names in his column. Hemingway, for instance, was changed to Mr. Hemingway. "There were a lot of names in the column, including about six dead people, and they were all changed. I mentioned Lincoln, but for some reason he was missed. I wrote them a memo and said, 'What's wrong with old Abe? How come he didn't get the Mr.?' Honestly, I almost expected to see Mr. Napoleon and Mr. Caesar in there. It was like a parody of copy-editing. I complained very mildly, and they said, 'Oh, sorry.' There was no 'We're sorry we made you look like a fucking idiot.' I would have burned with shame when I was editor of *Saturday Night* if we fucked up on somebody's copy and made someone look like an idiot. There was a carelessness in the air."

Fulford's first encounter with Richard Addis, shortly after the Englishman arrived in Toronto, was at the bar of the Four Seasons hotel, and Fulford, Canadian nationalist and able local historian, was hugely underwhelmed by the *Globe*'s British import. Fulford, astounded at Addis's apparent lack of knowledge of Canada and indifference to the country, laughs heartily at the memory of the meeting.

"He asked me what he should see in Toronto, so I told him. Then he asked what he should see in Canada, so I told him. I mean, can you imagine somebody taking a job in Australia and asking some Australian, 'What should I see in Australia?' Idiotically, I was being amiable, so I told him. I said for one thing take a weekend and go walking in Quebec City and you'll get some idea where the white man's Canada started. I told him to fly to Calgary and take the train to Vancouver, because you'll never see anything more spectacular. It was a strangely disembodied conversation."

Addis told Fulford he was in the throes of redesigning the *Globe*.

"But they redesigned it a little over a year ago," responded Fulford.

"Did they?"

Fulford still doesn't know whether Addis was kidding or whether he genuinely didn't know the newspaper had been recently made over. "If he was talking in code he was impossible to decode. Later I told someone who knows and likes him about the conversation. I said, 'He asked me, "What shall I see in Canada?"' and this person said, 'Oh, he was just testing you.' If that's true, I wish I'd told him to go to the Parliament buildings and listen to Question Period, or go see the High Arctic and get Pierre Berton to take you." (Addis might have appreciated the advice. He would eventually do something similar when he went on a northern canoe trip with his new best friend Margaret Atwood, her husband, and a few others.)

Fulford accepted Whyte's offer and defected from the *Globe* in December 1999. He was delighted, during a subsequent visit to a movie theatre, when a *Post* commercial, part of a series made by fallen theatre mogul Garth Drabinsky, appeared on the screen. The commercial featured numerous *Post* columnists in succession with a single word appearing on the screen for each one, apparently intended to sum up their journalistic attributes, and all against a dramatic musical background. "It was amazing. It was the Second Coming type music coupled with Citizen Kane editing. They kept throwing a word up on the screen like FEISTY, and then Christie would appear, and then the word TORQUEMADA and my picture. All my three daughters saw it and said, 'Dad, what's this about Torquemada?' I said, 'I don't know, and I am not going to ask!'"

Fulford knew, of course, that Tomás de Torquemada was the grand inquisitor in fifteenth-century Spain, and decided it was an over-the-top compliment on his abilities as a reporter.

◆ ◆ ◆

Compared to the patience, persuasion, and stroking Ken Whyte employed in hiring most of his marquee acts, Mordecai Richler, arguably his biggest catch, was relatively easy. It took one phone call.

"We're doing a paper," said Whyte. "Will you write for it?"

"Sure," replied Richler, a regular contributor to Whyte's *Saturday Night* magazine and columnist for the *Montreal Gazette*.

"We got along really well," remembers Whyte, "because we had worked for years together at *Saturday Night*. He wasn't that expensive to us because we shared him with the *Gazette* and he negotiated his deal directly with Conrad. He told me how he did it. He and Conrad sat down in London and started drinking, and Conrad said, 'We would like you to write for the *Gazette*.' He was already writing for *Saturday Night* and Conrad wanted something additional for the *Gazette*. Mordecai kept sitting there, and Conrad just kept offering more and more money. Mordecai said nothing and eventually it got up to a substantial amount, and he said okay. He was his own agent. I never met an agent for Mordecai in the eight years I worked with him. He did everything himself and did it well. He was an excellent negotiator and basically told you what you would have to pay, what the expenses would be, and take it or leave it."

Richler's *Post* columns were inconsistent, but Whyte had learned early in his dealings with the prolific writer that challenging the content of his work was pointless and, anyway, his less-inspired work was invariably better than most newspaper writing – or so Whyte decided. Recalling Richler, Whyte seems to forget his death at times and speaks in the present tense, with a fondness that isn't apparent for any other *Post* writer:

> I learned very early that you don't discuss content with Mordecai. He is capable of hack work and sometimes his column in *Saturday Night* was written, from one end to the other, in one sitting. Sometimes it would work really well and other times it was less inspired, but he is not a rewriter. You don't go back to him and say could you rewrite this. One time I had [*Saturday Night* editor] Barbara Moon rewrite him at *Saturday Night* and didn't send it back to him and it just ran edited. We had asked two or three times if he would mind suggestions

from us, and he said, no, he wouldn't mind. We would ask him to do changes and it would come back virtually unchanged. After a bit he phoned me and said, "Er, Ken, this column that you ran. It's not what I wrote and it doesn't sound like me." I said, "Well, we thought it could use some work, so we just had Barbara tighten it up a bit." And he said, "Well, it doesn't sound at all like me and, you know, Ken, nobody has ever done this to me before." So I had options: I could argue with him, I could say in future we will send it back to you after we rewrite it, or I could capitulate. I capitulated. That's just the way he works. It came out like it came out. You got what you got and usually it was very good. I loved him.

◆ ◆ ◆

Intense competition between the *Post* and the *Globe* brought a flurry of excitement to the Canadian book business, which got to play one newspaper off the other for excerpt rights – a bidding war Canadian-style that briefly doubled or tripled the going rate. Before the *Post* a writer could expect no more than $2,500 for a newspaper excerpt, but for a couple of years after the literary-minded Richard Addis got the *Globe*'s editor-in-chief job, the rates spiked and in at least one case reached $10,000.

According to book publishing convention, the publisher's representative negotiating the price for excerpts does not reveal to one bidder the identity of the other. But that didn't stop the *Post* or the *Globe* trying to find out.

It was all part of the fun, says one "negotiator." "I sometimes let the *Post* think it was the *Globe* when it wasn't, and that made them bid higher. That's my job. I didn't lead them to believe it was the *Globe*, but they would ask leading questions and I wouldn't answer them. So it was like, 'Can we assume the other bidder is the other national newspaper?' and we would both laugh knowingly. But I could have been talking about the *Hamilton Spectator*."

While still small potatoes compared to the United States or Britain, where excerpts go for hundreds of thousands of dollars, it was a nice little bonus for a few Canadian writers.

Excerpt rights aside, Addis was also able to attract a prestigious stable of writers to the *Globe*'s pages, his new friend Margaret Atwood, Rohinton

Mistry, and Michael Ondaatje among them. There were others, some occasional, some regular, including Rex Murphy, Ian Brown, Peter Gzowski, and Alberto Manguel.

Some writers, Atwood and Manguel included, refused to write for the *Post* because they objected to its politics. Atwood had walked the picket line with strikers at Conrad Black's *Calgary Herald* during a book tour, and Manguel, a homosexual, perceived the *Post* to be anti-gay.

Black wrote to one literary agent asking why so many writers were being placed in the *Globe* and not in the *Post*. The answer, he was told, was partly political, partly financial – the *Globe* was often prepared to pay more – and partly because Addis had been so remarkably successful in personally cultivating Toronto's literati.

But the *Post* had its own prominent literary columnists – most obviously Black's friend Mordecai Richler – and its own victories in the "my newspaper is more literary than yours" battle.

It started in the *Post*'s first week. The *Globe*'s Jan Wong and her editor, Sarah Murdoch, were attempting to arrange an interview with Tom Wolfe, whose book *A Man in Full* was one of the major publishing events of the North American season. Wolfe had agreed to do just one Canadian newspaper interview and left it to his publisher to decide which. The publisher chose the *National Post*'s John Bentley Mays, who, like Wolfe, had been raised in the American south. More important, Wong was told, the *Post* had promised to give the feature story prominent play, and anyway Wong's often acerbic Lunch With column had made her a pariah among book publishers.

The loss of the Wolfe interview was a wake-up call for the *Globe*, says Wong. "We wanted it, and thought we were going to get it, but we would not promise the publishers anything. We said, 'Well, use your brains. Of course he's going to get good play, but we are not going to promise anything.' There was a lot of gnashing of teeth, and then it went to John Bentley Mays. That's when we realized we no longer had a monopoly."

British newspapers, engaged in daily cutthroat competition, are masters at pre-empting each other's scoops, exclusive interviews often bought for large amounts of money. Both the *Post* and the *Globe* took lessons from that, and if one knew the other was going to get a major personality interview, the loser would find a way to paper-over the crack, usually buying an article from a foreign publication that had already interviewed the person in question. It wasn't difficult, and for the average reader probably didn't matter a great deal. But this was mostly about pride and not giving the other guy an inch.

17 KEN'S KIDS

"It was indicative of the newspaper war environment that people like me were being plucked out of nowhere and given these gorgeous gigs. It was a ridiculous, nutty period."

– Shinan Govani, columnist, *National Post*

Ken Whyte had a reputation for being negatively disposed to journalism schools, largely because he once told *Toronto Life* magazine that, given the choice of two graduates with equal qualifications, he would choose the one who had not graduated from journalism school. Such a statement, coming as it did from a high-profile editor, was, understandably, not well received in the corridors of journalism academia.

What Whyte really didn't like was Toronto's Ryerson University journalism program in general ("third rate," he says) and its magazine program in particular ("horrible"). It is often said that journalism is better practised than studied, and this was Whyte's working philosophy as he chose his B team to operate alongside his highly paid veterans.

The *National Post* was not a journalism graduate free zone, but Whyte assigned half a dozen raw prospects with no specific training to the Southam News office in Toronto during the summer of 1998. He left them with the impression that if they didn't totally screw up, they might get a job at the new newspaper.

He left the impression but, in typical Whyte fashion, did not state anything categorically. These were Ken's Kids, twenty-somethings who did not know how to construct a news story and had no preparation for the day-to-day general news bureau routine that could have a reporter at a criminal court trial one day, covering arcane Bay Street business news the next, and sports the day after. Whyte found others – or they found him – through Toronto's alternative press, through word of mouth, or through submissions he had received at *Saturday Night*. And for an editor who had been spending large on established talent, the untried were cheap hires, in some cases working for the relative pittance of $35,000 a year.

However he found them, and irrespective of the numerous, passionate opinions pro and con about the *National Post*, the newspaper certainly broke a logjam that had prevented the flow of young people into newspaper journalism. It was a logjam caused by cuts and hiring freezes, a lack of alternative employment for older journalists who tired of the business, and, most important, a lack of real, cutthroat competition, all of which had allowed individual newspapers to exist comfortably in their own niches.

Staticism had hit Canadian journalism. People were hunkered down and holding on to their jobs. Even the CBC's budget was being slashed by the federal government to the tune of hundreds of millions of dollars, and the prevailing atmosphere was grim. For the unhappiest, caught on career downslides, the traditional escape route into government jobs had been blocked, temporarily, by public-sector cuts. The symbiotic draining away of the unhappy had been especially well established in Toronto, where government and its numerous agencies had a seemingly insatiable appetite for skilled journalists to staff their media-relations departments. For their part, journalists no longer fired by a unique mission found happier, more secure environments where they were sure to earn significantly more money, work at a more leisurely pace, and emerge with a good pension. At the other end of the pipe, young journalism graduates had found entry-level jobs and seasoned enthusiasts from whom to learn.

For Whyte, there were other practical reasons for hiring young people, aside from the relatively modest salaries he had to pay them. "There had been a hiring freeze for five or ten years and there was a generation of young people who would normally have gone into newspapers. We wanted people who weren't too set in their ways. We couldn't get a lot of older, established people out of their jobs because there was risk involved and they had mortgages and kids and spouses with jobs in other cities. And there was still a feeling that it was all a bit of a joke and Conrad wasn't really serious."

❖ ❖ ❖

Chris Jones had earned a graduate degree in urban planning from the University of Toronto at around about the same time he realized he didn't want to be an urban planner. He was living at the graduate residence of Massey College, whose master was John Fraser, a former *Globe and Mail* correspondent who had preceded Whyte as editor of *Saturday Night*. Fraser, who had an acrimonious relationship with Barbara Amiel, quit when Conrad Black bought the magazine.

Jones told Fraser he was interested in writing, and Fraser, apparently impressed at the young man's thesis introduction, passed his name on to Whyte, who summoned him for an interview at the *Saturday Night* offices.

Jones dropped his resumé in a puddle on the way to the interview as a prelude to what he considered a disastrous encounter with the enigmatic editor. It apparently didn't occur to Whyte that Jones did not know that a new daily newspaper was under construction, and the two spent twenty minutes speaking at cross purposes.

"Ken put his feet on his desk and started talking about this newspaper, which I knew nothing about. He was talking about a newspaper, and I thought I was there for a job at the magazine. So I kept correcting him. He would say newspaper and I would reply and deliberately emphasize the word *magazine*. It was a terrible interview. He was very friendly, but we were on totally different wavelengths."

Jones was keen on sports, and Whyte, equally enthusiastic on the subject, wanted to know who Jones's favourite columnists were. He mentioned the *New Yorker*'s Roger Angell and the legendary *Washington Post* columnist Shirley Povic, who was to die a couple of months later at age ninety-two.

"What about Canadians?" asked Whyte.

"Stephen Brunt," responded Jones, under pressure.

"What about Cam Cole?" asked Whyte of his favourite, soon-to-be-hired columnist from Edmonton.

"Er, yeah, Cam's great," replied Jones, who had never even heard of him but felt that admitting it would scupper his chances to the get the job he wasn't even being interviewed for.

Jones answered a few questions about his favourite authors, and the interview, conducted more in the manner of a casual conversation, ended.

"I left thinking two things: that Ken was passionate about writing and that I would never see him again. I was going on vacation, and he told me to call when I got back, but I just dismissed that as politeness."

Whyte's ubiquitous assistant, Lisa Cooperman, called shortly afterwards, however, to offer him a job. Jones accepted the swift apprenticeship at the Southam News bureau along with several other prospects, including Jeannie Marshall, Katrina Onstad, Jennifer Prittie, Patrick Graham, and Shannon Black, Conrad's niece and, by common consensus, the best reporter in the group.

Jones clearly recalls his first day as a real-life newsman:

> It was pouring rain. I tried to look good getting there and there was Jennifer Prittie dressed immaculately in a pinstriped suit shaking the rain off an umbrella. I thought I was going to get my ass kicked. I was told to listen to a news conference by phone, something to do with the financial industry, which I knew nothing about. I was transcribing for a story [Southam business reporter] Theresa Tedesco was writing, but I couldn't hear the questions, just the answers and nobody identified themselves. I panicked and that was what the whole summer was like. I never really felt I knew what I was writing about. I covered a rape trial, did municipal government stories, and covered Curtis Joseph signing for the Leafs, but I never did quite master the inverted pyramid. I got caught up in it all, but because I had never wanted to work at a newspaper, I had the attitude that if it works, it works, and if it doesn't I'll do something else.

Katrina Onstad, a reluctant recruit, had been studying for her MA in English literature, freelancing on the periphery of the journalism business, writing for $50 an article in the alternative press, getting better paid by *Toronto Life* magazine, waiting tables, and interning at *Canadian Business* magazine. She had first met Whyte after submitting an article called "The Myth of Youth Crime" to *Saturday Night* and the two hit it off. She was on the verge of committing herself full-time to academic studies when Whyte called to tell her about the new newspaper. Says Onstad,

> Ken had been great to me, because I was pretty young. It was my first couple of years in the industry and I hadn't been to journalism school.

So we talked and he asked me what I was studying, and I said this eco structure of Alice Munro's blah, blah, blah about abortion and women, and Ken just rolled his eyes as if to say, "Oh, give me a break." He was totally uninterested, but I kind of liked that about him. He told me I should be part of this newspaper and I wasn't even sure if I really wanted to be. I heard the name Conrad Black and I could sense that it was going to be something of a mouthpiece for the right and I wasn't sure I was comfortable with that. And it sounded a little risky and I wasn't feeling that adventurous. So I said, "Okay, just call me when it comes out," but he became kind of persistent. He put his feet up on his desk, like he does, and put his hands behind head and said, "What would you most like to do? What would make you commit to journalism in this country?"

Onstad reached high and said she wanted to be an artsy pop culture columnist and, much to her surprise, Whyte agreed, or seemed to. It was June 1998 and they agreed to reconvene. "With Ken, things move either incredibly rapidly or incredibly slowly," says Onstad. "I left thinking, 'Wow, I have a new job,' and then I couldn't get him for like two weeks, and then I thought, 'Okay, screw that, it's not going to happen.' I had this opportunity to go to New York for a few months, which I decided to take and see if the paper existed when I got back. But it all seemed too good to be true, and people were raising their eyebrows and saying this will never happen. So I made my plans and then, of course, as soon as everything was solidified, Ken called me and said, 'Can you start next week?' And I said, 'Why? There's not even a paper,' and he told me he wanted his new hires to start training at Southam. In retrospect, it all seems a bit mad."

Onstad eventually joined her new colleagues in a back room at the Southam bureau and then became concerned, and increasingly confused, over whether she actually had a job at the new newspaper. "It was weird. I actually thought I had a job, and then it became clear that the Southam thing was more of a try-out situation. I don't know if I misheard Ken and I don't think he deliberately misled me. That's just Ken's kind of vagueness, and you sort of hear what you want to hear after a while, because you feel you have to hear something definitive. I wish I had recorded those conversations or something so I could hear it again exactly, but I thought Southam was a stepping stone to the *Post*. Then we heard we were going to be interviewed for these *Post* positions and people at Southam were suddenly telling us that nothing was certain. I was like, 'Well, why am I here?' It was a very strange summer."

Like many others, Onstad didn't know what to make of Whyte:

> The first word that comes to mind is *screwball*, but I can't decide if he's enigmatic or not that complex. He is incredibly bright and engaged. We talked about movies and art. He's a huge Woody Allen freak. He plays both sides of the fence and has the down-home Alberta-boy shtick, like I-don't-get-your-big-city-ways thing. Go to a Chinese restaurant with Ken and he'll order a grilled cheese sandwich because he doesn't like ethnic food. He has this chubby face and acts unsophisticated, but he's also very worldly and a freak for stories and ideas. But it seems to work for him. He has a kind of arrogance and doesn't seem to give a shit what people think of him, but I don't know whether that's true either. I don't know what it was about Ken, but I always felt I was the girl at the school dance and he was the football player, and many people at the *Post* felt that same aura. I would get literally tonguetied when he would come round and say, "Well, what have you got for me today?" He puts all the responsibility on you to be clever and to keep the conversation going.

The new recruits were placed under the wing of bureau chief Joan Walters, a popular boss who attempted to teach them the basics of news reporting by throwing them into a variety of assignments and familiarizing them with the daily grind of news bureau reporting, which demands well-honed reportorial skill and experience. The new "team" had little of either.

Whether real or imagined, the trainees felt an undercurrent of resentment toward them. "The bureau was a strange, bare bones place, like the netherworld," says Onstad, "and I sensed that we weren't particularly welcome. There was a schism between this weird little group of people that Ken had forced upon them and the people who worked there by choice. This was their workplace. So there was a divide between us, which I understand completely. And we were just doing such random things, like you would just come in at nine in the morning and have no idea what you were going to do. I thought I would be doing arts stuff and I was on this squeegee kid beat that summer because there was all that controversy about the squeegee kids and [Mayor] Mel Lastman had called them savages."

General news reporting often requires reporters to gain instant expertise in subjects they know little or nothing about. This was the aspect of bureau work that unnerved Whyte's young recruits the most. Squeegee kids getting the boot from local authorities was a relatively easy concept to grasp, but fluctuations in the bond market demanded a little more than a basic understanding of the human condition. Onstad recalls one story that was passed around like a hot potato before being assigned to Chris Jones, the youngest, more amiable member of the group.

"Something had happened with bonds – higher or lower yield, something good or bad," Onstad remembers. "We really had no idea. I said no, I'm totally unqualified to do this, I don't even know what you're talking about, I can't do it. It was the end of summer, and people were getting really fed up and everyone said no. And Chris said he would do it, and I just remember him in the backroom going, 'Does anybody know what a bond is?' And we're looking up the word in the dictionary, and we thought, hey, this is really a low point."

The group, feeling barely tolerated and unsure of where it was all going to lead, became close and, in most cases, remained friends with memories of the bureau as a common bond.

News agency journalists work for many masters and, unlike reporters employed by a specific newspaper, they usually have no idea how a particular story will be received or whether any newspaper will even use it. Because recognition is a huge part of the reward of being a news reporter, it takes a thick skin to work for a news agency, and because Southam had no newspaper in Toronto before Black started the *Post*, the bureau reporters were denied the instant gratification of being able to pick up that day's edition to see how the story they wrote the day before was played. It only accentuated the young reporters' feeling of disconnection, recalls Onstad.

"We were sort of floating around and nothing was ever really explained to us. Sometimes we'd go out for lunch and just kind of look at each other and go, 'Do you know why we're here? What are you working on today?' And someone would be like, 'I'm working on rewriting wire copy about the tobacco industry,' and then Chris would be doing something like a three-part story on graffiti artists, and you never knew where it was going, because there was no actual paper. So it would go off into the void and sometimes you'd get clippings on your desk and you'd be like, 'Oh, I appeared in the *Sault Ste Marie Bugle* this week!' It was just really strange."

As the launch of the *Post* got closer, and the lure of the new daily became irresistible, the anxiety increased. The fledgling newspaper reporters, still unsure of whether they had roles at the new paper, were called, one by one, over a period of weeks, to the *Post* offices at Don Mills. The last days, recalls Onstad, were tense. "You'd get this kind of tap on the shoulder. I can't remember who went first, but you'd come in one morning and someone would be packing their box and getting ready to leave and the rest of us would be trying to call Ken to get some kind of answer about what was happening."

Onstad's next visit to Don Mills was to meet newly arrived Englishman Tim Rostron, who had been appointed arts editor. The trip, as far as she was concerned, was to discuss her placement and a few other pre-employment details. After a long, arduous trudge from the nearest subway station, she arrived at Canadian journalism's unlikely new Mecca to meet her boss.

"I couldn't believe how many Brits were in the office. They should have had Beefeaters posted at the door. I was like, 'Am I in the right place?' The office was still sort of half-formed, with people banging things and building, but it seemed quite exciting. Tim said let's meet in the confectionary, and I just looked at him, and he said 'Oh, perhaps you call it the cafeteria.' He had arrived a couple of days before and looked a little shell-shocked. So we went to the confectionary and he clearly had no idea who I was."

Rostron, an import from the *Daily Telegraph*, was brief. He confirmed to Onstad that Whyte was keen on her work, flipped through clips of articles she had written and asked her what she would like to do for the newspaper. She gave him half a dozen ideas, which he seemed to like, and the brief encounter ended with a vague promise to meet again. "I was like, Oh my God, was that a job interview? Halfway into it I thought, I'm actually applying here, even though I had just spent three months training, and Ken had given me all these sort of half-big commitments. Other than that, it was a good meeting, I think we clicked."

It eventually became clear that Onstad's time would be split between the Arts and Life sections and she got to pack her box at the Southam bureau and carry it back to Don Mills, wearing the badge of honour that came with a job at the *National Post*.

What the trainees didn't know – or perhaps even think of – was that the hiring process was, to say the least, disorganized and they were at the bottom of the pile. Greater names were also left in states of limbo and fury. It's a defect deputy editor Martin Newland recognized. "We made a lot of enemies because we weren't equipped for the human resources thing. We would make a note ten minutes into the interview that we wouldn't be hiring a person but we would forget to tell them. We did our best, but loads of people got left by the wayside – some very important people. We were unpopular for taking key talent from the Southam titles but also unpopular because of the way we were perceived to have treated people we didn't want. If we had to do it all again, we would have a team to deal with that."

Newland had called Chris Jones in for an interview in the *Post* cafeteria with himself and sports editor Graham Parley. Newland said he wanted clear, concise stories written on deadline and Parley wanted magazine-style feature writing.

"I ended up going down the middle," says Jones, "because I didn't want to piss either of them off. So I said I could do both, which I couldn't."

Newland called a couple of weeks later with an unenthusiastic endorsement and terse invitation. "Ken sees something in you," he said. "I have no idea what, but you're coming to the *Post*."

Jones got several calls afterwards switching him from news to sports, from sports to news, and back again. He naively assumed they were fighting over him, which they were, but not in the way he imagined. Parley had reluctantly agreed to take Jones after Whyte promised it would not count against the sports department's hiring quota.

❖ ❖ ❖

Drag queen Enza "Supermodel" Anderson, onetime candidate for leadership of the Canadian Alliance, subscribed to the *National Post* and told the Toronto alternative newspaper *Xtra* that he fully supported the party's stand on beefing up Canada's military and police services, because "I just love a man in a uniform."

Enza is an acquaintance of gay reporter Mitchel Raphael, who contributed an edge to the *Post* that made Toronto's alternate publications nervous and helped cement the newspaper's reputation as an "out there" daily.

Enza was one loyal subscriber, but, in a way, so was the young man on Toronto's hustler strip who approached Raphael one day to discuss an article Raphael had written for the *Post*. Business was slow, so the hustler had kicked open a *Post* box, stolen a copy, and become engaged by a Raphael piece on the Toronto club scene.

"The drag queen, the bored hustler waiting for johns to show up, and Bay Street people. That was the *Post* readership," laughs Raphael.

A Torontonian from a well-to-do *Globe*-reading legal family, Raphael covered the gay scene and other non-mainstream cultural activity for the *Post*. He was one of many who in the spring of 1998 saw an ad in *NOW* magazine – an all-but-blank page with the words "All This Could Be Yours" – soliciting writers for the new daily. Raphael had done some work for alternative publications and freelanced for the *Toronto Star*, so he applied. The paper signed him up, and he started work at the *Post* at age thirty-one, around the average age of those who had been recruited from the Southam bureau.

Like many others, Raphael created his own beat at the *Post* and wrote on a variety of topics, from the rave scene, electronic music, Ricky Martin's sexuality, the drug ecstasy, or pre-operative transsexuals ("shemales") who wanted to keep their penises. Raphael called that one "my chick with a dick story."

Raphael ran into some resistance with a story inspired by a news story on a gay Web site that suggested 68 per cent of gay men thought Stockwell Day, then leader of the official opposition, was sexy. The basic thesis, according to Raphael, was that gay men have a history of eroticizing their enemies, and anyway, Day got huge points in the gay community for his infamous appearance in a wetsuit. "So I offered this broader piece about gay men and their enemies. It was classic *National Post*: gay men, Stockwell Day, Mark Walhberg, and Eminem all in the same story. They said, 'We'll ask Ken first,' and he said, 'Great, do it.' The *Post* captured the youth market. If you were young and hip and a newspaper reader, you read the *Post*, and that's a huge coup, because usually young people read the paper that their parents got. And when the *Toronto Star* is giving full-page ads to the big electronic music festival, you know they are worried."

On the face of it, an openly gay writer with spiked hair might not fit well in a house of right-wing ideology and small-c conservatism, but Raphael found the experience remarkably comfortable:

The liberal thing is that gays are just like us except it's two guys or two girls and they want marriage rights and to adopt and all that. Right-wingers perceive gay culture as just being different, which of course it is. I never pushed the "everyone is born this way" line and all that gay activist mantra stuff. I've always felt that we live in a democratic society and people can choose what they want. The *Post* sort of liked that I did the weird stuff – and not just the queer stuff, but rave and club culture. I remember Rebecca Eckler coming up to me after a few months and saying, "How do you get away with writing this stuff in Conrad's paper?" I said, "Rebecca, we can get away with anything we want in the first year. Whether we are or not, we're supposed to be the best journalists in Canada, so there's no way they're going to fire us in the first year, because it would be admitting they made a mistake. So enjoy the ride."

Raphael says the *Post* was instrumental in defusing the hysteria around electronic music, ecstasy, and the youth dance culture that was being portrayed with shock and horror in other media:

If these kids had been smoking pot, editors at the *Toronto Star* would have been rolling their joints for them. At the *National Post*, they may have been conservatives but they were conservatives in their twenties and thirties and it was very capitalist in that the person with the best idea won out. One editor asked me where he could score some ecstasy, and I remember one of the editorial writers pitching an editorial on raves, and Ken's response was "just run it by Mitchel first," so I felt great. And it's better for alternative radical voices to be in places like the *Post*, because that's whom you're trying to talk to and whose minds you're trying to open up. It doesn't matter whether people don't like the drug culture, gay culture, music culture, or fetish culture. What matters is they understand it.

Raphael, party animal by choice and occasionally by professional obligation, was double-booked the night of the *Post*'s glamorous first anniversary bash at the Royal Ontario Museum, having assigned himself to write about the Northbound Leather company's annual fashion show and fetish party being held the same night at the Docks. The two events presented a dilemma, the newspaper party being relatively formal and the fetish party demanding a more adventurous getup. Raphael settled for spiked hair and a rubber jacket.

The evening led him inevitably to Conrad Black, who seemed unimpressed, and into an intense discussion with Barbara Amiel. "Conrad knew me from the newsroom, when my hair was shaved on the sides and I had these wedges in them. It was called the disco ball. And now I had a halo of bleached blond longer hair in a ring of spikes. I always got this look from Conrad saying 'get a proper haircut,' but I got on well with Barbara socially. With Barbara it's like a conservative drag act. She could be such a serious diva, and loved by the gay community, if she shifted her politics a little. She said she liked my hair, so we had an intense conversation about hair products. I used Fudge, which was this Aussie brand, and she told me she used Bed Head, which is totally this urban downtown product. So we bonded on hair."

Raphael met a friend of a *Post* editorial writer at the ROM party and *they* bonded when the reporter noticed something bulging under the neck of the stranger's shirt. It was a dog collar. "I said, 'Oh, are you going to Northbound afterwards?' and he said yes. So I found a date at Conrad's party. That's the paradox of the *Post*: Tory editorial writer brings his gay best friend to Conrad Black's bash, who hooks up with the alternative reporter and heads off to the Northbound fetish party."

◆ ◆ ◆

The *Post* threw good parties. There were anniversary parties that began with the big expensive bash at the Royal Ontario Museum and subsequent anniversary celebrations that became progressively more modest as the hubris declined but twice included scantily clad newsboys wearing newsboy hats and newspaper bags. They came from a Toronto modelling agency recommended by Mitchel Raphael. There were *Post*-sponsored Toronto Film Festival parties, including one featuring a perfunctory appearance by Elton John and his boyfriend, David Furnish, from which *Post* employees were largely excluded. And there were regular boozy house parties where everyone, from the owner of the newspaper on down, was welcome.

At one film festival party favoured with an appearance by the actor Willem Dafoe, Raphael, opinionated in matters of music, caught the ear of

Lynn Munro, who was the newspaper's executive in charge of promotion and marketing.

"This music sucks," he said loud enough for her to hear. "Who's the bar mitzvah deejay?"

With the second anniversary party coming up, Barbara Amiel had suggested possibly booking The Supremes, but Raphael, sticking to territory he knew best, offered to get three people he knew who could dress like The Supremes to lip-synch their songs. "At that point Gordon Fisher walks by and Lynn says to him, 'Hey, Gord, what do you think of having three drag queens come to lip-synch to The Supremes?' He just smiled and rolled his eyes. I said you have to play something the twenty-year-olds from the *Post* will like and Ken will like and music that won't make Conrad want to put his fingers in his ears. In the end Barbara agreed to the deejay Daniel Paquette, who had a night at Buddies in Bad Times, the queer theatre in Toronto. He played dance mixes and a Captain and Tennille song. Ken came over after and said, 'I can't believe he played Captain and Tennille.' He also played the theme from *Love Boat*, and when Barbara and Conrad arrived she went up to the dee-jay booth and shouted, 'Great beats!' Daniel was impressed, because, oh my God, she is so fierce and had a reputation for bashing gays."

Shinan Govani, who had never studied journalism, was a former aide to an Ontario Conservative cabinet minister and barely twenty-seven when he started his daily gossip column at the *Post*. He left the Ontario legislature at Queen's Park, Toronto, and lived briefly in Washington at the height of the media fuss around the Bill Clinton–Monica Lewinsky affair, which gave him material for a piece he managed to get published in John Kennedy Jr.'s *George* magazine. Using the *George* article as a self-promotion tool, he marketed himself as a pop-culture journalist and into some freelance work in Toronto. It was the springboard he needed to make the monumental jump into Canada's new daily.

"I was a pop-culture writer with a thing for gossip. Ken read my stuff and saw something before I knew I had it. I knew I could turn a phrase, was manically social, and could be comedic on demand. When I worked at Queen's Park, I was never interested in policy issues but more the interactions and tensions between the various personalities. The newspaper war was a candy store for freelancers. You could sell almost any idea you came up with, but Ken offered me this gig as a gossip columnist, which I had never thought of before. One doesn't go to one's guidance counsellor at high school and say, 'I want to be a gossip columnist.' It's an extraterrestrial sort of thing."

Whyte told Govani he wanted a gossip column on current issues from all over the world, but one that didn't include "Canadian newscasters" or, indeed, any Canadians, unless they were Pamela Anderson or Jim Carrey.

"I would mix it up with my own digging and living the life of eating off napkins at parties. I covered music, fashion, society, politics, and I eventually started doing Toronto stuff, and there was an appetite for it. Gossip doesn't have to be vicious or tawdry, although in some cases it is. It's innuendo and suggestion with a narrative. It needs to play into the voyeur in all of us."

Despite his inexperience and relative youth, Govani was allowed to roam free and write about what, and whom, he chose – with the eventual exception of image-conscious Céline Dion, whose people threatened a lawsuit over a reference in his column to nude sunbathing, and Governor General Adrienne Clarkson and her husband, John Ralston Saul, who were often targets of darts. Govani was sent a message that the Clarkson–Ralston Saul references had become too regular and perhaps he might lay off them for a while.

"The *Post* enjoyed shit-disturbing and wasn't reverent. I was never told, 'Don't be as cheeky and bitchy as you are,' or never asked to leave out those annoying French phrases that I like to use. I was thrown into the pool and suddenly I was writing a daily column for a national newspaper. It was indicative of the newspaper war environment that young people like me were being plucked out of nowhere and given these gorgeous gigs. It was a ridiculous, nutty period. Young people are never likely to have the same opportunity again."

Like Mitchel Raphael, Govani did the party circuit and periodically bumped into the Blacks. And like many other *Post* writers, he was surprised when Conrad Black showed some recognition of his work. Given that Black was prone to calling the *Post*'s first executive editor, Kirk LaPointe, and asking him to do something to eliminate the number of typographical errors, it was clear he was reading his newspaper very closely. Still, Govani was not the first to be impressed or flattered by Black's remarkable recall and attention to detail.

"We met at the Elton John party. Conrad seemed to know me and we had a nice conversation. It wasn't, 'Oh, Shinan! How are you?' or anything familiar, but he was very pleasant. Conrad and Barbara are such characters in a country that has a huge shortage of characters. At the first anniversary, which was like 'Conrad's bar mitzvah' party, I remember thinking, 'Boy, these people are so confident and, boy, do they have money. Where does the money come from?' And at that party, Conrad gave a supremely confident and intoxicating speech in very eloquent language but basically he said, 'We're kicking everyone's ass.'"

◆ ◆ ◆

The *Post* launched many careers but few were more talked about than that of Rebecca Eckler, exponent of "me journalism," also, if the writer is female, known as "chick lit," "girl journalism," and "chick journalism." Eckler's shtick has been to make fun of herself and expose her personal life to the world – columns about her relationships, pregnancy, drinking . . . few things, seemingly, are off limits. Love her work or hate it – and both camps are well populated – she has developed into one of the best-read columnists in the country and inspired others, including her good friend Leah McLaren, columnist at the *Globe and Mail*, who Eckler says is more confident and secure than she is. The two share nasty e-mails they get from readers and regularly seek solace from each other when correspondence becomes especially vicious. Journalists are often encouraged to publish their office e-mail addresses. It's a subtle way of soliciting stories or information, but some readers feel it gives them carte blanche to insult, often obscenely.

The proliferation of "me journalism" moved the normally staid *Globe and Mail* political columnist Jeffrey Simpson to write an irritable satire on the subject titled "Welcome to Me, Myself and I." It ended: "Back in my carpeted office, I swept reports, documents, speeches, books into the trash. I closed my eyes. I began to reconstruct my childhood."

Eckler, obviously canny, naturally funny, and girlish-sounding despite being in her thirties, graduated from the Ryerson journalism program in 1996 and applied for summer internships at numerous newspapers, as graduating journalists usually do. The *Calgary Herald* was the only newspaper to offer her a job, so she went to Calgary for the summer, and two subsequent summers, working back in Toronto the rest of the year as a junior producer on Pamela Wallin's TV show, rounding up guests and generating ideas for the program.

"I had two or three interviews with the *Globe and Mail* and they wouldn't hire me. Nor would the *Star*. I swear on my life that I got a rejection letter from the *Globe* the day after the interview. It was like they sent the letter out before the interview."

Eckler had met Ken Whyte when she was working for a local Toronto community paper and he was editor of *Saturday Night* and living in an area of the city served by her newspaper. Whyte was the cover story. "It was kind of pathetic," remembers Eckler. "It was totally before the *National Post*. I was a student, and it was like, whatever, I'm going to meet this guy and interview him. I didn't do any research. I didn't think, 'He's the editor of *Saturday Night*. Maybe I could woo him and get a job.' I was just thinking about the $150 I would get for writing the story. When I first met him I thought, 'Oh my God, he's such a nice guy. So laid-back.' I had done lots of interviews before and he was the first person to ask me about myself. Later I sent him clippings from the *Calgary Herald* and he'd give me advice. I don't know why I did that, because I was never a schmoozer. We met again about a year later on Pamela Wallin. He was a guest twice."

She called Whyte at the end of the summer, sent more clippings from the *Herald*, and was hired to work on the *Post*'s Toronto section about two weeks before the newspaper launched. She met Whyte briefly at a pre-launch party and received a friendly greeting.

"What are you doing here?" he asked.

"I'm working for you," she replied somewhat puzzled.

"Oh, that's great," he said, somewhat vaguely.

"They called the Toronto section the baby section, because we were the least experienced. Martin Newland picked me out and encouraged me. I had done this story during the transit strike and he liked it. The idea was to stand at a bus stop, pretend I didn't know there was a strike, and find out how nice, or not nice, people would be. Some people were like, 'Yeah, the bus will be right along . . .' Martin said, 'We want you to do that on the Ontario election.' I was actually throwing up before the election, I was so nervous. I was writing about whether they were serving hot dogs or hamburgers and what the wives were wearing. It was a total learning experience. I was writing daily and being thrown in with these serious political writers who were like, 'What are you writing?' Some took me under their wing and explained the etiquette but others were really nasty."

Eckler developed her style and cemented her reputation, for better or worse, with a series of stories from Spring Break in Daytona in February 2000 – including a gutsy, first-person piece about appearing in a wet T-shirt contest – and, more infamously, a summer 2001 series from the Surf Diva School in San Diego, where she attended the all-female school, chronicled her attempts at becoming proficient on a surf board, and profiled some of her wackier fellow students. The series is often used as an example of the *Post*'s excessive spending, but Eckler says it only cost $800. "I was camping. It cost nothing compared to what other people spent. The only thing of mine that cost the *Post* a lot were my cellphone bills, but I got those under control."

Eckler was alone in the *National Post* elevator when she first met Conrad Black. "His wife had sent me a very nice note after the wet T-shirt contest piece, but he didn't know who I was. The elevator ride to the third-floor newsroom takes about three seconds, but it seemed a lot longer. I said, 'Oh, hi,' and he said something about the weather, but I didn't understand the word. I'd never heard it before. He made me so nervous. I asked him twice how he was, and the second time he said, 'I'm still fine.' I can't remember the word he used about the weather, but I remember running to my thesaurus to find out what he was saying. It meant springlike."

◆ ◆ ◆

Katrina Onstad became the *Post*'s TV critic for a while after asking to review *Felicity*, the new sitcom about a hip high-school student. "Ken came by my desk and said, 'Good piece,' and walked away and then [arts editor] Tim Rostron said, 'Right, we want you to write more about television from now on.' And that's how I became a TV critic."

Onstad eventually moved into movie reviewing and famously became one of the first journalists to leave the *Post* voluntarily. *MVP*, the movie about a hockey-playing primate, did it. She packed up and travelled to India shortly after the 2000 Toronto Film Festival. "I was burned out and felt I wanted to do other stuff. Movie reviewers have to sit through so much crap and the movie about the hockey-playing monkey was the last straw. I had seen a whole lot of other stuff and thought, 'Do I have to do this for the rest of my life?'"

Onstad's departure brought out Whyte's rougher, more petulant side. He didn't like her leaving and seemed to take it as a personal insult, harping contemptuously about his movie reviewer moving to India to live in an ashram. But when she returned to Canada, he hired her back anyway.

Onstad recalls meeting in Toronto with the talented young designer artist Leanne Shapton, who became the first designer of the centrespread Avenue section. Shapton, from Toronto, had been working in New York at *Harper's* and *GQ* magazines but was in Toronto trying to sell the *Globe and Mail* on the idea of a standalone book section and had received a frosty response.

"In New York," Onstad says, "if you have an idea, people will meet with you, but the Canadian thing is, 'You haven't paid your dues. We don't know who you are and the door is shutting now.' So I told Leanne about this new paper, gave her Ken's phone number, and told her to call him. We were out having breakfast and she went downstairs to a phone, called him, and came back and said, 'I'm gonna go meet him this afternoon.' And he hired her to do Avenue. That's why so many people are loyal to Ken. The paper presented a sense of possibility for young journalists who had been feeling discouraged and never quite knew what to aspire to."

Whyte recalls the phone call from Shapton. "She is perhaps the single most talented person who has worked at the *Post*. I had told Katrina that if she knew any bright young people they should give me a call. About a week later, I was sitting in the *Saturday Night* office, the phone rings, and this woman introduces herself as Leanne Shapton. And she says, 'I understand you're doing a new newspaper and I was wondering if it was going to have a book section, because if it is I would like to do the illustrations for the front of it.' It was a very specific and unusual request. I said it probably wasn't going to have a book section, and she said okay. That was going to be the end of it, and I asked her why she wanted to do an illustrated book section."

Whyte, a collector of old magazines, was surprised at Shapton's knowledge and impressed by the twenty-four-year-old's experience. "She had just left *Harper's*, where she was the assistant art director working with Tom Wolfe's wife, who is art director. She had not only been assistant art director but an illustrator, and we needed a designer to do Avenue. Leanne is the most wilful, stubborn, and single most difficult person I have ever worked with, but she was usually right."

◆ ◆ ◆

"It was like taking a warm bath," was how Shinan Govani described the heyday at the *Post*, shortly after he was laid off in September 2001. "Even when the layoffs happened, I couldn't be upset about it, because the *Post* had made my career. I was twenty-seven when I started and had been given extraordinary exposure because of the *Post* and met everyone in town because of the *Post*, so I was in pretty good shape. It was better to have been plucked and dumped than never to have been plucked at all."

Govani went to see Richard Addis after he was laid off. The *Globe and Mail* editor-in-chief was in the throes of drawing up a list of journalists he wanted among those who had just been dumped by the *Post*. The aim, as ever, was partially to add talent to the *Globe* staff and partly to inflict damage on the competition. He pumped Govani for information. "He was the anti–Ken Whyte and a most charming person," remembers Govani. "He asked me to do a big feature for the *Globe* and we spent a good hour together, because he wanted to know all the gossip at the *Post*. He seemed to be having a ball and enjoying the game. Richard had a very Raj approach to things. He asked me what I thought about the *Globe* buying the *Post* and turning it into the *Globe*'s Sunday paper, a lifestyles-type newspaper for the chattering classes, but I think it was a pipe dream."

Govani is now back writing his gossip column for the *Post*.

18 POLITICS AND THE POST

"The left-right-centre conceptualization of politics is about two hundred years out of date. When the *Post* conceptualized that as Unite the Right, it was a huge tactical communications error."

— Preston Manning, Reform Party leader

Preston Manning was furious at the constant attacks against his Reform Party in the pages of the *Globe and Mail*. What he considered to be an institutional blindness, and central Canadian bias, at the newspaper meant Reform was being labelled a rump western movement with no hope of national appeal. Figuring that his coverage couldn't get much worse, Manning arrived to meet the *Globe*'s editorial board during the 1997 federal election campaign ready to do battle. It is usual for electioneering politicians to meet with editorial boards, the people responsible for the comment pages of a newspaper, but it is not usual for a politician to tell these supposedly influential opinion makers that their newspaper is a naked emperor.

The *Globe* writers who had questioned Manning's national appeal and influence – especially, as they often pointed out, in Quebec – got a taste of their own medicine as five years of anger and frustration erupted in one damning, well-researched question: "How does a newspaper that only publishes in one language, and is only distributed in only one province, in any more than a token fashion, describe itself as a national newspaper?" It was the newspaper's Achilles heel.

Manning's handlers were mortified. The leader had not only broken the rules of journalist-politician engagement, he had also armed himself with the *Globe*'s circulation and readership numbers. He put his facts on the table and told the assembled *Globe* writers how many newspapers they circulated in Alberta, Saskatchewan, British Columbia, Quebec, and elsewhere. What, he asked, would your readership outside Ontario be if you subtracted institutional subscribers, libraries, and corporate offices? It was nothing they didn't know, but not necessarily something they wanted to hear.

Manning had his battles with the *Globe* but was realistic enough to know that news media are not always the impartial observers of the political process they pretend to be but participants in the game, driven as much by competitive concerns as ideology. Nor was the *Globe* always at odds with Manning's Reform Party, especially when it came to deficit cutting, the hot fiscal issue of the early 1990s.

The *National Post* came on the scene a year after Manning's harangue at the *Globe and Mail*, and although it provided a sympathetic and enthusiastic vehicle for conservative political views, Conrad Black's new baby did not automatically become Preston Manning's new best friend. According to the Reform leader's long-time aide, Rick Anderson, Manning's folksiness had little appeal to trendy salon conservatives.

"Ken Whyte and Preston had a distant relationship; they were ideologically similar but stylistically different. While Whyte was at the *Alberta Report*, the *Report* was at the forefront of the idea the Reform Party wasn't staunch enough. While Whyte was at the *Post*, the *Post* was susceptible to the idea that Preston wasn't trendy or telegenic and vulnerable to the idea that Reform stalled at the Manitoba border despite placing ahead of the Progressive Conservatives and NDP in Ontario in both 1993 and 1997. Underestimating Reform's Ontario strength was a classic central Canadian media problem and the *Post* practised too. It was a constant frustration for Preston and one of the things that undermined his ability to retain the leadership."

The phrase *Unite the Right*, used on the front page of the *Post*'s first edition, entered the nation's political lexicon the following day and stuck like a limpet to Manning and his grassroots movement. It was, Manning says, another chronic frustration:

The *Post* gave us a better shake, but when we were trying to launch the Alliance I never once used the phrase *Unite the Right*. The left-right-centre conceptualization of politics is about two hundred years out of date and inadequate for the twenty-first century. When the *Post* conceptualized that as Unite the Right, it was a huge tactical communications error on their part and on the part of the conservative side of the House of Commons, but once the *Post* had done that, there was little we could do about it. We had a pollster go out and ask people, including Reform supporters, whether they considered themselves on the right. Fewer than 15 per cent said yes. So if by uniting the right you were uniting fiscal and social conservatives what you would have is a right-wing NDP and certainly not a party with enough horse-power to become a government. With all the small Reform-oriented federalists, fiscal conservatives, and social conservatives you had the potential of getting six million votes and a governing coalition, but reformed federalism or democratic reform is neither the right nor the left nor the centre, and nor do the public think of it in those terms.

Manning spoke regularly to Conrad Black, who invited the Reform leader to the 1998 Bilderberg conference in Scotland, an annual gathering of international political and economic elites, the occasional European royal, legions of private bodyguards, and a few hand-picked working media types such as *New York Times* Middle East specialist Thomas Friedman or former *National Post* columnist Mark Steyn. Ralph Klein, Paul Martin, Mike Harris, Jean Chrétien, and Chapters-Indigo CEO Heather Reisman have all been invitees, breaking bread with the likes of Henry Kissinger, David Rockefeller, and other core members of the organization who are mostly international financiers, senior bureaucrats, bankers, industrialists, and aging politicians of rightish inclination. Depending on who you believe, Bilderbergers are a bunch of wealthy, Masonic-like power-brokers who rule the world by controlling all its money and manipulating weak-minded politicians; alternately, they are a bunch of wealthy, Masonic-like power-brokers who like to get together in some remote luxurious retreat with their privileged guests, drink fine wines, eat fine food, and prattle on for a couple of days about how they know what's best for everybody else in the world. Black is an enthusiastic Bilderberg attendee and, at the conference held at Versailles outside Paris in 2003, Canadian Alliance Leader Stephen Harper was a guest.

The Reform leader occasionally asked for Black's input and comments on concepts he was developing, speeches he intended to give, or articles he intended to write. The relationship, never personally close, began before the *Post* existed and continued afterwards, but despite a new hairstyle and laser-eye surgery that allowed him to cast away the clunky eyeglasses, Manning was not to be the *Post*'s chosen leader of the newly minted Canadian Alliance.

There was hot rumour in some circles that Conrad Black was toying with running for the Alliance leadership himself, but those who have done battle in the federal political arena doubt that the life would have suited the media magnate. "Conrad Black sees himself as an intellectual and a political player," says Rick Anderson. "At the intellectual level he has what it takes and then some, but why would he want to spend eighty hours a week and sacrifice his life and livelihood for that miserable existence. You've got to do the barbecue circuit and communicate in seven-and-a-half-minute speeches, three and a half of which is saying, 'It's great to be in Barrie, thanks for coming out.' You've got to do your heavy lifting in a few minutes, and if you don't do it just right, they say you didn't have a message, or didn't warm up the crowd."

Though he isn't known for communing with the hoi polloi, Black might not have done so badly on the barbecue circuit, but he chose instead to contribute to the affairs of the nation through the pages of his newspaper. His best weaponry failed to achieve the ultimate goal of dislodging Jean Chrétien's Liberals, but in the heat of ideological battle, the newspaper would influence the lives of most Canadians whether they read it or not.

Black says he never seriously considered running for Canadian office himself, though he had been approached by the Liberals, Tories, and, latterly, the Canadian Alliance to do so. "It is not an occupation to which I would take well. You know the old cliché about a person knowing his limitations. I wouldn't do well, especially in this country, where so much of it is a contest of who can – in the phrase of Lester Pearson – help more people in more ways, more constantly, and for longer than anybody else. It's a definition of government that is based more on taking money from people who have earned it and spreading it around to people who haven't earned it, and with insufficient regard to merit, in exchange for their votes. I don't think I could win a contest like that. Going out and proselytizing Canadians on the virtues of a more robust and individualistic set-up for the country was a bridge too far for me."

◆ ◆ ◆

Columnist Paul Wells had caused a bit of a stir at Southam's Ottawa office shortly before Christmas 1996 when he let it be known that Conrad Black – or more correctly Barbara Amiel – had summoned him by special invitation to the couple's annual pre-Christmas brunch. Wells had written a piece on separatists for *Saturday Night* that apparently caught Black's eye and may have been responsible for winning him the invitation.

It was a memorable occasion, and Wells, a reporter with a keen eye for detail, described to his colleagues the visit to chez Black with the relish of a world traveller telling tales of great adventures abroad to wide-eyed village innocents.

"The shrimp were the size of your fist and the curry was flown in from India. Mrs. Black greeted you on the way in, and Mr. Black would shake your hand on the way out. Barbara was entirely charming. She steered me to the journalists in the room – Ken Whyte, John Fraser, and Allen Abel were there. Fraser said, 'Have you seen this place?' and I said no, so he gave me a tour that ended in the library. It's cylindrical, three storeys tall, and has about fifteen thousand books. There was a video on the desk labelled 'Who Really Killed Vince Foster,' and there was a hand-carved wooden chair. Fraser said, 'That's a bishop's chair, and the last time I was in here, there was a bishop sitting in it.'"

Wells noticed former prime minister John Turner and movie director David Cronenberg among other famous faces. On his way out, he spoke to Conrad Black for the first time.

"Hello, Mr. Black, I'm Paul Wells. I'm a reporter from the *Montreal Gazette*."

"Oh, yes," said Black, "and *Saturday Night*. I admire your reportage."

"My what?" responded Wells, not quite able to hear in the cavernous entranceway.

"Your reportage," repeated Black.

"And then," recounts Wells, "he quoted from the piece I had written, including the last leg of the piece, which meant he had not only read all the way through it but also remembered the name of the guy who had written it. I was extraordinarily impressed. I sent them a little note thanking them for their hospitality and saying it was quite a novelty to have a proprietor who reads the product."

Several months later, Wells was in Montreal at the *Gazette* offices and noticed the editor's assistant feeding one of his columns into a fax machine. She said it was being sent to Black in London at his request but she didn't know why. Wells didn't know either, but since the parting compliment at the Christmas party was at least confident that Black's interest in his work was not a prelude to some ugly fate.

The call from Ken Whyte came shortly afterwards, and the two met for dinner at a Cajun restaurant in Toronto that Wells had suggested but neither of them especially liked. "I'm glad I didn't choose the restaurant," sniffed Whyte before making what Wells recalls was a "horrible pitch" for the new daily.

"Ken said he assumed I was going to work for him. It hurt my ego. I like to be wooed. I wasn't a name at that point. I was just starting out as a national columnist for the *Gazette*, so I wasn't read that much outside Quebec. I wasn't read that much inside Quebec either. Ken was insistent that we would produce political coverage different than anything else being done. I remember him saying that he didn't want to have a Jeff Simpson equivalent. He wanted a swarm of commentary with a centre of gravity well to the right, but nobody definitive, or anyone who thought they were definitive."

Wells, and *Globe and Mail* reporter Scott Feschuk, were Kenneth Whyte's first two hires for the *Post*'s Ottawa bureau. Feschuk had first met Whyte in 1993 in Edmonton, where Whyte was the newspaper's western columnist and Feschuk the *Globe*'s reporter in the province. Feschuk, by 1998 a parliamentary reporter and weekly political diarist at the *Globe and Mail*, sent an inquiring e-mail to Whyte when he heard about the new Daily Tubby. Wells and Feschuk, both in their early thirties, were developing the irreverent, cheeky style of writing Whyte wanted out of Ottawa and so it was that two writers with a comedic touch became his first hires for the *Post*'s parliamentary bureau.

Whyte told Wells to read Matthew Parris in the *Times* of London and Quentin Letts, then with Black's *Daily Telegraph*, both of whom were recognized as the best political diarists in journalism. Which means they observe well, write well, at best are irreverent, and at worst nasty.

It was, recalls Wells, a completely new experience:

> I was to be a British parliamentary sketch-writer type and write vignettes descriptive of actual events rather than navel-gazing thumb-suckers – the sort of stentorian crap that is the stock in trade of the Ottawa columnist. My job was to make fun of Parliament, and Scott's job was to make fun of everything else in Canadian politics. We weren't hired to be aboriginal affairs specialists, we were hired to be smartasses. Things evolved afterwards, but that was the original aim. I come from the *Montreal Gazette*, which is a wonderful paper but has a heavyweight obligation. It is the oldest newspaper in Canada, the only English paper in Quebec, and it's a newspaper where you are always told what you can't do. In the early days at the *National Post*, if you tried to explain why you couldn't do something, the editors would get mad at you, which was different from any newspaper I had ever heard of. Your bosses were egging you on and saying, "What, are you chicken?"

Whyte's opinion of Chrétien, initially formed during a profile he wrote for *Saturday Night*, was, to say the least, never high:

> It was just after I became editor of *Saturday Night*, in early 1994, and I did a piece on him, which, in all modesty, I think is still the best thing that's ever been written about him. At that time there was a media view of Chrétien that he was going to make government matter again and it was going to be an age of intellectual enlightenment and new ideas and purpose in government. I spent about ninety minutes talking to him at his office in Ottawa. It was abundantly clear that this guy was a manager who had no ideas at all. More important, he had no time for ideas or for planning. When I came into his office he had a clean desk. There was one pile in the corner. It was the end of the day and he always had his desk cleared. People brought him things, he got the work done, and that was it. There was no ambition

to it. He made a lot of biting comments about Trudeau and how if anyone mentioned the word *planning* around Trudeau you could keep his attention all day. It was abundantly clear he would be an unambitious, unenlightened prime minister who would make government matter a lot less. I had him pretty much pegged from that point.

Five weeks before the newspaper's launch, the *Post* sent Feschuk and Wells to a Reform Party meeting in Calgary to hone their *Post* style, contribute to prototype sections, and file columns for the Southam group of newspapers. The two had a lot of fun at the expense of Reform MPs, who were desperately and unconvincingly trying to play down obvious fissures in their political family and, most awkwardly, explain why so many of them had just decided to opt into the MPs' gold-plated pension plan after swearing to constituents during election campaigns that they would never join the herd of politicians grunting at the Ottawa trough. For any columnist assigned to snipe from the sidelines, it was easier than shooting ducks in a barrel, but Wells was initially unsure how far they could go. "So I went over to see what Feschuk had written, and it was something like: 'It would be all too easy to make fun of the Reform Party as they gather in the mountains a week before Parliament starts. So let's get started.' The conclusion I drew from that was that we were back at our campus paper again."

It was a pointed style that would meet with Black's approval, and Wells recalls with understandable pride yet another ego-boosting compliment from the proprietor, this time at the *Post*'s first anniversary party. "It's unfortunate that a writer of your talent has to function in a city of such pervasive political idiocy," he remarked.

"Whenever I ran in to him at public events for two years after I first met him, I would reintroduce myself. But that would always get the conversation off to a bad start, because he would be annoyed that I thought he didn't remember me. Then he'd talk politics, and his basic message was, Canadian politicians are such a sad lot that anyone who has to cover them has my sympathy."

Whyte would slowly build his Ottawa bureau, hiring hard news reporters such as the *Calgary Herald*'s Sheldon Alberts, an unrivalled specialist on the Reform Party and later the Canadian Alliance and the reporter who generated most, if not all, of the stories about Alliance infighting – stories picked up by other newspapers and TV news. Andrew McIntosh was a journalistic digger from the *Ottawa Citizen*, business writer Alan Toulin was inherited from the *Financial Post*, Joel-Denis Bellavance functioned as a generalist, Luiza Chwialkowska, also from the *Ottawa Citizen*, focused on the Supreme Court. Shortly before the *Post* launched, Whyte hired Robert Fife, a well-connected workhorse and a veteran of Canadian Press and the Sun newspaper group. Fife's name has appeared on the *National Post* front page more often than any other writer at the newspaper. And in the same Sparks Street office was a contingent of seasoned national reporters from the *Ottawa Citizen*, whose work would become a vital component of the *Post*'s Ottawa coverage.

Whyte's ambition for his Ottawa bureau had not changed since his early approach to the *Globe*'s Ed Greenspon. He wanted his reporters to explore new territory and break stories before anyone else, and especially before the *Globe and Mail*, which prided itself on influencing, if not setting, the national agenda. There were the pet subjects of the Reform Party's ugly transformation into the Canadian Alliance, the brain drain, tax cuts, constant lauding of the American system as a backhanded way of illustrating how Canada should be better, and, of course, criticism of the Liberal government, which would be achieved in the paper's first weeks both by Andrew McIntosh's investigations of the prime minister's business dealings and by the more simple journalistic technique of giving opposition politicians a vehicle from which to sound off. It is a rare journalist on Parliament Hill who hasn't telephoned an opposition politician seeking a self-serving, partisan opinion about a minor issue involving a governing politician or policy, received the expected response, and written an "Opposition Slams Whatever" story. It is easy, but on a slow day better than nothing. And whichever parties are in opposition, they rely on news media to provide material for Question Period. Newspapers were the research departments for the Liberals when they were in opposition against the Mulroney Progressive Conservatives, and the same applied to the Reform Party and Canadian Alliance. Opposition parties rarely produce independent original material.

But Chrétien's office also started to take notice and learned quickly that if an Ottawa story was on page one of the *Post*, the prime minister would likely be asked about it in Question Period.

Cabinet ministers push their own departmental priorities and battle constantly for funding at cabinet or pre-budget meetings. The *Post* benefited because some ministers were developing policies and funding studies – on national productivity, the brain drain, and such – that fit with the *Post*'s way of thinking and used the newspaper to generate public support for whatever policy they were attempting to push. For its part, the *Post* got stories revealing those studies and suggesting that some cabinet ministers, at least, were on the right track.

To critics, the *Post* promoted its right-wing agenda to the detriment of its journalism and its own economic well-being. In a country where the bulk of voters congregate in the centre, allowing either a dominant right- or left-wing agenda to influence news stories is a sure way to lose readers' interest and trust.

In the best traditions of wartime propaganda, the *Globe*'s Richard Addis sought out media writers, and anyone else of influence who would listen, and pounded relentlessly at what he perceived was the *Post*'s fundamental weakness. Says Addis,

> The *Post* could have won, but it made a few stupid mistakes. The first mistake was presenting the newspaper as too right wing. The whole flirtation with the Alliance and the support of Stockwell Day was a disaster, because Canada is a liberal country. In Britain you can do well with a newspaper whether you're on the right or left, because there are two very distinct political parties. Canada isn't like that; it doesn't have a political spectrum. You only have to be in the country ten minutes to realize that. So, to have a successful newspaper in Canada it has to be essentially a Liberal paper. The *Post* nailed its colours to Reform, Alliance, and uniting the right, and it was a hideous mistake.
>
> But it wasn't as bad as the other mistake they made, which was to allow the politics to dictate their news judgment. It's completely natural in Britain, but it doesn't work in Canada, partly because there aren't enough newspapers to choose from and partly because it goes against the North American model. People find it disconcerting. I saw to it that the *Globe and Mail* never had a political agenda on its news pages and was always balanced and fair. On our comment pages, where we could justifiably have a bias, we went for balance: one left, one right, one man, one woman, and keep mixing it up. So we could say that we embrace all views and we are the national debate. And

we deliberately and constantly referred publicly to the *Post*'s slanted news coverage and its way-out views and kept that in the public mind all the time and eventually people came to believe it.

This is one of the few areas of agreement between Addis and his predecessor, William Thorsell, who says the *Post*'s political bias, plus Conrad Black's well-known political stridency, conspired to make potential readers suspicious. "It limited their readership potential. I think an awful lot of people who said I'm not going to be a victim of Conrad Black's political agenda would read a headline and say, 'I know what they are doing.' They thought it was going to work with the readers, but I don't think it did. It gave too many people an excuse not to buy the paper."

To Whyte, the criticism was unjust and part of a continuing propaganda war waged by the *Post*'s opponents:

We had different news judgment and a different sense of what's important and of what's interesting. We have our prejudices and they have theirs, but we don't allow our prejudices to affect our news judgment any more than they do. Our political judgment and news judgment are significantly different. We wanted it that way and staffed the newspaper so it would be that way. But the notion that, because we are outside this consensus of what's news and what's important, we're more bias than anybody else is incorrect. There have been headlines in the *Post* that have been slanted or not entirely accurate, but I can point to the same things in the *Toronto Star* and the *Globe and Mail*, especially during election campaigns. As far as politics goes, it's not a question of us having biases and our competition have no biases, it's that we have different biases. Part of the problem of being outside the consensus is that you're an easy target for your opponents. They successfully labelled us biased and unreliable, at least in some people's minds. It wasn't just the *Globe*. Part of what we were founded to provide was an alternative to the rough consensus among the *Star*, *Globe*, CBC, and some major Southam papers of what constitutes news in the country and what's important and who was interesting and what the issues were. We wanted to stand apart from that and attack issues we thought were underplayed. You pay a price for being outside the mainstream, but you can't have it both ways. You can't stand apart from everyone else, because when you stand apart you're saying what they're doing is wrong and casting aspersions on their judgment.

Perhaps the truth is somewhere in between, because the *Post* also started a new trend, now commonplace, of spinning stories in a preferred direction not necessarily by twisting the facts but by placing a columnist with a specific, usually rightish, opinion on the front page alongside a legitimate news story. It helped mould the *Post* into a provocative political voice and provide ammunition to those who had decided it was a right-wing rag only worth reading if you threw away the front section first. But it's also true that the *Post* had a diversity of opinion – the predictable right-wing tub-thumper David Frum, the politically unpredictable Andrew Coyne, and the leftish likes of Roy MacGregor and Paul Wells.

Irishman David Walmsley, the *Daily Telegraph* import who became the *Post*'s political editor, says the *Post*'s inaugural Unite the Right story featuring the interview with Ralph Klein was known to only three people before it appeared – Whyte, his deputy Newland, and reporter Sheldon Alberts, who wrote it:

> We knew the story was going to be massive, something like Gorbachev Made Love to His Sheep and We've Got the Pictures. When I saw the Unite the Right story, I remember thinking, "Who the hell's Ralph Klein?" There is an extraordinary sense that the *National Post* was an evil behemoth with some big capacity to wreck everything that was uniquely Canadian, but in political terms the single point of the *Post* is to hold the politician accountable. The editor identified tax cuts as an issue and Chrétien identified with it too – astute, wily man that he is. He saw the growing momentum of his polls that were showing that people considered taxes were repressive and wanted more innovation. These were *National Post* mantras: dull subjects but they meant something to small business and the average punter. So Chrétien gave $5 billion away over five years in his budget and won an increased majority in 2000 because he adopted the *National Post* manifesto, which was the Alliance manifesto. I can't remember the

last time the Alliance had an original idea or asked a question in Question Period that wasn't taken from the *Post* front page or its main politics page. The *Post* has changed the landscape for every Canadian citizen because of its driven agenda.

When Walmsley met Chrétien at the annual Press Gallery dinner, the affair when leaders of the federal parties make speeches that make fun of themselves and each other, he introduced himself slowly and deliberately to avoid the potential comprehension gap between an Irish accent and a French-Canadian ear.

"I am David Walmsley," he said, "political editor of the *National Post*."

"Ah," replied Chrétien, "I will be mentioning the *National Post* in my speech."

"I hope it will be balanced," said Walmsley, sounding as respectful as he could.

"More balanced than anything in the *National Post* will ever be," retorted the prime minister.

❖ ❖ ❖

Politicians enjoy getting their names and points of view published in national newspapers, but as seasoned political communications specialists know, recognition in the *Globe and Mail* or *National Post* has a greater impact on the ego than on the average voter. Although a story in the *Globe* or *Post* can be important for the internal morale of a political party, a single story on the same subject that travels through a chain such as Southam (now CanWest) will hit the *Montreal Gazette*, *Ottawa Citizen*, *Calgary Herald*, *Edmonton Journal*, *Vancouver Sun* and *Province*, the *Saskatoon StarPhoenix*, *Regina Leader-Post*, *Windsor Star*, and the *Victoria Times Colonist*. The combined circulation of the *Globe* and *Post* is significantly lower than the cumulative readership of those local newspapers.

But for a while, Black also owned the Southam daily newspapers, which had become more receptive to conservative ideas, and any impact of the *Post* on government policy has to take into account the local and regional influences of Southam dailies across the country – and all other dailies for that matter, although for a period Black owned all but a few of them.

For a travelling conservative politician, it was all a refreshing change, as Preston Manning's adviser, Rick Anderson, noted:

> We found we were getting fairer coverage in Southam newspapers across the country and then there was a national paper shaking up the national agenda, putting the *Globe* on the offensive and shaking up the cozy club which represented 60 per cent of the coverage going the government's way, saying, "Here's what the government did and why the government is really smart, and here's what the opposition says." The *Post* was saying, "Here's what the government says, and here's what the other guys say." Well, more likely it was, "Here's what the government says, and here's why it is such a stupid, fucking idea." Before the *Post*, if the Department of Foreign Affairs had decided that Hezbollah shouldn't be on the banned list in Canada, there wouldn't have been a newspaper in the country capable of stepping away from the government's briefing, analysis, and spin and developing a serious argument as to why that would be wrong. The *Post* unleashed political journalism in Canada.

According to Jean Chrétien's chief of staff, Eddie Goldenberg, the *National Post* eventually became a topic of mirth inside cabinet meetings, partly because of its political predictability and, probably more important, partly because the Liberals won the November 27, 2000, election handsomely and, in the words of columnist Paul Wells, handed both the Canadian Alliance and the *Post* their teeth back.

On the road to the 2000 federal election, the *Post* had started by favouring Ontarian Tom Long for the leadership of the newly minted Canadian Alliance over Preston Manning and the telegenic former Alberta treasurer Stockwell Day. To win Canada, the *Post* figured, the Alliance needed a strong leader from Ontario who could win a bunch of the 103 seats in that province.

Long somehow came into possession of the *Post*'s subscription list, which took newspaper support for a political candidate to a new, unheard of extreme. Presumably, the list was considered useful for scaring up party memberships, which was an assumption based on the sketchy belief that *Post* readers were, for the most part, Alliance supporters.

Long, a senior adviser to Ontario Premier Mike Harris and an architect of the political marketing strategy known as the Common Sense Revolution, eventually flamed out when it emerged that his campaign workers had signed up at least seven hundred new members in the Gaspé region of Quebec without their knowledge. On further investigation, it transpired that most of them had never heard of the Canadian Alliance or Tom Long. The motive was money. Recruiters were paid five dollars for each new name they brought to the party.

It would have been a political miracle that an obscure right-wing politician from Ontario, leading a party that few people in Quebec had either heard of or cared a toss about, was able to attract more members in the heart of Quebec than the Bloc Québécois. And miracles, political or otherwise, tend to attract attention.

Jean Chrétien enjoyed every minute of it and couldn't resist predicting that the cemeteries in Gaspé would be empty on the day of the Alliance leadership vote because all the occupants would be out voting.

It was a debacle from which an embarrassed and apparently innocent Long couldn't recover. *Post* political editor David Walmsley delivered the news to Ken Whyte that the leadership bid of the newspaper's preferred candidate was about to collapse. "It was no bad thing when I went into the news meeting and said, 'Sorry, Ken, Tom Long has been buying memberships and his credibility is shot to pieces.' Ken may have batted an eyelid, but he never once suggested that we should do anything other than go with the story. We made mistakes and over-egged the pudding now and again, because that's what daily newspapers do. Sometimes they get it right and sometimes they get it wrong, but in the end we killed Long's candidacy by exposing the Gaspé story, even though he was the *Post*'s preferred candidate."

The *Post*, as part of its coverage, reported that Paul Terrien, a former speech writer for Brian Mulroney, had received a bogus membership card through the mail bearing the name Chul-Ran Jang, and Jean-Denis Pelletier, the vice-president of the Quebec wing of the Conservative party, had been re-baptized Jean Cook on his unsolicited, entirely bogus Alliance membership.

It would be an exaggeration to say that the *Post* alone killed the Long candidacy, but, more important, it did not shrink from treating him as it would any other candidate suspected of transgression. Supporting the owner's favourite politicians or political parties on comment pages is a traditional part of what newspapers do, but it only becomes dangerous when the owner, or the owner's editor, fails to apply the same standards of journalistic judgment to all politicians, irrespective of stripe.

After Tom Long's campaign for the Alliance leadership self-destructed, the *Post* turned its attention to Stockwell Day, who was a fresh face, at least, and had excellent geographic credentials. Born in Barrie, Ontario, Day spent much of his childhood in the Maritimes and went to high school in Ottawa and Montreal. And with a bit of work his French would be almost passable. The fix seemed to be in against Preston Manning, the creator of Reform and, if politics was remotely just, the natural leader of the Alliance. Day, playing his relative youth to the hilt against Manning (a rehearsal for a similar strategy he would employ so disastrously against Chrétien), looked more vital and had a comely smile that looked good on camera. Manning had transformed Reform into the Canadian Alliance partly to launder its socially extreme image, and many at the grassroots of his movement felt he had compromised too much in doing so.

Day, lay preacher, anti-abortionist, and generally what Preston Manning had been a dozen years earlier, made dubious political history on July 8, 2000, when he became Alliance leader after a drawn-out, media-unfriendly process. He got the keys to Stornoway, the high-end property supplied by the taxpayer to house the Leader of Her Majesty's Official Opposition. He won a by-election to become MP for Okanagan-Coquihalla in British Columbia in the early fall and made headlines at his first official news conference as an MP on Tuesday, September 12, 2000, when he appeared on a jet ski, in a wetsuit, to answer reporters' questions on a dockside in British Columbia. It was a carefully crafted photo opportunity and arguably one of the most misguided pieces of communications advice ever given to a politician. The purpose was to emphasize that youthful, macho image, but succeeded only in making the new Alliance leader a national laughing stock. The sight of him jet-skiing away afterwards with a plume of water apparently emerging from his rear end would be TV fodder for months.

There were hysterics at the *National Post*'s Ottawa bureau, where reporters were watching the news conference. It inspired the following column from Paul Wells, which the *Post* played on its front page:

> So there I was, sitting in my office yesterday in my chicken suit, practising the kazoo and wondering, for the thousandth time: "When

236 • CHRIS COBB

will Canadian politics produce a leader who speaks for regular folks like me?"

That's when the Ottawa bureau chief ducked his head in my door. He was sporting his regular Tuesday outfit, a yellow-and-black leotard with a golden cape and a *National Post* logo emblazoned across his chest. "Turn on the TV," he said. "Stock's on."

Sure enough, there he was on CTVNewsnet: Stockwell Day, boy leader of the Canadian Alliance, celebrating his election to the House of Commons and his imminent arrival at the centre of the national debate by holding a news conference.

On the shores of Lake Okanagan.

In a neoprene wetsuit.

With bare legs.

Hot off his still-smoking Waverunner. And I do mean hot. And I do mean smoking.

"We'll be respecting the citizens when we're in there," he said, referring to the House of Commons. "You'll see a change of decorum. . . . We're setting a new tone in the House of Commons, a new tone in Canada."

This was great. I called our chief investigative reporter in. He had trouble getting through the door, what with the inflatable rubber-duck life preserver he was wearing.

"Hey, Andrew!" I said. "Look! At last! Somebody who respects us."

The investigative reporter agreed it was wonderful news. As usual, he did this by cupping a hand under his armpit and making farting noises in Morse code . . .

Day was officially sworn in as an MP a week later, proclaimed himself the new sheriff, promised to shake up Parliament, and immediately did his best to alienate reporters in the Parliamentary Press Gallery by avoiding the scrums after Question Period and forcing reporters instead to go to a basement room usually reserved for news conferences. It was an effort on Day's part to control the messages news media pumped out, but reporters hated the change. Instead of the fast, frenzied, quote-grabbing scrum, it was long, drawn-out, and too often boring. Worse, reporters complained of missing deadlines. It was another communications misstep and even worse than the wetsuit fiasco, because it was chronically aggravating for the reporters he needed to win over – that any new leader of any party would need to win over. During the national election campaign, the *Globe and Mail* was generally hostile to Day and the *Post* generally hostile toward the Liberals. Stockwell Day had made one too many gaffes for unequivocal endorsement, the most famous of which during the campaign came at a stop at Niagara Falls to illustrate the north-to-south brain drain, that favourite topic of the *Post*. His analogy fell apart on the spot when a sharp reporter noted that the Niagara River drains from south to north, not the other way around, as Day claimed. It was a common-enough mistake, but potential prime ministers are supposed to be smarter than that, or at least hire smart people to give them the facts.

"I'll have someone look into it," said Day weakly.

The nation had more fun at Day's expense over his claims that Adam and Eve were real people and dinosaurs and humans roamed the earth together. This led the Liberal camp to spread the word that the Alliance leader thought *The Flintstones* was a documentary.

The *Post* reported, when other newspapers did not, the Internet petition sponsored by CBC Television's *This Hour Has 22 Minutes* a couple of weeks into the election campaign. The point of the petition was to poke fun at the Canadian Alliance's promise to hold binding national referendums on such contentious issues as abortion and capital punishment, if enough voters demanded them – a way of sidelining the more awkward aspects of Day's rightist, Christian ideology. The comedy show proposed a referendum to get Stockwell Day to change his name to Doris. Hundreds of thousands of people voted, reaching a pace of ten thousand an hour.

A *Post* opinion poll shortly before election day hinted that the country could be headed for a minority government because Liberal support was slipping. Another poll story, written by Robert Fife, suggested that the Liberals own internal polling was showing a similar pattern. This prompted an internal briefing note from Liberal headquarters to the party faithful accusing the *Post*, and Black, of a "not terribly secret vendetta" against Chrétien and the party. The story, said the note, was inaccurate and in conflict with what internal tracking polls were actually suggesting. The note was titled "Talking Points on the *National Post*'s Transparent and Failing Campaign to Elect the Reform Alliance" and also cited a recent article in the *Times* of London in which Conrad Black was quoted as saying, "By the time I get through with Chrétien, you'll be able to squeeze him through an eye dropper."

Black says he was overheard making the "purported" remark during a spring drinks party at his London home and it was reported inaccurately and out of context by a *Times* gossip columnist. "I never thought for an instant," he says, "that I was going to have an impact on the prime minister's career."

Chrétien emerged from the election with the largest majority of his career and workers with the prime minister joyously sang "I Shot the Sheriff" as they flew back to Ottawa.

Day did increase the Alliance party's popular vote, as the *Post* poll predicted it would, but the stunning failure in Ontario – with only two seats – began the erosion of Day's career as Opposition leader and the ultimate defection of a group of his most influential MPs into something called the Democratic Representative Caucus, which forged another alliance – with Joe Clark's Progressive Conservatives.

Efforts to unite the right were in a shambles, proof that any influence the *National Post* had attempted to exert in changing the nation's political landscape had failed – for the time being anyway. After an extraordinary display of political backstabbing, Day was forced to quit the Alliance leadership in December 2001. He tried to regain his credibility by winning the leadership back, but the following April he was senior foreign affairs critic and fellow Albertan Stephen Harper was the leader.

◆   ◆   ◆

During the federal election campaign, the *Post* had pounded away at the Liberal's claim that two-tier health care didn't exist and pointed to private MRI clinics as proof that they did. And then there was the continuing Grand-Mère story and the *Post*'s revelations in the last two weeks of the campaign that the prime minister had phoned the head of the Business Development Bank of Canada in an effort to get a loan for his most famous constituent, the hotel owner Yvon Duhaime. The bank was supposed to operate independent of government, as Chrétien had insisted it had.

In an editorial on election day, the *Post* was resigned to another Liberal government but urged voters to make it a minority:

For two years, the *National Post* has published stories about business and government transactions in the Prime Minister's riding. Here's a summary: A nearly bankrupt hotel once partly owned by Mr. Chrétien, and subsequently owned by a friend and business associate, received a large loan from the Business Development Bank of Canada, despite falling well short of the eligibility rules. The loans were approved after Mr. Chrétien personally intervened, pressuring the BDC president. Mr. Chrétien and his staff insisted for a year that the BDC was independent, but when we presented evidence of his interference two weeks ago, he shrugged and said he was just doing his job. This and many other incidents show that the Liberal government plays fast and loose with public money. There are five RCMP investigations ongoing into grants and loans in the PM's riding. The Auditor-General found $1-billion unaccounted for in what has become known as the HRDC boondoggle. A parallel system of government was discovered by which Liberal hacks oversaw the disbursement of public funds to ensure partisan compatibility. But still, the Prime Minister has refused to admit any wrongdoing, or to hold anyone accountable. Canadians deserve better. They deserve honest and competent management of their money and their government.

The editorial expressed disappointment with Stockwell Day and accused him of ignoring good advice and failing to tap into the wealth of talent and experience available to him in Ontario, but it said a minority government with Stockwell Day at the Opposition helm was better than another Liberal majority.

Political editor David Walmsley says the newspaper did its job but not enough people were listening. "The prime minister wasn't totally honest when he said he had had no contact with the Business Development Bank. He corrected himself after the *Post* ran the story. We nailed him during the election campaign and then he corrected himself and said it was normal behaviour for an MP. The *Post* pointed out to Canadians that the prime minister was telling them things that were other than the truth and we did that during an election campaign. He was returned with a majority, but I rested easy. We had done our job and Canadians made their choice. The prime minister didn't tell the truth but they voted for him anyway. That sums it up beautifully."

On the other side of the fence, Chrétien's inner circle was polling constantly, as is normal during an election campaign, and knew that the complex story was not registering with Canadian voters – at least not to the extent that it would affect the outcome of the election.

Eddie Goldenberg, the staunchest, most loyal among that inner circle, dismisses the stories. "Just what was Shawinigate? There was a lot of innuendo and no facts. It was a vendetta against the prime minister for being a small-l Liberal. The *Post* had been the most ideological newspaper we had seen in Canada for decades. I have no problem with the commentary or the editorials even though I don't agree with them, but I don't like the way they torque their news coverage and I'm looking forward to the time when I leave this job and no longer have to read it."

Goldenberg insists that the *Post*'s influence on government policy was zero. He says, for instance, the *Post* had nothing to do with pre-election tax cuts announced in the fall of 2000. They were just an inevitable part of the process after the federal deficit had been dealt with. Closer to the political truth is that the federal Liberals are masterful chameleons, and although the *Post*'s influence on the tax-cut issue can never be measured, the ruling party detected an increasing unhappiness in the country over high taxes, an issue the *Post* had championed from its first week of publication.

Peter Donolo, Chrétien's influential director of communications during the first year of the *Post*'s life and eventually the recipient of a plum patronage job as Canadian envoy to Milan, is equally dismissive. "The *Post* had a two-fold effect: to heighten competition for news and heighten sensationalism. It has been a reckless phase in Canadian journalism. The *Post* was three-quarters spin, one-quarter news, especially in its political coverage, and I think it lost a credibility battle very early on with the *Globe*. It never threatened the *Globe*'s status as the newspaper of record. The *Post* always had a political agenda. They were harsh on the prime minister and they created Stockwell Day. Four words sum up the *Post*'s editorial policy: Canada Bad, U.S.A. Good."

◆ ◆ ◆

Jean Chrétien's wife, Aline, refused to have the *National Post* in the house – a certain indicator that the newspaper's commentary and coverage in general, and Shawinigate in particular, irked everyone in the Chrétien circle. But it wasn't just the Liberals who were irritated by the *Post*.

Within a year, the Bloc Québécois was suing the newspaper for libel, Joe Clark was refusing to return phone calls from its political reporters and was walking away if *Post* reporters approached him outside the House of Commons, and New Democratic Party Leader Alexa McDonough was officially boycotting the newspaper. But it is the Prime Minister's Office, Ottawa's centre of power, that has the information and influence to make life truly difficult for any reporter or news organization it doesn't like. The preferred method of revenge is to give a scoop to a favoured reporter at the expense of another. Every parliamentary news bureau chief in Ottawa has heard the same question from head office: "Why didn't we have this story?" There is never a satisfactory answer to that.

And there are other, more subtle ways that people in power try to manipulate and manage the flow and nature of news. Sometimes it works and sometimes it doesn't, but they never stop trying.

Being on the prime ministerial hit list sometimes made life difficult for bureau chief Robert Fife, a reporter and manager under unrelenting pressure to generate splashy stories from his reporters for each of the *Post*'s six publishing days.

"I had a horrible relationship with Mr. Chrétien for a long time," says Fife. "I travelled with him for most of the 2000 election campaign, and he would never answer my questions nor would he answer the questions of other reporters if they were standing around me. So I became kind of isolated, and as the campaign went on, it got worse, because the *Post* was still doing the Shawinigate stories and the ethics counsellor was about to report on whether the prime minister had done anything wrong. I had close friends of Chrétien telling me, 'He's blaming you for this because you're the bureau chief.' Shawinigate was a good story and you can't ignore a good story. But even though I had a poor relationship with the prime minister's office, I still broke stories because lots of cabinet ministers talk to me. I don't really need the PMO."

Fife had an especially frosty time with Chrétien's senior communications adviser, Francoise Ducros, a lawyer by training who was the main bridge between the prime minister and the news media. "After the election, someone told me that Francie thought I didn't like her personally, which wasn't true, but I didn't have a good relationship with her. Some people assumed that the *Post*'s national bureau, directed by Conrad Black, was told to get the Shawinigate story and bring down Jean Chrétien, and that was encouraged by the newspaper war. The *Globe and Mail*, and other newspapers, deliberately left that impression."

It was Fife's exclusive story, published at the end of 2002, that quoted Ducros calling U.S. President George Bush a moron. After a frenzy of national and international publicity, she was forced to resign.

The chronic frustration for Fife, and reporter Andrew McIntosh, was the reaction of other news media to the Shawinigate coverage. All reporters enjoy having scoops and leading the pack on major stories, but a prolonged period out on a limb can be extremely lonely and unnerving. When a reporter is accusing the prime minister of nefarious dealings, and the furious prime minister is phoning the newspaper owner and accusing him of waging a personal vendetta, and the owner is calling the newspaper editor and telling him to make sure every detail published is accurate, the pressure on the reporter is immense. When other news media, opposition newspapers, and major TV networks are either casting aspersions on the story or ignoring it altogether, the pressure only intensifies.

It was, says Fife, a tough period:

> Other newspapers didn't follow what was a really good story, because they didn't want to give the *National Post* any credibility. They were involved in a newspaper war. The Opposition eventually picked up on the story, but not immediately, and even when it became an issue in the House of Commons, a lot of other newspapers didn't cover it. It wasn't just the *Globe* that ignored it but also other Southam newspapers. Eventually, CTV started covering it, but for the longest time the CBC didn't touch it. Columnist Lawrence Martin got onto it and began writing very thoughtful pieces, and when we entered the election campaign it began to be covered a little more. A lot of journalists are lazy, and it's a lot easier to go to a press conference, write your story, and go home. It's a lot harder to get on a phone, develop your own sources, and get ahead of the competition.

❖ ❖ ❖

Ezra Levant had the unique experience of being a *Post* editorial writer, a press secretary, a general mouthpiece for Stockwell Day, and, before that, an aide to Preston Manning. Most famously, however, he was the Alliance candidate in Manning's old riding of Calgary Southwest in March 2002 when newly minted Alliance leader and Calgary resident Stephen Harper decided he wanted to run there too. After an entertaining public scrap, in which Levant first refused to budge and the new Alliance boss hit his own first patch of turbulent infighting, the party bosses got their way and Levant stepped aside. But, again, it left the impression that Alliance opposition to the Liberal's gun registry was simply to ensure there was enough available weaponry for them to keep shooting themselves in the foot.

Levant had written for the *Alberta Report* and the Sun group when he met Ken Whyte at the United Alternative convention of February 1999 and, motivated by love for a woman in Toronto, asked if there was a job going at the *Post*. A few months later, Levant, at age twenty-seven, was an editorial writer at the *Post* under the tutelage of John O'Sullivan, a veteran British conservative of both the small- and large-c persuasion, a former adviser to Margaret Thatcher, editor-at-large of the *National Review*, and former assistant editor of Conrad Black's *Daily Telegraph*. Unlike anyone else on the *Post* editorial board, he was an experienced journalist. Like all good editorial writers, O'Sullivan's neo-con crew, average age around thirty, knew what they liked and didn't like, but they didn't always know how best to express their views with the written word.

Levant glows at the memory of working with O'Sullivan. "He was very lively and controversial and encouraged us to write outside of the conventional wisdom. We were the apprentices and he was the master. The high light of my day was going into John O'Sullivan's office while he edited my work and with every keystroke he would make a little comment. It was a real education, especially for those of us with no journalistic experience. We had the ideas, but he knew how to write."

In Levant's view, the *National Post* clicked in the West because Whyte and his team were the first news media out of Toronto that didn't treat the region – especially Alberta – like a colony. "Thirty years ago, the political news of the country came out of Toronto and Montreal. Quebec had the hot politicians like Lévesque and Trudeau and many of the hot new ideas. But now the crucible for creative political ideas in Canada is Calgary. The *Post* recognized that and shattered the cartel of what was considered news. The major news media didn't cover certain stories on conservative issues. They tut-tutted the rise of Ralph Klein and didn't cover the birth and growth of Reform properly because they thought it was an aberration from a different part of the country. The media class in Toronto didn't know anyone from the Reform party and it was a foreign thing to them."

So the *Post* attacked the Lloyd Axworthy school of foreign affairs, wrote about religion and spirituality, the ills of universal health care, the panacea of private health care, was pragmatic and often politically incorrect on aboriginal issues, and questioned whether people washing ashore off the coast of British Columbia should be welcomed into the country. And the newspaper placed itself firmly on the side of Israel in the wake of the second Intafadah.

Famously declaring himself a "Stockoholic," Levant had gone to work for Stockwell Day on Valentine's Day 2001 and walked right into a rat's nest of mutiny and some of the most vicious and public political backbiting seen in Ottawa for a generation. The Canadian Alliance was the story of the year, and for reporters who had covered most of the drab Chrétien years, it was a wonderful, long-overdue entertainment. Levant was employed as Day's communications director, which, in the circumstances, was like spinning for the captain of the *Titanic*.

Aside from suffering at the hands of such Alliance stalwarts as Deborah Grey and Chuck Strahl, who would lead defections from the party, Day was in a mess of personal issues, the most notable being the revelation that he had saddled Alberta taxpayers with a $792,000 legal bill to fight a lawsuit against him filed by lawyer Lorne Goddard after Day had written a letter to the Red Deer *Advocate* newspaper criticizing Goddard for defending a pedophile. Day took out a $60,000 mortgage on his house to pay the damages awarded Goddard and issued an abject apology to everyone.

In an unsuccessful effort to deflect some of the heat, Day called for an inquiry into Jean Chrétien's business affairs, saying Chrétien had tainted the office of prime minister, but within two weeks he was back on the defensive after the *Globe and Mail* published a story claiming he had met with a private investigator and paid him $6,500 to probe the affairs of Chrétien and other Liberals. At first Day admitted that he had met with the investigator, but two days later changed his mind and said the person was just one of many he met each day as leader of the Opposition.

And then, two weeks after that, came the "Day fends off calls to resign" stories as his deputy leader, Grey, and House leader, Strahl, boycotted their own caucus and urged Day to quit. The rebellious eight – Strahl, Grey, Jay Hill, Val Meredith, Jim Gouk, Grant McNally, Jim Pankiw, Art Hanger, and Gary Lunn – were to part company with the Alliance mother ship.

In a blatant act of political opportunism, Tory Leader Joe Clark offered an olive branch to the Alliance rebels, and throughout the summer of 2001 the situation for Day and Levant became worse. Grey, the Reform Party icon and its first MP, put the final nail in Day's political coffin when she joined eleven other Alliance MPs and left. On July 9, Day insisted he would stay on as leader, but on July 17 he stepped down and prompted the leadership convention that would be won by Stephen Harper.

After the hundred days that shook Ottawa, a bruised and battered Levant left Ottawa and began making plans to return as an MP, where more unexpected punishment at the hands of the news media would be waiting for him.

"The *Post* was tough on Stockwell Day," says Levant, "but the story was irresistible. It was the story of a mutiny. It was like having Eddie Goldenberg faxing confidential information to the media about Jean Chrétien. I have run it through my head a few times and tried to think how I might have handled it differently, but how do you put a positive spin on mutiny? I don't punish myself too much, because it was much more than a leadership or communications problem. It was a group of a dozen people who had decided they were going to destroy the party in any way they had to in order to get rid of the leader."

❖   ❖   ❖

Watching from his perch in Alberta at the University of Calgary, political scientist David Taras saw the *Post* grow large and influential on the western landscape. "It was a remarkable period in Canadian history. Conrad Black is part businessman, part politician, and part journalist, and to match what he did you really have to go back to the great newspaper barons like Randolph Hearst. In the first year, it brought new ideas into the debate, set agendas, and added a new perspective. It's been a controversial, interesting, passionate newspaper and, in the larger context, has meant a kind of Europeanization of the Canadian newspaper industry. It was also an extraordinary indulgence, but Black is a crusader. That's the way you have to look at him."

Taras, author of *The Newsmakers: The Media's Influence on Canadian Politics*, saw in the *Post* a link to the party press that existed for roughly four decades from the 1890s, when those in power and opposition forged alliances with newspapers. "The *Post* was in the delivery room when the Alliance was born and helped pull the baby out. Whatever happened in the Alliance party, you could read about in the *Post*, so it became a kind of party organ in the old way. It was so apparent and so extraordinary. It was like *Pravda*. All the machinations of the party and its executive were played out in the *Post*, but they weren't championing a particular person, they were championing the movement. The very fact they gave such prominence to the Alliance party was in effect showing their colours. Every headline shouted, 'This is important. This is what we should be caring about.' It incited the whole journalistic community and changed the temper and the climate. It became okay to be crusading and passionate and hold strong opinions."

Taras speculates that the *National Post* and *Globe and Mail* were never in competition journalistically, especially in the first year, because the *Post* began attracting a different political constituency – the politics of the Klein government in Alberta, the fractious politics of British Columbia, the politics of the Canada West Foundation, the oil industry, and Bay Street. "Think of the Alliance party system instead of the Alliance party. The system had its journalism supporters in *Alberta Report* magazine and Southam newspapers in the West, and it had fundraising support in the corporate community. It's a system that doesn't translate easily to another part of the country."

The critical yardstick from the West's point of view was the *Post*'s constant comparing of Canada with the United States. The newspaper's quarterly reports on how Canada was stacking up against the United States inevitably ended with the message that Canada was neither competitive nor productive enough and was overtaxed. In Alberta, that resonated, and Taras speculates that Whyte's Western sensibilities were part of the reason. "Western psychology is different. There was a sizeable immigration into Southern Alberta from the U.S.A. in the 1890s, and there are deep connections between the Canadian oil industry and American corporations, and those connections made the Alberta oil industry come alive. The emergence of Calgary isn't only because of oil. It is the focal point for free trade, the logistics hub for free trade between the west and the northwest. So there is an American republicanism in Alberta, which is more alive in Alberta than anywhere else in the country, and there is a populism that is part of the pioneering experience and part of the language and very powerful."

The *Post* also approached coverage of the Supreme Court from a different perspective and challenged the decisions of the justices, whom it considered otherwise unaccountable, and wrote about their personal lives. It was unheard of in Canada and caused significant consternation among the justices themselves, who began to explain their reasons for judgment in greater written detail.

Drawing direct lines between the *Post*'s political journalism and shifts in government policy is not easy. The Reform and Alliance parties have influenced the Chrétien Liberals and the *Post* was a supporter of the Alliance, but, as Taras says, the Liberals don't leave vacant political territory unoccupied for very long:

> The Reform-Alliance party went to Ottawa and was able to set the agenda on fiscal policy, government spending, law and order, Quebec sovereignty, and a series of other issues. So the Liberals played the old game, like they had done in the 1960s when they moved to the left to marginalize the NDP. Paul Martin in particular was smart enough to occupy a lot of the middle ground, and ground on the right, and marginalize the Reform-Alliance. The only way you get to the right of Paul Martin is to look absurd by becoming even more extreme. During the 2000 election, when Day was going on about tax cuts, Martin appears and says, 'Well, here are the tax cuts.' So the greatest influence of the *Post* may not have been on the Alliance but on the Liberals, because they knew the force of gravity was moving to the right and they had to occupy some of that space.

Something roughly the opposite happened to the *Globe and Mail*, which gradually edged to the political left as the *Post* puffed out its journalistic chest and boomed loudly that it was taking charge of all things right of centre. But as with most generalizations about the two newspapers, the real perspective is a little more complex.

Whyte is satisfied that the *Post* was successful in bringing a new set of ideas and priorities onto the national stage:

I don't think that any one news outlet dominates the conversations, but we have punched above our weight and in the first three and a half years were more effective at shaping the conversation than any other newspaper. I think we have had an impact on government policy. Tax cuts and the brain drain are the ones people most often point to. The government announced tax initiatives and scholarships to talented academics with the proviso they stay in the country. We thought nobody was paying enough attention to Canada's productivity problems. Our productivity was nowhere near our biggest trading partner. We made some editorial comment about this but also paid some attention to it in our news operation. Giles Gherson and Bob Fife found report after report from bureaucrats in the Industry department that Canada has a productivity problem. The problem existed, so we put it on the front page and gave it banner headlines, because we believe, and I think most Canadians believe, that Canada should be an affluent, prosperous, and productive country. In subsequent budgets more attention was paid to productivity than might otherwise have been. We did it all in the face of considerable denial by other media outlets. None of them agreed there was a problem.

Deputy editor Martin Newland, who returned to London as editor-in-chief of the *Daily Telegraph* in the spring of 2003, has a simpler analysis. "We made political reporting fun, and lots of other media in Canada picked it up. I don't think Canadian journalists were a bunch of lobotomized lemmings before we came along, but we did it differently."

It says a great deal about Canadians' political and social ethos that the *Toronto Star*, guided by its Atkinson Principles, was the *National Post*'s equal in terms of political bias, yet its journalism – supportive of the Liberals and championing of all manner of socially left-wing causes – is rarely criticized for being so. It also speaks to the effectiveness of the propaganda campaign launched against the *Post* by special interest groups, many of which found voice in the more established news media.

Conrad Black says his newspaper wore its political bias on its sleeve but no more than the *Globe and Mail* and significantly less than the *Star*. "The *Post* was a shock compared to what Canadians are used to. All the other papers were leftist so it stood up like a pikestaff in that regard, but in practice it was no more offensive than the others."

The *Post* was a "beacon for believers," but Black doubts it had much effect on either government policy or Canadian politics. "It encouraged those who believed in it and may have changed a few minds, I don't know. I wouldn't count on it, but I think it was a fine rallying place for that minority. But I doubt it changed anything. It had a marginal impact in some areas but was essentially preaching to the converted. But it was clearly a serious irritant to the prime minister, especially when it disclosed his own skullduggery in that business around the golf course in Shawinigan."

But Black concedes he has a more pessimistic view than most and especially more than his editor, Ken Whyte. "There was a difference in perception between Ken and me. I thought he was altogether too optimistic about achieving much in what is effectively a one-party state. He was trying to be helpful to the Alliance, but my reading of the Alliance was that it was never going to make it and the only way we were going to get anywhere with the policies we were proposing was to encourage and help develop a suitable faction within the Liberal party. When I was a young person in this country, the Liberals were in many ways more conservative than the Conservatives, but Ken, being an Albertan, was quite preoccupied with helping the Alliance, and I think in addition to assisting an enterprise that really had no chance, it accentuated the problem of the paper seeming to be partisan."

Black says his own larger-than-life public persona was no asset in the *Post*'s efforts to alter public opinion. "Too many people saw it as a power play by me personally," he says, "or a vendetta operation by me personally once we got going, or some kind of Hearstean or Northcliffean ego trip, or some unreasonable attempt to influence opinion. And that isn't a fair description of what we are trying to do, but that's not the point – that's what we were up against because we were absolutely affronting the conventional wisdom."

Black was long gone from the scene, and the *National Post* had long ceased its Unite the Right mantra, when it actually happened. In the early winter of 2003, Tory Leader Peter MacKay and Alliance Leader Stephen Harper joined forces to fight the Liberals as a united front. Typically, it didn't happen without argument or with unanimity, but it happened. Whether the unity boat eventually washed into port on the ripples made years earlier by the *Post* is anyone's guess.

"We set our egos aside," said Deborah Grey. "It's amazing what you can achieve when you set ego aside."

19   L'AFFAIRE GRAND-MÈRE

"You're not going to turn Canada upside down for $23,040, are you?"
— Yvon Duhaime, hotel owner, Shawinigan, Quebec

T he story, known as the Grand-Mère Affair, or Shawinigate, was about the prime minister, taxpayers' dollars, and how millions of those dollars found their way to ethically challenged businessmen in the prime minister's home riding. It was a complex story of many chapters with more twists than a tree root, and it pitched a newspaper personified by Conrad Black against veteran hardball politician Jean Chrétien in a high-stakes personal battle that Black, for all his wealth, influence, and power, would ultimately lose. He would lose in part because he resisted pressure from the prime minister and the prime minister's influential friends and refused to issue a cease-and-desist order to his editor.

Black had decided that the *Post* was performing well in its unofficial role as opposition to the Chrétien Liberals and had no desire to interfere in its coverage of the government, even though the more he read about Grand-Mère, the more he felt the *Post* was becoming a bore on the subject – as he puts it, "like the guy you encounter in a pub who talks about the same thing. It's a danger in newspapers."

But Black had mixed feelings. He recognized on one hand that it was a good story but eventually had some sympathy for Chrétien, despite the bad blood between them:

As scandals go, it wasn't much of a scandal. What irritated me was Chrétien's unctuous pretense that he was above all that.

I don't get particularly excited about the patronage system. It's not especially edifying, but that sort of thing goes on in politics. What I don't like is the hypocrisy of people who run a fairly traditional patronage operation claiming they are above it all.

Since we were the only effective opposition, I didn't really assert myself very much with Ken Whyte on the subject, even though he was a little naive about just how ferocious the response of the government would be, especially one governed on the traditional Quebec political ethic. Nobody else was going to make anything out of that issue, and it deserved an airing. There is no doubt that Chrétien lied to Parliament. There is no doubt that he interfered with supposedly non-partisan agencies. And there is no doubt he stood to gain modestly from the directed use of public funds.

The stories were written and reported by Ottawa bureau reporter Andrew McIntosh, whose interest had been sparked by a brief story he saw on the business news pages of the Quebec daily *La Presse* in 1995 reporting that the prime minister had sold his shares in the Grand-Mère Golf Club to a newly created Golf Division of the Delta Hotel chain. The Golf Division, McIntosh would later discover, didn't exist.

McIntosh, an investigative reporter from his days at the *Montreal Gazette*, and a senior researcher for author Stevie Cameron on her best-selling book *On the Take*, persuaded Whyte and Martin Newland that the story of Chrétien's business dealings in his home riding of Saint Maurice was worthy of investigation.

The reporter followed a long and complex paper trail, met secretly with highly placed sources, and wrote a series of stories that included allegations of forgery, computer tampering, and RCMP bias in favour of the prime minister and his aides. An unknown but obviously well-connected source sent McIntosh one key, super-sensitive document that arrived in the mail at his downtown Ottawa office. The leaking of that document sparked an RCMP probe into McIntosh's sources.

❖   ❖   ❖

The affair was dubbed Shawinigate, an amalgam of Chrétien's hometown Shawinigan and Watergate, which was the most renowned piece of investigative journalism of them all and the making of the *Washington Post*'s reputation as a journalistic organ equal to that of the *New York Times*. But the hook that caught and landed Richard Nixon failed to catch Jean Chrétien, who received two resounding endorsements at the polls while the story was hot. Watergate's easily understood, dramatic prelude – a burglary by a bunch of shady criminals of foreign persuasion – grabbed the American public's imagination. The allegations against Chrétien did not. Like the *Washington Post* with Watergate, the *National Post* had initially been alone in reporting on the Grand-Mère affair. Unlike the *Washington Post*, the *National Post* saw little long-term benefit for its efforts and would eventually drop the story altogether, but arguably the newspaper that had rapidly become known for its sexy, irreverent approach to news had nailed the most important story of the Chrétien regime – a story with the potential of cementing the reputation of Canada's start-up daily as a significant journalistic force.

McIntosh's first stories about the prime minister's investments in the golf club began appearing in the *National Post* on January 23 and 25, 1999, three months after the newspaper published its first edition, but the tale began more than a decade earlier.

In May 1988, Chrétien and two business partners bought the Grand-Mère Golf Club, near Chrétien's boyhood home of Shawinigan, from the paper company Consolidated Bathurst for $625,000. Chrétien, then a private citizen and businessman, was a director of Consolidated Bathurst. Next door to the golf club was a hotel, the Auberge Grand-Mère, which was also owned by Consolidated Bathurst.

When Chrétien and his partners bought the golf club, paying $208,000 each, the sale included goodwill, assets, and the ongoing business of the Auberge Grand-Mère but not the actual hotel building. That remained the property of Consolidated Bathurst.

In April 1993, six months before he was elected prime minister, Chrétien and his partners sold the business to Chrétien's old friend, the well-known local Liberal Yvon Duhaime. In December 1994, Duhaime bought the hotel building from Consolidated Bathurst for $225,000.

As McIntosh would subsequently discover, under Duhaime's ownership the Auberge Grand-Mère had got a $615,000 loan from the Business Development Bank of Canada (BDC) in 1997 and by the end of the next year had received a total of $1,028,799 in federal grants and loans from both the BDC and Human Resources Development Canada (HRDC). The BDC is a Crown corporation, and although its president is appointed by the prime minister, its day-to-day operations are independent from government. Or should be.

BDC officials rebuffed McIntosh's attempts to get more details of the loan and blocked his request for documents through the federal Access to Information Act. McIntosh appealed the decision and six months later received ten pages of the loan file. He appealed again and got the rest.

"I later learned from two confidential sources that my access request was handled by Jean Carle," McIntosh said in a court affidavit during the eventual RCMP probe. "Mr. Carle, who was at the time vice-president of public affairs at the BDC, had been director of operations for the prime minister."

A month after Chrétien was elected prime minister in 1993, he had sold his golf-club shares to Toronto real-estate tycoon and Delta hotel-chain owner Jonas Prince, who would later tell McIntosh that he had only bought an option on the shares and had never paid for them. Ownership of the shares was the key issue. If the prime minister owned shares in a property that had received federal grants, he was in a clear conflict of interest. It was a conflict Chrétien would continually, and vehemently, deny, and despite the murky question of who owned the golf-club shares, the prime minister remained adamant that Prince had bought them outright. Soon after being elected, the prime minister said, all his business dealings were in a private blind trust and he had nothing more to do with them while in office.

❧ ❧ ❧

McIntosh continued digging and reported that hotel owner Yvon Duhaime had a criminal record. The loan recipient had been convicted twice of impaired driving, in 1993 and 1995, and was convicted of assault in 1994 during a labour dispute involving workers on a picket line at a seniors' residence. Duhaime's company supplied food to the home.

McIntosh also found that Duhaime's company had owned another hotel, L'Hotel des Chutes, in Shawinigan, which was destroyed by a blaze on October 27, 1992. "Mr. Duhaime was the prime suspect in a criminal investigation after Shawinigan police strongly suspected that the hotel fire, which began on the roof, was deliberately set," McIntosh wrote in the *Post*.

"The Hotel des Chutes burned just after Quebec tax collectors obtained court judgments ordering Mr. Duhaime's company to pay $66,000 in business and sales taxes owing since 1990. As well, Hydro-Quebec, the provincial electrical utility, had just threatened to cut power to the Shawinigan hotel because Mr. Duhaime had failed to pay its power bills. 'It all made us very suspicious,' Claude Collins, a retired Shawinigan police officer, said. 'It's rare to have people saved by a fire. Usually, people are saved by fire-fighters.' "

(Duhaime had more bad luck with fire when arsonists struck Auberge Grand-Mère in early February 2004, causing, according to police estimates, more than $500,000 in damage.)

Duhaime had not been prosecuted due to lack of evidence, but, on the matter at hand, he freely admitted that being in the prime minister's riding helped him get both federal loans to renovate the Auberge Grand-Mère. "Mr. Chrétien," reported the *Post*, "cut the ribbon on the inn's new addition."

A major piece of McIntosh's ongoing investigation fell into place when another confidential source told the reporter that in April 1996 the prime minister himself had phoned Francois Beaudoin, president of the federal Business Development Bank, to discuss a loan to Yvon Duhaime. According to the *Post*, Chrétien met with the BDC president in May and they spoke about the loan again. The following September, the loan was rejected because the bank considered Duhaime a bad risk.

Chrétien persisted, phoning the BDC again in February 1997 to discuss a scaled-down version of the original hotel expansion, and shortly afterwards the bank approved the $615,000 grant. McIntosh also reported that Denis Tremblay, a senior aide to Chrétien, had attended a meeting at the Human Resources Department and several weeks later a grant of $164,000 was approved.

In June 1997, the Liberals won another election.

❖   ❖   ❖

Chrétien's defence would be unwavering: he was just doing what any MP would do for his constituency, especially a constituency that suffered the high unemployment rate of Saint-Maurice. And his staff grudgingly admitted that in his haste to do the right thing for his constituents, their boss might have been just a little naive in the process. It was possibly the first time in his distinguished forty-year political career that Chrétien had been described as naive.

The *Post*'s Shawinigate stories brought out the bare-knuckle political fighter in Chrétien, who started leaning on Black, calling him at 3 a.m. in Vienna to protest the treatment he was getting. Black, not an early-to-bed kind of guy, was awake when the call came. The two men had enjoyed cordial relations for twenty years, occasionally spoke about matters of state on the telephone, and dined together in Ottawa or London. But there was nothing cordial about the prime minister's angry early-morning call to Austria.

Black says Chrétien phoned him in total about half a dozen times, and despite a firm belief that the story was legitimate he concedes that Chrétien may have had a point:

> I thought we hammered it a little too hard, and beyond a certain point I had some sympathy for Chrétien. He was hypocritical and corrupt, of course, but he had a right not to be harassed on the point every single day with all the Shawinigan stuff. Of course it has never been properly examined what went on. In a proper two-party system I think Chrétien would have been out, but with that said, I think by attacking it almost every day the way he did, Ken in the first place harassed Chrétien unduly, and in the second place looked more like a Rottweiler than he would have wanted to look, and in the third place he underestimated the consequences. He is from Alberta, and I don't think he realized how nasty politicians, in essentially one-party jurisdictions, can get especially if they're from Quebec. Having been Duplessis's biographer, I knew something about that.

Chrétien's trusted aide, John Rae, an executive with Power Corporation and a major architect of the Chrétien election victories, telephoned Ken Whyte twice in late 1999 to express his displeasure, but according to the editor-in-chief, the conversations ended without any resolution.

Rae was also unhappy about a story played on page one of the *Post* connecting Power Corp. with business involvement in the Sudan. The United Nations had condemned the Sudanese government for gross human rights abuse and corruption related to oil revenues, and the United States had accused the country of sponsoring terrorism. Canada, the *Post* reported, had also been harshly criticized for not imposing sanctions on Sudan.

The *Post* revealed that Power Corp. had an interest in TotalFina SA, a French oil company with significant operations in Sudan, and that Paul Desmarais Sr., Power Corp.'s chairman and one of Canada's richest men, was a director of the French company. The CEO of Power Corp. was, and is, Chrétien's son-in-law Andre Desmarais, son of Paul. Rae was irritated at the *Post* for revealing Power Corp.'s Sudanese connections and emphasizing the company's political connections at home.

Black's message to Whyte after the early-morning phone call from the PM had been succinct: "I don't think the prime minister is too delighted, but it's up to you. Just don't make any mistakes."

The pressure on Whyte was mounting. "Rae had been calling me, and other pressure came from a variety of sources. Rae was dissatisfied with my response and made it clear he would be seeking redress through other channels. So I didn't hear anything for a week or two, and next thing you know Conrad was on the phone. Conrad handles those sort of things well, because he has had a lot of experience at it. He basically runs through all the facts, runs through your argument, probes, asks questions, and then asks what you think would be a reasonable way to address the concerns. So having the prime minister respond was a good way to address it. It made us look as though we were promoting a dialogue and allowing him to get his argument across."

Chrétien accepted the offer to explain his case and, in an impassioned response published on April 10, 1999, lambasted the *Post* on its own pages. Under the headline "THE PM RESPONDS," Chrétien vigorously defended himself.

A month later, the *Post* published two more McIntosh stories about federal grants and loans awarded to what was now Canada's most famous inn. They were based on documents the reporter had got from Human Resources Development Canada. The stories, McIntosh said in his Ontario Superior Court of Justice affidavit, did not support the prime minister's version. "The first story revealed how Mr. Chrétien had personally announced the $600,000 grant for the Auberge des Gouverneurs [a second hotel in his riding] three weeks before it had completed the requisite business plan and provided it to HRDC officials who were considering the application. The story quoted from documents showing that no review had occurred prior to the prime minister's announcement of the grant. The companion story revealed how René Fugere, a lobbyist in the private sector and an unpaid aide to the prime minister who represented him at public functions in Saint-Maurice, had helped secure a $100,000 grant for the Auberge des Gouverneurs from the HRDC's Transitional Grant Fund Program, even though the program's budget for that year had been exhausted."

The pounding Chrétien was taking in the House of Commons continued unabated until the summer break in June 1999, with opposition MPs accusing the prime minister of sullying his office and vote-buying with his efforts to secure loans and grants for his riding's businesses. Chrétien threatened to sue then Opposition Leader Preston Manning and Reform MP Jason Kenney but later withdrew his threat.

McIntosh wrote more during that summer, including a major article revealing that other businessmen in the prime minister's riding had received copious federal funding, including another grant awarded through HRDC after departmental officials had said there was no money left. In total, reported McIntosh, $6 million was invested in the Saint-Maurice hotel sector during this period. The prime minister said any support he was giving to local businesses was part of his job as an MP and invited reporters to go to his riding to see that the taxpayers money had been well spent.

◆　◆　◆

Early the following April, with the *Post* and others still raising questions over when the prime minister disposed of his golf-club shares, McIntosh found a sealed brown envelope in his morning mail containing an internal BDC loan approval form related to the $615,000 mortgage granted the Grand-Mère tour years earlier. The envelope was sent anonymously. The document contained one piece of potentially explosive information: a reference to a debt of $23,040 owed to JAC Consultants, the prime minister's own company. It appeared that the debt was owed at the time the inn got both the BDC loan and its grants from the federal Human Resources department. Given that the prime minister called the bank president about the loan and a member of his staff was involved in the Human Resources meetings when the grants were discussed, the document suggested that a clear line could be drawn between the loan and grants and the prime minister's own self-interest.

McIntosh immediately flew to Toronto to discuss the document with his editors and the newspaper's lawyers. The key question, and one that always faces a reporter who gets leaked documents, was its authenticity. Was it a forgery? Was it a set-up? Kenneth Whyte told McIntosh to find out.

The leaked document also referred to $46,563 that hotel owner Duhaime owed his father-in-law, whose construction company had built a banquet hall for him in 1996.

McIntosh decided to contact Duhaime and simultaneously fax copies of the document to the BDC, the Prime Minister's Office, and the prime minister's lawyers for their comments.

In a taped interview with Duhaime, whom McIntosh did not trust, the hotel owner admitted that he had owed the money to his father-in-law but balked at answering questions about the debt apparently owed to JAC Consultants.

McIntosh recalled the conversation in his Ontario Court of Justice Affidavit. "He then said: 'You're not going to turn Canada upside down over $23,040, are you?' I asked him to repeat his remarks as I wanted to make sure I had fully understood him. He repeated the remarks a second time. Mr. Duhaime then insisted he had not owed any money to Mr. Chrétien or his family holding company. . . . I did not take this denial at face value."

BDC officials sent two apparently contradictory letters to the *Post* in quick succession. One said the document, or at least the added footnote, was a forgery, because the bank had no record of the debt owned to Chrétien's company. The second letter said the newspaper was in possession of a stolen document and "should handle itself accordingly."

The prime minister's communications chief, Françoise Ducros, called *Post* senior management in an effort to persuade them not to publish a story based on the document and lawyer David Scott, in a letter to acting *Post* publisher Peter Atkinson, said the document was a forgery that effectively accused the prime minister not only of conflict of interest but of criminal activity. In a conference call with *Post* management on April 6, 2001, Scott repeated his contention that the document was an "obvious forgery."

The next day, bailiffs acting for BDC raided the home and cottage of former BDC president Francois Beaudoin looking for the original of the document leaked to McIntosh. They didn't find it, and the next day an outraged Beaudoin issued a statement demanding a public inquiry into the Grand-Mère affair, and McIntosh, worried that the BDC might obtain a warrant to search his home in Ottawa, moved his young children to a friend's house and hid the document.

Post managers decided not to publish anything based on the document until they were sure it was genuine, but events overtook them. The BDC letter sent to the *Post* claiming the document was a forgery had been lodged with the Quebec court that had issued the order allowing the search of Beaudoin's home. The letter was then a public document and immediately snapped up by reporters from competing media.

After a year or more out on a journalistic limb, McIntosh was now one of several reporters and columnists following the story and focusing on the RCMP's apparent unwillingness to investigate the loan and grants given to the Auberge Grand-Mère. Sun Media columnist Greg Weston was especially critical of the federal police force.

"Figuring out which of two documents was a forgery should have been a no-brainer," Weston wrote in his column, "even for the RCMP, whose record of investigating the Chrétien government has been borderline Keystone Kops. Instead, the RCMP immediately tried to hunt down the [wrongly] suspected whistleblower. In an act becoming any great police state, the Mounties raided the home and cottage of Francois Beaudoin, the former BDC president who was fired after blowing the whistle on the Grand-Mère loan fiasco.

Weston concluded his column, "Maybe it's time someone investigated the investigation."

Shortly after the police raid on Beaudoin's homes, McIntosh got a call from a source of earlier information in the case asking for a private meeting under the cloak of total confidentiality. The person claimed to have mailed McIntosh the loan authorization document but was nervous and anxious that the reporter destroy both the envelope and the document. If the RCMP got hold of either, explained the edgy informant, a simple DNA test could lead them directly to his/her door.

McIntosh insisted that the person describe the envelope and document, which they did, accurately. The reporter was almost convinced but still suspicious enough to warn the informant that if the document was a forgery, or a set-up, their confidentiality agreement would end and he would feel free to blow the informant's cover.

McIntosh refused to destroy either the document or the envelope but assured his informant that they were in a place where the RCMP could not get at them even though they were sure to try. On April 24, 2001, McIntosh published a story alleging that the BDC had violated its own internal criteria when it approved the $615,000 loan to the Auberge Grand-Mère and that Duhaime had received a preferential rate, a payment holiday, and had paid none of the bank's usual fees. The most serious violation, alleged the story, was that the BDC loaned the money to the hotel knowing that it had less than half of its value in collateral in the event of a default.

The *Post* published more stories in August, again based on documents from the secret source, that Jean Carle, the former director of operations for Chrétien and a BDC executive, had a generous clause in his employment contract granting him one year's salary if he chose to leave his job at the bank. The story stirred outraged editorial writers across the country into denouncing the bank, a publicly funded Crown corporation, for its generosity with taxpayers' money. It was one of the simpler aspects of the saga, concerning something readers could relate to. Who else gets a year's pay to leave a job voluntarily?

◆ ◆ ◆

The RCMP's hunt for the person who had leaked the allegedly forged BDC loan approval to McIntosh brought them to the *National Post* building in suburban Toronto in July 2001, where officers served Whyte with a search warrant and sparked a legal counterattack later joined by the CBC and the *Globe and Mail*. The RCMP, contending that someone had attempted to damage the prime minister's reputation by getting phony information published in the *Post*, demanded that Whyte find and surrender the leaked document and the envelope it came in so they could be sent for fingerprint and DNA analysis. The *Post*, and McIntosh in particular, had a duty to protect a source who had been guaranteed confidentiality and the CBC and *Globe* joined the battle in the cause of press and journalistic freedom.

(The long legal process that followed eventually ended in January 2004, when Ontario Madam Justice Mary Lou Benotto ruled in favour of the media groups and, by extension, set a significant legal prededent in favour of a journalist's right to protect confidential sources. She said that in issuing a search warrant similar to the one that allowed the RCMP to search Beaudoin's homes, a magistrate must consider that the majority of Canadians are informed about government and other taxpayer-supported institutions exclusively by news media, and the ability of journalists to consult confidential sources is a vital part of that process, Ironically, the decision was released, and overshadowed, during the scandal over an RCMP raid on the home of *Ottawa Citizen* reporter Juliet O'Neil, who had used a confidential source while reporting on the deportation and torture case of Syrian-Canadian Maher Arar.)

The *Post*'s own efforts to check the RCMP and BDC's claim that the leaked document was forged involved getting a look at the original but for fifteen months, the bank and Mounties had resisted showing it to them. It eventually emerged as part of the supporting documentation in the Mounties' search warrant and immediately sparked another controversy.

The document – the original loan approval form – carried the signature of Yvon Duhaime, and McIntosh, who had seen the signature dozens of times, immediately suspected it was forged. The *Post* hired a forensic expert to compare signatures and he detected numerous discrepancies, essentially confirming the reporter's suspicions. McIntosh then faxed the bank document to Duhaime, who not only confirmed that it wasn't his signature but said he had never seen the document before. Indeed, it was not the bank's practice even to show the approval form to loan applicants let alone get them to sign it. The *Post* reported the new developments in a page-one story on August 17, 2002, but the question of whether the prime minister's family company was owed $23,040 by Duhaime when the prime minister was lobbying the BDC to approve the $615,000 mortgage loan remained unproven. RCMP officers said the bank's computer system showed no record of it and neither did a list of suppliers owed money by the hotel owner. The official bank document, with Duhaime's forged signature, contained no reference to it either. But the leaked document sent to McIntosh did – a difference of six critical words.

Cries for a public inquiry from Opposition MPs were rebuffed by the government again, but the story didn't go away, re-emerging once more in the spring of 2003 during a cross-examination in the Superior Court of Ontario of lead RCMP investigator Roland Gallant by *Post* lawyer Marlys Edwardh. The court hearing was part of the effort to get the RCMP search warrant quashed.

Gallant revealed that France Bergeron, a BDC branch manager in Trois-Rivières, had told the RCMP two years earlier that the bank would never have approved the $615,000 loan without Chrétien's involvement. He also said that one critical page related to the possibility of money owed to the prime minister had been erased. The *Post* reported that story on May 12,

2003, and it sparked another predictable uproar in the House of Commons, with Chrétien again flatly denying he had profited in any way from the loan and suggesting that the *National Post* could put an end to the matter by releasing the leaked document and allowing the RCMP to prove it was a forgery.

"There is some documents that was falsified, and some don't want to give these documents back to the police to complete their inquiry," the prime minister told the Commons.

◆ ◆ ◆

In 2000, Andrew McIntosh won a major Canadian Association of Journalists award for his work on the Grand-Mère story – a significant acknowledgement by his peers. The Shawinigate coverage didn't bring down the government, but it did have some effect. In the summer of 2002, Chrétien announced an ethics initiative to prevent the kind of dealings between the prime minister, cabinet ministers, and Crown corporations that led to the Grand-Mère loan. Chrétien also promised to revisit his 1993 promise to create an ethics commissioner who would report to Parliament and not just the prime minister. That still hadn't happened when he left office in December 2003.

Ken Whyte recalls that he and his deputy, Martin Newland, were initially disappointed with the story:

> I remember Martin and I looking at one another after the first story came out. McIntosh had written it as an investigative piece, but at that point he didn't have very much, so it basically amounted to an amusing yarn about an investment gone wrong for the prime minister. So it ran as a news feature. It was okay, but not what we expected from our world-class investigative reporter after a month working on it. So it was vaguely disappointing. But bit by bit he kept hammering away at it and discovered more things and as he discovered more, we started to get calls.
>
> Conrad had always had reasonably good relations with Chrétien. He wasn't close to him, and he disagreed on a lot of policy items, but it was civil. It quickly became uncivil, but Conrad never said lay off the story. He was very insistent that we watch the tone of it and

that, if anything, we erred on the side of understatement, largely because these were very contentious matters and legally explosive and we could have got in a load of trouble if we had defamed the prime minister. But we were being very careful anyway, because we knew we were walking on eggshells. We were doubly cautious because of Conrad's insistence. It caused us problems with McIntosh. So there were a lot of tense moments in every direction, but there always is with a story like that. On the whole we did it pretty well, because it is such a rich, if complicated, story. I'm sure most people still don't really understand it, and that was always the problem. It was too complicated.

20 THE CIRCULATION GAME

"If you expand the size of the product and the size of your circulation, you add significantly to your costs. And if you don't get the advertising to justify that, you are in a black hole. The Black Hole: that should probably be the title of your book."
– Phillip Crawley, publisher, *Globe and Mail*

The *National Post* came out of the gate more quickly than even *Post* management expected, propelled by a mix of attractive subscription rates piggy-backed on Southam metro papers, cut-price offers, and targeted giveaways to more affluent neighbourhoods in Toronto, Ottawa, Edmonton, Calgary, and Vancouver. Certain households, chosen by postal code, got the newspaper free every day for three months, and in some cases a lot longer, depending on whether anyone at the *Post* remembered to stop it.

The newcomer, building on the 100,000 weekday circulation it bought from the *Financial Post*, had sold 30,000 subscriptions for a generously discounted $6 a month before the newspaper was launched and was soon boasting superior circulation figures over the *Globe* throughout the country, except in Toronto and Southern Ontario.

"We always said we would have one-third of our circulation inside Southern Ontario and two-thirds outside, which was the reverse of the *Globe and Mail*," says the *Post*'s first publisher, Don Babick. "We recognized we needed a critical mass in Toronto and Southern Ontario. The proportion was almost one-third to two-thirds. The original aim was a 200,000 daily circulation, which would have meant 130,000 outside Toronto and

Southern Ontario and 70,000 inside. As we got closer, we decided we wanted 100,000 in the Greater Toronto Area. It didn't have to be paid. We launched this paper on the basis that there would be a significant proportion of controlled circulation, as much as one-third."

Controlled circulation, a euphemism for everything that isn't a genuine paid subscription or a single-copy sale from a newspaper box or corner store, was key to the *Post*'s strategy: get the high readership and circulation numbers and establish fast credibility with the advertising community. How the numbers were achieved in the short term was less important than achieving them. Babick says it was immaterial at that stage whether people actually bought the newspaper and, if they did, how much they paid for it. In TV parlance, it was eyeballs the *Post* was after. In some cities, especially Toronto, casual newspaper readers were bombarded with free copies of the *Star*, *Globe*, and *Post*, making the effort of actually purchasing one an act of extravagance, stupidity, or charity. On some days, especially in early 2000, there were almost a quarter-million copies of free daily newspapers being handed out on the streets, gas stations, and coffee shops of the nation.

Conrad Black, who saw the Canadian newspaper war as a mini version of his own legendary price-cutting battle with Rupert Murdoch in Britain, wanted the gas pedal flat to the floor – not a strategy favoured by all his executives – but the *Globe* and *Star* were determined to match him copy for copy and spend whatever it took to prevent the *Post* from being able to boast readership supremacy especially in the Toronto region. It was a confrontation that, by some estimates, would cost the three papers combined more than $1 billion – a crippling burden for all three. The *Globe* entered the newspaper war economically healthy, and the *Post*, suckling on the cash cows that were the major Southam dailies, had time and money, but neither was ever likely to be in limitless supply.

Black says the initial outlay was about what he expected. "You don't start up a national newspaper in a country with five time zones and not spend some money doing it. The *Globe* confected this myth that the *National Post* was an open artery far beyond what a rational person, or any company, would endure, but it wasn't that bad. It was standard start-up costs, nothing more than that. I was pretty serene."

Part of those start-up costs included $1 million a year to fly a couple of thousand newspapers from the printing plant in Halifax to St. John's,

Newfoundland, six days a week. It was an essential, if ultimately cosmetic, expense if the *Post* wanted to call itself a national newspaper. Wherever the *Globe and Mail* left its footprint, the *Post* had to go. The wisdom of the decision had been confirmed to Don Babick shortly after he announced the *Post*'s launch. "One of the first calls I got after the announcement was from a CBC station in Cornerbrook, and the reporter asked, 'Will you be circulating in Newfoundland?' If I'd have said no we would have been accused of not being a real national newspaper. It's something you could cut back on in time, but in the early years we had to be there."

◆ ◆ ◆

Companies doing business with newspapers have different needs. Canadian Tire, The Bay, Sears, or Future Shop, and the like produce "free-standing inserts," which means those glossy flyers packed into the Saturday edition of most major newspapers. What those companies care about are reasonably accurate estimates of a newspaper's circulation so they don't waste money printing too many of their inserts. Whether a newspaper is selling for a dollar each or being given away is of no concern to them. Other advertisers buy space inside the newspaper for a fee according to the position and size of the ad and an expectation their ad will reach a certain number of readers.

The Audit Bureau of Circulation (ABC) measures the number of copies sold, based on independently audited information from each newspaper, and for the better part of the last century it was the only industry measurement. In 1986, the Newspaper Audience Databank (NADBank) emerged as an alternative means of measurement, estimating newspaper readership rather than the number of copies printed and distributed. NADBank gathers its figures through surveys, rather like opinion pollsters, and measures the number of people who read each copy distributed. NADBank surveys call back the same randomly chosen respondents a dozen or more times over a three-month period. If a household with two parents and two children over eighteen get a copy of the *Globe and Mail*, chances are that all four will spend time with the newspaper. If Aunt Gladys pops over each night and takes the well-thumbed *Globe* home to share with Uncle George, who is too cheap to buy a copy, that one copy could represent six readers. (Conventional wisdom has it that one copy equals slightly fewer than three readers.) Readership numbers aren't subject to the same rigorous verification as audited circulation and don't capture all newspapers, but advertisers prefer them, because they are nice and big and give some demographic dimension to the circulation figures.

According to a 2002 study by NADBank:

> 54% of adults 18+ read a newspaper on the average weekday;
> 60% of adults 18+ have read a newspaper the previous weekend; and
> 81% of adults 18+ have read a newspaper in the past week.
>
> Canadian adults spend an average of forty-six minutes reading a daily newspaper on the average weekday and eighty-seven minutes on the weekend. Males spend an average of forty-eight minutes reading a daily newspaper and females an average of forty-five minutes. On weekends, males average eighty-nine minutes and females eighty-five minutes.

The *Globe and Mail* was a member of ABC for decades but resigned in 1986 in protest because ABC refused to count bulk sales as part of a newspaper's circulation – only paid subscriptions, single-copy sales, and newspapers sold for 50 per cent or more of the official cover price counted. The *Globe*'s bulk circulation of some 30,000 to 40,000 was significant, because part of the newspaper's marketing strategy was to distribute cheap copies to higher-end hotels and airlines and into the hands of travelling business people. Aside from additional revenue, this exclusive niche was also a cleverly conceived selling point for the newspaper's advertising sales team.

But that desirable niche was also a prime target for the *Post*, the *Star*, and Conrad Black's Southam metro dailies, all of which began to muscle in. The battle, as *Globe* publisher Roger Parkinson recalls, quickly got vicious. "We had a huge and very important business with the hotels and airlines and were getting good money from them. And plus, they were our kind of readers. Then two things happened: ABC changed their regulations so that even a newspaper that cost a penny could be counted, so the *Post* wanted on the airlines and wanted us out. They went to the airlines, asked to come in, and tried to undercut us. They charged a penny per copy or something. So we had to go down in price too, because we had to stay on the airlines and had to stay in the upscale hotels. That business had been worth $3 million or $4 million, so it was revenue that came right off the top, but we had to compete and we had to win. We were not going to get knocked out of the hotels or off the airlines."

The *Globe*, which for years had produced its own internal circulation audits, reluctantly returned to the ABC fold in the fall of 2000 under pressure from the advertising community. It was the first time in a long time that advertisers had been able to exert any influence over the *Globe*, but with new competition in the market, and with that competition subjecting itself to a third-party audit, the situation had changed. ABC, in concert with tighter, more detailed audits, allowed any newspaper sold for a penny or more to be counted, and the *Globe*, personified by Parkinson's successor, Phillip Crawley, thought it cheapened the industry.

The *Post*, pressured to make a good early showing and to meet the expectations of advertisers who had bought space in the newspaper, thought differently. (Typically, a new media player that sells advertising on the promise of reaching a certain number of people has to offer compensation if it fails to reach those numbers. In the case of a newspaper or magazine, that compensation usually takes the form of extra free space.)

Increasingly, circulation figures became an expensive propaganda tool in the war between the *Post*, *Globe*, and, in the Toronto area, the *Star*. Much of the early groundwork for the *Globe*'s preparation for the newcomer had been laid during the latter days of Roger Parkinson who, along with other publishers in the industry, had been more focused on the number and type of readers his newspaper was attracting rather than the number of copies rolling off the presses. In the complex economics of newspapers, there is a point at which increased circulation becomes a drain on the bottom line. If you can charge $10,000 for a full-page ad with a daily circulation of 300,000, which translates to about one million individual readers, it's unlikely you can charge any more with a circulation of 350,000, especially if competitors with similar circulation numbers are offering cheaper advertising rates. A typical weekday newspaper costs between sixteen and eighteen cents in newsprint and ink alone – and around thirty-five cents for the fatter weekend editions. Add labour, delivery costs, and other overheads, and each copy of a newspaper costs more to produce than it does to buy.

In the mid-1990s, the *Globe and Mail* had about 10,000 newspaper boxes across the country but had been scaling back, especially around Toronto, where, before pulling some of them off the street altogether, the newspaper's circulation department fixed signs on them pointing to the nearest newsstand or corner store. Newspaper boxes are good, even essential, promotional tools but are an inefficient and uneconomical method of vending a newspaper. Vandalism is frequent, maintenance costs high, sales low, and people who actually buy copies from boxes sometimes take more than one. But with the *Post* looming, the *Globe*'s street-sale strategy had to be slammed into reverse. The box, and the equally uneconomical newspaper rack, suddenly became fashionable again. "We were heading into a circulation battle," recalls Parkinson, "so we bought a slew of boxes and we kept adding and adding. So if you wanted a *Globe and Mail*, you were going to be able to find it. We had to be very aggressive."

Part of the new aggressive attitude involved schmoozing retailers and newsstand operators to check whether they were happy with their relationship with the *Globe* and whether the newspaper was arriving on time and in a proper manner. The point was to ensure that the *Globe and Mail*, whether racked or otherwise, was prominently displayed. Vendors must have wondered why they were suddenly deserving of so much attention, especially in Toronto, because the other resident dailies were doing much the same thing.

The *National Post*'s black-and-gold street boxes displaying the paper's entire front page were more expensive than the traditional box, which shows only the half above the fold, but did make a significant splash on the streets of major cities. It was a *Washington Times* innovation spotted by Don Babick while he was at a Hollinger meeting in the U.S. capital. Newspaper designers have traditionally paid more attention to the top half of the front page because that was all single-copy buyers saw before laying down their fifty cents. In other words, the section of page one above the fold, containing what are perceived to be the top two or three major stories of the day, is a promotional tool unto itself. The *Post*'s full-length boxes, unusual for a broadsheet newspaper, demand total top-to-bottom design of the first page.

Babick and his fellow *Post* executives decided to order an initial 5,000, at between seven and eight hundred dollars each, and then some. So in Toronto the *Star* had to do the same. Allowing the other guy to boast more boxes on the street wasn't an option for anyone, and certainly not for the *Star*, in its own backyard.

Phillip Crawley was determined from day one to match the *Post* copy for copy to avoid even the vaguest perception that his newspaper had fallen behind. "Under the ridiculous rules we have in North America, circulation is whatever you want to make it – all you have to do is pay for it. So if you're prepared to spend the dollars to sell a paper for one or two cents, you can. But we said, 'If you're going to be stupid enough to spend all that money we will beat you on it.' It is literally throwing money away, because it devalues the whole product. And that really comes back to the damage Conrad Black has done to the Canadian newspaper market, because he had been prepared to sell this paper, ever since its conception, at a discount. It makes people feel that these papers are worthless, because they can get it on the street for nothing. People say to me, 'Yes, but you've done the same,' but whatever they do, we will do better."

Circulation and readership are two basic measurements newspapers do business by, but beyond that is a whole mess of complexities and enough smoke and mirrors to allow each newspaper to claim glory from the same set of figures – which, in shameless efforts at self-promotion, the *Globe*, *Post*, and *Star* did with great energy. Figures that before the newspaper war were considered barely worthy of public interest became front-page news and major stories in business sections. The stories were aimed at the advertising community, and as in most matters of newspaper self-promotion and notions of self-importance, readers likely remained indifferent.

Typical of the hype were the headlines that appeared in the *Star*, *Globe*, and *Post* on November 11, 2000, following the release the day before of a NADBank survey. All three found something to crow about.

"*STAR* BUILDS ON LEAD IN TORONTO NEWSPAPER MARKET: LATEST SURVEY PUTS READERSHIP WELL AHEAD OF RIVALS," said the *Star*.

"*POST* FASTEST GROWING, MOST TRULY NATIONAL NEWSPAPER: NADBANK READER STUDY," said the *Post*.

"NEWSPAPER READERSHIP ON THE RISE; NATIONAL LEADER THE *GLOBE AND MAIL* JUMPS 14 PER CENT, NADBANK STUDY SHOWS," said the *Globe*.

The *Post* story pointed out that the newspaper was now boasting the advantage in Ottawa, Montreal, Vancouver, and Edmonton and elicited a quote from one media buyer who said that if the Toronto readership figures were extracted from the equation, the *Post* actually had more readers. Which, to the casual observer, might have seemed like a hockey game ending 5-1 and the losing team announcing that they would have won if only the other team hadn't scored five goals. Still, the *Post* was getting

EGO AND INK • 271

good numbers, and was ahead in several major cities barely two years after its launch.

The *Star*'s readership stayed comfortably ahead of the pack in the greater Toronto area, and publisher John Honderich took pains to point out that the *Star* had lots of exclusive readership, a selling point to advertisers because it means that lots of people who read the *Star* weren't reading any other newspaper. In other words, Honderich would tell advertisers, if you want to reach our readers the only way to do it is through the *Star*.

In Toronto, in the year 1999/2000, the *Star*'s daily readership had edged up from 1.17 million to 1.24 million and slipped on Saturdays from 1.61 million to 1.54 million, ups and downs that were not especially significant.

The *Globe*'s Toronto weekday readership leaped from 366,000 in 1999 to 575,000 in 2000, and on Saturdays from 323,000 to 448,000.

During that same period, the *National Post*'s Toronto readership jumped from 296,000 to 349,000 during the week and on Saturdays from 191,300 to 233,700.

So there was some comfort for everyone, as there was the following spring, when the newspapers celebrated the release of the ABC figures:

"*NATIONAL POST* CIRCULATION SOARS AGAIN," said the *National Post* on its front page. Stories in the *Post* about *Post* circulation and readership numbers often included the word *soars*. It's a good word that fit nicely into big headlines.

"*GLOBE* STAYS ON TOP IN CIRCULATION WAR. *TORONTO STAR* AND *SUN* LOSE GROUND IN HEATED BATTLE FOR CANADA'S LARGEST MARKET," said the *Globe* in a report that admitted the *Post* had gained (though not *soared*) but only because it had increased its bulk sales by 34 per cent.

The *Post*'s front-page story did not go into much detail beyond attempting to justify the use of the word *soars*, which became *surged* in the body of the story, to describe its increase in copies sold. But it did take a swipe at the *Globe*'s "quality of circulation" and made the dubious boast that the *Post*'s circulation was of better quality because it sold fewer discounted copies. Another story on the same subject inside the newspaper delved more deeply into the bulk sale minutiae but made the point that, through whatever method, the *Post* had moved within a hair of overtaking the *Globe*.

The unvarnished ABC figures tell the story of an industry engaged in a high-stakes game of chicken or perhaps even Russian roulette. Producing any commodity for thirty-five cents and selling it for one cent has inevitable repercussions. In the words of one Southam executive, "It all went crazy."

Audited ABC figures (rounded off to the nearest thousand) for the period ending September 30, 2000, show that the *Globe and Mail* had average bulk circulation of 83,000, Monday to Friday, and 79,000 on Saturdays. Of that bulk, 73,000 copies were sold Monday to Friday for five cents or less, and on Saturdays 70,000 copies were sold in the same price range.

In that same period, the *Post* had average bulk sales of 54,000, Monday to Friday, and 55,000 on Saturdays. More than 36,000 were in the five-cent-or-less category, six days a week.

A year later the *Globe* was bulking by 81,000, Monday to Friday, but had upped the ante to 101,000 on Saturdays – 72,000 of Monday to Friday copies in the one- to five-cent category, and on Saturdays more than 90,000.

In this last period of Conrad Black's involvement in the *National Post*, his newspaper had 85,000 in the Monday to Friday total bulk category and 106,000 on Saturdays. More than 70,000 of those newspapers were sold for five cents or less, Monday to Friday, and more than 67,000 on Saturdays.

Another year on, in the first full twelve months of CanWest Global control of the *Post*, the costly bulk sales and giveaways dropped dramatically and the *Globe*'s followed suit.

But even ABC, with its close auditing, wasn't catching all the giveaways. Commuters on the streets of Ottawa, Toronto, Vancouver, Montreal, and other major cities couldn't walk from their bus stop to the office without a free newspaper being thrust at them. In late 2000 through the spring of 2001, the *Post* was selling 75,000 Saturday papers nationally in a promotional deal with PetroCanada, which gave them away to customers.

The various interpretations of the same sets of figures cut little ice with the advertising community, which has access to the same numbers and does its own crunching. Hugh Dow, head of the advertising house M2 Universal, began commissioning his own reader surveys, largely to stay current in a dynamic market confused by propaganda from the opposing forces. It was clear, he says, that the *Post* and the *Globe* were engaged in a battle of selective interpretation. "If you read the *Globe and Mail* article on the latest ABC numbers, it's a totally different story to the *National Post*, and you think, 'Is this the same audit'? And, yeah, it's the same audit, but they're being selective in terms of what numbers they're using. And a great deal of it was exacerbated by the *Globe and Mail*, which reported with great glee any time there was any kind of whiff of what the *Post*'s financial situation was."

What the advertising community gleaned from the *Globe*'s enthusiastic coverage of the *Post*'s deficits, and its owner's eventual financial difficulties, was a sense that the *Post* was hungry and willing to make deals. "A hungry media owner wants revenue and is prepared to negotiate a discount," says Dow. "Generally speaking, a media owner who is enjoying great success with revenue flowing in is not prepared to discount, or negotiate. We like hungry media owners."

From the advertising buyers' perspective, the *Post* had not only opened the door to deal-making and the ability to play one newspaper against another, but had injected energy into a staid Canadian newspaper market. "The newspaper industry prior to the arrival of the *Post* was mature and somewhat lethargic," reasons Dow. "There was no major innovation, but even before the arrival of the *Post* we started to see the reaction from the incumbents, particularly the *Globe* but also the *Star*, so without question the arrival of the *Post* stirred things up, both nationally and locally, and led to a better and more vibrant and certainly higher-profile newspaper industry. And Conrad Black is followed with a great deal of interest; almost everything he ever says or utters or speaks about seems to be reported. And so he was seen as the champion, and for many years one of the things we have looked for are champions of media – someone who raises the bar and challenges the status quo. We have them in the television business, but before Conrad Black we were hard-pressed to find visible champions in newspapers. And without question, he changed the face of the newspaper business in Canada."

David Harrison, another veteran Toronto advertising executive, saw immediate practical benefits in the *Post*. "The *Globe* improved its business practice, like making sure an ad ran on the right day on the right page, which is something that is strangely important to us and they weren't very good at it."

The *Post*'s apparently impressive 2001 figures caused euphoria among its staff, and some started to talk about achieving the incredible and bringing the *Globe* to its knees. More vivid imaginations saw a scenario where the Thomson Corporation, obviously almost done with the newspaper business anyway, would call it quits, hand over the smoking ruins of its franchise to Conrad Black, and head off into the sunset while the business of amalgamating the *Post* and *Globe* under one title was quickly achieved by the victorious Southam/Hollinger forces.

It all brought an uncharacteristically sober response from *Globe* publisher Phillip Crawley, who said, essentially, that the *Globe*'s self-imposed reduction in bulk sales had caused the gap to narrow. Then he added a sombre warning: "The Canadian newspaper industry is fast approaching a day of reckoning, when economic realities will force a return to more normal consumer pricing."

He had no idea how fast.

◆　◆　◆

Black did not care for the *Post*'s own marketing and advertising campaign, which he though crude and unsuitable. One billboard, featuring a dog peeing on a competitor's newspaper box, offended him almost as much as another depicting a toilet bowl full of bricks and some boast suggesting this was the effect the *National Post* was having on its competition.

The *Post*'s then publisher, Don Babick, didn't agree. "Conrad didn't like the dog pissing on the newspaper box, but he didn't get it. I thought it was brilliant and irreverent and what the *Post* was all about: 'If you don't like us, piss on you – you don't have to read us.'"

Black wasn't especially offended by the crudity, but he did think it sent the wrong message. "I thought the general theme of the advertising was defensive. We were certainly a hellraiser of a paper stirring things up, but I thought the line we should be taking was, 'We're the best national paper, buy us,' and we should stop being a kind of mustang or maverick buzzing around and disturbing and afflicting the powerful and, in fact, set out our stall as a first-class distinguished paper. I don't think our advertising did that."

Black ordered the campaign changed from the start of 2000 and turned to theatrical impresario Garth Drabinsky, who would produce some spectacular work for the *Post*, including the series of cinema ads featuring the newspaper's name writers that had so surprised Robert Fulford. "Garth was having his legal problems," says Black. "He is a friend of mine, at loose ends and happy to do something. He is a promotional talent, so I thought, let's give Garth a try. We brought Garth in when he was down on his luck and under indictment in the U.S.A., but he is a talent and you stick with your friends."

Babick – who had encountered Drabinsky in Vancouver when Babick was publisher of Pacific Press (the *Vancouver Sun* and *Province*) and Drabinsky was marketing the Ford Theatre – was less thrilled at the prospect. He turned to his deputy, Gordon Fisher, to handle the details. "I knew Garth relatively well. He is an inspiration but tough to control, so I said to Gordon, 'Here's where I pull rank. You get to deal with Garth, because if I have to, I'll probably kill him.' But Garth is a brilliant marketing guy and challenged us to do different things. He didn't move the needle a great deal for us except for a little bit in Toronto."

◆ ◆ ◆

The *Post* was pushing hard on all fronts, but neither *Globe* publisher Phillip Crawley nor his then-boss, Stuart Garner, have too many good words to say about the effort. They seem passionate in their belief that, in Crawley's words, Black set aside normal business judgment to launch a money-losing newspaper, for which there was no business rationale, in order to use that newspaper to pursue a political agenda. It was a message Crawley repeated countless times in interviews and speeches.

Garner, now long gone from the paid employ of Thomson, has no ready answer when asked if the *Post* had any redeeming aspect:

> I have to think carefully, because I don't want it to sound trite. I was keenly aware, given the enormous amount of favourable publicity Black was getting, that the biggest danger we faced was a loss of self-belief. In other words, we would defeat ourselves . . . the enemy within and all that. So I was always looking for that. The coverage of what was going on was definitely anti-*Globe*. Whatever the *Post* did or said was forgivable; whatever the *Globe* did or said wasn't. But like a lot of things in life, it had as much to do with the preparations as it did with the execution. If you run a soccer team and you let your players spend all week playing snooker and they turn out at three o'clock on a Saturday, it's no surprise if they get thrashed. If you spend the week

analyzing the strengths and weaknesses of the competition and do your training – you've got a lot better chance of winning. What we did prior to the Black launch was vital.

Black sees it differently. He claims to have been "pilloried" by the CBC and others, especially in the run-up to the *Post*'s launch, and he sniffs at the negative assessment of his business acumen. "I am not one to invoke the Marquess of Queensberry rules, but they overreacted, didn't they? We were interrupting their cozy little monopoly. Those speeches Crawley used to give attacking me personally and attacking my wife. I never responded, because I thought it was pretty bush-league stuff for the traditional national newspaper owned by the wealthiest person in the country. They were shaken by what we did, and if you calculate the circulation accurately, we got awfully close to them. We did have advantages outside of Toronto, there is no doubt about that, but on the other hand, they are the *Globe and Mail*, for God's sake – the best established title in the country."

The *Post* did get close to the *Globe*, and edged ahead of it in British Columbia, Alberta, and Manitoba, where the newspaper was especially well received. It is true, too, that the *Post* seriously upset business for the *Globe*, which had been in the luxurious position of being able to raise its cover price in a deliberate effort to cut circulation and reduce production and distribution costs. The *Globe* was able to do this knowing that a trim of its circulation numbers would not compromise its advertising rates because it had its own unchallenged niche. In 1997, the year before Black launched the *Post*, the *Globe* made around $40 million profit, which was about 20 per cent of EBITDA (Earnings Before Interest, Taxes, Depreciation, and Amortization), otherwise known as operational cash flow. For a major daily newspaper 20 per cent is a healthy average, although in smaller markets throughout North America, the Thomson Corporation and Black's Hollinger had been known to squeeze 40 per cent and perhaps slightly higher by pressing two corporate thumbs on a newspaper's throat and squeezing aggressively. While $40-million profit is a good place to be, it is not, and was not, an unassailable position. Fortunately, the Thomson organization, one of the world's most successful, efficiently run media corporations, was prepared to dig deep into its well-stocked pockets to defeat Conrad Black. It was business, but it was also personal. The company had divested itself of its North American newspapers in favour of electronic delivery of information and had made a remarkably profitable transition. But for reasons that can only be speculated at, Thomson kept the *Globe* as its lone newspaper, took it into battle against Black, and watched the profits dwindle. And then the phone company, with wads of money and an agenda of its own, came by to make a deal.

It was September 2000 when Bell Canada Enterprises (BCE) formed a joint venture with the Thomson family's private holding company, Woodbridge, and the *Globe*'s parental pockets got deeper. Bell, led by the expansion-smitten CEO Jean Monty, had paid $2.3 billion for the CTV network earlier in 2000 and wanted the *Globe* and its content as part of an overall convergence strategy, a similar model to the one that would motivate CanWest Global's move into the newspaper business. Bell, owners of the Sympatico Internet portals, had the means of transporting news and information at high speed, and the *Globe and Mail* had quality content. It was an expensive expansion strategy that would ultimately lead to Monty's exit as Bell chief and a reversal of corporate strategy that would effectively put the *Globe* up for sale yet again, with Thomson having first refusal on the venerable daily.

At the *Toronto Star*, where the corporate coffers were also well stocked but paid circulation was slipping, executives watched with interest as the phone-company reinforcements arrived at the *Globe*.

"Everybody wondered who was going to run out of money first," recalls *Star* executive managing editor James Travers. "Our assessment was that the *Globe* was not a rich property and was basically being kept alive by Thomson. It wasn't losing money, but neither was it making much. We knew that BCE hadn't bought the *Globe* to shut it down. It was a significant asset to them and it really changed the game. We figured before that it wouldn't take much to move the *Globe* from profit to loss, whereas to do that to the *Star* you would have to take out a huge chunk of revenue. So we always thought the *Globe* was the most vulnerable and we decided that at the end of the day it would be in our best interests if the *Star*, *Globe*, and *Sun* were left standing. The Toronto market had been carved up and there existed three newspapers that were comfortable with one another."

Globe publisher Phillip Crawley confirms that the partnership with BCE did not affect Thomson's determination to crush the *National Post*. "Thomson sold the *Globe* to BCE and retained nearly 30 per cent, but if you see the way Thomson and Woodbridge operate you will see that their involvement is much more than that of a 30 per cent partner. They are very active and their presence and active support have been continuous. The people here feel they have two very-well-resourced companies behind the newspaper. If the *Globe* had been an individual newspaper, on its own, we would have felt more vulnerable, but Thomson has spent many millions of dollars supporting our company."

❖ ❖ ❖

"If you don't get the advertising dollars," Phillip Crawley points out, "where else is the money coming from? It isn't from circulation when you sell at a price that doesn't even cover the distribution cost. The normal cover price barely covers costs. So you get less circulation revenue than you should be getting, and it puts all the eggs into the advertising basket. Conrad Black played the cheap circulation cards, and to do that he had to win big on the advertising side."

But he did not win big.

In the months before the launch of the *Post*, Conrad Black and his executives had worked hard courting the Toronto advertising community, hosting lunches and receptions, and Black personally hosted a garden party at his Toronto home for members of the city's corporate elite. The event inspired Black's wife, Barbara Amiel, to write an account in her regular *Maclean's* magazine column several weeks before the *Post* launch:

> I am married to the chairman of Southam Inc., which is launching a new national newspaper in Canada later this month. I may also write a column for said paper, and if that paper is a financial success, I'm hoping my husband's income from it will subsidize my obscene dress bills. (Of one thing you can be sure: someone will take that last sentence out of context.)
>
> Last Monday, I arrived at my Toronto home, jet-lagged to death, to see a large white tent flapping on our front lawn. About 150 CEOs and spouses/partners or pet seals had been invited to dinner that night to celebrate the upcoming launch of the paper and hear my husband give them a pep talk about advertising in it.
>
> With six hours to the arrival of potential underwriters for next spring's wardrobe, I looked at the tent. It resembled something out

of MASH: a bare structure, huge expanses of rubberized nylon flapping over a dull anthracite-colored carpet. All that was missing was stretcher beds and IVs. Where were the decorations, the whimsy, the clever touches that make a large event intimate, I asked rhetorically? Rhetorically, because there was no one in sight to answer the questions.

After some searching, a reluctant person called an "events" coordinator appeared. "Why is this tent so horrid-looking?" I asked nicely. "The group," he informed me solemnly, "decided the evening should have a corporate look." The only look that came to mind was Oxfam or possibly the wedding tent for Le Corbusier's daughter. I began a search-and-rescue operation to salvage the evening. Six hours later, we hadn't re-created the Hanging Gardens of Babylon, but the Gobi desert motif was softened.

In January and February of 1998, Black's executive team had met regularly with advertising industry executives, who had been positive about the prospects for a new daily supported by the existing Southam infrastructure, and while nothing was guaranteed, Black's people were persuaded that if they built it, advertisers would come and, most crucially, the national advertising pie might grow. Among advertisers, there was an element of self-interest at play: a new competitor might reduce newspaper rates for advertisers, who for years had complained of an arrogant take-it-or-leave-it attitude, especially at the *Globe and Mail*. In the midst of a buoyant economy, the prospects looked good for an energetic, professionally produced newcomer capable of quickly establishing itself as a major player – especially in Toronto, one of the western world's most competitive newspaper markets, with four established dailies, a vibrant ethnic press, and, for a time, three free tabloid dailies targeting the commuter trade. The Greater Toronto Area represented a quarter of Canada's population and roughly the same amount of the nation's economic clout. To get a comparable, proportional market in the United States you would have to clump together New York City, Chicago, Detroit, San Francisco, and a couple of other cities.

Hugh Dow, one of Canada's most prominent advertising executives, was one of several people in the industry sought out for advice by Black's team in late 1997. The Toronto area, he told them, would be a tough nut to crack.

Advertising support was enthusiastic in the *Post*'s first weeks but quickly diminished as the novelty wore off. Reporters, section editors, and copy editors began referring to the newspaper as an "ad-free zone," a state that threw early editorial strategies into disarray but, on the positive side, allowed for beautiful-looking news pages, packed with long, detailed news stories and features. It was a treasure trove, especially for those readers with time to read it.

The *Post* had started with a branding policy that required all stories to be labelled as written by *Post* staff – a British daily newspaper tradition that required a staff of rewriters to pull together reporting from other sources and produce stories written in-house. This work, together with stories filed by the newspaper's own reporters, was to comprise the bulk of the *Post*'s news section.

Kirk LaPointe, part of the early newsroom leadership, recalls when the reality set in:

> We needed rewriters and we needed a hell of a lot more reporters. That was really evident after the first week. All the advertisers wanted to be in the paper in the first day. We turned down advertising and convinced ourselves that we were going to have to fight editorially to make sure we didn't go beyond the 30 per cent threshold for advertising and be shouting with the advertising guys, telling them, "You can't take that space."
>
> I hate to say it, but within ten days we were saying, "Where are the ads? What's happened here?" There were days when there would be fourteen or fifteen totally open pages. Advertisers had bought for the first week and were supposed to be coming back later, around Christmas. What that did, almost instantly, was change the best-laid plans of the place to do medium-range journalism. We had six days of newspapers and we needed everybody every day. We only had about twelve or fourteen reporters, and it wasn't enough. Suddenly we were commissioning a lot of freelance pieces and leaning on our Ottawa operation and demanding that all our national correspondents write every day. We were backtracking on what we told them would actually happen. A lot of them thought they were there to be news feature writers and to do special projects. We had to tell them, "No, no, no. You've got to be on the file tomorrow and if it's anything less than twenty inches, we're screwed." That was the first real

change in the nature of the paper, and it was driven by the sad economic situation.

It got better, sort of, and advertising revenue gradually built over the next two years. In its hottest year, 2000, the *Post* was generating $130 million in revenue, comprising $98 million in advertising revenue and $32 million from circulation. Significantly, only about 15 to 20 per cent of the *Post*'s ad revenue was from the Toronto–Southern Ontario market whereas the *Globe and Mail*'s take from that lucrative geographical pot was around 40 per cent or more. By some estimates, the *Globe and Mail*'s total revenue around that time was in the $250 million range.

The *Post*'s expenses, largely from the burden of producing and distributing tens of thousands of copies each day by essentially giving them away, also climbed. In that same period when $130 million was coming in the door, $190 million was going out. And the war being fought on the journalistic and circulation fronts was equally brutal, if not more so, on the advertising front.

The *Globe and Mail* had put enormous effort into sharpening its approach to advertising sales, a push that began toward the end of the Parkinson era and continued with intensity under Crawley. The newspaper's advertising team won several national awards during the height of the newspaper war.

The *National Post*, building on revenue it had inherited from the *Financial Post*, had done reasonably well in attracting some of the bigger business advertising – banking, automotive, high-tech, and other corporate accounts, but made no inroads into the lucrative classified ad market in Toronto locked up over the years by the *Star* and, most everywhere else in the country, by Southam's own major metros. The *Globe* had a relatively modest number of classifieds but cornered the career-advertising market. At the height of the war, and the economy, the *Globe*'s classified and career ads were worth $75 million. The *Post* had only $2 or $3 million of that business.

Despite the many advantages that the Southam infrastructure offered the *Post* across the country, there were also press limitations, especially in Calgary and Vancouver, and limits to the number of A-section pages and the amount of colour, and colour advertising, that sections could accommodate.

Still, *Post* publisher Don Babick insists that everything at the *Post* was according to plan and the rhetoric coming from the enemy camp was nothing more than what the *Post* expected:

> There was a price war going on and everyone was discounting. We were behind but on track. We weren't off the rails. We became a success faster than anyone thought, and faster than we thought, but the model doesn't quite work if you have circulation building ahead of the advertising and you have to catch up. We had great readership when we first came out, and that shocked everyone. In our first NAD-Bank we had almost one million readers a day, including 400,000-plus in the Toronto market. In our first official ABC audit we came out with 268,000 paid circulation, and we said from the beginning that we needed 300,000 nationally. Criticizing our business model was a logical position for the *Globe* and *Star* to take because saying anything other would have given the *Post* credibility. The *Globe* went into this war making a lot of money and the *Post* caused it to lose a lot of money, but we never went into this saying we would displace the *Globe*. We thought the market was big enough to support two national newspapers.

With circulation, printing, and marketing costs sucking up the *Post*'s revenue and the costly relaunch of *Saturday Night* magazine in May 2000 as a free weekly insert in the *National Post*, the newspaper was ill prepared for the onslaught of an economic slowdown, which began to show itself in the fall of 2000 and hit hard in 2001. The advertising market shrunk by millions of dollars for all newspapers and what Babick describes as "a rising airplane" was dragged back to earth by an ailing economy.

Conrad Black is adamant that the *National Post* did not get the advertiser respect or support it deserved and speaks bitterly of overly cautious business people – the like of which he entertained in his MASH tent shortly before the launch:

> Large sections of the business community, in that pusillanimous manner of Canadian businessmen, bought into the theory that it was an assault on the cocoon that they lived in and were comfortable in, and

this was essentially a hobby horse of mine rather than the cost-per-thousand argument we were presenting them. We used to have all sorts of dinners with these advertisers and we made some headway, and I want to exempt some, because some were very supportive and helpful, but in every case we were not asking for charity; we were giving them a proper cost-per-thousand argument. I made it clear at every meeting I went to that I did not ask for one cent of business on other than hard-headed commercial grounds.

But the fact is that Canada is not only a smug country but a fearful country, very afraid of change and particularly afraid of it if the change, as it was portrayed in this case, is something that, if adopted, would accrue to the benefit of a controversial individual. And the degree to which it was my paper, and therefore something many people wouldn't wish to support, was a problem for it.

Yes, says Black, he knows many of the business people he is criticizing, but "the fact that you know someone, and have a civil relationship with them, doesn't necessarily translate into two cents, let alone sizable amounts of money. Advertising was respectable, a little less than we'd hoped for, but it was respectable."

Despite its hip image, the advertising business is not one to embrace change readily, and that rigid attitude also militated against Black and his new daily. David Harrison, president and CEO of the Toronto media management group Harrison, Young, Pesonen and Newell, was one of several advertising executives sought out by Black's executives for pre-launch advice. He believes that if the *Post* did not attract the advertising it deserved, as Black claims, agencies whose business it is to spend clients' money on the myriad of media alternatives were at least partially to blame:

The advertising business claims to be creative, off the wall, flaky, and edgy, but it is, in fact, among the most conservative businesses in the world. For new media to gain acceptance is extraordinarily difficult. It is very easy to not say yes and just to wait and see. We will never be criticized for not saying yes. Advertising is a cold, commercial activity, which is only interested in how many eyeballs it can get for how much money. Anyone who paints it differently is mistaken. We are about spending our clients' money as efficiently as possible, and there's a lot of media out there. The *Post* looked great, it was fantastic, but we sat back and waited. The ad community always liked the *Post* and thought it was a good product. Everybody saluted the flag when it went up the pole and Conrad is an admired figure – controversial perhaps, but admired. People thought it was a great idea, but they didn't spend their money. I don't think the industry necessarily saw the need for another newspaper, but competition is always good and if someone wanted to start another national newspaper, God bless them.

The crucial battle for all media, whether newspapers or TV, is for a piece of what Harrison's industry colleague Hugh Dow calls the advertising pie. "It's a battle for a share of the advertising dollar whether it's the newspaper business, television, or radio. The advertising pie is not going to grow because of forty-five new digital television services, or because a new magazine or newspaper suddenly becomes available. Revenue comes from one pie, because most advertisers allocate a certain portion of their sales, or marketing efforts, toward advertising, and that's not going to change because of the availability of a new player."

◆ ◆ ◆

The *Toronto Star*, focused on keeping its own local franchise out of harm's way, had been heavily into the bulk sale and giveaway game and had hired prominent advertising executive Tony Pigott to work on the newspaper's image.

Pigott, who became Canadian branch president of the multinational advertising company J. Walter Thompson, repackaged Canada's largest daily as a local newspaper for five million people and an essential buy for anyone who wanted to understand and enjoy life in Canada's largest city. A companion message was sent to the advertising community: If you want your ads to reach the Toronto masses, the city's local paper is your vehicle.

Through its then-pollster, the Angus Reid Group, the *Star* had been tracking public reaction to the *National Post* from the first day it hit the streets. The news Reid delivered to the *Star* was mixed, but in essence told the story of a new newspaper in the Toronto market that had been well received and, within six months, was registering a "reader satisfaction" level as high as the *Star* and the *Globe*. Early *Post* readers in Toronto, many of whom were getting the newspaper free, were not necessarily prepared in the early months to give up their regular *Star*, *Globe*, or *Sun* but had been pleasantly surprised by the *Post*'s content.

And the *Post*, warned Reid, was proving attractive to younger, well-educated readers who had the potential of pulling advertisers away from the *Globe* and *Star*. The bottom line was that the *Globe* and *Star* were in no immediate danger but neither could guarantee the loyalty of their readers.

The *Star* analyzed the *Post* three ways to Sunday and decided it needed to: sharpen its coverage, especially its local coverage, and become more attractive to visible minorities; beef up its Sunday edition, largely to deter the *Post* or *Globe* entering the Sunday market; and attempt to attract more young women readers – something the *Post* had done in short order.

"Occupy the City" and "Make the Other Guy Die" became the *Star*'s war cries.

Star publisher John Honderich says he was determined not to reduce advertising rates or discount, even if his newspaper lost a portion of the advertising pie. "The *Post* and *Globe* got into significant discounting and did incredible deals. We didn't do that and we felt that strategy was the right one. A full-page ad in our paper is $20,000 to $25,000. The *Post* was offering these at $2,500. If you undercut, you undermine your own rate structure, especially if you are the market leader. Our fundamental strategy was to maintain our circulation levels, maintain our promotion and our editorial focus. There is a psychological aspect too: We are number one. We are not going to panic. We are the *Toronto Star* and are not going to change our course because of this new interloper. I was insistent upon it."

It suited Honderich's purposes that the newspaper war was invariably characterized as a *Globe-Post* conflict. "Everyone said the *Star* wasn't really involved, but I never believed it for a moment. We were affected, and just as much under the gun, as the *Globe*, but our public posture was different. It served us well not to be out there saying, 'We're nervous, we're under the gun.' The *Globe* did some of that and it didn't serve them well at all. The *Globe*, by its actions, was signalling to the market that they were confused and were trying to reinvent themselves. They ultimately got it right, but there were times when they looked disorganized and lacking in focus."

◆ ◆ ◆

Conrad Black's long-time and influential partner, David Radler, an early skeptic about the wisdom of launching a new, full-blown national newspaper, withdrew to focus on the company's other businesses – notably the *Chicago Sun-Times* – after he had completed the deal for the *Financial Post*. He had favoured taking the *Financial Post* and its established brand and gradually building on its existing circulation and advertising.

Radler had earlier seriously considered building the *Ottawa Citizen* into a national franchise – "I always thought it was crazy that the *Washington Post* wasn't taken nationally but the *New York Times* was" – and played with the idea of turning the *Financial Post* into a *Wall Street Journal*–style daily with a little sport and lifestyle, an option that was to be tried almost disastrously by the *National Post* for a few days following the terrorist attacks in New York City and Washington, D.C., on September 11, 2001. Says Radler,

> I never viewed the new newspaper as competing with the *Globe and Mail*. I knew the *Globe* had a lock at that time on some of the financial aspects of Canadian business, but the old *Financial Post* was just as powerful a tool. But I was supportive of whatever they were doing at the *National Post*. I thought it was a great newspaper. I thought we had a market of our own, a right-of-centre market that the *Globe* was never going to get and still won't, the same kind of people who listen to talk radio. Canadian newspapers don't service that portion of the public. So I don't know whether we could have done anything differently. I never thought chasing the *Globe*'s circulation figures was going to yield anything positive, and in the end both of the papers were spending a lot of money over nothing. But second-guessing is easy. During one of the few meetings I sat in on, Conrad was proposing some hard-headed strategy to increase circulation and I doubled him up, I didn't think he was being tough enough. So who am I to say anything?

But with the privilege of hindsight, Radler says the *Post*'s monumental leap from 100,000 to 300,000 circulation in twenty-two months created impossible expectations. In the long term, he thinks, a more moderate, gradual approach, and fewer freebies, would have reduced crippling losses and may have been in the better interest of the newspaper.

Those nagging doubts about the circulation strategy were not confined to Radler. Some of the newspaper's executives, including publisher Don Babick, now feel a wiser strategy may have been to stalk the *Globe* from behind rather than jump immediately on its back and try to wrestle it into submission. The more subtle approach might have prevented the *Globe* from becoming as aggressive as it eventually did. Or so they figure.

"It was close enough that we were able to battle for advertisers," says Babick. "We never had to beat them, but euphoria took over and we thought, 'Holy Christ, we're catching them, let's see if we can pass them. Lets keep going.' And then, boom, the *Globe* woke up."

Black, who had been through it all before in his circulation war with Rupert Murdoch in the United Kingdom, had been heartened by the *Post*'s initial success and saw no reason to stop the advance. It was a calculated risk, but then again, so was starting the newspaper in the first place. "It's what you get in these circulation wars and not quite as insane as what we had to deal with in England. It cost a lot of money but couldn't have been avoided. We were aiming for at least 200,000 and we got there pretty fast. We wanted a solid franchise with enough people reading it as a primary or exclusive read to have a proper argument for the advertisers."

"It had absolutely nothing to do with Conrad Black. . . . This was not payback time."
                        – Eddie Goldenberg, chief of staff to Prime Minister Jean Chrétien

On one side, the most powerful newspaper proprietor in Canada, and on the other, the nation's most powerful politician. It was a knightly scenario that took place over the summer of 1999 with spoils of ego, prestige, and position riding on the outcome. Conrad Black is not a sympathetic figure to most Canadians, so when he and the prime minister crossed swords it was not going to hurt the ruling Liberals. To the casual observer, it seemed as though the prime minister had been handed a heaven-sent opportunity to skewer the owner of the newspaper that had been publishing damaging stories about him. Chrétien and his closest aides were suitably aghast that such a base motive could be ascribed to them or their leader, and in the absence of any secret memo proving a link, it is unlikely there will ever be any proof that the *Post*'s aggressive reporting of Shawinigate and the prime minister's move to block Black's peerage are anything more than coincidence. But circumstantial evidence suggests otherwise.

In early 1999, Black had been nominated for a peerage by then leader of the British opposition, the Tory William Hague. It is traditional in Britain that the opposition leader gets to suggest a few names for the annual honours and, on that particular occasion, Black was one of five on Hague's list. Things proceeded normally from there. Black was a British resident, proprietor of the *Daily Telegraph* (dubbed the "Torygraph"), and while no enthusiastic supporter of British Prime Minister Tony Blair's Labour government, was a natural choice for elevation to the House of Lords, which is a landing place for most British national newspaper owners. Curiously, despite their apparently close relationship, the former Conservative prime minister Margaret Thatcher had not been the one to offer Black his peerage. Nor had her successor, John Major. For his part, Black insisted he had never lobbied for the peerage, but when it was offered he figured there was no reason to turn it down. He had never discussed the business with Jean Chrétien but being a Canadian citizen had commissioned some private legal research that confirmed his right to become one if he chose.

The prime minister had other ideas.

Publicly, the process played out simply enough. On June 2, 1999, the British High Commissioner in Ottawa, Sir Anthony Goodenough, wrote to the Canadian Honours Policy Committee via the Department of Foreign Affairs advising it that Conrad Black would be named a peer seventeen days hence. The committee is chaired by the Governor General's secretariat and is comprised of representatives from Foreign Affairs, National Defence, Canadian Heritage, and the Privy Council, the prime minister's own department.

A story about the peerage appeared in the *Globe and Mail* on June 8, which was the first Chrétien and his inner circle had heard about it. Two days later, the Canadian government faxed its official objection to London, but that notice failed to reach 10 Downing Street. On June 14, Prime Minister Tony Blair was busily signing a note of congratulations to Conrad Black, informing him that he was about to become Lord Black, pending the approval of Queen Elizabeth. It took three more days for Canada's objection to reach a Downing Street desk, whereupon an apologetic Blair had to telephone Black to tell him his name was being struck off. It was a monumental embarrassment for Black, who was understandably furious. He immediately contacted Chrétien's office demanding to speak with the prime minister, who was en route for Bonn, Germany. Chrétien returned the irate Mr. Black's telephone call from Bonn, presumably knowing what it was about. Black gave the prime minister forty-eight hours to remove the roadblock to his peerage, but Chrétien was unmoved. During that conversation, according to court papers subsequently filed by Black, Chrétien mentioned his ill treatment at the hands of the *Post*.

To block Conrad Black's peerage, the government used the 1919 Nickle Resolution, usually described as "little known" but was, more correctly, actually "unheard of," except by those who specialize in arcane aspects of government machinery and political history. The Nickle Resolution asked the British government to refrain from "conferring any title of honour upon any of your subjects domiciled or ordinarily resident in Canada." The Nickle Resolution was just that, a resolution of Parliament, but never a law.

The resolution was sponsored by Conservative MP William Folger Nickle, who, according to distant relative James Travers, by then national political columnist for the *Toronto Star*, drafted the resolution as some noble effort to protect Canadian constitutional rights.

On September 14, 1999, Travers published an inspired column in the *Star* that gave an unrivalled perspective on the Nickle saga. He wrote, in part:

> Black's argument is that the Nickle resolution is irrelevant because it never passed the Senate and only applies to Canadian residents. Black, it seems, is as Canadian as maple syrup when it comes to buying Canadian newspapers but as British as bangers and mash when a peerage is up for grabs. Chrétien cited precedents, including Nickle's backbench resolution, when he announced in June that Canada would scupper British Tory party efforts to secure a place for Black in the House of Lords. . . . Adding a marvellous sub-plot to this melodrama is the public perception that Black's charge to join the titled classes has tripped over an egalitarian and vaguely republican resolution propagated by the anti-monarchist left. The truth is so different there should be room in Black's heart for the man whose resolution may keep him a commoner.
>
> History's verdict is that Nickle's motivation was self-interest and a keen appreciation of the prestige and power that a peerage would bring. In a fit of pique and in the absence of then prime minister Robert Borden, Nickle highballed his resolution through the Commons after failing to secure a knighthood for Daniel Gordon, the principal of Queen's University and his father-in-law. That failure had implications for the academic and fund-raising rivalry with

Montreal's McGill University and for an already strained family relationship. Nickle's revenge was to ensure others didn't get what his family had been denied. His resolution asking the King to refrain from giving titles to Canadian residents swept through the Commons on a wave of public sentiment he did not share. Nickle's duplicity is a bit of a family embarrassment – W.F. Nickle was my grandmother's sister's father-in-law. So forgive some disappointment that Nickle and Black might well have been cut from the same bolt of Savile Row cloth. Nickle, who became Ontario attorney-general as well as mayor of Kingston, was a deep blue Conservative who in business and politics took full advantage of his birth into the ranks of the privileged. . . . Nickle's great, unwitting contribution was to harness, albeit for his own purposes, the antipathy towards the English class system that has wafted around this country since before Confederation. As Prof. P.B. Waite puts it: "Canadians didn't like people putting on airs in a country where there are none. There are no airs in Saskatchewan." London, of course, has cornered the market on airs and Black's nose for them is so obvious that further comment is as unkind as it is unnecessary. Those who want more will have to wait for the trial, one that seems inevitable since Black's pockets are deep and Chrétien has ours.

Chrétien's unearthing of the Nickle Resolution produced an inevitable, yet ultimately unresolved, debate among constitutional experts. One posting on the Monarchist League of Canada message board quoted Prime Minister R.B. Bennett: " '[I]t being the considered view of His Majesty's government in Canada that the motion with respect to honours, adopted on the 22nd of May, 1919, by a majority vote of the members of the Commons House only of the thirteenth parliament, is not binding upon His Majesty or His Majesty's government in Canada or the seventeenth parliament of Canada.' " "Sounds pretty definite to me," added the correspondent.

Liberal Senator Anne Cools jumped to Black's defence and pointed out that the president of France had recently granted the Ordre Royale de la Legion d'Honneur to Quebecer Robert Gagnon, an honour similar to that awarded René Lévesque in 1977. For good measure, she mentioned the knighting of Supreme Court Chief Justice Sir Lyman Duff in 1934; the knighting of conductor Sir Ernest McMillan in 1935; Sir Bryan Irvine in

1986; and Sir Neil Shaw and Sir Conrad Swan, both in 1994. Swan was an adviser to Prime Minister Lester Pearson. The Canadian government challenged none.

Chrétien stubbornly insisted that, in his interpretation, the Nickle Resolution "directed that the practice of bestowing titles of honour by foreign governments on Canadians be discontinued."

Key to the lawsuit Conrad Black would file against Chrétien a few weeks later was his assertion that officials in the Canadian government had assured him there would be no objection to him receiving the peerage on condition that he became a dual citizen by taking out British citizenship and did not use the title in Canada. According to the *National Post*, those officials were mid-level bureaucrats in the Privy Council Office, but the PCO said none of its officials had spoken either to Black or his staff.

With publication of the Honours List looming, Black applied for expedited British citizenship and it was granted a couple of weeks later.

Behind the scenes, the peerage battle created enormous strain between the Prime Minister's Office and diplomats at the British High Commission, who were caught unwillingly in a domestic spat they had no interest in being part of.

Officials at the High Commission had one overriding concern: to avoid, at all costs, having Queen Elizabeth dragged into the fray and risking her embarrassment. And so it was the last straw when Chrétien's office sent a message to Buckingham Palace, via the Governor General's secretariat in Ottawa, advising Her Majesty that the Canadian government did not want her to bestow Conrad Black, a Canadian citizen, with a peerage. Or, in the words of Eddie Goldenberg, senior aide to Chrétien, to transmit the message that if Black did get his peerage "the Canadian prime minister would not be amused."

Approaching Buckingham Palace in this way was well within the rights of the prime minister of Canada but the message effectively forced the Queen of England and Canada into the impossible position of choosing the side of one or other of her prime ministers. The British were not about to drop that dilemma in the royal lap. "It was jolly complicated," says one British diplomat. "We were desperately trying to come to an arrangement the Canadian government could live with but found ourselves in exactly the position we were trying to avoid."

❖ ❖ ❖

Black launched his lawsuit against Chrétien in August 1999, seeking a token $25,000, accusing the prime minister of "abuse of power," and claiming that he had no right to intervene with the Queen to block his appointment. Black's legal team intended to bring Chrétien to the stand to explain himself; Chrétien's legal team said the matter had no place in the courts and it was the prime minister's prerogative to act as he did.

In a few paragraphs of opinion that were the journalistic equivalent of British and German troops meeting in no-man's-land for a Christmas game of soccer, the *Globe and Mail*, led, incidentally, by two Englishmen, came out full force in Black's favour:

> If newspaper baron Conrad Black wants to be a lord, what's Prime Minister Jean Chrétien's goal? A sheik comes to mind, given the petulant way he has used his authority to thwart Mr. Black's ambition to join the British House of Lords. On Thursday, Mr. Black retaliated by slapping the Prime Minister with a lawsuit for "abuse of power" and asking for $25,000 in damages. Good for him.
>
> The argument presented last June by Mr. Chrétien is made of pretty thin gruel. He exhumed an octogenarian resolution, introduced into Parliament in the days when Canada was trying to establish its independence from Britain. The so-called Nickle resolution, which was never passed by the Senate or given royal proclamation, asked the British monarch not to confer titles on Canadian citizens. It didn't say Canadian citizens couldn't accept titles; it merely asked that they not be given.
>
> So what is the problem? The honour of being made a life peer was offered to Mr. Black as a British, not a Canadian, citizen. Since Canada allows dual citizenship, it recognizes that there is no conflict in private citizens accepting the duties and obligations of citizenship in another country. Why then can't they accept the honours as well?
>
> Mr. Black suggests in his lawsuit that Mr. Chrétien was motivated not by nationalism but by personal pique after *The National Post*, one of Mr. Black's newspapers, wrote a series of highly critical articles about the awarding of federal grants – what some might call the

patronage equivalent of a life peerage – to businesses in the Prime Minister's Shawinigan riding.

The dispute between Mr. Black and Mr. Chrétien is for the courts to decide. What is of greater importance is the Prime Minister's apparent use of his own high office to settle a score with a powerful critic. That sort of arrogant despotism is archaic in a modern democracy.

Black appeared on television to explain his case and told CBC news anchor Peter Mansbridge that he was fighting on a matter of principle and, contrary to all popular opinion, the prospect of becoming a member of the British House of Lords was not a major preoccupation for him.

Black reiterated that Foreign Affairs officials in Ottawa had recommended he apply for British citizenship if he wanted to become a British peer. In doing so, he could also retain his Canadian citizenship. "That was the Canadian government's recommendation. I followed the recommendation. Then the Prime Minister of Canada purported to intervene and claim that the Queen of the United Kingdom could not confer an honour on me as a citizen of the United Kingdom for services rendered in the United Kingdom. The Canadian government gave us advice, we acted on that advice, and they reneged a week later. That is the core of this . . . the Nickle Resolution is a sideshow."

There was no doubt in Black's mind that Chrétien was simply out for revenge. To him the link was obvious between the Shawinigate coverage and the prime minister's intervention. In his interview with Mansbridge, he also repeated his view that the prime minister had abused his power and had given "wilfully erroneous advice" to the Queen.

He also defended the stories his newspaper had published. "I read the entire file to make sure I hadn't missed anything and I don't think our coverage was unfair. . . . I mean, if we had defamed him, if we really had done anything other than point out the facts, then I certainly would have asked the editor to be much more careful and to publish corrected pieces, if we had been unjust. And not because he was prime minister. We're not in the defamation business. As is well known, I've often been libelled myself, and I've often sued myself. I've sent and received a great many libel writs, and I'm very sensitive to the virtue of always having truth as a defence."

As a sort of joke in one of their last conversations, Black told Mansbridge he had mentioned to Chrétien the idea of becoming both a Canadian senator and a British Lord, but the prime minister didn't seem to get the "esoteric" nature of the remark.

As the interview drew to a close, Mansbridge asked, "Do you think the public cares about this?

"No, and I don't see why they should."

"Or does it have any impact on the way the public sees you?"

"I can't judge that. If you'll pardon the ghastly expression, my image is of a Frankenstein monster that's been lurching about for twenty-five years, and I have absolutely no idea what animates it at times. But I think a good many people see this as a case of an individual abusing political office for petty reasons and overreaching his jurisdiction. And as we take his evidence and that of those around and beneath him, I think the impression is going to be reinforced."

◆   ◆   ◆

Shortly afterwards, on November 8, 1999, 230 newly unionized workers at the *Calgary Herald* went on strike after a year of fruitless negotiations. Their timing may not have been the best. Although the *Herald* employees claimed they were asking for roughly the same contract that already existed at other Southam newspapers, including the *Ottawa Citizen* and *Montreal Gazette*, Black decided to use favourable Alberta labour laws to bring in replacement workers to bring the striking union members to their knees. "We're amputating gangrenous limbs," he said famously of his employees. "If they have the grace of conversion and want to function as employees instead of staging an NDP coup d'etat in the newsroom, they'll be welcome."

The acrimonious strike, covered copiously and, for Black, unflatteringly on the pages of the *Globe and Mail*, ended eight months later with decertification of the union bargaining unit and buyout packages for those who wanted to take them. Most did. In what was a generally creditable period of ownership of Canada's major daily newspapers, the *Herald* strike was an ugly blemish, largely because the strikers – mostly long-serving and loyal employees with a record of good relations with pre-Black management – were able to generate widespread support and sympathy. But as with all strikes, they were eventually forgotten. Once the decision to strike had been taken, they were essentially at Black's mercy and he showed no inclination to offer any.

It didn't help Black's public image as the aggrieved party in his battle with the prime minister.

❖ ❖ ❖

Ontario Supreme Court Chief Justice Patrick LeSage ruled in March 2000 against Black's claim, saying that Chrétien was within his rights to advise the Queen as he had done. The matter was not one for the courts, said LeSage.

Black appealed. In May 2001, the Ontario Court of Appeal unanimously upheld LeSage's ruling. A few days later, Black announced that he was giving up his Canadian citizenship. "Having opposed for thirty years precisely the public policies that have caused scores of thousands of educated and talented Canadians to abandon their country every year," he said, "it is at least consistent that I should join this dispersal."

Conrad Black returned to Canada as Lord Black of Crossharbour in November 2001, and, in a speech to members of the right-wing think tank the Fraser Institute, reflected on Shawinigate, the peerage, and his decision to renounce his citizenship:

> The *National Post* had exposed the fact that the prime minister had improperly influenced a government agency to make grants to a commercially dubious hotel in his constituency. It is adjacent to a golf course in which the prime minister had an interest and he had misled Parliament about it.
>
> As we were exposing this story, the prime minister deliberately gave false advice to the Queen of the United Kingdom and Canada, that I was ineligible under Canadian law for the British peerage to which I had been nominated. The British government had initially asked the Canadian government's view of this as a courtesy, and Ottawa had suggested that I seek British citizenship and be a dual citizen. I did so.
>
> The Canadian Prime Minister then used the fact that I was a dual citizen, and the fact that the Queen cannot choose between conflicting

advice from two prime ministers, to both of whom she is technically Chief of State.

I had not lifted a finger to achieve this honour and to become a member of what is certainly the most talented legislative chamber in the world. But the honour having been offered, I wasn't disposed to be deprived of it in this outrageous way. I was assuredly happy to be asked. As I am not under the illusion that I have any aptitude for electoral politics and this is almost certainly my only chance to be any kind of legislator, and as it is a fascinating time in British politics, I wished to accept. I sued in Canada for recognition of my rights as a citizen of the United Kingdom . . .

Four years later, Black sounded significantly more philosophical about the affair and said his departure from the country was nothing to do with Chrétien but rather a desire not to "spend the rest of my life fighting an uphill battle":

I could have lived without a peerage, and if I had been an enthusiast of the course I was on in this country I would have stayed here. I was in my fifties, and I had fought for twenty-five or thirty years and was tired of it, and doubtless many of the people whom I had been engaging were rather tired of me, too. So we got a rest from each other. I didn't renounce my citizenship for the sole purpose of becoming a peer. If that had been the case, I could just have waited until Chrétien left. He was attempting to intervene in the affairs of another country and create a second class of U.K. citizen consisting of one person, who would uniquely be solvent, adult, sane, unincarcerated, but ineligible for an honour in that country because Chrétien didn't want that person, i.e., myself, to have that honour. This is completely illegal. I am technically a lawyer and in my day the Court of Appeal in Ontario was arguably the most distinguished bench in the country. We used to say that cases should be appealed from Ottawa to Toronto instead of the other way round. But that bench just rolled over for the regime . . . they took the maximum time to deliberate before saying they didn't have jurisdiction. That was the most disillusioning thing of all to me, that where the federal government is concerned it isn't really an independent court system any more and the implications of that are potentially serious.

In the midst of it all, Black saw an opinion poll saying that 64 per cent of Canadians thought Chrétien was doing a good job. "It was then I thought that I have given it a good try but I have got to go. I wish the country well, but I don't belong here."

Black has said he would consider coming back to the Canadian fold when a new regime took over in Ottawa. "I wouldn't say no. I think Paul Martin will make a good prime minister."

Has Martin expressed an opinion to him about the peerage issue?

"The answer is yes, but it would be indiscreet of me to tell you. Lots of people have expressed an opinion on it and that includes the leaders of both major parties in the U.K. and the Queen of both countries. But I am not at liberty to quote them."

Despite the effective ban through tax laws on foreigners owning Canadian newspapers, Black says it is not a major obstacle to any future ambitions he may have: "Roy Thomson owned newspapers in Canada for years, and he was a British citizen."

But despite reports to the contrary, he no longer owns the special passport granted when Brian Mulroney made him a member of the Privy Council. "Mulroney made a number of people privy councillors, who were not in public life – Paul Desmarais, Charles Bronfman, Maurice Richard, and myself. You get a special passport. Some foreigners have the same, Nelson Mandela and the Duke of Edinburgh among them. It served as a passport while I had it, but my information is that the prime minister required that it not be renewed. He had no grounds to suspend or withdraw it, but he was able to prevent it being renewed. It is lapsed now."

On Black's wall in London is a cartoon published by the *Toronto Star* after he announced he was leaving Canada. "It's of me paddling a canoe past a beaver which is holding a life preserver in one hand and a Canadian flag in the other. I found it quite touching."

"Conrad Black improved the quality of newspapering across the country. And he was still pretty much getting abused for it. I think he should be a lot more bitter than he is."

— Kenneth Whyte, editor-in-chief, *National Post*

K en Whyte was on vacation at a rented cottage in late August 2001 when, at about four o'clock in the afternoon, Conrad Black phoned and left a message. Whyte was instructed to call Black's personal assistant in Toronto, Joan Maida, to make an appointment for Black to call again. The formality, and Black's urgent insistence, was unusual. The *Post* editor suspected immediately that something serious was afoot. They connected a short time later, when Black was in his car and on the way to dinner with his friend Cardinal Emmett Carter. "Are you sitting down?" Black asked.

Black then delivered the bombshell that CanWest Global, controlled by the Asper family of Winnipeg, now owned 100 per cent of the *National Post*. The 50-50 partnership struck between the Aspers and Black the previous year was over, and Black's baby was now legally adopted by the Aspers. Whyte, always in the loop when major decisions were being made about the *National Post*, didn't see this one coming.

"Are we still on speaking terms?" asked Black.

The formal public announcement about the transfer of ownership was due in less than ninety minutes, at seven o'clock. Whyte, deep in affluent

Muskoka cottage country, was a two-and-a-half-hour drive away from the *Post*'s office in the Toronto suburb of Don Mills.

"Perhaps we'd better talk later," he said to Black. "I should get to the office." He managed the journey in one hour and forty minutes, anxious to be with the staff when the announcement was made, but he was still fifteen minutes late. His thoughts raced as quickly as his car. "I was driving back and thinking it had been a great three years and I'd had a great time. I had no regrets and had been happy about the way everything had turned out. I could leave with my head up but thought I'd hear the Aspers out and see what they wanted to do. If we were compatible, the adventure would continue."

When Whyte walked into the *Post* newsroom he found people confused, saddened, and distinctly on edge. Reporters, copy editors, and section heads, all dedicated pioneers who had worked ten- and twelve-hour days for three years, were angry that Black was deserting them. There had been plenty of unease when CanWest made the deal to buy Black's Southam newspaper chain and with it half of the *Post*. But as far as anyone could tell, the Asper-Black relationship seemed to be working well, despite an early, well-publicized tussle with the new joint owners over the *Post*'s coverage of Jean Chrétien. But that evening, for the first time since the *Post* first rolled off the presses almost three years earlier, a sense of betrayal, uncertainty, and depression hung in the air. The bubble had burst.

◆ ◆ ◆

Black had handed over the second 50 per cent in exchange for CanWest releasing $500 million worth of vendor take-back notes that Black and his indebted company desperately needed. The notes were part of the deal the two companies made when CanWest bought the Southam group. According to Black, CanWest executives had it in their power to block the release of the notes if they chose to.

In the days that preceded the final deal, Black and his Hollinger executives had explored the possibility of buying back the Aspers' 50 per cent, but with a crippling debt load and the prospect of owning the *Post* as an independent newspaper without access to the advantages of major Southam newspapers now in CanWest's hands, it was not an option.

Losing the *Post*, says Black, was a blow. "It was my baby and I was very attached to it. You have to be careful mixing commercial and emotional matters, but, yes, it was very unpleasant."

◆ ◆ ◆

The Aspers, led by the late family patriarch Israel (Izzy) Asper, had built their multinational company CanWest Global from modest Winnipeg beginnings and developed it into one of the world's most successful independent television companies. They were not newspaper people, but according to CanWest president and CEO Leonard Asper, the desire to get into the print business ran deep in the company history – back to when Izzy Asper was in partnership with financier Gerry Schwartz. The pair had a basic strategy that focused on four areas: financial services, energy, transport, and communications. Before they dissolved the partnership in 1984, Schwartz and Asper had come close to buying several different newspapers, including *FP* Publications, which at the time owned several newspapers, including the *Globe and Mail* and the *Winnipeg Free Press*.

Spurred by the media fragmentation of the early 1990s, the Aspers began thinking beyond their lucrative TV business and considered buying Sun Media newspapers, the group eventually bought by the Quebec printing media conglomerate Quebecor.

While Izzy Asper, a long-time columnist on tax issues for the *Globe and Mail*, had always loved newspapers, it wasn't until 2000, one year after his second son, Leonard, became president of the company, that it happened. Conrad Black announced he wanted to unload some of his company's smaller newspapers – those with a circulation of less than 100,000. Leonard, driven by a belief that various media fragments could be linked in a profitable chain, was in Vancouver at the time with his father and other CanWest Global executives. They were in the midst of preparing for Canadian Radio-Television and Telecommunications Commission hearings into the company's plan to buy the broadcast outlets of WIC (Western International Communications). "It became clear," said Leonard Asper, "that owning one TV network was no longer going to be sufficient in terms of the relationships with advertisers, viewers, or readers. So we started to develop a strategy that said we should be in all the major media, from print to TV, out-of-home ads, and radio. As the 1990s progressed, the Internet became a part of that."

Black had put his smaller newspapers on the block to ease his company's debt, but as is invariably the way when newspaper groups change hands, the outcome was entirely unpredictable and the deal snowballed.

There were signs that Black had become increasingly uncomfortable with the way the newspaper war was shaping up and, according to *Globe and Mail* publisher Phillip Crawley, made overtures to the opposition in an effort to bring an end to the ruinous, giveaway battle they were engaged in. "When the numbers weren't going his way," says Crawley, "and it became clear to him that he wasn't going to overtake the *Globe* in circulation or get the ad returns, he finally said that it is probably a good idea if we get more sensible about things. It was pretty clear that things had got so bad that he was looking for some sort of release."

The offer from the Aspers, in early spring 2000, came as a total surprise, says Black, who, in addition to his other problems, was labouring under the short-lived prejudice on the stock market that companies engaged exclusively in the newspaper business were essentially run by Luddites. This was the frenzied period of the Bell Canada Enterprises move into TV and newspapers, and Quebecor's purchase of the *Sun* newspapers, cable giant Videotron, and the TVA network, all of which was preceded in the United States by the elephantine and ultimately disastrous amalgamation of AOL-Time Warner. Convergence of media was hip for a few brief years, and companies that grew too big too fast began to wobble. In the case of AOL-Time Warner, the union was doomed to collapse in a shambles of lost millions and bitter recriminations, but not before Wall Street, enchanted by the bigness of it all, had decided that it had seen the media future and wanted to go along for the ride.

"Our company was U.S.$1.95 billion in debt," says Black. "We had the assets, but we couldn't get any upward movement on the stock price. It's an American-listed company, and the Americans in the first place were not very impressed with Canada, and in the second place newspapers were out of fashion. It was the peak of the Internet boom and you could hardly step out of doors without people telling you that you were like a silent movie or black-and-white TV set. There was no glamour in the stock, and we had to get the debt down because when the economic boom ended we would be seriously overexposed. So we had to sell something and allowed that we would entertain offers for some of the papers but didn't have the desire to sell as many as we did. Then Izzy phoned and said, 'Would you consider selling some of the larger ones?' and I said, 'Conceivably.'"

Izzy Asper's phone call followed another phone conversation weeks earlier between the two men, when Asper was at his home in Palm Beach. The discussion then had been about joint ventures between the Hollinger and CanWest Web sites.

Izzy and Leonard Asper flew to New York, where they met with Black and Hollinger vice-chairman Dan Colson. The CanWest executives surprised Black and Colson with an offer for the entire Southam newspaper group, including the *National Post*, which Black had no intention of selling. But the Aspers were adamant that they wanted the *Post* and made it clear that without it the $3.2-billion deal would fall apart or be significantly scaled down, likely back to the Saskatchewan papers.

Leonard Asper recalls,

> It was "an evolutionary discussion that started with the Hollinger announcement, but at the time we were looking at the *Winnipeg Free Press*, which was being sold by Thomson; we studied whether we should acquire that. About two weeks before Hollinger made its announcement, Izzy had been talking to Conrad about some sort of alliance between canada.com and global.com. They had renewed acquaintances on the telephone, and when Hollinger made the announcement we said we weren't interested in those [smaller] newspapers but it would be nice if we had the *Winnipeg Free Press*, *Regina Leader-Post*, and *Saskatoon StarPhoenix*, if they would pump up that threshold from 100,000 and include some of the larger smaller papers, if you will. So Izzy called Conrad and said, "What do you think?" Conrad said, "We hadn't been intending to do that, but we'll give it some thought." Then we thought, "Well, boy, we've got television stations in Alberta, what if he threw in the *Calgary Herald* and *Edmonton Journal*?" So another call was made, and at the Hollinger end the response was open. Finally, our senior management group and Izzy sat down and decided that maybe it would be best if we bought the whole thing. All the Southam newspapers were in cities

where we had TV stations, so why not? That was April-May of 2000 and it got the negotiations going. Then we had to ask ourselves, "What about the *National Post*?"

The Aspers decided that despite the *Post*'s status as a start-up newspaper, it was a vital part of their future strategy – a fact that was often overlooked in the subsequent predictions of its imminent demise. First, the *Post* was a seller of national advertising, the prime revenue source of CanWest's Global television network, whose advertising ratio is about 85 per cent national, 15 per cent local. Similar local relationships would link Global's city stations and the Southam dailies in cities such as Montreal, Vancouver, Calgary, and Edmonton.

"The *Post*," says Leonard Asper, "also gave us access to a good, difficult-to-reach demographic that was complementary to what Global was offering, which was more middle-of-the-road and mainstream. In the business of advertising it is important with all this fragmentation to be able to walk into an advertiser and say, 'Whatever you're looking for, I've got.'"

The younger Asper says his company was also attracted to the deal because of the access it gave them to a bank of top-quality journalists at the newspapers. "The strength of having access to the quality journalists at the *Post*, and the metros, would have a very salutary effect on the quality of news we could generate at the TV stations. In the end it's about how good your content is, and journalists in the newspaper business are typically quite studied in their fields, because they produce long, detailed, and thoughtful reports, whereas TV is a more hit-and-run kind of medium. We also felt we could bring some of the entertainment value to newspapers to help boost sagging circulation."

But Asper does concede that initially Black appeared to have no interest in parting with the *National Post*. "He felt it was unfinished business for him, so, yes, it was a sticking point for a few weeks, but because the deal was progressing quite rapidly, and there was goodwill all around, we came to a compromise. And he did recognize that the *National Post* had a relationship with the metro newspapers through printing, shared content, shared advertising opportunities, and cross-promotion. And it was the only newspaper with a Toronto presence. So we sawed it off at 50-50."

The biggest deal in Canadian media history was worked out in detail through a series of faxes, e-mails, phone calls, and personal meetings between Asper, Black, and their executives. It took about four months of intense, back-and-forth negotiations from wherever on the globe Izzy Asper or Conrad Black found themselves. And remarkably, in an industry where gossip is the stuff of life, news of it never leaked, even though there had been at least a couple of clues.

After the WIC sale was finalized, Izzy Asper himself dropped a hint that there was more to come, but a call the CanWest chairman made to author and columnist Peter C. Newman was a bit of a giveaway. "I need your book about Conrad. I've lost my copy. Please courier me a copy as soon as possible," said Asper.

Newman sent him a copy of *The Establishment Man: Conrad Black, a Portrait of Power*, published two decades earlier. "At the time Izzy called me, rumours were swirling around that something might be up between him and Conrad," Newman told the *National Post*. "Izzy's call confirmed to me that he was now serious about getting together with Conrad. So I told him I felt it was really important that he reread my book on Conrad so that he could get a full picture of who he really was and where he had come from."

And a story by *Toronto Star* business writer Gillian Livingston on July 31, the day of the official announcement, came frustratingly close to spoiling the Aspers' surprise. It is clear from reading the story that Livingston knew something was happening, but her inquiry was batted away by a Hollinger spokesman who said some sort of announcement about something might be forthcoming in ten days or two weeks. CanWest officials refused comment, but Livingston reminded her readers that the Aspers had spoken previously of informal talks with Hollinger and there were rumours of possible CanWest newspaper purchases in the Western provinces.

The Canadian newspaper industry had been through so many upheavals during the previous dozen years that any scenario, however incredible, could not be discounted. Except, perhaps, one that involved Conrad Black giving up total control of his beloved *National Post*, the only newspaper he had created in a long and storied career, and selling his entire Canadian empire to the Asper family of Winnipeg, owners of the so-called Love Boat Network.

◆ ◆ ◆

At the official announcement in Toronto on July 31, Izzy Asper was effusive in his praise of Conrad Black, whom he described as "one of the world's greatest businessmen."

"In less than two years, Conrad Black has made a miracle," said Asper of the *National Post*. "I can think of no greater miracle in the twentieth century than the *National Post*."

Black wasn't there but later told a *Post* reporter, "I didn't want to sell him any part of the *National Post*, but I couldn't fault his logic, and this is the formula that we arrived at to reconcile his ambition to be in Toronto with my absolute refusal to sell the *Post*."

In exchange for their money, the Aspers got thirteen metro dailies, a 50 per cent share in the money-losing *National Post*, and an agreement that Black would stay on for five years as chairman and publisher with the deciding boardroom vote in the event of a tie. It wasn't an arrangement the Aspers particularly liked but a compromise that was probably essential. "I thought we would give it a go on that basis," says Black, who also grew to dislike the arrangement.

Shortly afterwards, in January 2001, Don Babick left the *National Post* to become president of the Southam newspaper company. "I had no interest in being the publisher of a newspaper half-owned by Conrad Black and half-owned by Izzy Asper. I'm not sure how you win that battle. How do you handle a Monday-morning conversation when one of them phones at 10 and the other at 10:30? They're both bigger-than-life figures, so I said, not me."

When the dust of the deal settled, after suggestions that Black had taken the Aspers to the cleaners and/or the Aspers had got themselves a superb deal at the expense of a financially wounded Black, it became clear that the agreement between the two companies had been more symbiotic than overly advantageous to either side: newspaper company in search of buyer meets television company in search of the future. Black, who had often said that the value of the Southam newspaper chain would be significantly enhanced if it had a foothold in Toronto, was proven correct, and CanWest, with a stronger drive and better chance than most to make the illusion of convergence a reality, got the jigsaw pieces. The two were meant for each other. On August 1, the day after the deal was announced, the *Globe and Mail* gleefully ran a front-page cartoon of Izzy Asper, with a maple-leaf

bib, feasting on a Thanksgiving turkey in the likeness of Conrad Black –
devouring the enemy, the *Globe*'s enemy that is.

◆ ◆ ◆

Leonard Asper compares the financial adjustments that led to Black relin-
quishing the final 50 per cent of the *Post* to buying a house and having to
deal with the bills that were the responsibility of the previous owner arrive
in the mail after the deal is closed. "There were amounts owing on either
side, so we all just sat in a room and said, 'Let's call it a wash.' I don't think
any of us could tell you to the exact dollar amount, but there was enough
on either side for us to say, 'You take that and we'll take this.' And Conrad
felt the *Post* was progressing and was in good hands. It was always our
desire to own 100 per cent even though we settled for 50-50. Every deal at
50-50 is always less easy to manage than where someone has a majority
stake, but we had no quarrels with Hollinger."

Black's explanation is a little more complicated but appears to amount
to roughly the same thing. The problem was "technical," he says, and
involved vendor take-back notes that were "part of the consideration we
took from CanWest":

> CanWest could go to an arbitration process if we sold the notes, or
> sold participations in the notes, and because it's fair to say that their
> financial advisers had somewhat mismanaged further debt under-
> writing for them in the autumn of 2000, those notes were not accept-
> able by the banking community as collateral. So we found ourselves
> once again in the position we thought we had got out of: having an
> inconvenient structure of debt. We could sell participation in those
> notes all right, but we needed approval from them to do it, so I made
> that arrangement with Izzy Asper. The deal was I would sell him the
> other half of the *Post*. In order to realize about $500 million of these
> notes that's what I had to do, so I did it. They could have held it up
> indefinitely and capriciously if they had wanted to. So what we got
> for the *Post* was what we got for the first half of it, and of course we
> recovered the cost of the *Financial Post* and more. I didn't want to do
> it, but on the other hand it was an anomalous arrangement and more

anomalous than I had thought at the time it would be. I thought it might be more of a successful arrangement than it had been.

In the world of mega business deals, the bitterest enemies are often moved by convention and convenience to make complimentary remarks about each other in public, but Black seems to have entered the deal with genuine admiration for Izzy Asper – an admiration that appeared to be mutual. "There is, ideologically, no particular difference between Izzy Asper and myself," Black said two months before the CanWest founder passed away in October 2003. "I had known him a long time, and before I knew him I followed a little his career as a party leader in Manitoba. He was for the flat tax and that sort of thing. He was well ahead of his time in many ways. And of course he is very friendly with the government, and I thought it could prove the best possible platform from which to get a successful arrangement for the *National Post*, namely a small-c conservative who is in good standing with the Liberal party."

◆ ◆ ◆

The sale to the Aspers of the other 50 per cent the following August had come together over four or five days, and the aftermath was frenetic for editor Ken Whyte.

Whyte eventually heard both sides of the story, from the vendor and the buyer. Joint ownership, the CanWest executive chairman told him, had been difficult, and the two sides sometimes disagreed with what needed to be done with the newspaper. But more important were those other issues related strictly to the business transaction between the two. It had been decided to deal with everything at once.

Whyte subsequently had several conversations about the sale with Conrad Black, who told him that hanging on to the *Post* and running it as a daily newspaper independent of the Asper-owned Southam newspaper chain would have been fiscal suicide.

"I told him I was disappointed we weren't going to be a part of Hollinger and under his direction any more," Whyte says, "and I told him I understood his reasons, but also told him we would all have trouble accepting it. They spent that last week trying to figure out how to hang on, but they would not only have been competing against the *Globe* and *Star* but against Southam, too. All those earlier advantages of having Southam would evaporate and they would be paying commercial rates for everything, including the printing presses and distribution. It would have affected everything, even rack placement at airports. There are so many ways we are entwined. So the losses would have been more – $60 million a year or more – and he would have had to absorb all the losses instead of sharing them."

A few weeks later, Conrad Black and his wife, Barbara Amiel, invited Whyte to their home on the Bridle Path on the Labour Day weekend of 2001. The three had coffee – Amiel drinking her favourite instant brand. "I sat with them in this enormous garden and it wasn't a buoyant conversation. They were obviously upset, because they were going through another round of media abuse and it was abundantly evident that they were genuinely attached to the *Post*. Barbara in particular was very upset. She doesn't have much time for Canada, but she was upset about losing that attachment to it. She had been receiving calls from some of the Toronto establishment. People had called and said, 'Oh, it's such a sad thing that you sold the *Post*. It was a great thing for Canada, and this country is just unthinkable without it.' Barbara said if they were so concerned about the *Post* and its importance to the country, they should have given it more advertising support."

Whyte's emotional attachment to Conrad Black was stronger than most editors might ordinarily have for the proprietor of their newspaper. In fact, most editors don't have any emotional attachment to the proprietor. But Whyte had begun to write for *Saturday Night* magazine only after Black bought it, and he moved from Edmonton to Toronto to edit the magazine only because he wanted to work for Black.

But he says he didn't feel betrayed by Black's departure. "After the first sale, I remember [columnist] George Jonas saying, 'You must feel like those Vietnamese soldiers on the ground watching that last helicopter fly off the roof of the U.S. embassy.' But I understood why Conrad did it. He had to make a deal and it was a very good deal. He had to put some of his papers on the market to clear his debt and he ended up with a deal he couldn't say no to. In his heart he would rather have kept us. You've got to be a grown-up about these things. We work for properties that are owned by people, and if you have a business you can sell it. Betrayal doesn't enter into it. If he had said to me, 'I am never going to sell this paper,' then I could say I was betrayed, but he never said that. I have read through his history. He is a businessman and a very shrewd one."

During the meeting in Black's garden, Black tried to reassure the *Post* editor that he would get along with the Aspers. He was also keen to know what people at the *Post* were saying about him.

"It was a brilliant, beautiful day," recalls Whyte, "and we talked for a couple of hours. They wanted to know what the journalists and others at the *Post* were saying. He wasn't disillusioned, because he isn't a guy with illusions, but he was disappointed. His demeanour never really changes that much. He will get angry sometimes, and at other times he is a little more buoyant, but generally he is a very solid personality. He never gets morose. He always puts a good face forward and always has good manners. He had done an ambitious thing in trying to launch the *Post* and he wasn't getting credit for any of it.

"He had improved the quality of newspapering across the country and enlivened and broadened the debate on public policy across the country. And he was still pretty much getting abused for it. I think he should be a lot more bitter than he is."

◆ ◆ ◆

Whyte's doubts about working with the Aspers were partially rooted in the column published on March 7, 2001, by David Asper, Izzy's elder son, and CanWest's chief of the newly acquired print operations. It was a vigorous defence of Jean Chrétien and, by extension, an attack against the editorial policy of his own newspaper, which he lumped in with others who had been "having a remarkably unfair go at the Prime Minister over alleged financial misdealings in Shawinigan."

The column was distributed and published in all the major Southam newspapers and, it is fair to say, generally not well received by any of them. Conservative Leader Joe Clark, who was leading the charge against Chrétien in the House of Commons, was outraged (Asper had referred to him as "desperate for attention Joe Clark") and Chrétien himself denied he had exerted any influence in the matter.

In writing the column, and having it published in the family-owned newspapers, David Asper did nothing he was not entitled to do and nothing that Conrad Black had not done dozens of times when he disagreed with some article or editorial position taken by one of his own publications. The only difference, perhaps, was the context.

The Aspers had created a storm of local and national protest when they fired respected and popular *Ottawa Citizen* publisher Russell Mills the previous year, apparently for one feature article detailing Chrétien's alleged misdeeds and an editorial calling for the prime minister's resignation. The firing was cast as the bullying act of a mighty Liberal Party–loving media owner crushing dissent and became not just a major Canadian story but an international one, covered in dozens of newspapers from the *New York Times* to Australia's *Sydney Morning Herald*. The firing of one Canadian newspaper executive has never before received, and likely never will in the future receive, such wide, condemning attention.

The other part of the picture was the CanWest editorial policy in which the company periodically distributed must-run editorials from its headquarters in Winnipeg to its newspapers, opining on various matters of domestic public policy and on Israel, a subject close to the hearts of the Aspers and about which they have firm opinions. But the editorials, labelled in the newspapers as corporate opinion, became a long-running story in other media and put huge pressure on CanWest, which eventually significantly reduced their frequency without any formal announcement.

Looking back on the early days of CanWest's newspaper ownership, Leonard Asper says his family was open and honest when they chose to express an opinion through their newspapers and have not interfered with news coverage:

> The record will show that the coverage of the prime minister [Chrétien] didn't change, but what we do oppose, and find odious, is pack reporting where the entire media community decides someone is guilty or innocent – a devil or a hero – and fails to look at both sides. We come from a legal background as a family and perhaps that's why we have that sensitivity. We believe there are usually two sides, if not three, to every story, and we thought there was too much of a mood in the [*Post*] newsroom that the purpose of the paper was to bring down the government or the prime minister, whichever the case may be. In our view, the purpose of a newspaper is to inform the public – present the public with the facts and not editorialize

through headlines or in news reporting. News should be news and opinion should be opinion and clearly marked as such. We felt that some of that distinction was lacking. We believe that the purpose of a newspaper is to inform and in its editorial pages try to lead public opinion in a way it sees appropriate. That was really it. We have never interfered in news coverage of the prime minister, and when we did disagree we were open about it. We came out openly and said, "We think this has gone a bit too far." A lot of good has been done by this government, and a lot of not-so-good, but it isn't all black and white.

The Aspers were satisfied with the small-c conservative positioning of the *Post* when they assumed control of the newspaper, despite Ken Whyte's initial concern that there would be a conflict. Izzy Asper visited Whyte and *Post* managing editor Hugo Gurdon shortly after the sale was finalized. "He had a list of twelve things that he believed in," Whyte says. "Hugo and I made notes, and afterwards we went out and checked and balanced to see if we'd editorialized on any of them. On all of them we were in agreement. We thought they were too close to the Liberals and they thought we were too close to the Alliance, but on the issues, we agreed."

◆ ◆ ◆

Leonard Asper and Conrad Black both spoke to staff at the *Post*, on August 24, 2001, the day after Asper's company got outright control of the newspaper. "This is the finest newspaper in Canada, if not the world," Asper said. "We believe that. We don't intend to mess with that."

More ominously, Black admitted that cost-cutting at the *Post* was inevitable, irrespective of who owned it. "If such economies are imposed, unless they are absurdly draconian, people shouldn't think, 'This wouldn't happen if Hollinger was still here.'"

The axe fell a few weeks later, on September 17, at the end of a long and exhausting week of covering the terrorist attacks in New York City and Washington, D.C. Among those left in the *Post* newsroom, the day became known as 9/17.

Employees were laid off, *Saturday Night* magazine was temporarily killed again, and the Weekend Post, Arts and Life, and Sports sections disappeared, along with most of their staffs. Most people understood it was all part of an effort by the Aspers to save the newspaper from extinction, but it didn't soothe the hurt, nor assuage the anger, much of which was directed at Black.

Leonard Asper was back at the *Post* again the day of the layoffs and recalls the day vividly:

> It wasn't pleasant. I knew in my heart that this was the beginning of a positive move for the folks at the *Post*, though I don't think they could possibly have seen it that day. But I did feel like the stepfather who was being introduced to the family and was clearly not someone they had either chosen, knew, or, quite frankly, had a lot of respect for. At that time, and to some extent today, we are still seen as purveyors of Bart Simpson and lowbrow television, even though I know quite the opposite is true. When I was describing my family's history in the newspaper business – my father wrote five hundred columns for the *Globe and Mail* and the *Winnipeg Tribune* and had a long history as a journalist – I could see in the faces it wasn't a message being received. There was clearly shock, but I did sense a hint of hope at the end of my comments, that someone was going to get behind the *Post* for the long term. On the other hand, many in the room felt jilted and it was awkward with both Conrad and I there. He was trying to tell them they were in better hands, and I was trying to tell them they were in better hands, but I think they felt that the party was over.

Sports editor Graham Parley, spared the axe but left with no department to run, went home to consider his future. He didn't have to wait long. Barely a week after the sections were cut, they were reinstated, following negative reaction from advertisers, especially car sellers. Given that the *Post*, along with all other newspapers, had been temporarily reorganized to cover the September 11 tragedy, it isn't clear whether most readers even realized the sections had gone before they were put back again. And according to polling commissioned by Toronto advertising executive Hugh Dow, the dip in readership was minimal.

But war being war, the *Globe and Mail* and *Toronto Star* didn't hesitate to point it out, and in time most readers knew whether they noticed or not.

It damaged the *Post*'s reputation, compounded the impression that Black had walked away from a sinking ship, and regenerated the predictions of eventual demise.

The decision to drop sections of the paper and focus on the *Wall Street Journal* model of a newsy A-section and solid business coverage was an effort to cut costs and refocus the newspaper, but was a mistake, admits Leonard Asper. "We did some research and surveys among readers and advertisers and somehow it came back that no one felt there was much value in the Sports and Arts sections, or didn't see them as important as the front and business sections. We made a mistake. For some reason the research wasn't as accurate, as history showed. There is a thud factor in the newspaper business. If it gets too small, people think they're getting a flyer and don't want to pay full price for it or they may cancel altogether. It's not that you or I read everything in the newspaper, but psychologically we feel it has to be a certain volume for us to feel we are getting our money's worth. Maybe we were a bit superficial in our analysis of the research, and it was clearly a mistake, but we did everything necessary to rectify that."

After Black's departure, newly installed publisher and CanWest veteran Peter Viner held a meeting for senior staff, and for the first time since the *Post* began publishing he laid their predicament on the line. Arts editor Peter Scowen, who, along with many of his colleagues, was critical of Black but grateful for the three-year trip he had provided them, found Viner's presentation a relief. "He was very straight. He sat us down at a table and said, 'I know you must be worried about your jobs,' and he tried to give us as much information as possible, so we could make up our own minds. It was the first time we had got an honest talk about the paper. I said, 'What do we do as managers? We are stuck with very low morale when before we had this dream situation where we could go and do anything we wanted and there were no limitations.' He said, 'You were living in a fantasy world, Disneyland. This is the reality, now go do your job.' I found that reassuring. No bullshit."

In the bars, coffee shops, and on the phone lines, the analysis among employees and former employees continued. Scowen's opinion, typical of many, was that the business side of the newspaper hadn't been aggressive enough. "They spent all this money on marquee writers, but it seems to me they should have spent ten times as much on a marquee sales guy from a major Toronto newspaper. They never set up a competitive advertising department and didn't develop an advertising team that was used to that kind of competitive market. It was a call-taking culture. They should have gone to the *Star*, identified the most important salesperson there, and offered them $1 million to come and work for us. We had major advertisers we dealt with editorially who didn't know who their sales rep was at the *Post*. I'm still pissed off about it."

Publisher John Honderich, watching the goings-on from across the city, could barely believe it when Black left the *Post*. "I was stunned when he walked away. I know his career is dotted with exits, and I know the numbers were huge and he hates losing money, but he had never started a newspaper before. At some level I could understand the financial imperative, but his ego was so completely involved in this, and he had made such a personal stand. I was shocked. I think it was quite humiliating for him and I think the reaction of the journalists at the *Post* spoke volumes. There was this great investment and he was going to do all these things, and he turned around and sold it all. It's hard to characterize it as anything else but a retreat."

❖ ❖ ❖

Thursday, August 23, the day Conrad Black announced he had sold the final piece of the *Post*, was Richard Addis's birthday. The *Globe* editor logically decided that the *Post* had handed him a windfall of high-profile *Post* journalists as a gift. Addis, who had periodically attempted, and failed, to hire *Post* stars in an effort to knock a hole in their line-up, took out his little list of names and started phoning. "I called up a dozen people at the *Post* and tried to hire them all, because I thought they might be wobbly. Many were. I had lots of lunches and meetings and sent job letters out, but in the end I didn't get anyone. I thought they were all mad. They were like the Taliban. Some said they liked the *Globe* and would be happy to come and work for me and accepted the offers, then something happened: the cult leader Ken said, 'If you leave you will break the spell and it will be your fault.' It was very clever of him. I tried to hire Christie, Robert Fulford, David Walmsley Andrew McIntosh, Marina Jimenez, Alison Uncles, lots of them."

Whyte knew that Addis was trying to poach his staff; most of them told him. After the *Post* layoffs, Whyte knew, too, that Addis would be back for another attempt. From the *Globe*'s point of view, the period of uncertainty was a perfect opportunity to finally skewer the wounded enemy and get rid of it for good.

Whyte's success in persuading all of Addis's targets to stay was another example of persuasion as only Whyte could persuade, but it was also clear that loyalty to the newspaper's founding editor was an immense, if irrational, factor in most of the decisions. But before he persuaded others to stay, Whyte had to decide what he was going to do himself:

> My immediate concern was to settle people down and wait for real information. Martin had been at a wedding in Malta, and when he got back I talked with him, Christie, Alison, Mark Steyn, Andrew Coyne, and Paul Wells . . . ten or twelve people who were not necessarily targets but people who for me are a big part of the *Post*. I went out with Christie and we had a three-hour discussion about whether it was worth carrying on. People like Christie get offers all the time and could just pick up the phone if they wanted to leave. When I was making my own decision about what I was going to do I went to talk to the Aspers and hear from them what they wanted. Did they want me around and on what terms and how was it going to work. After I got that settled, I wanted to know what those others were planning to do. If they weren't going to stay, it wasn't going to be the same for me. So that influenced my decision about whether I was going to stick around. By the time the poaching had started, we had all decided, especially the core group of editors, that we were going to try to make it work.

Martin Newland put it more succinctly. "At the *Post*, if someone gets an offer, they are so terrified of hurting us they blurt it out. They judge everything at the *Globe* by their own tight-arsed newsroom. Addis thought we were like a cult."

"We are [still] a conservative newspaper, but we're not trying to get anyone elected or unite any particular party. We are not torquing the news to pull down the prime minister."

— Matthew Fraser, appointed editor-in-chief of the *National Post*, May 2003

Kenneth Whyte kept in regular contact with Conrad Black during the first eighteen months of CanWest's full ownership of the *Post*. Black, by then a minority shareholder and CanWest board member, urged the increasingly unhappy and restless editor-in-chief to hang in. It would get better, he said.

By the spring of 2003, the *Post* was on its way to a $23-million loss, forcing Whyte and publisher Peter Viner to produce a cost-cutting plan aimed at slashing the losses in half while maintaining a viable national newspaper capable of holding its own journalistically. Advertising revenue had slumped to around $69 million, down $5 million from the previous year, and by May it was getting worse and showing no prospect of recovery. CanWest decided that $23 million was too much to lose.

But the rift between the new owners and the newspaper's senior editors wasn't just about money.

Whyte and his deputy, Martin Newland, had been vocal in their criticism of a new company policy that effectively removed much of the *National Post*'s exclusive use of its own news stories and its often clumsily exercised right, since day one, to claim the best from the rest of its sister newspapers. Under the new arrangement, all newspapers in the CanWest group would share most news stories, a move Whyte and Newland saw as an effort to impose the TV network business model on their newspaper. During the U.S.-led invasion of Iraq in the spring of 2003, when all the company's newsgathering resources were pooled, their dismay increased.

The *Post*'s demands on the metro newspapers had been a chronic irritation for many metro editors. Whyte and Newland had always urged their subordinates to phone "the shires" (as Newland liked to call them) to get dibs on the good stories being worked on by fellow reporters in the Conrad Black empire. In the early weeks of the *Post*'s life, some reporters at the sister newspapers received calls from *Post* editors and "rewrite" people – reporters employed to retool wire stories in *Post* style – asking for notes and phone numbers of sources. The purpose was for *Post* writers to take the reporter's raw material and write the story themselves. This was predictably perceived as a gross insult, whether intended or not. The practice met too much resistance and was stopped within weeks, but not before it cemented an image of the *Post*, among its sister newspapers, as arrogant and condescending.

What did continue was the exclusivity the *Post* commanded over its own stories, together with the right to use any story it chose from anywhere else in the newspaper group. If, however, the *Post* claimed a story from the *Vancouver Sun*, for example, for the front page of its national edition, the story would not be in the edition of the *Post* circulated in Vancouver. In those other cities, sister newspapers would not get the original story and would have to wait to publish a follow-up piece the day after it appeared in the *Post*. It was never a perfect or consistent system, and many of Whyte's fellow editors considered it detrimental to both their own newspapers and to the spirit of co-operation that was supposed to exist in the Southam newspaper family. It wasn't a totally one-sided arrangement. The upside for reporters who wrote stories appropriated by the *Post* was exposure in a national newspaper, which is an ego boost, and, in some cases, a chance to get an issue onto the agendas of politicians and policy-makers, who tend to be impressed by national coverage.

So the relationship between the *Post* and other newspapers in the group was undoubtedly odd, and often strained, but had somehow worked most of the time, especially while Conrad Black owned all the newspapers and wished it to be so. Whyte and Newland were adamant that keeping the *Post* exclusive and distinct was the only way for it to survive and thrive journal-istically. The newspaper was, and is, a second-read newspaper for sub-scribers who receive it as part of their subscription to the *Vancouver Sun*, *Ottawa Citizen*, *Montreal Gazette*, and others in the CanWest chain. Whyte and Newland reasoned that if their newspaper featured the same stories available to readers of those metro publications, it would eventually make the *Post* irrelevant.

The new owners did not agree.

Costs continued to spiral, and circulation had declined to 243,000 from a 327,108 high, albeit in large part from a cut in the infamous giveaway and almost-giveaway bulk sales. Cutting back on those meant immedi-ate savings.

But for CanWest, which had bought the former Southam newspapers from Conrad Black to pursue the company's goal of converging TV, Internet, and print, it was illogical to have two or more reporters in its employ chasing the same story on the same day even if they did, ostensibly, work for different newspapers. Didn't it make more sense to have two or three reporters chasing two or three separate stories and then share the prod-uct of their labours? Wouldn't lack of duplication simply mean more and better journalism?

CanWest CEO Leonard Asper reasons that the *Post* has plenty of exclu-sive editorial content and maintains that no newspaper, or TV news broad-cast, is comprised totally of exclusive material:

> It's true that newspapers need unique content and to a great extent today the *National Post* content is unique from that which is in the metros. But on the other hand, there is a lot of content, Canadian Press and Associated Press, that plays not only in the *National Post* and the metro papers that are part of the CanWest family, but also in the *Globe and Mail* and *USA Today*. All newspapers have generic content and their own proprietary content. It could be just as true that someone at the *Vancouver Sun* writes an article that is submit-ted to Canadian Press and it appears in the *Globe and Mail* and *Toronto Sun*. It happens all the time in newspapers and it happens in the television. CTV and Global may have the same news-sharing arrangement with CBS, and on any given night both will be airing

the same coverage. So I have never believed that every line of a newspaper has ever been unique and distinct from another newspaper, but its uniqueness lies in its columnists, its sports and arts coverage. There was, and is, very little crossover in those areas.

◆ ◆ ◆

On May 1, 2003, Kenneth Whyte was told he was being "transitioned out of the company."

Newland, who had a clause in his original contract giving him the option of leaving with full compensation if Whyte resigned or was fired, was also dismissed, along with other managers in the advertising and marketing departments. Publisher Peter Viner, a veteran of the CanWest group, was asked to head the company's radio development.

Many of Whyte's colleagues, who had watched him grow more disillusioned and disengaged, had been expecting it.

David Asper was installed in the newly created position of *National Post* chairman, and Bob McKenzie, former publisher of the St. Catharines *Standard* in Ontario, assumed the duties of publisher. The Aspers turned to Matthew Fraser, a *Post* columnist, author, and Ryerson University professor, to replace Whyte and decided to integrate the newspaper's advertising sales force into its central media sales department.

Putting an Asper in overall control of the *Post*, and his name on the newspaper's masthead, was a symbolic statement, Leonard told staff the following day. "The Asper name is on the line," he said. "We're here to praise the *Post* not bury it." He referred to the *Post*'s sniping competitors as the "Axis of Snivel," and reminded everyone that similar skepticism had greeted the Global TV network when it first started and, perhaps more pertinent, *USA Today*, which took a dozen years and many millions of dollars before it turned a profit and achieved its current status as a cash cow.

CanWest, seemingly determined to keep the *Post* alive, launched a three-year break-even plan. Leonard Asper, a believer that an ailing company has to be stripped down before it can be rebuilt, says disagreement over the exclusivity of *Post* news stories wasn't the only reason CanWest decided to remove the founding editor and push ahead with a major managerial reorganization. "It was one issue on which we continually disagreed, but in the end we believed the paper needed a management change and a different kind of approach. In order for the *National Post* to survive and continue to be an alternative voice, we felt it had to have a new managerial direction."

What he didn't expect was the exodus of name columnists and key editors that followed. The loyalty to Whyte and Newland, evident when *Globe* editor Richard Addis had attempted his raid a year or so before, was now writ large.

Ottawa columnist Paul Wells went to *Maclean's* magazine; freelance columnist Mark Steyn switched his focus to other publications; reporter Robert Benzie and managing editor Alison Uncles left for the *Star*, as did sports columnist Dave Feschuk; author and columnist David Frum decamped; and Christie Blatchford went with great fanfare to the *Globe and Mail*. Steyn, on his own Web site, and Frum, in the *National Review*, both wrote columns explaining that they had withdrawn their services from the *Post* because, in essence, it wasn't like it used to be and they didn't like what it had become. (Frum would, however, change his mind and reappear.)

Fraser says the impact of the defections was minimal and the *Post* got barely half a dozen e-mails from people who cited the departing columnists as a reason for cancelling their subscriptions. "It was difficult to manage from a morale point of view," reports Fraser, "but from a strictly business perspective it had no effect whatsoever – which perhaps should be a lesson to all journalists who think of themselves as stars. No one individual can sink a franchise."

The big-name departures from the *Post* came as a shock, admits Leonard Asper. "I didn't appreciate the loyalty, I guess, to Ken and Martin. I can certainly understand how they generated loyalty, but I had hoped that we as the *National Post* team would continue to fight it out and prevail – the little engine that could, the underdog, the David against Goliath. I was upset that some of the people didn't want to stick it out and abandoned ship in the middle of the game. Given what I thought existed in the journalism community – loyalty to one another – I would have thought the people who left the *Post* would have stuck by their brothers and sisters."

The relatively limited, sometimes turbulent, experience as owner of most of Canada's major newspapers has left Leonard Asper with mixed feelings:

> It is an intellectually stimulating, exciting business, and I really enjoy the people. You can walk through a newsroom and get a conversation going with anyone on any subject. You build your product from

scratch every day, and every day you have to go back and build a new one. There are disappointing factors. There is less company loyalty than there is professional loyalty. We saw that with the editorial row we had, where people who were part of the CanWest company turned against us. I was surprised that would happen. The *Montreal Gazette* writers, for example, withholding their bylines, and people within our own company writing columns criticizing us. We come from a culture where the company is a family, and a family keeps its squabbles internal. But I do empathize with people in the profession who have had dozens of owners over the past ten, twenty, or fifty years, and I can see how that lack of loyalty, or sense of family, with the proprietors exists. I do think there is an unhealthy suspicion of big business and proprietors in general in the profession, but that has to be worked on.

There is a disconnect, he suggests, between some newspaper columnists, staff writers, and proprietors. "They think it's none of our business to care what they write, but on the other hand, it is our name on the masthead."

And Asper, head of the most influential media conglomerate in Canada and vendor of news, information, and entertainment to millions of Canadians, feels standards generally have slipped:

I do think there is a sloppiness that has crept into journalism. More and more, news is editorialized, and I think that is a tragedy. News is not nearly as objective as it used to be, or should be. I have spoken to a number of people about this and look at it as both a customer and someone whose name is on the masthead – and also as someone who has been the victim of some of that from the *Globe and Mail*, who have made no secret of their intent to denigrate CanWest at every opportunity. So that is something about newspapers I find troubling. No one minds being criticized, but use of argument ad hominem, or the use of negative adjectives to describe a factual situation, that seems to be creeping into news coverage. It comes back to the separation of church and state. News being news, and editorials and columns marked as such. By and large it is a good and noble profession, but like the accounting or law professions we have to uphold higher standards.

◆　◆　◆

Matthew Fraser was already personally and professionally acquainted with both Izzy and Leonard Asper and had spent time with the family patriarch at his Palm Beach estate in February 2003. Fraser, whose wife had died that January, was at a crossroads, not quite knowing what he was going to do with his life or career. He had no ambition to become editor-in-chief of the *National Post*, and says that during their time together in Palm Beach, Izzy Asper was a perfect host, and treated him with great kindness, but did not mention anything about the top journalism job at the national newspaper.

"We talked about the meaning of life and lots of other things," says Fraser, "and we got to know each other quite well."

Fraser's appointment in the spring of 2003 coincided with the owner's commitment to put the newspaper on an even financial keel, hack away at its losses, and try to generate more revenue. "In a strictly business sense it was a turnaround," he says. "The paper was losing a lot of money and the cost structure was completely out of control. It was a labyrinthine maze. To be fair to Conrad and Ken, the *Post* was a start-up, and start-ups have to spend a lot of money to create a lot of religious zeal and enthusiasm about the enterprise. But there is always a second phase where you have to take the enterprise to the next step. The victim, or sacrificial lamb, is often the founder himself. So in that respect the *Post* was not out of the ordinary."

Fraser inherited journalistic responsibility for a newspaper he felt had too often "torqued" news stories to achieve its core political ambition of uniting the right and unseating Jean Chrétien's government. In keeping with the views of the new owners, the *Post* would remain small-c conservative in its outlook, maintain its cheeky, irreverent flavour, but dump the anti-Liberal campaign. Coverage of the Grand Mère affair, which, as chairman of CanWest's publications committee, David Asper had famously attacked in his *Post* column of March 2001, was consigned to history.

David Asper's point was that the Grand Mère coverage had been unfair and unproven and had continued despite the fact that Chrétien was cleared of wrongdoing by federal ethics counsellor Howard Wilson and that the RCMP had decided against an investigation. "TO CHRÉTIEN'S ACCUSERS: PUT UP OR SHUT UP" was the headline above Asper's column, which also ran throughout the CanWest newspaper chain. It was followed the next day by a Mark Steyn column in the *Post* vigorously defending the newspaper's Grand Mère coverage. ("SHAWINIGAN SHENANIGANS:

OUR INVESTIGATIVE REPORTING HAS BEEN AS SOLID AS IT GETS.")
The Steyn column was seen as an official response by a rebellious newsroom management to the new part-owners. It was still several months before
the Aspers would take full control.

As is common with all newspaper owners, CanWest eventually sought
an editor-in-chief with similar views to theirs on a range of key issues.
Indeed, Conrad Black would not have chosen Kenneth Whyte had the two
not shared the same conservative ideology.

"Ken was very committed to the united-right ideological crusade, and
the *Post* was quite hostile to the prime minister," reasons Fraser. "That
was the crusade upon which the missionary zeal of the *National Post* was
founded. By late 2000, Jean Chrétien was re-elected with a massive majority and the mission failed. In retrospect, it might have been a very smart
thing to do if it had succeeded, but it failed in 2000 and so it looked stupid.
That's when the start-up phase of the *Post* encountered its first major obstacle. It was a rude awakening. The prime minister outsmarted Conrad Black,
the wind in the *Post*'s sails began to lose strength, and the founding religion of the *Post* began unravelling. We are [still] a conservative newspaper, but we're not trying to get anyone elected or unite any particular party.
We are not torquing the news to pull down the prime minister."

Uplifting dampened spirits and answering questions about the new owners were among the first tasks that faced Fraser, a long-time journalistic
observer of CanWest Global as well as a family acquaintance.

The Aspers, he says, were largely unknown and misunderstood, partly
because they had never taken time to ingratiate themselves with Toronto's
powerful media elite. "When the Aspers had 50 per cent of it, and Ken was
running the paper, the Aspers were not invited into the building, so to
speak. The staff didn't really know the Aspers except what they had read.
When Ken and Martin left and the Aspers came into the building, the staff
realized that David Asper was a really likeable guy and not this meanie or
brute they had been reading about in the *Globe and Mail*. That helped the
Post turn the corner in terms of morale."

In hard-nosed business terms, Fraser says the Winnipeg Aspers think
like most media owners. Any gulf with the central Canadian media establishment is sociological. "The Aspers have not spent a great deal of time
in the care and feeding of the media elite. They don't cultivate members
of the intelligentsia or media clique in Toronto and were never creatures

of the salon. They paid the price, to the extent that the Toronto media elite likes to be cultivated and lionized. They never really felt the Aspers wanted to get to know them, and they felt no inclination to get to know the Aspers. Hence this muted hostility. And, of course, the Aspers own Global TV, which is regarded with some condescension by the *Globe and Mail*, CBC, and *Toronto Star* group. The media elite is venal, and always has been."

◆ ◆ ◆

Conrad Black called Ken Whyte the day he was fired and the two reminisced about their time at the *Post*. As Whyte recalls it,

> Conrad mostly just talked about the achievements of the *Post* and said it was a great thing to have done and that he believed it made a serious difference in Canadian journalism. I thought from an editorial point of view that nothing is ever perfect, but it would have been unreasonable to expect anything other than what we achieved at the *Post*. Conrad always has a great sense of occasion with these things. I had talked to him for over a year about wanting to get out, and every time I had that conversation with him he encouraged me to stay and keep it going. He didn't say I was acting unreasonably to the demands of the Aspers, or the circumstances, but he always played a bit of the devil's advocate. So the last conversation was mostly congratulatory. He said two things about the paper: He said the paper that we had started and worked on was more or less finished, but in terms of the commercial options the way the Aspers were going was probably the only chance they had of an escape. He never believed that going back to the *Financial Post* was viable unless you wanted to invest another $50 million. Shut-downs are horribly expensive. Nobody quite realizes how much it costs. The severance payments, breaking business contracts . . . they were looking at between $40 and $60 million, not including write-downs. It would have wiped out any profit they had so was never a serious option.

Whyte is convinced that his *National Post* has left an indelible mark on Canadian journalism and former *Post*ies are now working in every corner of news media in the country – as well, of course, as those still at the paper.

"Everything that is happening in journalism in Canada now is in reaction to, or out of, the *Post*," he says. "When the *Toronto Star* goes looking to change itself, where does it turn? Graham Parley, Peter Scowen, and Alison Uncles. The *Globe* hasn't produced a writer of its own in five years. The closest they came to it was Leah McLaren, and they only made her a columnist after we tried to hire her."

What would he have done differently?

"Everything," he says. "You make hundreds of decisions a day and some work out and some don't. On the whole, the only things I can second-guess are some of the difficult personnel decisions. Letting people go is a hard thing to do, and I still find that haunting. But the paper was what it was and we are proud of what we did."

Shortly before he returned to England, Martin Newland offered this assessment of what the Black-Whyte-Newland tenure at the *Post* had achieved. "We shook 'em up in terms of how to present a news package. We made 'em angry and made 'em laugh. We showed that in journalism, you can set your own course and be proactive. But the thing I really enjoyed was working with the people at the *Post*. We spent a couple of years circling around each other and then came together in a new way of doing journalism. That was fantastic and something I'll never do again."

◆ ◆ ◆

There was a story on the journalist grapevine after the Whyte-Newland firings that they had suffered the indignity of being accompanied by security guards when they were allowed back into the office to collect their belongings the Saturday following their dismissals. It wasn't true. "That was all blown out of proportion," says Whyte. "There was just a very nice human resources person."

As Martin Newland emptied the contents of his office into boxes, he came upon a photograph of himself in a spontaneous, albeit pretend, amorous embrace with photography editor Denis Paquin at a *Post* Christmas party. Paquin was dressed as Buzz Lightyear. Newland went out into the newsroom and put the photograph on Paquin's desk. He then took his final opportunity to place little messages on certain desks – messages, he says, that "let them know I cared."

After so many layoffs, a gallows humour had developed among the people who remained – a humour that manifested itself in a plastic potted plant that was ceremoniously placed on the chairs of the departed. Newland had also taken to putting the plant on chairs of people who had irritated him or otherwise met with his temporary disfavour. On this, his last visit to the *Post* newsroom, he hunted down the plant and placed it on his own chair.

Newland had tested new motorcycles for write-ups he published in the *Daily Telegraph* back in England, and he did the same a few times in Toronto. When newsroom colleague and fellow motorcycle enthusiast John Racovali arrived at work on Monday, the black motorcycle helmet Newland had brought from England was sitting on his desk. A yellow Post-it note was stuck to it: *Raco*, it read. *For You.*

Racovali, who had already been reduced to tears at Newland's departure, was deeply touched, and he kept the helmet on his desk for another six months before using it on a trip through the northern United States. "I sent Martin an e-mail saying I had finally got some use out of it," says Racovali. "I still miss him. Those of us who started at the *Post* together developed this real connectedness and were so in tune with each other's thinking. I remember an unusual thing. A week before he left the paper he came up behind me and started massaging my shoulders. He leaned forward and whispered, 'Raco, good old Raco.' I wonder if he knew then he was leaving and whether it was his way of saying goodbye."

Newland's memory of his last morning in the *National Post* newsroom remains vivid. "The place had a feel and a smell, and because so much of your soul and sweat, happiness and exasperation went into it, it was an incredibly pathetic moment to be there. Ken and I were sheepish, like two naughty, farty schoolboys who had just been expelled and were cleaning out our rooms. But saying goodbye to that place was really upsetting. There were only the two of us. A couple of TVs were on because some bugger hadn't turned them off on Friday. I felt angry and humiliated. I was unemployed. Canada provided so many things in terms of new experience and comfort, both professionally and in our family life, but it was all coming to an end. Like I always do, I kept joking and talking too much, but I was completely gutted and terrified."

On October 27, 1998, the day the *Post* launched, Conrad Black had phoned and left a warm message on Ken Whyte's voice mail, congratulating him on the first edition. "Ken, it's Conrad Black speaking. It's about ten past one on Tuesday. I'm really phoning essentially to congratulate you. It was a damn good paper. I'll not produce yet another cascade of superlatives, but it was a tremendous ramp up to a very great undertaking, and I think it was as good a launch as we could possibly have expected. The opening paper was very hard to criticize and, obviously, I get partisan comment pretty much, but all comment I've heard, even from some people I would trust to be objective and frank, has been positive. I think it's a tremendous achievement. I would be remiss if I didn't say that with a certain amount of specificity toward you and a slight degree of formality. You have a first-class team there and they have a first-class leader. You don't have to phone back, but I'd be happy to hear from you."

Whyte had kept the message on his machine, and now, before they left the building for good, he called Newland into his office and played it for him. The two listened to Black's message, left almost five years before on a day as euphoric as this was depressing.

Then Whyte erased it.

"I have given new meaning to the term *struggling author.*" – Conrad Black

C onrad Black was at the height of his power and international prestige when he launched the *National Post* in October 1998. Five years later, in the wake of a devastating Delaware court judgment, his reputation was in tatters and his personal fortune at stake in future legal battles.

A drawn-looking Black spent six hours on the stand at Delaware Chancery Court on February 20, 2004, fighting for his right to sell Hollinger Newspapers on his own terms and denying that he and fellow executives took millions of dollars in unauthorized payments from Hollinger International. The allegations, he said, had "horribly defamed" him: "I have been characterized and stigmatized as an embezzler. I am trying to retrieve my reputation as an honest man."

Judge Leo Strine was not impressed. In a scathing attack, he cast Black as a cunning, calculating bully of a chief executive who wilfully misled his company directors and shareholders. Black, he said, was "evasive and unreliable. … [I]t became impossible for me to credit his word." The judge's harsh assessment came down like a hammer blow on Black's claims that he was an honest, defamed man. The judgment stirred suggestions of possible criminal charges. Black issued a statement respectfully disagreeing.

Black had earlier launched an $850-million action against former chair-man of the U.S. Securities Exchange Commission (SEC) Richard Breeden and independent directors who had been part of the Hollinger committee investigating the company's finances.

In his suit, Black claimed malicious media coverage has left him a "social leper," a "loathsome laughingstock, pilloried and mocked merci-lessly in the media throughout the world." Lord Black also claimed to have been "spurned by and shunned by persons who had personally accepted my hospitality in London, New York, and Palm Beach."

Black promised to pay back, by the summer of 2004, the $7.2 million he received, as did his long-time associate David Radler, who got the same amount. Radler also resigned as the company's chief operating officer and publisher of the *Chicago Sun-Times*. Further payments of $600,000 each had gone to directors Peter Atkinson, who also promised to pay it back, and Jack Boultbee, who was fired after refusing to return the money and then sued the company for wrongful dismissal, demanding U.S.$12 million and insisting he had been told the payment was authorized. Half of the total amount of U.S.$32.15 million went to Hollinger Inc., the parent company of Hollinger International. Black later changed his mind about returning the money, saying he had been duped and that Hollinger documents proved it.

News of Black's woes broke while he was promoting his new biography of Franklin D. Roosevelt. Predictably, reporters were more interested in the scandal than in the book, which was receiving overwhelmingly positive reviews. "I urge you," Black told the swarms of reporters who descended on his book signings in New York and Toronto, "no matter how addicted you are to representing me as having been shamed, disgraced, and chased out as a scoundrel, to contemplate the possibility that there's just a chance I might be innocent. As time will prove I am."

And with equal loquaciousness he remarked to a reporter with the *Financial Times* of London, "This is a greenmail effort accompanied by a comprehensive media smear-job, which some elements of the so-called working press . . . have swallowed with what our defamers consider heart-warming gullibility."

Fighting words, but followed by more bad news.

Shortly before Christmas 2003, on another front, Black "took the Fifth" at the Securities Exchange Commission in New York, refusing to testify under the U.S. Constitution's Fifth Amendment right against self-incrimination. His lawyer, John Warden, said Black and his legal advisers needed more time to prepare their defence. The SEC, newly aggressive following major corporate scandals in the United States, launched a major investigation into financial irregularities at Black's company shortly after the unauthorized payments were revealed.

As part of the deal with CanWest, Black's Hollinger had agreed to cover six months' worth of losses and other costs at the *National Post* to the tune of $22.5 million. A dispute over the unpaid cash resulted in CanWest suing Hollinger companies in December 2003.

Documents filed in the United States as part of a lawsuit by Hollinger shareholders accused Black and his fellow executives of "a stunning abuse of authority" and accused them of diverting to themselves "hundreds of millions of dollars" of Hollinger funds.

Cardinal Value Equity Partners, which held 1.75 million Hollinger International shares, had begun asking for board meeting minutes and other company documents as early as the summer of 2003. The documents revealed "a troubling reality," claimed Hollinger's shareholders, and suggested that accused Hollinger executives were treating the company "like their personal piggy bank" while its blue-ribbon directors simply agreed to anything asked of them without independent analysis, fairness opinions, or extensive discussion.

The high-profile board included former U.S. ambassador and White House defence adviser Richard Perle and former U.S. secretary of state Henry Kissinger. Perle described the Hollinger collapse as "a tragedy."

The suit describes transactions where the board allegedly rubber-stamped sales of Hollinger assets to companies controlled by Black and other Hollinger executives, paid them non-compete fees, or raised their compensation without question in a series of deals that cost Hollinger $300 million or more.

According to the *New York Times*, the board approved the sale, for one dollar, of two publications to a company controlled by Black and David Radler. The explanation for the sale of the newspapers, which had negative cash flow, was that a dollar was fair market value. "But there was never any independent valuation of the properties," said the *New York Times*. "Nor did the committee even discuss, the suit alleges, why a company controlled by Black should sell properties for so little, if a second company controlled by Black obviously believed they could be made profitable. At that same meeting, the committee also agreed to raise by more than 7 per cent the annual management fees paid to Ravelston, a company controlled by Black. In the previous year, the company had been paid $24 million. The management fees paid annually to Ravelston included fees for both management services to Hollinger and Black's compensation. But there was never any independent analysis of the payments, review of their propriety, or discussions of whether those services could be obtained for less money from other companies. The meeting, which took a half hour, also approved raises for the fees paid to board members without any explanation or review of the propriety of the raises.

"As to Black's perks, Hollinger's accounting firm, KPMG, told the board that it was difficult to assess whether Black's use of the corporate jet was for personal or business reasons. Nevertheless the audit committee agreed to continue to pay for the jet 'for security reasons.' The audit committee also approved payment of 300,000 Canadian dollars, or $232,955, that had been spent to staff one of Black's homes as well as previously undisclosed payments to Black's wife, who was also a board member."

Black had also irked shareholders when he used company money to buy a collection of Franklin D. Roosevelt's letters, memos, photographs, and other artifacts supposedly for U.S.$8 million – a figure later alleged to be U.S.$12 million. Information about the U.S.$4 million discrepancy, leaked to the media by Hollinger insiders, was sketchy, but Black maintained that he had not used the materials extensively in writing his book and the purchase was a corporate investment, as the acquisition of a valuable painting might have been. The new regime at Hollinger decided to sell the Roosevelt collection, along with a condominium apartment used in Chicago by David Radler.

Amid the complexities of the SEC investigation, the shareholders' lawsuit, corporate resignations, and the still to be proved allegations were some more tangible manifestations of the British peer's decline.

He put his Palm Beach estate up for sale, listing it at U.S.$36 million. The pale yellow winter retreat covered 17,000 square feet and included six bedrooms, nine bathrooms, an elevator, a library, a cinema, and a swimming pool. Black also began entertaining offers, in the $20-million range, for his ten-bedroom mansion in London.

Gordon Paris, the new chief executive of Hollinger International, ordered the company's private jets (used primarily by Black and Radler) grounded, and asked questions about other expenses, such as the Rolls-Royce Black and his wife used to get about in London.

But to show that he could retain his renowned sense of humour even in the face of such dire prospects, Black dryly told reporters on his Roosevelt book tour, "I have given new meaning to the term *struggling author*."

◆ ◆ ◆

If Phillip Crawley's disdain for the *National Post* is little more than competitive posturing, his pretence otherwise is very convincing. Take him at face value and the *Globe and Mail* publisher is unremitting in his indifference to the quality of the newspaper and in his insistence that it is nothing more than the product of a rich man's vanity.

"Most of the circulation was subsidized," he says, "because they couldn't get people to pay a decent price and they couldn't sell the ads. When the final denouement came, the sense of betrayal among the journalists who had been hired to fight the good fight was palpable. Christie Blatchford articulated it: this was their champion deserting the field. They had some good individual journalists, which is inevitably going to be the case. You cannot monopolize all the best stories and all the best ideas as much as you might try. But, by and large, my impression was that it was a highly puffed-up operation which needed to come down to earth, and it came down to earth with a crashing thump."

When asked if there was anything he liked – even a teeny bit — about the *Post*, he sighs, and after thinking a moment turns his answer into corporate self-congratulation. "Competition makes you perform better and generally sharpens the wits. It shakes the complacency out of journalists, salespeople, and everyone else. Did it make the *Globe* staff rise to the occasion? Yes it did. They were very clear what their values were and they were going to defend them. It made the Thomson family appreciate the *Globe*'s virtues and they were determined to defend them. And that, of all the things, was the single biggest difference: the Thomsons stuck by the *Globe*, and have been 100 per cent solid in their support of the *Globe*, and still are. That consistency of support, from Ken Thomson down, has been very important and something that Conrad didn't bargain for."

But Crawley, aggressive defender on the soccer field, focused thumper of a tennis player, long-distance runner, would surely shrivel from boredom if the *Post* wasn't around to take a kick at every day. On the way out of his spacious office, past the photocopied pages of *Frank* magazine on his secretary's desk, he is asked to consider the possibility. (An interview, of course, is never over until the elevator doors close and the reporter disappears from sight.) Crawley contemplates the question for a few seconds and just smiles.

James Travers, the former *Star* executive managing editor who steered his newspaper's initial editorial push before and immediately after the *Post* launch, has no doubt that Conrad Black's daily made the *Star* a better newspaper, both internally and externally, and created a livelier newspaper out of the *Globe and Mail*. "There was the *Star* way and every other way, and the *Star* way was always the best way. So it was a bit of a revelation at the *Star* when some parts of the *Post* were as good as they were. We were going to have to make real strides in terms of quality. It was a wake-up call, and despite being the largest newspaper in the country, the way it thinks makes the *Star* inward. Everything is judged on the standards of the *Star*, and suddenly there was another standard, and some of it was very good. People who had been around the *Star* for twenty-five years figured they were damn good journalists and had the whole thing figured out, but then suddenly they started thinking, 'Jeez, maybe there is stuff here I haven't thought about.' We started a training system that had never existed at the *Star*, and we started to work on photojournalism and design. We had a million things on the go. We brought in external help, people from the U.S. to do courses. It wasn't part of the *Star* culture. Our feeling was that without disturbing the core readership it was a great opportunity to start working on journalistic standards and edge the quality up and start doing a few non-traditional things."

❖ ❖ ❖

Several months before his business world began collapsing, Conrad Black he said he had few regrets about the *National Post*, beyond having to sell it. But there were one or two things he would do differently. He regretted the newspaper was perceived as being pro-American and anti-Canadian.

And using his newspaper to promote a new political party was not necessarily what he had in mind at the outset.

"I would be a little more insistent than I was on being a little more subtle in some areas – being ambiguous about whether we were trying to promote an alternate party or alternate thinking within the governing party. Too many people got the idea that the paper was always critical of Canada, and it certainly wasn't what Ken [Whyte] and I wanted the perception to be. I think I would assert myself more than I did, to try to avoid that perception. Beyond that, we gave it a good go. We did better than I expected to do financially and about as well as we thought we would in terms of the opinion climate. The whole soft left establishment of the country locked arms and it was like a Venus flytrap closing in us. But we made our gesture. It was intense and interesting and worthwhile. A newspaper can be serious and fun and well written and a critical success. From scratch it was an ambitious undertaking. I think it will be remembered by journalists who were active at the time, and especially those who worked at it, all their working lives rather fondly. It was a high-class, high-quality product, and I think everyone associated with it was proud."

◆ ◆ ◆

The birth of a daily newspaper is a rare event to be celebrated, and its death a passing to be mourned. Journalists, circulation staff, and advertising salespeople who work for the *Globe and Mail*, the *Toronto Star*, the *National Post*, and any other newspaper across the land know that is so. Competition is good; monopoly is bad, always overpriced, and invariably more tedious for readers.

Many say that the national newspaper war has been won by the *Globe and Mail*, and to some extent that is clearly true. But as long as the *Post* is still publishing, the war continues.

If the *National Post* buckles under the weight of debt and, as many have been predicting since its first week of operation, disappears, there will be few cheers to be heard inside the competitors' offices, except among the corporate types who occupy the boardrooms and the executive suites.

Most people in the newspaper game are content to battle it out on a daily basis. They fight to get better stories than the other guy, and to get major stories before the other guy. And they battle to sell more copies. But they don't want to defeat each other. The last thing they want is to wake up one day and find that the competition has packed up and gone away. Playing in a league of one is no fun.

When CanWest Global CEO Leonard Asper says the *National Post* is "good for Canada" he is speaking with a degree of self-interest, but he's also correct. For better or worse, whether you agree with it or not, the *National Post* has become a voice in Canadian national affairs.

In newspapers, tomorrow is everything.

Leonard Asper insists his company will do what it takes to take to keep the *Post* alive.

"Perseverance and commitment are a big part of it," he says. "Part of the issue with the *National Post* in the last year or so has been the consistent and vicious rumours, mostly from the *Star* and its owners and the *Globe* and its owners, that they were going to bury the *Post*. But every day the *Post* doesn't go away is further assurance to our readers and our clients that we are not going away. I remember twenty-five years ago the Baton and Eaton families were quite vocal in Toronto about how Global could never survive and how CTV was going to bury Global, but here we are. We have made all the cuts it is prudent to make at the *Post*. Now the approach is to strengthen the content and the promotion, but mostly content. It is now going to win on the ability of the content to generate circulation. With the last round of cuts we now have an appropriate cost base. We have a loyal minimum of 250,000 subscribers, and that will increase. Now it's a question of staying the course and moving down the field five or ten yards at a time, adding a thousand people here and two thousand there, and reaching out to advertisers who haven't been in the paper before and getting others back to where they were in 2001 before they lost some confidence – and making sure there is enough content to generate new advertising categories. There are no deadlines. It is a long game and we are going to win it."

CHANGES

The following list accounts for just some of the people mentioned in this book who have moved on to other jobs.

Richard Addis, assistant editor and design editor, *Financial Times*, U.K.

Donald Babick, consultant

Michael Bate, pursuing a musical career

John Bentley Mays, art and architecture critic and columnist

Christie Blatchford, columnist, *Globe and Mail*

Scott Burnside, freelance journalist, Atlanta, Georgia

Susan Delacourt, Ottawa bureau chief, *Toronto Star*

Dave Feschuk, sports columnist, *Toronto Star*

Scott Feschuk, speech writer for Prime Minister Paul Martin

Joe Fiorito, city columnist, *Toronto Star*

Gordon Fisher, president of news and information, CanWest Global Communications

Chrystia Freeland, deputy editor, *Financial Times*, U.K.

Stuart Garner, chairman, NewsStand Inc., international electronic newspaper delivery

Paul Godfrey, board member, CanWest Global

Edward Greenspon, editor-in-chief, *Globe and Mail*

Chris Jones, writer, *Esquire*

Douglas Knight, president and CEO, Knight Paton Media Corporation, consultants

Kirk LaPointe, managing editor, *Vancouver Sun*

Ezra Levant, founding publisher, *Western Standard*, a conservative magazine

Roy MacGregor, columnist, *Globe and Mail*

Colin MacKenzie, managing editor, *Globe and Mail*

Preston Manning, travelling academic

Martin Newland, editor-in-chief, *Daily Telegraph*, U.K.

Graham Parley, sports editor, *Toronto Star*

David Radler, president and majority shareholder, Horizon Publications Inc., a private newspaper company

Mitchel Raphael, editor-in-chief, *fab*, Toronto gay scene magazine

Peter Scowen, entertainment editor, *Toronto Star*

James Travers, national political columnist, *Toronto Star*

David Walmsley, executive producer, newsgathering, CBC Television

Paul Wells, columnist, *Maclean's*

Kenneth Whyte, visiting scholar, McGill University, Montreal

ACKNOWLEDGEMENTS

My wife, Margot Sunter, carried the family burden during my absences, physical and otherwise, while I was working on this book and was a constant source of inspiration. I couldn't have done it without her and neither would I have wanted to try. Our children, Jeremy and Rhiannon, helped keep life in perspective, occasionally conspiring to haul me from the computer in crude wrestling holds or playing their lyrically sanitized Eminem CD cranked loud enough to smoke me out.

Many people gave generously of their time and insight as I attempted to piece this story together. Most are quoted or mentioned, and are part of the story in ways large and small, so I won't repeat all their names here. Others provided useful insight in exchange for anonymity, an arrangement that is never totally satisfactory but sometimes necessary. These included one prominent individual with whom I had lunch in Toronto. After we parted, the person called after me and cautioned, "And don't even thank me in the acknowledgements, either." I am grateful to them all, named and otherwise.

I am especially indebted to Kenneth Whyte and Edward Greenspon. I met with Mr. Whyte over several Sunday evenings on the terrace of Toronto's Granite Club for a series of interviews that began shortly after

Conrad Black's departure from the *Post*. Mr. Greenspon invited me into his home and in subsequent telephone conversations he read patiently from his diaries and described a flirtation with the *National Post* that his loyal colleagues and gut instinct ultimately derailed. As *Globe* columnist Hugh Winsor noted, some journalists are just "*Globe* people."

Thanks to Richard Addis, who arrived at my house in the Governor General's car with the Governor General's chauffer driving it. He had spent the night at Rideau Hall at the invitation of Adrienne Clarkson and her husband, John Ralston Saul. Mr. Addis's contract at the *Globe* had expired and he was to return home to London a short time later. He reminisced candidly over several entertaining hours about his Canadian newspaper battles.

Jan Wong's observations of newsroom life are priceless and everyone should go to lunch with her at least once.

After more than a year's back and forth, Conrad Black agreed to an interview during August of 2003, shortly before his much publicized decline in fortune. Lord Black spoke at length and with good humour about the *Post*'s failings and elaborately of its successes. I would be remiss if I didn't also thank his personal assistant, Joan Maida, with whom I exchanged scores of phone calls and e-mails. It is often the lot of journalists to deal with gatekeepers of rich, famous, or powerful people and the worst of those gatekeepers rarely resist dismissive condescension, especially when the journalist is in the throes of deadline desperation and being necessarily persistent. Ms. Maida was never less than respectful, helpful, and straightforward in her dealings with me.

Leonard Asper, whose company, CanWest Global, came to loom unexpectedly large in the Canadian daily newspaper business, was genial and generous with his time. His perspective on the *National Post* specifically, and the newspaper industry in general, was especially insightful and instructive.

Special thanks to Graham Parley of the *Toronto Star* and Lynn McAuley of the *Ottawa Citizen*, whose reputation within our business as inspiring and skilled editors renders superfluous anything I could say here. And special thanks also to *Ottawa Citizen* editor-in-chief Scott Anderson, who thoughtfully said to me at the outset, "If there's anything I can do to help . . . "

Stevie Cameron opened doors for me in Toronto, including her own. Aside from many personal kindnesses, she introduced me to Linda

McKnight, a consummate professional who was always there to help. David Staines, ever generous toward struggling writers, gave me a kick in the pants, hopefully to some affect, and Alex Schultz, my editor at McClelland & Stewart, was enthusiastic from the outset and an ideal working partner.

I also wish to acknowledge CBC-TV, *Ryerson Review of Journalism*, *Toronto Life* magazine, and the *Toronto Sun*, all of which I referred to during my research.

Julie Dove did splendid work transcribing interviews, and Tina Cobb, co-proprietor of the Tree Top Eco Shop in beautiful Kimberley, British Columbia, waited too long for me to visit. But I got there.

Chris Cobb, Ottawa, March 2004